THE EVOLUTION OF JEWISH THOUGHT

*FROM BIBLICAL TIMES TO
THE OPENING OF THE MODERN ERA*

*

THE EVOLUTION
OF JEWISH THOUGHT

FROM BIBLICAL TIMES

TO THE OPENING

OF THE MODERN ERA

*

JACOB B. AGUS

ABELARD-SCHUMAN
LONDON NEW YORK

To the loving memory of
REUBEN AGUSHEWITZ
philosopher and saint, and
BERNARD SHORE
father of my life's
companion

First published in 1959
Library of Congress Catalog Card No. 59-5612

Manufactured in the United States of America

PREFACE

ANYONE who sets out to achieve a comprehensive philosophy of life will sooner or later encounter the theme of this book: the unfolding of Jewish thought from its beginnings in antiquity to the modern period. Jew or Christian, rationalist or romantic, liberal or socialist, nationalist or internationalist, a citizen of the West can hardly understand the roots of his own mentality without taking into account the fascinating spiritual Odyssey of the Jews. Small in numbers and weak in organization, the Jewish people loomed neither large nor important in the political and military affairs of the concert of nations. But their faith and culture are imbedded inextricably in the texture of Western civilization.

Judaism may well be regarded as the spiritual "heartland" of Western man. It has been loved and appreciated or maligned and hated, but it could never be ignored by the master-builders of our culture. The high priests of European culture in nearly every age were keenly aware of the continuing impact of the Jewish faith, and many of them were impelled to recast the historic image of Judaism into the pattern of their own philosophy. The masses of people were similarly conscious of the crucial role of Judaism and its unique place in the contemporary scheme of things. Projected into the very center of the drama of human civilization, the Jewish faith was frequently the hurricane eye of popular frenzy and demagogic devilry. No religious culture was so systematically misrepresented and misunderstood as was Judaism. Friends in their blind devotion and ardor as well as foes in their bigotry and hatred tended to overlook the fullness and complexity of this great historic faith. Attackers and defenders have shared the same glib assumptions; in particular the notion that Judaism is uniform and unchanging, monolithic in its ideology, and frozen into rigid, unyielding patterns—crystal-lized and fossilized.

In this volume, we propose to show that Judaism in nearly every age resembled an Oriental tapestry in the plenitude of colors and shades it embraced and unified. The comparative unity of law and custom concealed the great diversity of thought and sentiment. Within the authentic field of Jewish consciousness we recognize an unending struggle between the self-exaltation of romantic nationalism and the self-dedication of prophetism; between the austere appeal of ruthless rationality and the beguil-ing seduction of self-flattering sentiments; between the gentle charm of moralistic and pietistic devotions and the popular pre-ference for routinized rites and doubt-proof dogmas. The mighty tensions within the soul of contemporary Western man were reflected faithfully and clearly in the currents and cross-currents of the historic stream of Judaism.

In the following chapters, we consider both the unifying bed-rock of the stream of tradition and the diverse currents within it. The sources of the diverse contemporary ideologies are thus ex-posed to view. And although the story of the rise of Reform and Conservative Judaism is reserved for another volume, hardly a chapter of this book is irrelevant to the intellectual ferment in Jewish life today. The one bias which we consciously embraced in the writing of this volume was the attempt to read the annals of the past in the light of our contemporary concerns.

No one, be he Jew or Christian, can write of Jewish thought with absolute detachment. Yet a high degree of objectivity is in itself an expression of the inner impetus of the philosophical current in Judaism. To love God is to seek to know Him, asserted Maimonides, and the Talmudic sages affirm: "The seal of the Holy One, blessed be He, is truth." The greatest contribution of Judaism may well be its insistence that the Divine Will can only be illumined by the Divine Light within the human soul: the double light of intelligence and conscience.

This volume was designed neither for the uninstructed reader nor for the professional scholar, but for the advanced student of Judaism or of general thought. Whereas an elementary know-ledge of the Jewish faith, of Jewish history and the evolution of Western civilization is assumed, we eschewed the use of technical terms familiar only to students of philosophy, and have chosen to call this volume "The Evolution of Jewish *Thought*" rather than of Jewish philosophy or theology. We have sought to grasp the issues from within, focusing attention on the conflict of aspirations and sentiments underlying the formal façade of ideas and rites. While it was impossible to avoid altogether the issues of literary and historical criticism, we have reduced such speculations to a minimum. Nor have we attempted to trace in detail the process of evolution of ideas in Judaism. Our main concern was the portrayal of the great plateaux in the ongoing and ascending curve of the Jewish faith.

To do justice to the many-sidedness of the Jewish tradition, we have included movements and personalities that are usually omitted in a history of Jewish philosophy. Qabbalah and Hasidism are included; aspects of Spinoza's mighty labors are explored; the Qaraitic offshoot is studied; and the slow severance of the Christian and Jewish faiths is traced. At the same time we were obliged to leave out some outstanding personalities and works in our concentration upon drawing the general outlines of Jewish thought.

In the Epilogue the reader will find a discussion of the questions that naturally arise in the mind of a thoughtful reader when he approaches the study of Judaism. Some may even prefer to read the Epilogue before the other chapters. All readers will do well to remember the sage remark of the Talmud: "The end of a project is first in conception."

May I hereby express my thanks to Joyce Engelson of Abelard-Schuman, who edited the manuscript with meticulous care and devotion.

CONTENTS

9

great reward of every single Commandment in Judaism – Flexibility of a true faith and the credentials of Judaism – Reasons for the Commandments – Israel and mankind – The infinite love of God – Residues of superstition – Arame's anti-intellectualism – Defense of the naïve faith of the people – Concept of an "intelligent nature" – The cosmic status of Israel and the role of Torah – Defeatist mood of Ya-abetz – Philosophic speculation a hindrance to survival – Substitution of Qabbalah for philosophy

CHAPTER ONE

THE PHILOSOPHY OF THE
OLD TESTAMENT

How did the revolutionary concepts of monotheism take hold of the Jewish people? Did the transition from paganism to monotheism take place suddenly, so that the religion of Israel was from the beginning identified with the national consciousness of Israel? If such were the case, we should have to regard the occasional lapses from pure monotheism as exceptional and superficial deviations on the part of marginal elements. We should then interpret the making of the golden calf as the work of a tiny, noisy minority; the denunciations of the prophets as due to the perfectionist zealotry of impassioned souls; the building of temples for the gods of King Solomon's wives, the Baal worship in the time of King Ahab and the idolatry of King Menasheh as foreign importations that never struck deep roots in the hearts of the people.

It is certain that the introduction of monotheism upon the stage of history represented a tremendous advance over the ways of thinking and living that are native to humanity. Though the cultures of paganism come in a thousand varieties, they share in certain common elements that are contradicted by the monotheistic mentality. Monotheism is a deep and mighty spiritual revolution that begins with a series of affirmations concerning God and ends by transforming the entire structure of human society. This marvelous reorientation of the human soul achieved its first triumph among the children of Israel some time during the Biblical period, roughly from the fifteenth to the fourth century B.C.E. In later centuries, a similar metamorphosis was to transmute the spirit of the Greco-Roman world, through the emergence of Christianity, and still later, the lands of Western Asia and Northern Africa were to be similarly affected by the rise of Islam. The first and original revolution took place within the heart of Israel. But how?

To the fundamentalist Jew, the answer is clear and simple. It was the Lord Himself who revealed the fullness of truth to Adam. Gradually, through the steady degeneration of humanity, idolatry proliferated in diverse forms. However, a few great men remained loyal to the truth. In the course of time, only the descendants of Shem, son of Noah, cherished the true tradition. Abraham, belonging to the tenth generation after Noah, was the recipient of direct revelation from God. Thereafter the truths of Judaism remained in the possession of the descendants of Abraham until the appearance of Moses, through whom the Divine Torah in its entirety was given to the children of Israel. Following the death of Moses, the variations in Israel's spiritual life consisted only in periodic oscillations between loyalty and rebellion, faithfulness to Israel's peculiar heritage and surrender to the lure of alien gods. The prophets did not present new truths; they sought only to inculcate the spirit of devotion to the Torah of Moses. There was no evolution in the advance of Judaism from Moses to Ezra and from Ezra to Hillel, only periodic backslidings that were due principally to foreign influences, with the people returning to the Torah of Sinai, under the leadership of judges and prophets, scribes and sages.

In direct opposition to the fundamentalist point of view, the classical school of Bible criticism, deriving from the massive labors of hundreds of scholars, postulated a progressive evolution of monotheistic thought that was primarily achieved by the great literary prophets. Down to the rise of the prophetic school in the eighth century B.C.E., the Israelites were monolatrous but not monotheistic; i.e., they worshiped one god, in the belief that, in the land of Israel, only the "God of Israel" was the Supreme Master, but they did not assume the existence of only one God in the entire universe. The prophets were mighty men of genius, who gradually transformed the thinking of the people, and out of prevailing folk traditions created the wondrous saga of the Pentateuch dealing with the creation of the world and the early history of Israel. The Pentateuch is composed out of several diverse documents (J.E.D. and P.) that were collated and edited by Ezra and his disciples (circa 400 B.C.E.). Accordingly the magnificent spiritual wonder of monotheism was the work of " God-intoxicated " individuals who hammered out their ideas on the reluctant anvil of the primitive culture of the Israelites, molding the unlikely material into the pattern that was shown to them on the mount. And this struggle of prophetic genius and inspiration against the pride and prejudice of the people, recurring in various forms for many centuries, was climaxed by the appearance of Jesus and the tragedy of his repudiation.

The central pillars of "higher criticism" or the Graf-Wellhausen theory, as it came to be known, have been considerably undermined by the progress of Biblical study. The patriarchal age, as described in the book of Genesis, is now believed to represent authentic traditions. Monotheism obviously antedated the appearance of the Hebrew prophets in the eighth century. How, then, did it arise? Kaufman, reflecting the accents of modern Jewish nationalism, propounded the theory that monotheism constituted the natural expression of the national spirit of Israel. From the beginning of its appearance upon the stage of history, the Jewish people was endowed with a " peculiar " orientation of mind and heart, which gave rise to the intellectual concepts and moral sentiments of monotheism. Not only the prophets and priests, but also the people generally were so deeply permeated with the idea of one God that they could not even understand, much less surrender to, the pagan mentality. Idolatry and all its works were utterly foreign to the Jewish soul. All the stories of Israel's " backsliding " were for the most part exaggerated by the perfectionist zeal of the prophets. Occasionally, kings imitated foreign fashions in Divine worship, for political and social reasons, and the women of Jerusalem were from time to time seduced by the surface glamor of Canaanite practices and superstitions. But these deviations were empty of real content, devoid of deep roots in the national tradition and confined to marginal elements of the population. Like the white foam on ocean waves, idolatry in Israel had high visibility, but it was ephemeral and superficial.

In this chapter we deal with the philosophy of the Holy Scriptures as a whole. Hence we have to deny ourselves the pleasure of tracing the evolution of monotheistic thought during the Biblical period. However, since ideas never entirely lose the stamp of their origin, we need to bear in mind the various theories concerning the origin and evolution of the Jewish religion. In general, we follow the interpretations of Kaufman and Kassuto, though not in all respects. We do not assume that the "national soul" of Israel was fashioned in a unique mold and we do not look upon paganism and monotheism as if they were totally disparate worlds of thought. As will appear in the sequel, we recognize that paganism and monotheism are polar concepts, with the pattern of thought of the prophets and the people falling somewhere between the two opposite poles—the prophets tending in the direction of monotheistic spirituality, the people occupying various stages in the direction of paganism.

This does not mean that monotheism arose spontaneously among the people. There is no reason to doubt the appearance of Moses as a "servant of the Lord," who launched both the people of Israel and the God of Israel upon the stage of history. A covenant was concluded at Sinai which had the effect of fashioning a peculiar nation, committed to the abolition of paganism and all its works. The image of the first prophet served as the symbol of "messengers" that God had promised to send unto His people. These "messengers" were first the judges and later the literary prophets. This image of the "servant of the Lord" became also the archetype of the future Redeemer, the Messiah.

Kaufman summarizes his conclusions: [1]

> Before their entrance into the land of Canaan, there arose among the tribes of Israel a religious movement which brought about their unification into a religious-national covenant. This movement resulted from the appearance of a new religious idea, which contained within itself the negation of paganism. Its symbol and its banner was the name of God (YHVH). The creator of the movement was a prophet-messenger (as distinguished from the "prophetizers" of the ancient world). He was the messenger of the new God, the herald of the new idea, the prophet of the one, exalted God. His religious message was clothed in a national form, fashioning a "people of God" out of the tribes of Israel and setting before them a great national task. His appearance led the people to expect prophet-messengers. Thus the prophetic kingdom of God was founded. He planted in the soul of the people the seed of the new idea, and as this seed grew and flourished, the wellsprings of mythological thought were gradually dried up. Prophet-messengers, like Moses, arose in Israel in every generation. They nurtured the Israelite religious idea, incorporating it into the life of the people.

By degrees, prophetic monotheism in its full majesty became the religion of the people, especially so after the Babylonian exile.

At no time, however, were the prophets so remote from the people as to interpose a hiatus between them. The prophets were not a band of esoteric teachers, separating themselves from the multitude. They spoke *for* the people as well as *to* them. The contemporaries of Isaiah or Jeremiah were certainly not all the "seed of evildoers"; else they would not have treasured the words of their preachers. On the other hand, the inclusion of any one book into the Hebrew canon did not necessarily mean the widespread incorporation of its precepts into the life and thought of the people.

The polarity of monotheism and paganism is evident in the entire domain of spiritual life. Metaphysically, monotheism asserts that God transcends nature, and is not identical with or part of it, while paganism includes the gods within the realm of natural forces. Yet the distinction is not absolute. For in the Bible there are lingering references to the Canaanite myths concerning the Lord's conquest of the god of the sea. And in the higher pagan religions, the gods are not regarded as fetishes of wood and stone, but as spiritual entities governing the forces of nature. Thus, too, monotheism postulates a host of angels, including Satan, alongside God, while in the higher forms of paganism, there was always a dominating figure, a "father of the gods." In monotheism, God is not subject to the variations of mortal life; hence there is no mythology or theogony in the Bible. But in the Holy Scriptures we are told of God's being bound by oaths that He had taken and also of His rejoicing and His mourning, of His anger and His relenting, of His "hiding" and retiring and of His descent to the earth. Most importantly, perhaps, in monotheism, man serves God by doing His will in humility, piety and devotion, not by placating Him through gifts of various sorts. But even among a deeply monotheistic people there will be many who will seek to "appease" God's wrath by ritual devices and external acts rather than by "returning" to that state of heart and soul which is in accord with God's will. The tension between paganism and monotheism is therefore actually infinite in extent and duration. Man is born pagan, and he becomes monotheistic only imperfectly and partially.

The teachers of Israel presented their all-encompassing philosophy of life by way of editing and transmuting the literary tradition of the people. They did not embody their teaching in an abstract system of ideas, but they directed the impetus of their inspired genius toward the reshaping of the prevailing tales, myths, and traditions. The people of Israel derived from Babylonia, dwelt long in Syria and Palestine and resided for several generations in Egypt. They were acquainted with the myths and theologies of the greatest civilizations of their day. They cherished songs and stylized stories, similar to those of the Canaanites, in which there were celebrated the creation of heaven and earth, the emergence of mankind and man's fall from grace, the story of the Deluge, the emergence of their ancestors and the faith that they taught. The national literature of Israel came closer to Biblical monotheism than that of their neighboring nations, but it was still replete with pagan residue. In the Holy Scriptures we see a thorough retelling and re-editing of the ancient traditions in the spirit of the Biblical faith of the teachers of Israel. In keeping with the ancient pedagogical methods, abstract ideas are not presented in philosophical terms, but by way of symbols and pictures, stories and incidents. And the intent of the Holy Scriptures can be inferred as much by the portions that the inspired editors left out, as by the incidents that they incorporated in the body of the sacred tradition. The full significance of any Biblical doctrine or practice can be appreciated only when it is studied in the light of the contemporary pagan notions and practices.

The story of the Deluge is a case in point. The Babylonian version of this tale has many points in common with the Biblical story. In both versions we read of a decision on the part of the gods to destroy mankind and all living things by means of a flood; of the saving of one man and his relatives, together with representatives of all living species, by the interposition of a god who instructs the favored man to construct an ark and to gather in it those that are destined to be saved; of the downpour of the flood waters, the floating of the ark and of its final resting on a mountain peak; of the sending of birds from the ark to learn if the waters had receded; of the bringing of sacrifices by the saved man, after he leaves the ark; of the acceptance by the gods of the sacrifices that the saved human family offers; and of a blessing that the gods confer upon the children of man.

The differences between the Biblical and the Mesopotamian story are equally striking. According to the Mesopotamian account, the god Enlil engineered the Deluge because the noise of humanity disturbed his sleep. According to the Gilgamesh tale, the decision of the gods to annihilate mankind was altogether arbitrary. In contrast, we note that in the Biblical tale, the human sins of adultery and robbery were the cause of the Divine decision to punish mankind. By the same token, the saving of the favored man in the Mesopotamian myths was not motivated by his piety or saintliness, whereas, in the Biblical story, Noah was saved because of his righteousness.

In the tale of Gilgamesh, we read of a division of opinion among the gods, of their trembling in fear of the elemental forces of nature that they had let loose and of their gathering " like flies " to enjoy the fragrance of the sacrifices brought by the small, human family that was saved. In the Biblical story, One Will judges, decides, rewards, and punishes. And this One Will is guided by the principle of absolute justice. It remains but to add that, in the Mesopotamian myths, the hero of the flood is elevated to the rank of god, whereas, in the Bible, the boundary between the human and the Divine is impassable and irrevocable. Thus, the Biblical story of the Deluge illustrates how the raw material of Near Eastern legendry was transmuted by the inspired genius of the Biblical authors. They clothed their divine teachings in the cultural notions and practices of their day because they sought to mold the life of a whole people. Not content with the establishment of an esoteric society of saints and sages, they set for themselves the high task of transforming the people of Israel into " a people of priests and a holy nation."[2]

Is it possible to speak of a Biblical philosophy of life? Does not the Hebrew Bible contain many diverse views regarding the nature of God, of man, and of the good life? Indeed, it is possible to cite Biblical verses in proof of many and differing views concerning man and God. Several of the books of the Bible bear the individual stamp of their authors. Nevertheless, it is incontestable that the Holy Scriptures conveyed to countless generations of people a philosophy of life that was sufficiently precise for their daily needs. We must learn to distinguish between logical consistency and the compatibility of diverse ideas in countering the actual pressures of life. The unifying thread that runs from Genesis to Chronicles in unbroken sequence through legend, law, prophetic utterance, and pious psalmody is the quest for the good life, so as to be pure in the sight of God. Speaking of the divine choice of Abraham, the Torah states, " in order that he might command his children to keep the way of the Lord to do justice and righteousness."[3] In the light of this yearning for the fullness of human dignity, the lore of the past was recast and reinterpreted; in the light of a covenant with the one God, the laws of social life were amended and a marvelous set of utopian principles was enunciated. Inseparable in the Biblical view were the yearning for the good life, the acknowledgment of the one God, and the covenant of the people of Israel with the Creator of heaven and earth. The unity of the Biblical world view is that of a quest, a faith, and a sense of historical commitment.

Does this view of the unity of the Biblical message contradict the doctrine of divine inspiration? Not if inspiration be taken in a nonliteral sense, as applying to the inner core of meaning. When we read a great poem, we recognize that the truth of its message is relatively independent of the worth and weight of any single syllable, or word, or figure of speech. As we study the evolution of ideas in the Biblical span of one thousand years, we find that the Word of God came to be heard with ever greater clarity. By the same token, we learn to recognize the Word of God in the pages of our Holy Scriptures with ever greater distinctness, as we pursue our own quest for the good life in the spirit of truthfulness, humility, and reverence.

In the richly variegated and panoramic view of life that the Holy Scriptures present to our gaze, there is but One Hero, the Lord God. In Him the quest for the good life has its source, motivation, and fulfillment. All human figures are heroic only insofar as they serve His will, as willing servants, as faithful messengers, or as involuntary instruments. The patriarchs are not heroes in their own right; they happen to be beloved of the Lord. The prophet is His messenger, approximating the vision of a hero, but no prophet, not even Moses, is the image of perfection. The people of Israel are His " portion," and the entire travail of mankind has meaning only by reference to His will.

Hence our analysis of the implicit philosophy of the Holy Bible must begin with the idea of God. The next focus of our attention will be the people of Israel, for it is through their tragedy and destiny that the character of God is manifested in the actual course of history. Lastly we shall deal with the character of the good life, as it is portrayed in the Bible. For it is around three luminous foci that Jewish piety was concentrated from the very beginning—God, Israel, and Torah.

The central theme of the Holy Scriptures is sounded in the opening sentence of Genesis: " In the beginning, God created heaven and earth." God is the Creator and Master of the universe. All the things that the eye can see and the hand can touch are the works of God. But He is beyond and above all that is material. And He is not an abstract idea, but a living being. To the Israelites, God was conceived principally as the ideal personality. If man was created in His image, it is because the image of Him constantly assumed by the writers of the Bible is that of a perfect personality, freed from the inescapable limitations of flesh and blood.

In the first place, His power is unlimited. Sarah is rebuked for momentary skepticism with the query, *Ha-yipaleh me'adonai dabar?* " Is anything too wonderful for the Lord? "[4] There can be no limits to His power, since all existence was wrought out of nothingness by His Word. Darkness and evil do not represent forces opposing light and good, for He is the author of these negative phases of existence as well, even though it is light, not darkness that He pronounces to be good.[5] The power of God is manifest in the creation of heaven and earth and in the invariable operation of the laws that He set for the elements of nature. " The heavens declare the glory of God and the firmament showeth His handiwork: "[6] " When I behold Thy heavens, the work of Thy fingers, the moon and the stars, which Thou hast established; What is man that Thou art mindful of Him? And the son of man that Thou thinkest of him? "[7] On rare occasions the power of God is revealed in special " signs " and miracles, such as the plagues of Egypt and the miracles in the desert. For the basic principle of the Biblical conception of God is the absence of any limitation upon the absoluteness of His power.

Allied to God's attribute of power is His infinite wisdom, which is not limited either by the impenetrable darkness of fate or by the unpredictable whims of chance. The thoughts of men are to

Him even as an open book. His wisdom is compounded of a hierarchy of ethical and esthetic values as well as an all-embracing knowledge. Therefore, His wisdom was occasionally envisioned as a positive, ethereal entity that functioned as the loyal companion of the Lord, as it were.

> The Lord made me as the beginning of His way, the first of His works of old. I was set up from everlasting, from the beginning, Or ever the earth was. When there were no depths, I was brought forth, When there were no fountains abounding with water. . . . Then I was by Him as a nurseling; And I was daily all delight, playing always before Him, Playing in His habitable earth, And my delights are with the sons of men.[8]

The Wisdom of God was incorporated into the structure of the universe, but it is not possible for man to rediscover His wisdom by his own efforts and observation, save only by faith, humility and reverence.

> Trust in the Lord with all thy heart, And lean not upon thine own understanding. In all thy ways acknowledge Him, And He will direct thy paths. . . . The Lord by wisdom hath founded the earth, By understanding hath He established the heavens.[9]

Another corollary of the infinity of God's power is His eternity. Since no elemental or primeval power exists which was not created by Him, He is both first and last.[10] In this doctrine, the repudiation of pagan mythology is complete and uncompromising. For the genealogy of the gods plays a most important role in every pagan system. Almost universally, the ruling gods of the pagan world were second- or third-generation gods, having come forth out of the primeval chaos, or out of the primitive semigods, antedating the emergence of the present world. Manifestly, if the gods are the scions of a more primeval, impersonal substance, then they might be expected to sink back into its dark formlessness at some future time. There is no trace of any such conception of *Götterdämmerung*, the twilight of the gods, in the Bible. God is not only immortal, enduring as long as the world, but He is eternal, first and last, outside the flow of time and the change of the seasons.

As the ideal personality, God is the judge and active ruler of the universe. Thus, Abraham exclaims, " Shall not the judge of all the earth do justly? "[11] In contrast to the Greek ideal, which projected the perfect personality as a being utterly self-sufficient, content, and unconcerned with any person or thing, the Israelites conceived of perfection in the active terms of practical sainthood. Thus Aristotle portrayed the Deity as being aloof from all earthly matters, busying Himself with the most perfect of all conceivable occupations, namely, the contemplation of His own perfection. In Scriptures, on the contrary, the Lord is portrayed as the "judge of the entire earth," descending to examine the corruption of Sodom and beholding with profound sympathy "the poor, and him who is of a contrite spirit, and who trembleth at my word."[12] Free from the limitations of the human judge, He looks to man's inward self, and His judgments are "righteous altogether." "For man looketh on the outward appearance, but the Lord looketh on the heart."[13] Since His judgment is conceived as taking place in this earthly world, the problem of the wicked prospering and the righteous suffering presented a sorely perplexing dilemma. To be sure, the prophet Isaiah warned that it is impossible to escape His judgment by fleeing to Sheol, the nether world; but, then primarily, His dominion is exercised in this world, not in the shadowy and insubstantial realm of post-mortem existence. Hence, the poignancy of Jeremiah's outcry, "Why is the way of the wicked prosperous? "[14]

The corresponding problem of the suffering of the righteous is treated at length in the Book of Job, and in scattered psalms and prophetic passages. The standard and authoritative answer, in spite of numerous challenges and rebellious utterances, remained unshaken; to wit: Ultimately, even in this life, the righteous are properly rewarded and the wicked are punished according to their deserts. So the Psalmist declares, "When the wicked sprout forth as the grass and the workers of iniquity flourish, it is only to be destroyed forever."[15] And the author or the editor of the Book of Job supplies the final answer to all who doubt, by relating that Job was compensated for his misfortunes by receiving from the hands of the Lord twice the number of children and the possessions that were taken away from him by Satan.[16] Modern commentators believe that the last chapter of the Book of Job was a later addition. The original author would not have accepted so facile an ending. After all, the righteous may suffer not only temporarily, but throughout their lives. Apparently the original author satisfied Job's quest for understanding by having God appear to him out of the storm. It was sufficient for Job to know that God was with him. We cannot comprehend the inscrutable ways of God, but the righteous are certain that God shares their sorrows and hopes. The companionship of God is the good man's consolation.

Suffering is not the mark of sin, for people may bear the burden of grief laid upon them by the unfathomable wisdom of God for some mysterious purpose, or they may bear the guilt of others, either individually or collectively, as the "suffering servants."

> Surely our diseases he did bear, and our pains he carried; Whereas we did esteem him stricken, Smitten of God and afflicted. But he was wounded because of our transgressions, He was crushed because of our iniquities; The chastisement of our welfare was upon him, and with His stripes we were healed.[17]

These verses were applied by the early Christians to their Saviour. But the life of nearly every prophet could have served for Isaiah as the prototype of his vision. The prophet is a messenger of the Lord, yet he is frequently abused by his contemporaries. Those who do God's work in this world must be willing to endure misery and humiliation, waiting long and patiently for their vindication. Nevertheless, since God is just, He stands by the side of His servants, and He is certain to compensate them for their sacrifices. The reward of the righteous may be long delayed, but it will not be denied.

This concept of the Lord as the merciful judge, whose verdicts may be understood only when seen against the background of centuries, led to the view of God as the author of the drama of human history. When the affairs of mankind are viewed as a whole and properly understood, then the judgment of God is seen to be just and inexorable. This insight made it possible for the Biblical authors to contemplate the vicissitudes of their own time "under the aspect of eternity," and to build up an impressive philosophy of history. The agonies of the Israelites in Egypt were to be understood as preparatory training for their destiny as "a people of priests." The dross of their character, conceived chiefly as arrogance, had to be purged in the crucible of Egypt, in order that they might emerge as a humbled and spiritualized people, aware of their kinship with all who are downtrodden and oppressed.

"But you hath the Lord taken and brought forth out of the iron furnace, out of Egypt, to be unto Him a people of inheritance as ye are this day."[18] Purified in the crucible of pain, the children of Israel could be expected to love the stranger and to understand the soul of the slave.[19] "Behold, I have refined thee, but not as silver; I have tried thee in the furnace of affliction."[20]

Arrogance is indeed the chief sin of the nations, a circumstance which accounts for the generalization, "Before the breakup, greatness is attained."[21] Sennacherib, the ruthless empire builder of Assyria, was the "rod of the Lord's anger," the instrument of His chastisement.[22] But, he did not realize his place in the divine scheme of things, as a tyrant rarely does, and he therefore allowed his ambition to drive him to his eventual destruction through the avenging anger of another human instrument. Thus, every potentate is entrusted with a divine mission, and woe betide him if he oversteps its boundaries. Within his proper limitations, however, not only a king in Israel, but a conquering emperor like Cyrus is called a *mashiach*—"an anointed one [of the Lord]," chosen to be the instrument of His will on earth.[23]

The Biblical conception of history embraced in its vista the whole of mankind, not merely one nation or one geographical position. God concluded a covenant (*b'rith*) first with Adam, then with Noah, then with Abraham, "father of a multitude of nations," lastly with the children of Israel. So the Bible transcended the mental world of contemporary paganism by projecting the concept of one humanity. All men are descended from one family. Through the delusion created by pride, they sought to build the tower of Babel, and they were scattered to the ends of the earth and made to speak in many languages. In the end, the original situation of mankind will be reinstated. The "covering" will be removed from the faces of men. All nations will learn to speak a "clear language."[24] So we see that the Scriptures represented the tragic dynamism of the human drama as being not a conflict of the gods or their capriciousness, but the unfolding consequences of human arrogance and folly, rising again and again to challenge the will of God.

To be sure, the implications of God's concern with all nations were not always clearly realized and consciously affirmed. Some scholars maintain that the doctrine of God's universal providence was a late development. Thus, King David believed that he could not worship the God of Israel outside the land of Israel.[25] But, while other lands were "unclean" and unfit for worship, the Lord in Jerusalem was believed to hear the prayers of all people.[26] While the Holy Land and the people of Israel were God's "portion," His concern for the moral life of all humanity is stressed in the tragedy of Sodom and in the mission of Jonah. In the major portion of the Scriptures, idolatry was conceived as a sin only for the Israelites, on account of the covenant concluded with them, but crimes of morality were punished by God throughout the world. Thus, the book of Deuteronomy speaks of subordinate gods as being assigned by the one God to the various nations.[27] However, the literary prophets repudiated this assumption and projected the hope of the eventual conversion of all men to the worship of the one God. Long before the prophets asserted their conviction that all men are obligated to serve the one God, the Israelites came to believe that His concern and His Providence extended to all mankind.

A direct implication of the concept of God as the judge of mankind and the author of human history is the doctrine of the "day of the Lord," which is proclaimed with passionate intensity by a succession of prophets. On that climactic day, all the accounts will be settled, as it were, and all wrongs will be righted. It will be a day of judgment for individuals and peoples, a day when the full majesty of the Lord will be revealed, and His justice will be asserted. As one reads the prophets, one cannot fail to be impressed with the sense of urgency that the vision of the "day of the Lord" evoked in their minds. It was not a prophecy for distant days, but for the "here and now," for "the day of the Lord is near," and His judgment will be final and devastating.[28] The Biblical conception of history implied that the justice of God is carried out, first, by means of the actual unfolding of the divine design in the rise and fall of empires, and secondly, through a sudden, overwhelming and all-embracing day of judgment, when all accounts are to be righted with one stroke. Manifestly, the two phases of this conception were not contradictory, and the second phase was viewed as achieving that which the first left undone.

Two phases are implied in the concept of the "day of the Lord"—one of punishment, the other of the state of redemption that follows the ordeal of destruction. The first phase is well exemplified in Jeremiah's vision. "Take this cup of the wine of fury at My hand, and cause all the nations to whom I send thee to drink it. And they shall drink, and reel to and fro, and be like madmen, because of the sword that I will send among them."[29] The state of redemption that will follow God's chastisement will consist in the "repentance" of all nations and their being accepted by God as His "portion."

> And the Lord will smite Egypt, smiting and healing, and they shall return unto the Lord, and He will be entreated of them, and will heal them. In that day shall there be a highway out of Egypt to Assyria, and the Assyrian shall come into Egypt, and the Egyptian into Assyria; and the Egyptians shall worship with the Assyrians. In that day shall Israel be the third with Egypt and with Assyria, a blessing in the midst of the earth; for that the Lord of Hosts hath blessed him saying: "Blessed be Egypt my people and Assyria the work of my hands, and Israel Mine inheritance."[30]

Associated with the doctrine of the "day of the Lord," but rising immeasurably beyond it in sublimity of conception, is the belief in the advent of the Messiah, at the end of days. As described by Isaiah and Micah, the Messiah will be a "branch out of the stem of Jesse," a king of Israel, but immensely more than a mere king. Primarily, he will be the ideal human personality, perfect and Godlike, but human and mortal. He will execute judgment with a divine intuition, "judging not according to the sight of his eyes and rebuking not according to the hearing of his ears."[31] With his advent, a new age of human life will be ushered in. Along with the perfection of the human personality, as symbolized in the Messiah, there will be attained also the ethical perfection of human society and perhaps also of the animal kingdom. Absolute peace and perfect justice will prevail across the entire face of the globe, and "the spirit of the Lord will cover the earth as the waters cover the sea."[32]

Zion or Jerusalem will be the spiritual capital of the world, with all the nations coming to it, not to pay political tribute, nor simply to acknowledge the supremacy of the God of Israel, but to learn the ways of the Lord. They will not then abandon their separate ways of worship, for, according to at least two prophets, it is possible for the several nations to worship the one true God, through the refinement of their own respective cults. "For all the nations will walk each in the name of its god, and we shall walk in the name of the Lord, our God," says Micah; and the prophet Malachi declared, "for in all places, incense is burned and offerings are brought to My name."[33] Other prophets, especially Jeremiah and Deutero-Isaiah, looked forward to the abandonment of idolatry on the part of all mankind. "Unto Thee shall the nations come from the ends of the earth and shall say: 'Our fathers have inherited nought but lies, vanity and things wherein there is no profit.' Shall a man make unto himself gods, And they are no gods?"[34] As to the religion that all nations will accept, Jeremiah asserts that it will take the form of intensified inward piety, a "new covenant" that will be written upon the tablets of the heart, and Micah described it in memorable words: "He hath told thee, O Man, what is good; and what doth the Lord require of thee? Only to do justice, and to love kindness, and to walk humbly with thy God."[35]

The Messianic age is represented as a magnificent victory for the people of Israel and a vindication of its historic role as the "suffering servant" of mankind, but it does not necessarily imply a position of political pre-eminence for the Jewish people. It is the faith of Israel that will be proven true, while the people of Israel will attain only a central position of spiritual influence, because theirs is the task of serving as a "light unto the nations" and witnesses unto the Lord. To be sure, they will be reassembled in their own land, where they will be once again free and united, respected and beloved, but this is a consummation that is expressly promised to all other deserving peoples.[36]

No doctrine in Judaism is as deeply rooted in the inherent logic of monotheism as the belief in the Messiah, and none reflected so sensitively the changing moods and fortunes of the Jewish people. Since God represents the absolute unity of pure justice and infinite power, it is impossible to escape the conclusion that His kingdom will one day be fully established. The original state of the world when it emerged fresh from the hand of the Creator must be re-established in a paradise-like society.

In the prayer of King Solomon, the ideal age is believed to be in the present.[37] God has fulfilled His promise. In the books of Leviticus and Deuteronomy, edited in the latter years of the Judean kingdom, the fourfold link between sin, exile, repentance and redemption is asserted.[38] To this chain of deliverance, the prophet Ezekiel adds the motive of the "sanctification" of the Holy Name. The prophet Amos still speaks of the coming of redemption, rather than of a redeemer.[39] In the prophecies of Isaiah, the house of David was portrayed as the central symbol of the Messianic age. All of mankind was to share in the glories of the Messianic kingdom. Jeremiah stressed the inwardness of piety in the days of redemption.[40] But it was Deutero-Isaiah who gave the Messianic hope its most glowing expression, describing it as the mission of Israel to be a "light unto the nations."

Yea, He hath said: "It is too light a thing that thou shouldst be My servant to raise up the tribes of Jacob, and to restore the offspring of Israel; I will also give thee for a light of the nations, that My salvation may be to the ends of the earth."[41]

The conversion of all men, not merely of the Jewish people, was now affirmed as the hope of Israel.

Also the aliens, that join themselves
to the Lord, to minister unto Him.
And to love the name of the Lord,
To be His servants,
Everyone that keepeth the Sabbath
from profaning it,
And holdeth fast by My covenant:
Even them will I bring to My holy
mountain,
And make them joyful in My house
of prayer;
Their burnt offerings and their sacrifices
shall be acceptable upon Mine altar;
For My house shall be called
A house of prayer for all peoples.[42]

However, the prophets did not urge the launching of an active, organized missionary effort for the purpose of converting mankind to monotheism. God will bring about the consummation of His design in His own good time.

What is the nature of God and how is His being to be conceived? In the Holy Scriptures, we are told on nearly every page that God is the most fundamental reality, but not what He is.

God is conceived as an ideal personality, but without a material body; He may not be represented by any image, because He is unlike all things. Scripture speaks of the radiance "beneath His feet,"[43] of His perceiving the fragrance of sacrifice,[44] of His riding on the cherubim,[45] of His occasional anger, regret and reconciliation,[46] of His right hand and the smoke of "His nostrils."[47] But all these expressions were to the Biblical authors hardly more than poetic representations. In every prophetic vision, the voice of God is heard distinctly, but only the radiance about Him, or the "carriage" beneath Him is seen.[48] The cherubim above the veil of the Holy Ark were probably intended to represent the cloud within which the Lord is hidden.[49]

Though they were not metaphysicians or logicians, the prophets realized intuitively that the being of God can be conceived by people only as the source of the imperatives of action. Thus, when Moses asks to see the divine glory, he is told "that man may not see Me and live."[50] However, he is permitted to see the Lord from the back, as it were; the content of what he has seen is then described by Moses in words of moral action: "The Lord, the Lord, God merciful and gracious, long-suffering and abundant in goodness and truth; keeping mercy unto the thousandth generation, forgiving iniquity and transgression and sin . . ."[51]

Similarly, in Elijah's vision, God is in the "still, small voice," not in the fire, wind, and storm that preceded it.[52] The voice of God is heard in the inner recesses of the soul, though His felt presence is always preceded by or associated with overwhelming physical phenomena, such as the thunder and fire on Mount Sinai, the cloud of glory resting on the sanctuary, the pillar of fire and smoke in the desert, the radiance beneath His feet observed by the elders of Israel, the complex "divine carriage" with wheels within wheels perceived by Ezekiel. Though Isaiah writes of his seeing the Lord, he describes actually only the events associated with the divine presence, "whose train filled up the temple."[53] It is by means of audible commands that the Deity communicates with the prophets, for the dialogue is the one instrument by which two minds commune with each other.

To be sure, there abounded in ancient Israel bands of ecstatics and "prophetizers," to whom "inspiration" evidently came in the delirium of a fevered frenzy. But the true prophets of Israel steered clear of irrational, ecstatic babbling and identified the voice of God with the imperative of a superlatively keen conscience and with the rare experience of holiness. In sum, the Biblical conception of the Deity is that of a living personality, infinite in power, wisdom, and goodness; at times, retiring and "hiding," at times, coming close and "brightening" its countenance; occasionally, traveling and resting; observing all men and choosing some among them as objects of special interest and love; given to inscrutable and wrathful decisions, but ever ready to be reconciled. He is spirit, with all the fathomless depth of a Soul of souls, not simply a mind nor an abstract absolute, a disembodied ghost, or a soulless principle; He is free from all the weaknesses and impulses that are associated with flesh and blood, but He lacks none of the powers of a personality.

The Biblical conception of God commends itself with overwhelming immediacy to spiritually minded people, even as it presents a perpetual challenge to the most subtle and speculative philosophers. Its very simplicity and universal appeal make it difficult for us to comprehend the tremendous revolution which it brought about in the minds of men. From the moment of its appearance in the titanic spirit of Moses, it marked the birth of an unending revolution, a dynamic movement for freedom, justice, and human dignity. Immense and wide-ranging are the consequences that flow from the assertion that the will of God is supreme in heaven above and in the earth beneath. The power of God is conceived in the Scriptures as being so absolute as to preclude the existence of other gods, no matter how inferior, battling against Him. Accordingly, all the phenomena of nature as well as the happenings of history cannot be explained either in terms of a struggle between divine forces, or by recourse to the blind processes of fate to which even the gods must yield, or by pointing to the resistance offered by the forces of chaos to the execution of the divine will. The whole range of existence was part of one plan.

The uniqueness and supremacy of God evoked the feelings of majesty and sublimity, as well as the feeling of absolute love and devotion. Only that which is divine is noble. "The lofty looks of man shall be brought low, and the haughtiness of men shall be bowed down, And the Lord alone shall be exalted in that day."[54]

More practical were the implications that Jeremiah drew from the feeling of divine sublimity:

> Thus saith the Lord, Let not the wise man glory in his wisdom, Neither let the mighty man glory in His might. Let not the rich man glory in his riches; But let him that glorieth glory in this, that he understandeth and knoweth Me, that I am the Lord who exercises mercy, justice and righteousness, in the earth. For in these things I delight, Saith the Lord.[55]

In polar opposition to the divine will, there was ranged not an elemental force, but the obstinacy of human nature. It was the very freedom and consequent pride of man that account for the rebellion against God and the long train of evils flowing from it. Idolatry is frequently identified with human pride.[56] Though idolatry was a cardinal sin only in the case of Israel, all nations were to be punished for their wilfulness and arrogance.[57] Hence the rise and fall of nations and the ebb and flow of Israel's fortunes. While in virtually all pagan philosophies, matter or chaos was primary and therefore more ultimate than the gods, in monotheism, the Deity, representing and championing all the values of the spirit, was absolutely supreme, save as it was controverted by the free and obdurate wills of men.

The revolutionary import of the monotheistic conception derived from its fateful synthesis of absolute power with the totality of spiritual values. The exaltation of God implies the exaltation of man's spirit and the ultimate conquest of the demonic impulses slumbering in the depths of the human psyche. For God is the projection on the canvas of infinity of the lines of spiritual growth in human nature. The doctrine of man being fashioned in the "image of God" implies that man is truly himself only when his soul is turned toward God in utmost devotion and trust. In the Scriptures, man is more likely to be evil than good when he does not trust in God.[58] This emphasis is particularly evident in the claim that all forms of evil are associated with idolatry. Only those who "cleave unto the Lord" or keep the "way of the Lord" can live the good life. The Biblical conception of God implies a conception of man which is neither naturalistic nor dualistic, neither idealistic nor pessimistic, but God-centered. To "walk before Him" is the source of all goodness, or, to use Biblical terms, God is holy and all human goodness derives from holiness.

The totality of spiritual values is designated by the Biblical writers as the realm of the holy. God is frequently referred to as "the Holy One of Israel."[59] The seraphim in Isaiah's vision declare Him to be thrice holy.[60] Many of the laws in the Pentateuch are prefaced with the introduction, "And be ye holy, for I, the Lord, am holy."[61]

There is a dimension of mystery to the concept of holiness, since the surface of the human mind can only glimpse but not fully reflect the "image of God." Hence, the irrational and the mysterious enter inevitably into the context of the holy. In our Holy Scriptures, many rites and taboos were invested with the valance of holiness. A living faith can hardly dispense altogether with ritual observances, and every rite symbolizes by its irrationality man's reverence for the unknown. Nevertheless, there is an endless tension within the feeling of holiness between the rational and the ethical elements, on the one hand, and the emotional, nonrational elements on the other hand. We may describe this tension as the struggle between the priestly and the prophetic conceptions of faith. Thus, in the Pentateuch, ritual observances are listed side by side with moral commands. The literary prophets, one and all, emphasized the centrality of the moral imperative in the life of holiness.

The opposite of *Kedushah*, holiness, was *tumeah*, uncleanliness. In the concept of *tumeah* we easily discern the same tension between the ethical and the ritual denotations as in the concept of holiness. Acts of moral depravity are "unclean," but some animals are also "unclean," as are the corpses of the dead and certain bodily discharges. In the Biblical period, the priestly and prophetic elements were kept in an uneasy balance. Though the spell of "ritual uncleanliness" was powerful and pervasive in the religion of Israel, we seldom encounter the implication that *tumeah* represented a diabolical dominion of darkness, opposing the rule of the one God. For the priestly mentality, which is of course common to monotheism and paganism, the "unclean" and the holy are the fundamental polar concepts. In the post-Biblical period, the laws of ritual "purity" proliferated and invaded many aspects of daily existence. While our sources for the period from Ezra (400 B.C.E.) to Hillel (40 B.C.E.) are very meager, we find that there was a continuous struggle between those who sought to expand the application of the "purity" laws and those who sought to restrict the domain of purity to the priesthood.[62]

The attribute of God which proved to be of decisive importance in history is that of His stern jealousy. The second of the ten Mosaic commandments enjoins the Israelites, "Thou shalt have no other gods beside Me."[63] Elsewhere, they are commanded, "And the name of other gods you may not mention."[64] The readiness of the Lord to forgive "iniquity and transgression and sin" is reiterated again and again. But, at the same time, the Israelites are bidden to remember "that the Lord, thy God, is a jealous God," and, that in spite of His infinite mercy, He "will by no means clear the guilty; visiting the iniquity of the fathers upon the children, and upon the children's children unto the third and fourth generation."[65]

Moved by the logic of this conception, the Israelites proceeded to destroy the Canaanite sanctuaries and idols. The progressive penetration of this concept into the thinking of the people brought about successive stages of iconoclasm among the Israelites, leading to the steady purification of the religion of Israel. Consequently Saul exterminated the diviners and the sorcerers. Jehu annihilated the worshipers of Baal in the northern kingdom; Hezekiah abolished the copper serpent made by Moses, Josiah terminated the practice of worshiping at the high places, and the prophets ridiculed the "golden calves" made by Jeroboam, preaching an impassioned crusade against the last vestiges of idolatry in Israel. In their terminology, idolatry is described consistently as a form of harlotry, with God as the jealous husband who is confronted with an unfaithful wife, "straying after" a multitude of worthless lovers.[66]

The uncompromising jealousy of the God of Israel has been derided by unfriendly critics as an expression of the uncharitableness and intolerance of the Israelites. In the ancient pagan world, the votaries of any one god were generally accommodating, yielding a measure of deference to other deities, and becoming resentful only when the invasion of foreign gods threatened to usurp the place of their own favored deity. The impassioned intolerance of the Israelites seemed to the ancient pagan to be an expression of inhospitality and unfriendliness.

Actually, monotheism could not have become the source of a

dynamic revolution on behalf of all the values of the spirit if it had repudiated the doctrine of the unyielding jealousy of the Lord. Judaism would have dissolved in the syncretistic cauldrons of antiquity, losing all its revolutionary fervor and moral impetus, if the prophets had not been convinced that the implacable wrath of God would pursue those who grant the slightest concessions to the worship of other gods, " that are not gods." A modicum of jealousy is inherent in man's fundamental commitment to the values of the spirit. The heathen nations of the ancient world were able to change gods, in keeping with the rise and fall of political fortunes, and to recognize fundamental identities in the myths and rites of other peoples because their gods did not represent the totality of man's higher aspirations. But the God of Israel was unique, even as the demands of the spirit are pure and exacting.

Truth is inherently jealous, incapable of yielding sanction to folly, however innocuous on the surface. And the worship of the pagans was by no means an innocent pastime. It was intimately associated with sexual immorality, the intolerance of strangers, the cheapness of human life, the subordination of conscience to ritual mumbo-jumbo, the institution of pitiless slavery and the persistent corruption of the fiber of society generally. Consequently, we find that it was precisely the doctrine of God's jealousy that functioned as the most potent factor in the growth of Israel's monotheism. While Aaron's tolerance would have permitted the degeneration of worship, through the employment of the image of the golden calf, the consciousness of the Lord's wrath led Moses to emerge as the incorruptible champion of the invisible God.[67] Samuel's awareness of the inexorability of the divine will impelled him to express one of the fundamental classical statements of emergent monotheism: " Behold, to obey is better than sacrifice, and to hearken than the fat of the rams."[68] The stern zealotry of Elijah prevented the worship of the Lord from sinking down to the base level of Canaanite religion.[69] All the literary prophets who fought valiantly for social justice, for the perfection of the individual and of society and for all the values of the spirit, derived their inspired zeal from their clear perception of divine jealousy. Their keenest perceptions of the truths of religion were associated with the call to return to the purity of the worship of the Lord.

From cover to cover, the Holy Scriptures affirm that the one God had "chosen" the people of Israel to be "His own treasure."[70] Mythological deities were connected with natural phenomena, geographical locales or tribes, by quasi-physical ties. They were personifications of one or more of the life-giving forces, or they dwelt in certain places where they wielded dominant authority, or they were the ancestors of an association of tribes. In any event, their connection with their worshipers consisted in necessitous bonds, deriving from their inherent nature. Not so the God of Israel. Since God was absolutely free, His choice of the Israelites was uncaused, motivated solely by His own inscrutable will. His was the initiative in selecting Abraham as the object of His solicitude, and the mystery of his own nature remains the source of His motivations. The Deuteronomist explains the choice of Israel as follows: "Not because ye are more in number than all the nations did the Lord desire you and make choice of you; for ye are the fewest of all the nations. But, on account of the love of the Lord for you, and because He keepeth the oath which He hath sworn unto your fathers."[71] The choice of Israel was, therefore, a free act of decision on the part of the living God.

The meaning of Israel's chosenness is that it alone is legally pledged to worship Him. While God's rule extends over all the world and all mankind *ought* to worship Him, only the people of Israel is *obliged* to spurn the worship of idols and to observe His specific commandments. Other nations may be punished for their arrogance, or for their infraction of the rights of others, as Nineveh was threatened, Egypt chastised and Sodom destroyed; but they are not usually punished for the sins of idolatry except in the final judgment of the "day of the Lord," or when idolatrous arrogance overreaches itself. Israel alone is wedded unto the Lord, dedicated to function as "a kingdom of priests and a holy nation."[72] "You only have I known of all the families of the earth; therefore I will visit upon you all your iniquities."[73] The objects of worship of other nations are described variously as fetishes of "wood and stone," or as the heavenly bodies created by God, or as secondary divine entities distributed by the Almighty to serve as objects of adoration for the other nations.[74] Therefore the universal God limited His sphere of worship, either by His own choice, or because of the recalcitrance of other nations, to the people of Israel. However, not only His rigid rules of justice, but even His benign compassion is tendered to all peoples, as is illustrated especially in the Book of Jonah.

Since the choice was made largely by God, it cannot be revoked, save by His will, which is unchanging, for " God is not a man that He should lie, neither the son of man that He should repent."[75] God is not, as among the pagans, a quasi-physical ancestor, but for this very reason the bond between Him and the people of Israel is even more enduring, deriving from the irrevocable will of the Almighty. " Can a woman forget her suckling child, not to have mercy on the son of her body? Yea, should these even forget, yet would I not forget thee."[76] The irrevocability of the covenant between Israel and the Lord is one of the fundamental convictions of the Biblical authors. For one moment, the seed of Moses is considered as a possible substitute for the seed of Abraham, but this possibility is immediately rejected.[77] A " messenger of the Lord " is considered for a while as a possible substitute for the Lord Himself going among His people, but this threat is withdrawn after the entreaties of Moses, " Let the Lord, I pray Thee, go in the midst of us; for it is a stiff-necked people; and pardon our iniquity and our sin, and take us for Thine inheritance."[78] If Israel should sin, it will be severely punished, but the bond will not be repudiated. A " remnant " will return, and that remnant will be so purged and purified as to remain eternally loyal. Or the Lord will endow the Israelites of the future with " a new heart " and a " new spirit," making with them a " new covenant," so that they might serve Him with whole-hearted devotion.[79]

What is the relationship of Israel, the " treasured people," to the totality of the divine plan for mankind? Broadly speaking, we may discern two distinct answers to this question. In the Five Books of Moses there is scarcely any reference to the divine concern with the destiny of other nations and with the forms of their worship. When they commit immoral and antisocial crimes, as did the people of Sodom and Gomorrah, they are destroyed, and when they obstruct the divine will, as did the Egyptians, they are punished, but the Pentateuch does not hold out the promise of God for the eventual inclusion of all mankind within the circle of His people. The closest the Pentateuch comes to this teaching is in the verse, " and all the nations of the earth will see that the Name of the Lord is called upon thee and they shall be afraid of thee."[80] The patriarch Abraham is represented in Aggadic literature as a dedicated missionary, breaking the idols in his father's house, championing the cause of monotheism before Nimrod with reasoned arguments, and using the hospitality of his house as a means of demonstrating to wayfarers the truth concerning the one God. In the Pentateuch itself, however, there is no mention of Abraham crusading for his faith. Nor does Joseph in Egypt utilize the power of his position to change the faith of the Egyptian people. In the same spirit, Moses' message to Pharaoh is concerned solely with the liberation of the Israelites and with their sacrifice to the Lord in the desert. In all the passages dealing with the future, there is no mention of the other nations of the world, save as agents of the divine wrath or as rebels against the Lord, or as spectators of Israel's glory. Israel's designation as " a people of priests " implies the obligation to represent the truth to the rest of mankind, but not the task of bringing about their complete absorption into the monotheistic society.

On the other hand, the literary prophets view the history of Israel against the backdrop of humanity as a whole. As the Lord took the Israelites out of Egypt, He took the Arameans out of Kir and the Philistines out of Kaphtor, but to the Israelites He assigned a special task, to be His witnesses unto the children of man and be " a light unto the nations."[81] In the end of days, all the nations of the world will recognize the supremacy of the Lord, abandon their idols, and turn in worship to the God of Israel. On that day, " the Lord will be one, and His name One."[82] Mankind will learn the ways of peace and justice and they will be grateful to the people of Israel for their teachings. The mountain of the Lord's house will be exalted, in their eyes, above all sacred places, and they will stream unto it, to learn of the Lord's ways and to walk in His paths.[83] They will join in the pilgrimage festivals honoring Zion as the spiritual capital of a divinely enlightened world.[84] Assyria and Egypt, the ancient enemies of Israel, will repent of their former militaristic policies so that the Lord will regard them too as His portion and His dwelling-place.[85] This consummation will be attained by the gradual penetration of divine truth, not necessarily by the acceptance of

38

Israel's rituals and patterns of worship. At the end of days, the glory of Israel's destiny will be gratefully acknowledged by a transformed humanity. Israel will then be revered as " the suffering servant" that travailed for the sins of mankind.[86] In the meantime, Israel, mindful of its spiritual destiny, must learn to rise above the national rivalries of its time. Isaiah counseled Judah to resist the hosts of Sennacherib, while Jeremiah counseled surrender to the King of Babylonia; quite apart from their respective views of the changing international situation, as prophets, they thought of Israel as being above the normal rise and fall of empires, functioning chiefly in the domain of the spirit. "For thus hath said the Lord Eternal, the Holy One of Israel: In repose and rest shall ye be helped; in quietness and confidence shall be your strength."[87]

The divine choice of Israel has its counterpart in God's arbitrary selection of the prophet, the land, the sanctuary, and the ritual. The prophet, unlike the ecstatic bands of " prophetizers " that abounded in the ancient Near East, is not primarily a mystic, trained in the art and wisdom of sacred yogas, who rises to the exalted state of religious ecstasy by dint of special skills and exercises. He is not a person who has chosen prophecy as a profession or as an art, but one who has been chosen by the Lord and entrusted with a special mission. God's choice was entirely His, undetermined by man's wisdom and power. Jeremiah was selected from birth for prophecy, Isaiah was assigned his mission while praying in the Holy Temple, Moses assumed his task with great reluctance, Jonah even sought to run away from the Lord, and Amos asserted proudly that he never sought the office of prophecy and that he is not a member of any prophetic guild.[88] Remnants of " prophetizers," as distinguished from prophets, were still to be found in Israel in Biblical times. They were apparently practitioners of " prophetic frenzy," of the type then current in the Near Eastern countries. But the characteristic institution in Israel was that of the prophet, as the messenger of the Lord, expressly chosen by Him for a specific purpose. Even the disciples of the prophets do not rise to the position of their masters by natural succession; Elisha and Joshua are themselves specifically chosen. Moses declares that whenever the people in Israel should be in doubt, " A prophet I shall cause to rise among you like myself," who would render the final and authoritative decision.[89]

The land of Israel was similarly chosen by an arbitrary decision of the Lord. The reason for the divine choice of the land is nowhere explained, save by the Deuteronomist who points out that it is suitable for faith, since its dwellers are compelled to look constantly to heaven for the gift of rain.[90]

Once the land was chosen, it became the abode of the Lord, and those who were banished from it thought that they were denied the opportunity of sharing in the " portion of the Lord."[91] God is everywhere, so that His power and His word can never be evaded, but His holiness is peculiarly restricted to the land of Israel. The Levites refused to sing the song of the Lord on strange soil, and it was comforting for Naaman to feel that when He bowed down in the temple of Rimmon, he kneeled on the sacred soil of Israel.[92] When Ruth and Naomi were in the land of Moab, they were subject to the providence and punishment of the Lord, but presumably they were freed from the obligation of worshiping Him. However, when they entered the borders of the Holy Land, Ruth felt called upon to declare, " Your people is my people and your god is my god."[93]

Like the people of Israel, its land and its prophets, the Holy Temple was chosen by the will of God. The movable sanctuary of the desert served as the focal center of the amphictyony of the twelve tribes before the conquest of the Holy Land was completed. Located in Shiloh, the sanctuary was built in the form of a tent, housing the Holy Ark that was conceived as the special dwelling place of the Almighty. Capped by the cherubim, the Holy Ark contained the tablets of the law, the symbols of Israel's covenant with the Lord, and the Lord was occasionally addressed as " He who sitteth [on] the cherubim." When the divine voice spoke to Moses, it seemed to issue from that hallowed spot.[94]

Later, when the tent-sanctuary at Shiloh was destroyed, various places came to be regarded as central places of worship, until the Holy Temple in Jerusalem was built by King Solomon. Thereafter all other sanctuaries sank progressively in value and esteem, since the Jerusalem temple was now the chosen place of worship. Many centuries were to elapse before the reform of Josiah in the year 621 B.C.E. Occasioned by the finding of the book of Deuteronomy, this reformation established the Holy Temple as the only sanctuary in the land. However, the germ of this thought was already contained in the earliest documents of the religion of Israel.

In the prayer of King Solomon, dedicating the Holy Temple, the universality of God's rule is emphasized again and again, and His dwelling place is said to be beyond the containment of the heavens and the heavens of the heavens. Nevertheless, the temple was the spot chosen by the Lord as the gateway for all prayers addressed to Him. It was in that house that the Israelites were to pray, and to that house that their prayers were to be addressed, wherever they might be.[95] Even if they should be exiled to other lands, their contact with the Almighty would be re-established if they directed their prayers " through the land which Thou hast given to their fathers and of the city which Thou hast chosen, and toward the house which I have built unto Thy name." God is everywhere, but by His free choice, the Holy Temple was to be the place where " His eyes and His Glory" might be found at all times. So the paradox was asserted: the Lord whom the heavens and the heavens of heavens do not contain has chosen to " dwell " in the Sanctuary and to speak to Moses " from between the two cherubim."

The covenant between the Lord and His people was based upon the laws of the Torah. The numerous rites were ordained by the fiat of the Lord; they are therefore expressions of His free nature, not, as in paganism, part of the life-cycle of the gods. The observance of the laws is accordingly a " sign " or action-symbol of the submission of Israel to His will. Many of His laws are described as expressions of His Absolute Justice and His mercy; some of the commandments were expressions of the goodness of the Lord and of His solicitude for the welfare of His people; but some commandments are not motivated by any reasons and are attributed to the inscrutable nature of God's will. This is especially true of the laws governing the ritual of the sacrifices of the Day of Atonement and the rituals of purification —laws which fall roughly within the province of priestly practice and supervision.

The reason most frequently assigned for the observance of the commandments is that they serve as a reminder of the covenant and of the Exodus. The ideas evoked by the performance of the rites were not merely historical incidents, but the interpretation of them which implied that every worshiper was part of the historic community that was "chosen" by the Lord, in order to testify to His name. In the version of the Ten Commandments given in the Book of Exodus, the Sabbath is described as a sign of the covenant and a weekly re-enactment of the triumph of liberation from slavery. The great festival of Passover is, of course, specifically motivated by this purpose, as is the festival of Sukkoth. But, almost every other *mizvah* was also described as *zaicher liziath mizrayim*—a reminder of the Exodus. The observance of wearing fringes on one's garment, of leaving the soil fallow every seventh year (*shemittah*), and of the dietary laws are all grounded in the same basic principle, that is, they serve as reminders of the intervention of God in behalf of Israel at the time of the Exodus.[96]

It was assumed that this miraculous series of events transformed the Israelites into "sons" of the Lord, who must forever be distinguished, in their practices, from the rest of mankind. Hence, the motivation for the rite of circumcision is that it might be a "sign of the covenant."[97] Thus, too, some pagan practices are especially forbidden on the general principle of their being characteristic of the lives of those who are not "sons" of the living God. "Ye are children of the Lord your God: ye shall not cut yourselves, nor make any baldness between your eyes for the dead."[98] A stirring awareness of the ubiquitous presence of the Lord is given as the reason for a number of ethical and ritual commandments, such as reverence for one's parents, the observance of the Sabbath, leaving the grapes of the undressed vines for the poor, the prohibition of usury, the injunction to accord equality of treatment to strangers and to help the widow, the command to revere the aged and to assist the impoverished.[99]

We may summarize the specific motivations of the Biblical precepts as being, first, the terms of a covenant which was drawn up by the Lord and His people; second, as being signs and reminders of the covenant and of the Exodus; third, as constituting the means whereby Israel is to be distinguished from the rest of the nations. These three categories of motivation refer to the people of Israel as the basic unit. In addition, the individual Jew was to be guided in his personal life by the awareness of the immediate presence of God. While most of the rites and cere-

monies described in the Pentateuch were practised long before
the Holy Scriptures were composed, the new interpretation that
was given to them by the prophets and the scribes endowed them
with fresh significance. For the soul of a religion is expressed
not in its ritual but in the spirit which motivates its worship.

These motivations, we must remember, blended together in the
Holy Scriptures. The will of God is furthermore assumed to be
at all times consonant with man's striving for happiness. The
divine purpose in granting the Torah to His children was to have
them live a good and happy life here on earth. In this world that
was fashioned by His fiat, human goodness and human happiness
go hand in hand. "And the Lord commanded us to do all these
statutes, to fear the Lord our God; that it might be well with us
at all times, and that He might preserve us alive, as it is at this
day. And it shall be righteousness unto us, if we observe to do
all this commandment before the Lord our God, as He hath commanded us."[100]

To the literary prophets, the core of the divine will is the duty
to cultivate the inner qualities of piety. Hence the need of ranking ethical imperatives above ritual observances. While the
prophets did not oppose the practice of religious rituals, as is
sometimes supposed, they insisted that the pursuit of truth and
kindness in humility and love was the ultimate purpose of God's
laws and they protested against the tendency to abuse rituals by
treating them as mechanical actions that are automatically effective. Therefore Isaiah rebuked the people of his day for their
naïve belief in the efficacy of mere fasting: "Is not this the fast
that I have chosen? To loose the fetters of wickedness. To undo
the bands of the yoke. And to let the oppressed go free and that ye
break every yoke?" [101]

The emphasis of the prophets on the goals of morality as constituting the essence of the divine intention served to inspire the
revolutionary ferment of progressive religion in all future ages.
In every age, sensitive souls were encouraged by the prophetic
example to recognize the promptings of their keen conscience as
the reverberating echo of the divine call. Nevertheless, it was not
the intention of the prophets to abolish all forms of ritual, for
they derived their inspiration from the fluid Mosaic tradition of
their day, which included a vast number of rites and institutions.
The prophets rebuked the people for the slightest deviations from

the worship of the one God, for the least infraction of the Sabbath, for the non-observance of the "Sabbath of the Land," for the failure to render the proper tithes to the temple and the priests.[102] Ezekiel, who stands in the direct line of prophetic tradition, foretells the restoration of the sacrifices and the temple and prescribes intricate regulations for them.[103] The prophets illumined the ideal pole of Jewish consciousness, but they were not immune to the attraction of the opposite pole. Their faith shared in the characteristic tension of Judaism between the self-dedicatory mood of a rational-ethical faith and the self-sanctifying piety of the priests and the people.

When the civil and criminal code of the Holy Scriptures is compared with the codes of the Babylonians, Assyrians and Hittites, some interesting conclusions may be clearly inferred. In the first place, we learn that the legal system of the Bible was built on the massive foundations of a complex and rich legal tradition in the Near East thousands of years old when the legislation of Moses was begun. The import of Biblical legislation may be better understood if it is viewed against these ancient codes, which are frequently more detailed than the terse verses of the Pentateuch. The Biblical precepts appear at times to have been amendments or modifications of existing legal traditions.

Secondly, the creative *élan* of monotheism is manifested in the manner in which the ancient laws were modified in Holy Writ. While the Israelites shared in the legal tradition of the ancient world, they reworked the cultural context of this society in keeping with their fresh religious insights. Thus, the genius of monotheistic faith is to be seen not so much in the static panorama of Biblical law as in the dynamic moralistic impetus of Biblical legislation.

For instance, the principle of equality of all men before the law is affirmed in the Bible, in contrast to the then prevailing practices. The Mosaic insistence on the *lex talionis*, "an eye for an eye," is to be interpreted primarily as a protest against the ancient laws which distinguished between the punishment meted out to a commoner and to a nobleman, or between the satisfaction due to an ordinary person and to a man of substance.[104] The same observation applies to the Biblical precepts, "a soul for a soul," or "thou shalt not take ransom for the life of a murderer." Mem-

44

bers of the aristocracy were then not subject to the same laws of retaliation as were the common people.

The sense of individual responsibility was strengthened and brought into focus in the legislation of the Bible. Children were no longer regarded as the appurtenances of a householder, but as individuals in their own right. Thus, the laws of Hammurabi call for the killing of the builder's son, if, as a result of defective construction, the house caved in and the children of the residents were killed.[105] New light is thus cast on the verse, "fathers should not be killed for the sins of sons, and sons for the sins of fathers."[106]

Another example of the prevailing principles of inequality and family responsibility is revealed in the following citation from the code of Hammurabi:

"If a seignior struck another seignior's daughter. . . . If the woman died, they shall put his daughter to death. . . . If it was a commoner's daughter . . . he shall pay two shekels of silver."[107]

In the same ethical vein, Biblical legislation drastically softens the punishments that were meted out to criminal and civil offenders. While Near Eastern legislation itself reveals a slow tendency in the direction of leniency, the Biblical authors virtually effect a revolution in the merciful treatment of thieves, robbers and defaulting debtors, eliminating altogether the penalty of bodily mutilation.

The Biblical laws concerning sexual offences and the structure of the family reveal an intense passion for moral purity.

The exceedingly rough justice of the Middle Assyrian Code, which permits the father of a virgin to attack the wife of the man who raped his daughter, was inconceivable within the Biblical frame of ideas.[108] The permission that was granted to a soldier's wife in the Assyrian code to marry someone else if he had not returned in two years, and then the subsequent permission for the wife to return to her former husband when he reappears, is regarded by the Bible as an intolerable "uncleanliness."[109] The leniency of the Hittite code in permitting the husband to save his wife, an adulteress, from the death penalty is not paralleled in Scriptures, since marital infidelity was regarded as a sin against God, not only against the husband. It was probably in keeping with this passion for family purity that the laws of adoption which figure so prominently in the Near Eastern codes were not mentioned at all in the Bible. Impassioned zeal for family purity led to an exaggerated concern for an uncontaminated family tree, a concern that is best illustrated in Ezra's expulsion of the "foreign" wives and their children.[110] We must remember, however, that Ezra's action was not representative of the policy of later Judaism.

From all the above it is evident that the emergence of monotheism among the Israelites led to the development of a new and vigorous ethical and religious culture that challenged the pagan world at every point of contact.

CHAPTER TWO

THE CONSOLIDATION OF JUDAISM

IN the second period of Judaism, covered roughly by the documents contained in the Talmud and the Midrashim, the focus
of interest is shifted from speculations concerning the Deity to a
detailed study of His commandments. After the reforms of Ezra
(circa 430 B.C.E.) the victory of monotheism in Israel was absolute
and complete. Legend told of the capture and annihilation of the
evil desire for pagan worship by the members of the Sanhedrin.[1]
During the days of the Second Commonwealth there was no
longer any doubt in the minds of the people that " the Lord, He
is God." But, what is it exactly that the Lord requires of His
people in their day-by-day living? This question became the
dominant concern of the architects of Judaism.

While the institution of prophecy was still alive, the ancient
documents containing Mosaic traditions were collated and edited.
Jeremiah was in his prime when Deuteronomy was " discovered "
in the year 621 B.C. It is, in all probability, built around a very
ancient core, dating at least in part to the time of Moses. But
under the reign of King Josiah, 638-608 B.C.E., the Book of Deuteronomy was made into a state document. By the time Ezra arrived
in Judea with the express authorization of the Persian Government to institute laws for the new community and to lay the
foundation for the renewed worship of the " God of heaven,"
the Five Books of Moses and the Book of Joshua were already
compiled, more or less in their final form. The Talmud compares
Ezra to Moses, as a Torah-giver.[2] He is believed to have changed
the script of the Torah from the old Hebrew to that of the then
modern " Assyrian " script, and to have instituted the regulation
that portions of the Books of Moses were to be read and translated
in the Aramaic vernacular on Mondays, Thursdays and Satur-
days.[3] A new " sure covenant " was drawn up by Ezra and signed
by the heads of the Jewish community, in which they undertook

" to walk in God's law," to tax themselves for the maintenance of the temple, to observe the Sabbath and to refrain from inter-marriage with their pagan neighbors.[4]

The promulgation of the Books of Moses as the constitution of the new Judean Commonwealth had the effect of terminating the institution of prophecy. While the Deuteronomist urges the Israel-ites to consult prophets in the event of doubt, Ezra and his contemporaries seek guidance in the diligent study of the written documents.[5] The living but temperamental and unpredictable instrument of the Word of God that the prophet had been was now replaced by the rigid but certain book. This development was inevitable, since the written letter of the Torah could not but set firm limits to the protean revelations of the prophet. In the Book of Deuteronomy, the authority of the prophet was limited only insofar as he could not urge the worship of other gods. Now that the Torah of Moses was standardized, it appeared that the prophet could not controvert any of its numerous pre-cepts, which in turn could be stretched by interpretation to cover almost every contingency in life. " A prophet is not permitted to institute any new ordinances in our time."[6] Furthermore, there soon arose a class of scholars, known as scribes, who pre-empted the prerogative of interpreting and applying the words of the Torah. Thus, the prophet, as the living organ of dynamic revelation, passed quietly from the scene of post-Biblical Judaism.

There is no record of any struggle for survival waged by the last of the prophets, nor do we detect any awareness of a sudden break in the manner of God's dealing with the children of Israel. Pro-phecy was never ruled out in theory. On the contrary, prophecy loomed large and radiant on the Jewish horizon as the glory of the past and the dawn of the Messianic future. Simon the Has-monean was made head of the Jewish Commonwealth and high priest " until there should arise a prophet of truth."[7] But for everyday living, short of the advent of the Messiah, the Jewish pattern of piety had become crystallized and hardened, and the learned sage took the place of the inspired preacher. Since the books of the law contained the terms of Israel's covenant with the Lord, the scribes proceeded not to preach in general terms, but to teach in detail the precepts and doctrines of the Word of

God so that the entire "community of Jacob" might possess its rightful "inheritance."[8] The synagogue arose out of the labors of the scribes; hence its uniqueness as an institution which is dedicated to instruction as well as to prayer, sharing in the qualities of both a philosophical society and a temple of God.

The natural organic growth of monotheistic piety transformed the prophets into scribes, and the scribes, sticking closely to the literal text of the Torah, into sages claiming authority to interpret its deeper meaning. "Pharisaism is applied prophecy," says a modern scholar.[9] The Talmud phrased it more simply: "Prophecy was taken from the prophets and given to the sages."[10] The eloquent exhortation of titanic personalities gave way to the persistent interpretation and legislation of a large body of saintly men who flourished in the two centuries from the reforms of Ezra to Simon the Just and who were known as the "Men of the Great Assembly."[11] The creative spirit of Judaism found expression in circles of learned and saintly men, who sought to spell out for themselves and for their contemporaries the meaning of "walking in the ways of the Lord," and who aspired to attain the divine favor of the Holy Spirit (*Ruah hakodesh*).[12]

The imposition of a law requires an organized structure of authority. During the days of the First Commonwealth, the ritualistic laws were administered partly by the representatives of the king and partly by the priests, who were organized into twenty-four subdivisions and a governing, hereditary hierarchy. Many of the dietary and "purity" regulations were restricted in their application to the members of the priesthood.[13] During the first centuries of the Second Commonwealth, the study of Torah was taken to be a universal obligation, the range of the "purity" laws was extended beyond the priesthood, and there was no royal power. The Biblical division of labor among priest, wise man, and prophet was no longer sufficient for the practice of Judaism as a religion of Torah. "For there will not cease Torah from the priest, advice from the sage and the word from the prophet."[14] The vacuum left by the disappearance of the prophet and the absence of a sovereign could be filled either by the enlargement of the authority and scope of the "wise men," previously the instructors of the youth in moral wisdom, or by the extension of the sway of the priests outside the walls of the temple, or by the creation of a new authoritative body that would function as the highest religious arbiter of the newly reconstituted community.

Actually, all three possibilities were realized to some extent. The high priest achieved a dominant position in the Second Commonwealth, functioning almost continuously not only as the custodian of the Holy Temple but as the actual head of the Jewish community. When the curtain of history in Palestine lifted, following the conquest of Alexander the Great (332 B.C.E.), the high priest was in full charge of the Province of Judea, in both its spiritual and temporal aspects. Many, if not all, of the high priests served as heads of the high court, the Sanhedrin, which met in one of the halls of the Holy Temple. Ezekiel's suggestion for the appointment of a Nasi, or prince, seems to have been disregarded.[15] Even in the New Testament period, the high priest still headed the Sanhedrin, at least officially. But morally the high priesthood lost its standing in the eyes of the people, first as the result of the assimilationist policy of Jason and Menelaus, members of the old Zadokite family, and later when the Hasmonean kings proved unacceptable to the pietists. So, during the two centuries preceding the common era, religious authority shifted progressively and decisively to the rising new class of scribes and sages.

The scribes absorbed the ancient function of the teachers of "wisdom"; that is, a class of instructors common to many civilizations in the Near East. The Proverbs of Solomon, the Books of Ecclesiastes and Job, as well as the Wisdom of Solomon and Wisdom of Ben Sira, were the productions of these scholars. As teachers of the people, their prestige depended entirely upon their reputation for scholarship, integrity, and piety. In contrast to the priests, they were, therefore, a society founded on Torah and living for the sake of Torah.

In the course of time, the rift between the aristocrats of birth and the aristocrats of Torah-learning grew ever wider. While the former guarded the written Torah as a work of static perfection, the latter lavished their ardor and acumen upon the dynamic task of interpreting the Holy Scriptures, refining their methods of exegesis from generation to generation, and expanding the law by degrees to mountainous proportions, for, as the rabbis put it, "there is no study session without an innovation."[16] The "words of the scribes" and their ordinances were regarded as divinely inspired and designated as the Oral Law, a category which the dominant section of the priesthood, the Sadducees, rejected with vehemence. To the Sadducees, the Written Law alone was sacred, while for the needs of daily guidance they relied on the decrees of their judges. If the policies of the entrenched priesthood had prevailed, the Pentateuch would have become a revered but irrelevant relic, while the life of the people would have been determined by a combination of priestly orders and secular laws. The Pharisees or lay teachers sought to fashion the total life of the people in the mold of the divine law, so as to create a Torah-society, thoroughly imbued with the Word of God. For these folk teachers, life and the divine teaching were coextensive, without any neutral or secular domain.[17] However, the gulf between the Pharisees, the masters of interpretation who succeeded the scribes, and the Sadducees, guardians of the priestly tradition, did not appear in the open until after the consolidation of the Hasmonean dynasty, in the latter part of the reign of John Hyrcanus (135-104 B.C.E.). Up to that time, it may be assumed that the masters of the lay schools of learning sat with the heads of the priesthood in the Gerousia, the Assembly of the Elders, and in the Sanhedrin.

The central source of authority for Jewish law was the Sanhedrin, which had its headquarters in the Holy Temple, though it is probable that in the first century of the common era the Pharisees had their own high court, in addition to the official Sanhedrin of the high priest. The Talmud relates that the Sanhedrin moved out of the temple some forty years before its destruction in 69 C.E., in order to be free from the onerous task of imposing death sentences upon a multitude of murderers.[18] The historic realities that this tradition reflects cannot now be deciphered with certainty. It appears that by the time the Talmud was edited, the bitter struggles for the control of the judiciary institutions of Palestine were forgotten by the people and the folk image of the Sanhedrin was bathed in a rosy glow. Following the destruction of the temple, the Sadducees disappeared from the scene and the highest legislative and interpretative functions devolved upon the assemblies of the Pharisaic sages, which were presided over by the Hillel dynasty of *nesiim*. The Talmud mentions the many " journeys " of the Sanhedrin, the transfer of its residence from place to place.[19] Later still, when the center of

51

gravity in Jewish life shifted to Babylonia (after 250 c.e.), a strong measure of both temporal and spiritual authority continued to be exercised by the Exilarchs and the Geonim (up to 1038 c.e.). In theory, however, the re-establishment of the Sanhedrin remained the goal and the hope of Judaism.

The Torah was conceived as having been given directly and explicitly and in its entirety to Moses. Not only the precepts contained in the Five Books of Moses and those mentioned in the prophetic writings, but even the non-Scriptural ordinances of the Oral Law were, according to the Pharisees, transmitted verbally to Moses at Sinai. This belief may be understood in two different ways—either as implying that every single discovery, interpretation, and enactment of later years was specifically known to Moses, or as teaching the divine origin of those principles which the authorities of subsequent generations employed as the basis for their enactments. The former version does not merely attribute total omniscience of all future events to Moses, including, say, the events of Hanukkah and Purim, but it also affords a blanket authority covering all the ordinances of the rabbis, and it does not admit even in theory that the flow of time introduces any modifications in the structure of the law. Apparently both views found adherents. The masses of the people probably understood the divinity of the law in the static or literal manner, while the great sages suggested from time to time a dynamic and progressive concept of revelation. For example, the Midrash inquires, "Did Moses learn the whole Torah? Is it not said of the Torah that its measure is longer than the earth and wider than the sea? How could Moses learn it in forty days? But the Holy One, blessed be He, taught general principles to Moses."[20] In this view, both the Written and Oral Laws were divine in their general principles, but human in their detailed teaching.

In addition to the practices comprised under the heading *Oral Law*, there were certain rabbinic enactments, *takkanoth*. The basic intent of these rabbinic laws was to "build a fence for the Torah"; that is, to add an extra margin to the injunctions of the Torah so as to lessen the danger of their violation. In such spheres of the Law as the Sabbath, the dietary laws and the regulation of ritual purity, the range of rabbinic prohibitions was immense.

Nevertheless, it would be wrong to assume that the efforts of the rabbis were directed solely to the end of increasing the burden of the law. The later Pharisees alleviated many of the injunctions of the Sabbath and of *Shemittah*, with the express purpose of rendering the law more suitable to the exigencies of life.[21] The range of the "purity" laws, which in the first century was staggering and very troublesome, was gradually narrowed. The awesome taboos, relating to vows, were brought under control.[22] The Torah is "not in heaven," to be kept aloof from the realities of the market place and immune to the rigors of logic, asserted a liberal sage of the second century; it is *of* God, but *for* living people. Therefore the sages are entitled to set aside any one law of the Torah, if such a course of action is deemed important for the Jewish faith as a whole.[23]

We note two opposing tendencies among the Pharisaic teachers. In the main, they thought of themselves as *preservers* of the deathless divine law, not as its *molders*. A leading teacher of the beginning of the second century accounted it a high merit for one not to have taught anything which he did not specifically hear from his masters.[24] And yet we do also encounter statements which reflect a more dynamic conception of the Oral Law. A later Midrash tells the parable of two servants to whom their master gave some wheat and flax. One servant tended the wheat and flax with zealous care, while the other servant made bread out of the wheat and a tablecloth out of the flax. Will not the master prefer the latter servant to the former? Manifestly, some Pharisaic sages deemed it their duty to discern and implement the ideals of Torah rather than to preserve inviolate the letters of the law.[25]

In the Biblical period, the religion of Israel confronted the ideas and realities of the pagan world; in the Talmudic period, Judaism confronted itself. For most rabbis the great ideas of monotheism receded into the background and the law in all its complexity became the sole subject of endless meditations and elaborations. Their philosophy of life was expressed indirectly in the reasons they assigned or assumed for the various precepts of the law. Thus, we must turn our attention to the study of *taamai hamizvoth*, the reasons for the Commandments. What was the divine purpose in imposing the law upon His people? What is accomplished in the soul of the worshiper and in the world at large by the observance of the Commandments? Is it the purpose of the Commandments to train good and pious people, or is it also to achieve a high cosmic end? Is the law perchance a supreme end in itself, with the world in all its immensity and complexity serving merely as the necessary background for the law, projecting the stage for the drama of human obedience and revolt? It is easy to see that the answers to these questions are far more indicative of the real philosophy of the Talmudic sages than any occasional abstract pronouncements concerning the faith of Judaism. The law forms part of a vast tradition of religious belief and speculation, and its meaning can only be understood in the light of the totality of the sacred tradition. The word *Torah* means teaching, tradition in its entirety, a tradition containing both explicitly and implicitly a vast body of ethical and theological instruction, as well as laws.

We have seen that, to the Biblical authors, the observance of the Mosaic laws was a " sign " or a symbolic expression of loyalty to God, in opposition to the loyalty that might be shown to other gods. Those who " cleave " unto the Lord will want to " walk in His ways," thereby acknowledging His dominion in their lives. The prophets did not deal with details of observance. They cautioned against rebellion and disobedience, assuming that those who are loyal to any god will express their loyalty in one form or another. Thus, to the Deuteronomist, the purpose of the divine laws is " to walk in His ways, to love Him and to cleave unto Him,"[26] with the meaning of " cleaving " being taken from the realm of human loyalties, indicating the desire to be in the camp of God, in a world where many gods have their respective camps of followers.

Later, as the full meaning of monotheism was unfolded in Jewish consciousness, the challenge of the worship of other gods faded into the background. The purpose of the laws had to be understood, then, in terms of the relationship between God on the one hand, and mankind or the people of Israel on the other hand. Since God was envisioned as the ethically perfect personality, His laws had to correspond to the requirements of human goodness. But only a fraction of the Torah can be justified in strictly ethical terms. As an expression of the divine Will, the law may be expected to range beyond the limits of human comprehension, but the will of God for mankind must ultimately relate to human needs. The all-perfect God, completely sufficient unto Himself, cannot possibly be in need of anything that men may or may not do.

In answer to this dilemma, the Talmudic sages offered the following replies:

(a) The purpose of the law is nothing but ethical perfection. for goodness and humility is all that God demands of man.

(b) It is the building up of a fund for merit in behalf of the Israelites. In heaven, people are rewarded for their good deeds. The Torah offers so many opportunities for divine service, and hence for reward to an especially favored people.

(c) It is the inscrutable will of the Deity. God is so far beyond the reach of man's comprehension that we cannot hope to understand the reasons for His Commandments.

(d) Every precept is a " sign " of being a follower of God and a mark of the homage that is due to Him.

(e) The law is a purpose unto itself, constituting part of that divine wisdom which is the supreme end of existence. It need not be justified in terms of its effect on the lives of men. Human life was ordained for the sake of the law, not the other way round.

(f) The world is so constituted that many good effects follow quasi-automatically upon the observance of the Commandments and many evil consequences result from their violation, for there is a mystical correspondence between the heavenly realm of divine essences and the domain of earthly realities, between the laws of Judaism and the physical laws of the universe.

Upon reflection, the reader will notice that these categories of explanation are not mutually consistent. However, each category may recommend itself to the different moods of a pious man. Taken together, these explanations reflect the inner tension within the life of the Jew between humanism and nationalism, between rationality and mysticism, between self-dedication and self-exaltation. Let us now proceed to study more closely each category of explanation.

The attempt to account for the details of the law in terms of ethical perfection constitutes the prophetic strand in the pattern of Talmudic piety. Man's humility and his consciousness of living under the judgment of the Almighty constitute the essence of all ethical virtues. When a soul is about to descend to this world, an oath is administered to it, requiring the soul " to be wicked in his own eyes even if the whole world assures him that he is righteous."[27] So Job, who is presented as a saintly man in universal terms, bearing no relation to the ritual of Judaism, is described as eschewing self-righteousness and as bringing regular sacrifices to the Almighty, to atone for the involuntary sins of his children.[28] In Judaism, awareness of the reality of God and reverence for Him form the indispensable foundation of the good life, even when it is described in universal terms. " The beginning of wisdom is the fear of the Lord."[29] Piety is the crown of all virtues.

Bearing this Biblical conception of the good life in mind, we find many passages in the Talmud, expatiating upon the theme that the purpose of the Commandments is to ethicize and spiritualize the human personality. The following selections are typical:

(1) Commenting upon the maxim, " Would they had forsaken me, and kept my Torah," one rabbi declares: " By their occupying themselves with it, the light contained in it will bring them back to good standing." The implication of this comment is that there is an innate spirituality in the Torah, which responds to man's inescapable needs. Out of the doing of God's will comes the understanding of it.[30]

(2) A similar thought is implied in the remark: " He whose wisdom is greater than his deeds, to what may he be compared? To a tree, the branches of which are more extensive than its roots, which the southern wind might easily uproot and overturn on its faces. But he whose deeds are greater than his wisdom, to what may he be compared? To a tree, the roots of which are greater than its branches. It might well withstand all the winds of the world."[31] The term *deeds* refers to the performance of *mizvoth* which, like roots, give forth the fruit of wisdom. They also make for stability of character, integrity and tenacity.

(3) Since piety is an essential virtue of the perfect personality, one reason for the *mizvoth* is to provide man with the opportunity to express his yearnings for the nearness of God. Commenting upon the verse, " and to cleave unto him," the question is asked, " But how is it possible to cleave unto Him, for, behold, He is a consuming flame. It means, therefore, to walk in His paths. As He is merciful, so be you merciful; as He is a doer of kindnesses, so be you one, etc."[32] God is conceived as purely ethical in His " ways " and the *mizvoth* are ways of approaching Him: so many avenues for the yearning to come nigh to Him. In this passage, piety is represented as being an " imitation of God." This ideal is stated by Plato in several places. The sages apparently found the Greek ideal to be fully consonant with the Biblical ideal of " walking in His ways " and " cleaving " unto God. Yet they were conscious of the impropriety of using the principle of imitation of God on all occasions. For God is " jealous " and men must not presume to embrace this quality.[33]

(4) The great philosophical sage Rabbi Joshua Ben Hananya pictures the Lord as remarking, "If you should say, 'He who observes the Sabbath, what gain does he bring to Me?' Then learn from this verse: 'Happy is the man who will do this and the son of man who will hold onto it, guarding the Sabbath from desecration and guarding his hand from doing all kinds of evil.'[34] From this you learn that he who observes the Sabbath is removed from sin." The effect of Sabbath observance is to keep man from all forms of sin.[35]

(5) Many *mizvoth* give expression to the truths of monotheism, thereby helping to impress their veracity and significance upon the mind of the worshiper and upon the people of his generation. So, the Sabbath is a testimony to the creation of the universe: "He who desecrates the Sabbath testifies before the One who spoke and the world came to be, that He did not create the world in six days."[36] In the same manner, another rabbi explains the meaning of the Sabbatical year of agriculture, as having been ordained "in order that you might know that the earth is mine."[37] In the same spirit another rabbi comments, "Respect the *mizvoth*, for they are my messengers," i.e. symbols of His authority.[38]

(6) Many rites are expressions of the humility of the Almighty in "contracting" His presence or in reducing His demands; their effect was therefore to induce the feelings of humility. The fact that the Creator of the universe deigns to regard the sanctuary as His dwelling place is an expression of His "contracting" Himself (*zimzum*) for the sake of man. In the same manner, the offering of sacrifices in the temple was an expression of the thought that, while the whole world belonged to God, He, in His goodness, limited Himself and his demands, as it were, to a mere token, thus setting an instructive example for mankind to follow.[39]

(7) Some *mizvoth* are intended to convey specific lessons. For instance, the prohibition of the use of iron in the building of the altar was meant to teach the supreme value of peace; the fact that the thief was punished more severely than the robber, in that the former had to pay double, or four and five times the value of the stolen article while the latter was asked only to return the goods he took, is because the former implied that he feared men more than God.[40] The reason the slave's ear was punctured, if he refused to leave his master at the expiration of six years of servitude, was to convey the thought that "the ear should be deservedly punctured which heard the Lord declare at Mount Sinai, 'My slaves they are, slaves of mine they are, not slaves of slaves.' "[41] The prohibitions relating to the woman during her menstrual periods are motivated by the desire to make her husband love her the more.[42] On the other hand, the reason given in the Torah for the prohibition of the use of blood ("for blood is the soul") is, by implication, rejected by one of the sages. He argues as follows: "If the Torah warns us, 'only be strong not to eat the blood, for the blood is the soul,' using such strong language concerning a *mizvah* which is the lightest [least significant] of all the *mizvoth*, it is in order that we might infer the importance of the other *mizvoth* that are so much more significant."[43] Thus the Commandment which is described in the Torah as of highest importance is esteemed by this rabbi, who classifies the

mizvoth according to their spiritual significance, as being of the least value.

(8) Some *mizvoth* are motivated by the historical circumstances that prevailed in the time of Moses. They fulfilled an educational function during the formative stages of the Jewish religion. The entire institution of sacrifices was designed for the purpose of weaning the Jewish people away from the worship of other gods, according to a third-century rabbi.[44] This remark did not imply for its author the obsolescence of the sacrifices or their irrelevance, for he remarked elsewhere, " The Lord desires the sacrifices of Israel."[45]

The second category of motivations for the *mizvoth* constitute a rejoinder to those who felt the law to be a burden or a yoke. Why should God, Who desires only goodness from the rest of mankind, demand so much more from the Israelites? The prophet Amos gave the classical answer to this question: " You only have I known of all the families of the earth; therefore, I will visit upon you all your iniquities."[46] The principle implied by Amos is that of *noblesse oblige*. It rings truly and nobly in respect of duties to mankind, but it is not a satisfactory explanation of ritual obligations. Certainly, if, as a leading rabbi affirmed, " the pious among the nations of the world have a share in the world to come,"[47] what do the Israelites gain by taking upon themselves the yoke of rituals in addition to the precepts of righteousness? In answer to this question the sages maintained that through the performance of the *mizvoth*, the Israelite was offered the opportunity of accumulating a treasury of merits, entitling him to special rewards in this life and in the hereafter.

An oft-quoted remark reads: " The Lord desired to favor Israel [endow it with merit], therefore He multiplied for them Torah and *mizvoth*."[48] In other words, ritual practices are enjoined in order to make possible meritorious service, which in turn leads to additional rewards. In line with this thought, it is suggested that the Israelites in Egypt were given two *mizvoth*, the blood of the Passover sacrifice and the blood of circumcision, in order that they might acquire at least some religious merit, " for people do not obtain rewards save through the performance of deeds."[49] Similarly, in commenting upon Abraham's question, " How shall I know? "[50] the thought is put forward that Abraham did not doubt the divine promise, but that he wanted to know the nature of the merit whereby his descendants would be found worthy of the Holy Land. The answer of the Lord was, in effect, " With the merit of the sacrifices."[51]

The rabbis cautioned against the tendency to assess separately the merit of each *mizvah*, warning that "you do not know the rewards of the different *mizvoth*."[52] Perhaps, too, different people derive merit from diverse *mizvoth*, so that you do not know from which *mizvah* life comes to you.[53] Some rabbis taught that every *mizvah* creates a protecting angel, as it were, and every sin an avenging spirit.[54] Hence, the *mizvoth* are calculated to create a host of protecting powers around the faithful Jew.

From the point of view of acquiring merit it might be more advantageous to experience emotional resistance in the performance of the Commandments than to observe them out of habit or even in joy. To be sure, as a rule, the sages regarded the service of God in love and joy as being superior to any other motivation. Nevertheless, in order to see the total picture we have to take account of the naïve strand of piety which was concerned with the acquisition of merits through *mizvoth*. Thus, a rabbi of the first century declared, "How do I know that a person ought not to say, 'I don't want to eat the flesh of a pig, I don't want to enjoy the forbidden types of sexual intercourse,' but he should say instead, 'I want these things, but what can I do, when my Father in heaven has already decreed that I may not do these acts.'"[55] Hence, another reason for the laws of sacrifice may well be this need for the accumulation of merit. "Said the Holy One, blessed be He, 'I labored to ordain sacrifices in order to multiply your chances for the gaining of merit.'"[56]

The merit acquired through the performance of the *mizvoth* is so vast that the gift of Torah is irrefutable proof of the profound love of God for the people of Israel. "An additional measure of love was accorded to Israel, through the gift to them of the wonderful vessel [Torah]."[57] To be sure, the Torah was also offered to other nations, but not through the same compulsions of history as those by which it came to Israel. "But why? Because they are my sons. . . ." The Lord is represented as calling upon the angel of death and addressing him as follows: "Even though I appointed thee a 'cosmocrator' over the world, you have no right to touch the people of Israel. Why? Because I made them into a god [immortal]."[58]

The accumulation of merit by the observance of the Commandments is sometimes conceived in quasi-physical terms, as being accompanied by a mystic transformation of the soul of the worshiper. The purpose of the *mizvoth* is frequently described as being *lezaref*, to purge or to purify mankind. This purgation of the faithful is achieved in a manner known only to God, the Creator of the souls of men. It is not a natural or logical reaction, visible on the surface of things or subject to rational scrutiny. This thought is best illustrated in a frequently cited Midrash, where the question is asked, " What does it matter to God if the ritual bath [*mikvah*] contains exactly forty *seah* [20 gallons], or whether it contains forty *seah* minus a small amount? " The answer follows, " From this we learn that the *mizvoth* were given only for the purpose of purging mankind." The manner in which the question is put is intended to exhibit the nonrational quality of the Commandment. The effect of this irrational element is then explained in terms of its mystic effect upon the soul.[59]

The abundance of nonrational elements in the rituals of Judaism was sometimes attributed to the inscrutability of the divine will. It is not for man to presume to comprehend the reasons of the Almighty for His Commandments. " It is not the dead body which inherently renders things unclean, nor is it the water [of the red heifer] which renders things clean. But, the Holy One, blessed be He, said, 'A decree I proclaimed, a law I ordained. You do not have the right to speculate concerning them.' "[60] A magical, mechanical effect resulting automatically from the performance of the rituals is here expressly ruled out. But then the right of the King of Kings to order decrees that men may not question is affirmed as an absolute principle. God chooses to dwell in darkness. Not only His essential being, but also His will and plan for human life, are impervious to the twin lights of human conscience and intelligence.

One rabbi inquires, " Why were the reasons for the *mizvoth* not revealed? " And he replies, " Because the reasons for two *mizvoth* were revealed, and the greatest man of the world was misled by them." The reference is to King Solomon, who took many wives and acquired many horses in the belief that he could withstand the blandishments of the women and the seductive appeal of the land of Egypt.[61] King Solomon's melancholy failure is proof of the danger of revealing the reasons for the Commandments.[62] It was also felt that the Torah must be regarded as one organic structure, built on the foundation of belief in divine revelation, and that if the slightest component part of the law is questioned, the entire edifice may crumble. "Any legal document of which two or three words are regarded as inapplicable is rendered inoperative in its entirety."[63]

Does the principle of divine inscrutability invalidate the prophetic insight that morality and piety constitute the essence of the will of God? Not entirely, since the ritual laws supplement but do not supplant the teachings of the prophet. The divine law may be nonrational and amoral, though not antirational and immoral. Nevertheless, a certain limitation of the validity of the human sense of right and wrong is implied in this doctrine. This is illustrated in the homiletic comment on the verse, " Be not righteous overmuch,"[64] which cites the error of King Saul, who did not obey Samuel's order to kill all the Amalekites and, following the bent of his moral feelings, spared the life of King Agag.[65]

We have noted in the previous chapter that the major explanation of the *mizvoth* in Biblical times was their function as " signs " of Israel's covenant with the Lord. The mental picture evoked by this concept is that of a multitude of nations worshiping their respective gods, and the people of Israel separating themselves by means of signs which attest to their worship of the one God. To be sure, God is King over the entire universe, but only the people of Israel accept His dominion in their hearts. In submitting to His Kingship, they also agree to refrain from the practices of other nations, which are inevitably associated with idolatry. Consequently the Torah warns, "And in their laws ye shall not walk."[66] In the Roman world the distinction between the religious and the secular domains of life was exceedingly tenuous; therefore, the deepened consciousness of the uniqueness of Jewish monotheism led to steadily rising barriers between the Jews and the other nations.

There were two schools of thought in regard to the advisability of either raising or lowering the barriers between Jews and Gentiles. Prior to the destruction of Jerusalem in 69 c.e., the intensely nationalistic school of Shammai triumphed over the Hillelite moderates and by sheer force caused a number of precepts to be adopted, designed to make social intercourse between Jews and non-Jews exceedingly difficult. In this spirit, Gentiles were declared to be defiling; their bread, their milk, their oil and wine were prohibited.[67] At the beginning of the third century, when relations between Jews and Romans improved, some of these restrictions were relaxed, but only with the greatest difficulty.[68] We may state as a general rule in the history of Judaism: Persecution and pogroms tend to intensify Jewish isolationism, and a kind, tolerant atmosphere is likely to bring to the surface the liberal trend in Judaism.

What was the purpose of God in creating the world? That He entertained such a purpose is an obvious inference from the conception of Him as an ideal personality, rational and ethical in all His actions. According to the ethical concept of His perfection, His purpose could only be the good life of humanity. If, then, morality be extended to embrace piety and the practical precepts of religion, we arrive at the conclusion, frequently reiterated in the literature of this period, that the Torah (strictly speaking, the life of Torah), is the purpose of creation. This conclusion follows also from the conception of God as King, Who created the world for His own "glory."[69] He attains the height of His "glory" when His Kingship is acknowledged and He is freely worshiped; for while all else is determined by Him, the human individual is free to obey or to rebel against the will of God. "All things are in the hands of heaven save the fear of heaven."[70]

The concept of Torah as the supreme value of creation is reflected in numerous passages in Talmud and Midrash. Expressed first by the prophet Jeremiah in the words, "Were it not for my covenant, day and night, the laws of heaven and earth I should not have ordained,"[71] this doctrine is asserted in several variations. "We infer," said a rabbi of the third century, "that the Holy One, blessed be He, stipulated a condition with the works of creation; to wit, if the Israelites accept the Torah, well and good; if not, I shall return the world to its pristine void and chaos."[72] Another rabbi comments, "For 978 generations [prior to the creation of the world], the Torah in written form lay in the lap of the Holy One, where it joined in the chants of the angels of the Presence."[73]

The term *Torah* was applied at times to the ideal essence of divine teaching of which the Scriptures were a reflection in the mirror of time. The heavenly counterpart of the Torah was not unlike Plato's realm of ideas.[74] Occasionally, however, the Torah is regarded not so much as an ethereal entity, but as the pious life of men and women, bearing its stamp. Thus, the doctrine of the supremacy of the Torah is not necessarily in contradiction to the principle of the supreme dignity of human life. The supreme worth of life according to the Torah is affirmed in the assertion that it is for the sake of the saints that the world was created.[75] A folkloristic variant of this is the belief that " the world cannot exist save by the presence in it of thirty saints," or in some versions, " thirty-six saints."[76]

Since Israel is the only people loyal to the Torah, the statement is frequently made that the world was created for the sake of Israel, and that its continuous existence is dependent upon the conduct of pious Jews.[77] " There is no disaster that comes upon the world save through Israel,"[78] as punished for its failure to maintain itself as the spiritual foundation of humanity. " It was in the Torah that the Lord looked when He created the universe."[79]

By a subtle change of emphasis, the Torah is sometimes represented not as the pattern of the good life, but as the end and the purpose of life. The *mizvoth* need not be justified in terms of human values, but vice versa. The highest ideal of life is study of the Torah for its own sake. " He who occupies himself with the Torah for its own sake protects the entire world."[80] As the great sage of the second century, Rabbi Meir, summarized it, " Whosoever labors in the Torah for its own sake merits many things; and not only so but the whole world is indebted to him: he is called friend, beloved; it clothes him in meekness and reverence . . . and it magnifies and exalts him above all things."[81] The Talmud records a lengthy dispute between the Shammaite and the Hillelite schools concerning the priority in the hierarchy of values of learning or of performing the *mizvoth*. The assumption of both schools is that the Torah is a supreme end in itself. The point in dispute was whether the Torah was to be conceived primarily as an intellectual entity or as a pattern for human living.

The concept of Torah as the supreme end of creation in the mind of God was sometimes allied with the belief that the rituals possessed a quasi-magical property effecting reactions that reverberated throughout the cosmos. It is important to distinguish between the concept of Torah as the purpose of creation and the view of the *mizvoth* as mystic rites, surcharged with cosmic potencies; for while the former belongs to the mental world of pure monotheism, with all causes and effects being achieved solely by the supreme will of God, the latter operates in the mental domain of theosophy, in which rites produce occult effects automatically, or through physical laws.

A clear mark of the theosophic attitude may be seen in the attribution to God of the practice of performing the "*mizvoth.*" For example, when the assertion is made that the Lord prays, wearing *tallith* and *tefillin*, the implication is that the act of praying brings about beneficent effects apart from the will of God. Thus the Talmud pictures God as praying to Himself, "May it be willed that My mercies prevail over My anger." The same passage describes the Lord as desiring to be blessed by men, so that He might be "aided" by their efforts.[82]

This mechanical conception of the efficacy of ritual is especially marked in some passages referring to the institution of the sacrifices. A third-century scholar imagines God as saying, "I did not create a better advocate for rain than the sacrifices."[83] Characteristic of this line of reasoning is the assumption that the rites of sacrifice are essential to the very existence of cosmic order; hence, the sacrifices could not possibly have been discontinued when the Holy Temple was destroyed.

"'To build up the sanctuary'—by this is meant the sanctuary of the realms above, the sanctuary in which the youth, whose name is Metatron, sacrifices the souls of the saints in order to atone for the people of Israel in the days of their exile."[84] Vicarious atonement by the saints has taken the place of atonement by the ritual of animal sacrifices. "The Holy One, blessed be He, inflicted agonies upon the prophet Ezekiel, in order to purge the sins of Israel."[85] We read too that the blood of King Josiah, spilled when he was shot at by the Egyptian soldiers, "atoned for all Israel."[86] Conceived in the same spirit is the principle comparing the observance of a fast to the bringing of a sacrifice. Consequently a Babylonian rabbi of the fourth century used to pray, following a fast, that in view of his loss of fat and blood through fasting, the Lord might see him "as a sacrifice, lying upon the altar, and accept him."[87]

We must not forget that the prophetic emphasis on inwardness is found in the Talmud side by side with this theurgic conception of sacrifice. The rabbis declared, " Greater is the performance of charity than all the sacrifices."[88] And, " He who does charity in secret is greater even than our teacher, Moses."[89] Rabbi Johanan Ben Zakkai, who established the Academy at Jabneh, following the destruction of the Holy Temple in 69 C.E., declared, " We have one means of atonement that is like sacrifice—the performance of deeds of kindness."[90] A leading rabbi of the early part of the third century declared that the dining-room table takes the place of the altar when poor people are invited to share in our repast.[91] The offering of prayers was usually regarded as an acceptable substitute for sacrifice: " He who prepares himself properly, washes his hands and puts on *tefillin*, recites the Shema and prays, is regarded by Scripture as if he had built an altar and brought a sacrifice upon it."[92]

Regarding the Torah as the ideal pattern of the universe, the Talmudic sages were troubled by the fact that only the Jewish people were loyal to the Word of the universal God. Is not the doctrine of the election of Israel unfair in its implications? Legend had it that the Torah at one time was offered by God to all the nations of the world. But even this answer was not completely satisfactory. Is not the culture and faith of every nation the product of a peculiar conjunction of historical circumstances? Was not Israel's acceptance of the Torah therefore due to its having been properly conditioned for that event by the processes of history? To meet this objection, the sages pointed out that the Israelites accepted the Torah voluntarily and individually in the very teeth of relentless persecution, and that they had continued to demonstrate their individual loyalty, even in the face of martyrdom, through many centuries.[93]

This line of reasoning is presented in the following beautifully embellished homily: In time to come, the Lord will come down from heaven and assemble all the nations of the world for judgment before Him. With the Torah in His lap, He will inquire, " Who among you can justify his life by reference to this book? " Then the Persians, the Greeks and the Romans will come forward and say, " Many wars we have led, many bridges we have built— and we did it all for the sake of Israel, that they might occupy themselves with Torah." But the Lord will refuse to accept this answer. Then the nations will say, " But how were we to live by the Torah, since it was never revealed to us? " To which the Lord will reply that the Torah was offered to all the children of men, though it was accepted only by the children of Israel. To this argument the nations will again reply that Israel had accepted the Torah under duress, since, according to a Talmudic legend, the Lord lifted up the mountain of Sinai and held it above the Israelites, as an inverted tank, saying, " If you accept the Torah, well and good, but if not, you will be buried here." To be sure, the Israelites proved their individual loyalty in later years, but initially the Torah came to them through the providential processes of historical necessity. The Lord, being just, will be compelled to recognize the cogency of this defense, but He will offer to the Gentiles a new test, saying, " One commandment I have, which is called *sukkah*; go ye now and prove to me that you can observe it." Thereupon, all men will be tested individually; they will build their *sukkahs* (booths) and stay in them a while. But the Lord will cause the sun to shine with great heat, causing the arrogant and the impatient to boot the *sukkah* with contempt and go out. " Will this test be fair? " inquires the Talmud, and it replies, " Yes, for all Israelites too are tested in this manner. Besides, even if the weak and unworthy go out of the *sukkah*, do they have to treat it with contempt? "[94]

The point of this fantasy is that Israel passes the divine test so long as it remains loyal to the true faith in spite of being treated as a despised minority. The sin of the wicked among the nations consists in their contemptuous treatment of the *sukkah*, the symbol of the homelessness and insecurity of a scattered minority. They will be accepted and forgiven, however, if they learn to sympathize with those who are oppressed and rejected.

Many Aggadic statements could be cited, reflecting this current of thought, and implying that in one way or another the nations will be punished for their repudiation, not of the Torah as such, but of the ethics of the Torah.

The Torah consists of a set of universal principles applicable to all mankind, coupled with the particular rites that are obligatory only upon the people of Israel. The former category of precepts is designated as " the seven commandments of the sons of Noah," for, according to the sages, God concluded a covenant with the sons of Noah, or mankind generally, implanting His Word in their mind and heart.

As to the laws and principles contained in the Noachide category, there were many variations and differences of opinion.[95] All the lists contain an injunction against idolatry, but it remained a matter of dispute as to whether the service of other gods, in addition to the one God, constituted an act of sin for the Gentiles.[96] The belief in one supreme Deity was accepted, in one form or another, in the "higher" cults of the Hellenistic world, especially in the synthesis of neopaganism with neo-Platonism, which became semiofficial doctrine in the declining years of the Roman Empire.[97] In the Persian Empire the revival of Zoroastrianism led to the worship of the god of light and goodness, the Creator and the ultimate Redeemer, though in theory an independent and opposing diabolical force was postulated. In these circumstances, it is strange that the doctrine of the Noachide laws was never formulated in detail, so as to determine its applicability to the nations among whom the sages lived and worked.[98] Here again we encounter the polar tension in the soul of the Jew between liberal universalism and narrow dogmatism. The assumption running through most of the Talmud is that the Romans were pagans who did not observe the Noachide principles, but the contrary convictions were also voiced.[99] From history we know that the Zealots regarded the Roman eagles and banners to be "unclean" idols, and that they risked their lives in order to prevent the "defilement" of the Holy Land and especially of Jerusalem.[100]

In the early medieval period we note a similar difference of opinion concerning the nature of Catholic Christianity, which then included iconolatry and the adoration of the saints. The French school of Talmudic commentators maintained that all Christians were monotheists, even though some of them added the worship of other beings to that of the one God, since Gentiles are not obligated to worship in the same strictly monotheistic manner as are the Jews. On the other hand, Maimonides, living among the Moslems and sharing their prejudices, maintained that the Christians of his day could not be included in the category of those who observe the Noachide laws, even though their faith serves the purpose of preparing the world for the ultimate attainment of the "kingdom of heaven." The European disciples of

67

Maimonides, principally Rabbi Menahem Mameiri, embraced both Christians and Moslems in the category of monotheists or semiproselytes.[101]

The doctrine of the Noachide commandments was actually a legal application of the prophetic principle that the pagan nations might contribute to the advancement of the kingdom of God, even while they retained their own customs and rituals.[102] This principle weakened the impetus of Jewish proselytism, since the rabbis did not believe that they "saved souls" from the fires of Gehenna when they accepted proselytes into the faith of Israel. It was possible to be numbered among "those who feared the Lord," observing the Noachide laws, without embracing Judaism in its entirety. The Mishna records a dispute between the two great masters at the Academy of Jabneh, Rabbi Eliezer and Rabbi Joshua, concerning the question whether "the pious among the nations of the world possessed a share in the world to come."[103] The vast number of "God-fearers" on the fringe of the Jewish community in the first century of the common era attests to the wide acceptance of this doctrine.[104] However, special merit was ascribed to those who were completely converted to the faith of Judaism and were thus voluntarily subjected to the full weight of the yoke of the law. By the rites of circumcision and baptism, Gentiles were accepted into the Jewish faith and made part of God's collective instrument for the ultimate spiritual conquest of mankind. Characteristic is the rabbinic circumlocution for the ceremony of conversion, "to be brought under the wings of the *Shechinah*," reflecting the belief that the divine presence, in an especially intense and real sense, dwells within the congregation of Israel.

Heretofore we have dealt with the concretization and consolidation of the law, which took place in the Talmudic period, devoting considerable space to this development because the law in all its casuistic minutiæ overshadowed all else in the thinking of that age. "From the day when the Holy Temple was destroyed, the Holy One, blessed be He, possesses in His world only four ells of *Halachah* [law]."[105] As we now come to the evolution of the idea of God, we recognize, to begin with, that the rabbis did not attempt to carry the harsh rigidity and bright exactitude of legal reasoning into the domain of theological speculation. They set out to regulate the concrete actions of the Jewish people, leaving a considerable measure of freedom in the realm of ideas. Only rarely and in the heat of controversy did they succumb to the fever of dogmatism.[106]

In general, the sages operated with the Biblical concept of God. But as masters of calm reflection and meticulous scholarship, the rabbis could not possibly speak of God in the same intuitive and authoritative tone as did the God-intoxicated prophets. They were men of sober faith, pragmatic and judicious, suspicious of the wild rhapsodies of the emotions and fantastic flights of fancy. Schooled in the arts of dialectic and reflection, though not in the discipline of Greek philosophy, they took note of the difficulties in naïve belief even though they distrusted the pride of intellect and the zeal of dogmatism. While they did not insist on niceties of definition or strive for the perfection of systematized thought, they perceived and formulated the paradoxes in monotheistic thought, which in future centuries and in fully developed form, were to occupy the minds of Jewish, Christian, and Mohammedan theologians.

The first paradox with which they dealt, they described as the contrast between "the greatness of God and His humility." In philosophical parlance, the question would be posed in terms of the transcendence of God and His immanence. So, we read in the Scriptures of the immensity of the Lord, of His dwelling in the highest of the heavens, and at the same time we come across passages which describe the Lord of the universe as "descending" to see the evil of the Sodomites,[107] or as "passing" before Moses, who hid in the crevice of the rock,[108] or as "walking" in the Garden of Eden,[109] or as speaking to Moses from between the cherubim on the Holy Ark,[110] or of His glory as descending visibly in a cloud upon the Sanctuary,[111] or of His sitting on a throne, surrounded by a host of seraphim,[112] or of His appearing as "a still small voice," preceded by a storm, an earthquake and a fire.[113] In particular, the Sanctuary of Shiloh and the Holy Temple of Jerusalem were regarded as the dwelling-places of God in a special sense. It does not require a philosophically trained mind to be troubled by this contradiction between a God Who encompasses the universe and one Who moves from place to place, withdrawing, as it were, from the rest of the cosmos, and demonstrating

His special concern with certain individuals. The intuitive genius of the prophets was exercised in expanding the power of God beyond the outermost reaches of the heaven and in deepening His love for the lowest and weakest of all mortals. As the reflective heirs of the mystical prophetic tradition, the rabbis faced the task of retracing the path of intuition in logical terms, so as to render it comprehensible in the ordinary light of day.

It was easy enough for the Talmudic sages to perceive this contradiction in moral terms and to interpret it as an illustration of the superb humility of the Deity. The Almighty condescends to interest Himself in the lives of the poorest and the humblest, for the most exalted being is morally perfect and therefore also the apotheosis of humility. "Wherever you find the greatness of the Lord," one rabbi moralized, "there too you find His humility."[114] The Lord teaches us the lesson of humility. From the ethical point of view, this is indeed a fine homily, implying that the movements of God in Scriptures were not to be taken in a literal sense. On the other hand, the rabbis were not prepared to concede that the nearness of God in certain chosen places and to certain favored individuals was always to be interpreted in a figurative, allegorical sense. The ethical interpretation of God's greatness and humility should be construed as an instructive homily, not as a logical solution.

One way of resolving the difficulty, for the Talmudic sages, consisted in an extension of the doctrine of the Lord's power. Almighty as He is, cannot He "contract" Himself so as to speak to a man, even "from between the hairs of his head"? Is there aught that is too difficult for Him? His motive in so "contracting" His being is to be revealed to men according to "their power" of conception, not according to "His power."[115]

Nevertheless, the rabbis did not feel content with this solution, chiefly because of the dangers implicit in a possible extension of its implication. If the Lord does indeed "contract" His being so as to descend to the level of human comprehension, why cannot we assume that He will go to the extreme of assuming a human form? Profound rabbinical reverence demanded the pure exaltation of the Deity, guarding His being from any taint of anthropomorphism or earthliness. At the same time, they felt constrained to account for the Scriptural references to His nearness and to satisfy their yearnings for the Lord's closeness, the feeling of His immediate, all-redeeming presence.

In these circumstances, their legal training came to the aid of the sages. Accustomed to weigh the full significance of each word in the Torah, they applied the same method to the Scriptural verses which imply the Lord's presence among men. The verb *shochon*, "to dwell," was thus turned into a noun, *Shechinah*, "presence," implying that an emanation from the Supreme Being or a special effulgence of divine radiance was made to dwell in certain places. In this form, the *Shechinah* dwelt in the sanctuary and in the Holy Temple. It remained an open question whether the *Shechinah* in this specific sense continued to dwell on the Holy Mount after the destruction of Jerusalem, or whether it was removed step by step, in proportion to the rising anger of the Lord.[116] In any event, in this specific sense, the *Shechinah* was neither merely a euphemism for the Deity, nor just a created spiritual substance, but a quasi-material, though normally invisible, extension of the Deity, serving as a mark of His special favor for Israel and as the instrument of His contact with His people. The official Targum, the Aramaic translation of the Bible, uses the expression, *memra d'adonai*, the Word of the Lord, or simply, the Word, as a translation for the name of God when its occurrence in the text seems to imply bodily features or to ascribe locomotion to the Lord of the universe. Since God communicates with Israel through words, the *memra* is an equivalent expression for the *Shechinah*, in this sense.

Once the emanation of God, in *memra* or *Shechinah*, was postulated, it was natural for the rabbis to generalize this phenomenon, and to assume that this divine aura extends to all holy phenomena. Thus, when man and woman are united by the bonds of love, the *Shechinah* dwells with them.[117] In this more limited and generalized sense, the *Shechinah* is said to attend wherever ten people are gathered in prayer and even where one person studies the Word of God or prays to Him in purity of devotion.[118] It sits by the bedside of the sick, as an expression of the Lord's sympathy with the agony of mortals, and also because the sick are likely to be repentant.[119] In a more intense form, it surrounds as a living fire those who study the secrets of the Torah.[120]

In both its special and general senses, the *Shechinah* dwells in

Israel, so that a convert is said to enter under the wings of the *Shechinah*.[121] A liberal sage declared that the *Shechinah* rests on Gentiles as well as Jews, in accordance with one's deeds.[122] However, we frequently encounter the contrary assumption: that the *Shechinah* is restricted to Israel.[123] A third-century rabbi expatiated on this theme in this way: "Three things Moses asked of God, and God granted them to him—that the *Shechinah* shall rest on Israel, that it shall not rest on the worshipers of the stars, and that he might know the ways of Providence in dealing with the righteous and the wicked."[124]

Associated with this doctrine of the *Shechinah* is the conception of *Ruah hakodesh*, the Holy Spirit, which is the instrument of revelation. Although the two expressions are sometimes used interchangeably, the latter term is used specifically to denote the inspiration of the canonized Scriptures. As the instrument of prophecy, it disappeared from the life of Israel with the last generation of the prophets, Haggai, Zechariah and Malachi.[125] There are, however, occasional statements to the effect that prophetic insights are implicit in the teaching of the sages.[126] On rare occasions, we are told, the sages were privileged to receive a *Bath Kol*, the echo of a divine voice.[127] Thus the long and bitter controversy between the schools of Shammai and Hillel was resolved by means of this divine echo which declared, "Both opinions are the words of the living God, and the law is like the house of Hillel."[128]

The tension between the rational and the mystical concepts of divine inspiration is illustrated in the following tale: In the Academy of Jabneh (circa 100 C.E.), when Rabbi Eliezar sought the assistance of various miracles and of a *Bath Kol* in support of his views, the rabbis sustained his opponent, Rabbi Joshua, who objected to the intrusion of miracles in a discussion of law, declaring, "It [Torah] is not in heaven."[129] In the opinion of most sages at Jabneh, God speaks chiefly through the insight and reasoning of those who live by His Torah.

Manifestly, the concept of God that prevailed among the rabbis of the Talmudic period was both transcendent and immanent. God was at once remote, beyond the furthest reach of the human mind, and near, to those who are broken of heart. Many stories are told concerning sages who prayed for rain without results, but when they became brokenhearted, their prayers were heard and accepted forthwith.[130] But He Who is so nigh to the humble is also " the place of the universe and the universe is not His place."

What is the process whereby the transcendent Deity becomes the immanent *Shechinah*? We may assume that detailed speculations concerning this problem occupied no small part of the esoteric lore that was jealously guarded by the sages and designated as *Ma-asai Merkabah* and *Ma-asai Bereshith*, the former referring to Ezekiel's description of the divine carriage and possibly containing a theory of emanation, the latter referring to the first chapter of Genesis and possibly containing a Jewish version of the theory of ideas. Many passages in the Talmud tell of the zeal with which this sacred lore was guarded and the care with which it was transmitted by word of mouth to trusted disciples. We may assume that much of the lore that appeared in post-Talmudic times as proto-Qabbalah and Qabbalah had its source in these secret traditions. The rabbis were agreed on the unworthiness of bold speculation concerning the Deity and on the implicit dangers of such a venture.[131]

Apart from these theosophic speculations, there were current some analogies suggesting how the different phases and appearances of the Deity were possible. One rabbi pointed out to an interlocutor that reflections which appear in differently shaped mirrors may either magnify, diminish, or otherwise distort the true object.[132] Even so, God is one, while the reflections of His being that come to us from our varied experiences and insights are many and diverse. If the sun is in the heavens, reasoned another rabbi, while its effect is felt everywhere, why should we not assume the same power in the case of the Creator and Master of the sun?[133] Another popular analogy was of an open cave by the shore of the ocean, being filled by the flowing tide and emptied by its ebb, and still another analogy of the relation of God to the universe was that of a human rider to his horse.[134] More frequently, the Deity is viewed in the guise of a king, who is at the same time a loving father and who deals with men in accord with their deeds. He may sit on the " throne of justice," weighing mankind in the scales of strict law, in which case the world as a whole is surely found wanting, or He may sit on the " throne of mercy," overlooking the sins of mankind and dealing with mankind in love.[135]

One Talmudic analogy must be considered with great caution. It compares the Deity to the human soul in these five respects: filling the whole of the body, perceiving yet being itself invisible, feeding (i.e., keeping alive) the whole body, being pure, and dwelling in the innermost chambers.[136] In the Hellenistic world, there was current the Stoic conception of *anima mundi*, the soul of the world, which pictured the Deity as the sum and substance of the laws prevailing in the universe. The rabbis did not think of God as the world's soul, in the sense of being the expression of the totality of its powers and functions. They envisioned the soul as " pure;" i.e., as being derived from the heavenly spheres so that wickedness is foreign to its true nature.[137] The soul is independently existent, having entered the body from without.[138] In this nonpantheistic sense, the rabbis thought of the Deity as the ultimate source of all physical power, yet separate from the world; immanent in the world of men, yet " pure " and holy.

Primarily, the Lord is the righteous judge. In His administration of the affairs of men He judges mankind as a whole, weighing each generation in His scales of justice. But He does not neglect to balance, with utmost care, the reward and punishment of every person. " The Holy One, blessed be He, does not neglect the reward of any creature."[139] While in Scriptures, divine justice is conceived as being carried out in this earthly life, we find that in the Talmudic period there is a growing realization of the inadequacy of this conception.

In this connection, the doctrine of the resurrection of the dead played a most important role. Associated with it in varied contexts were the hopes for the advent of the Messiah and the belief in the ultimate emergence of a sinless and painless, ultrajoyous and supraphysical type of existence known as the "world to come." The leading motive in the eschatology of the Talmud is the absolute justice and the infinite mercy of the Almighty. Thus, when a person dies, his soul is brought before the bar of judgment; the first question asked of it is, " Did you deal righteously with your fellow men? "[140] If completely sinless, it goes to paradise; if it has sinned, it must be purged in purgatory for varying periods. But neither heaven nor hell are more than transitory phenomena. " The punishment of the wicked in hell does not exceed twelve months."[141] In comparison with full-blooded earthly life, post-mortem existence was for the sages vague and shadowy. They wondered whether it is possible for the Deity to judge the soul separately from the body, which is at least partly responsible for the misdeeds of the person.[142] In this way they evolved the doctrine of the resurrection, reuniting body and soul, either for final judgment or for the final enjoyment of the delights of life, in the "world to come."

Fashioned out of the amorphous stuff of hopes and dreams, "the world to come" appeared to different rabbis in varying forms, reflecting the whole gamut of human taste. One much quoted passage describes the "world to come" as offering neither food nor drink nor any other of the bodily pleasures, but as an ethereal domain, in which "the righteous sit with their crowns upon their heads enjoying the radiance of the *Shechinah.*"[143] On the other hand, other passages portray the delights of future existence in fanciful (albeit very earthly) terms, maintaining "that there is no difference between this world and the days of the Messiah, save in the freedom from the oppression of governments."[144] The terms, "days of the Messiah" and "world to come" were not identical. It was believed that following the Messiah's reign, "the world to come" would be revealed as a heavenly form of life. Yet in many periods the three protean hopes tended to blend into one dazzling vision.[145] The resurrection of the dead was to take place some time after the advent of the Messiah and before the emergence of the "world to come."

Since it is not in this earthly existence that all accounts are balanced, human suffering may be viewed not as punishment for sin but as a sacrificial offering of the righteous. It need no longer be regarded as a mark of divine displeasure, nor even, as in the Book of Job, need it be attributed to the inscrutability of divine wisdom. Paradoxical as it may seem, suffering may well be an expression of divine love, especially so if it is conducive to prayer, the study of Torah, or the attainment of a humble and contrite spirit.[146] The love of God may decree the punishment of people in this world, for the small sins that no mortal avoids entirely, in order that they might enter paradise and the "world to come" without any prior agonies in purgatory.[147] The Jewish people of any one generation may suffer for the sins of their ancestors, just as they generally benefit by the accumulated "merits of the fathers," or from the merits of their contemporary saints.[148] Imputed merit serves as a counterbalance to imputed sin. Thus all men must die because of the sin of Adam and Eve, which rendered the human body mortal even if, perchance, their lives are completely sinless.[149] One sage maintains that the serpent injected "corruption" into the human race, from the effects of which the children of Israel were freed when they accepted the Torah at Sinai.[150]

In the wisdom of Providence it may also be necessary for the righteous of every age to suffer for the sins of their generation.[151] Not only is the gift of the Holy Spirit denied to deserving souls if their contemporaries are unworthy, but the righteous are made to endure pain and death in order to atone for the sins of others.[152] The people of Israel as a whole may be expected to share the lot of the righteous and to advance by their suffering the cause of God's kingdom. For "those who endure pain in joy bring salvation to the world."[153] We have already referred to the passage describing Metatron or the archangel Michael, the heavenly "prince" of Israel, as sacrificing the souls of the righteous on the heavenly altar, in order to atone for the sins of Israel.[154] The Messiah is also portrayed as bearing upon himself the sins of his people.[155]

The doctrine of the Messiah loomed large in the consciousness of Jewish people during the Talmudic period. While the esoteric and apocalyptic literature was devoted almost entirely to speculation concerning the Messianic period, the literature of the Talmud is very restrained and cautious in its comments on the "hope of Israel." Nevertheless, it can be assumed with certainty that the Messianic hope dominated the consciousness of pious Jews, rising to crescendo heights of feverish expectation from time to time, especially during the Bar Kochba rebellion (131-135 C.E.).

While this doctrine was not congealed into a rigid dogma by the codifiers of the law, it was doubtless a focal principle of normative Judaism. The hope of the Messiah was incorporated into the standard prayerbook, even in its earliest sections. From the beginning there were two phases to the Messianic hope—on the one hand, the restoration of the Kingdom of Israel, the achievement of national power under a son of David, and on the other, the triumph of the religion of Israel and the conversion of the nations to it, with the consequent attainment of ethical perfection for the individual and for society.

The nationalistic and spiritual phases of the Messianic hope were closely intertwined in the minds of the sages. However, we may assume that most of the sages were generally inclined to emphasize the universal spiritual features of the Messianic age, while the common people were more prone to favor the national aspects of the era of redemption. The fact that Bar Kochba, the leader of Israel's last desperate rebellion against Rome, could have been regarded as the Messiah is proof of the potency of the national-military phase of the Messianic idea. But the intermingling of ideas and motives is evident in the circumstances that Rabbi Akiba, the most influential sage of his generation, favored the claim of Bar Kochba to the Messiahship and yet taught that, following his triumph, the Messiah would sit on a throne to the right of the Deity, Who would also be seated, in order that they might judge the world together.[156] We must remember that in the minds of the people, the national, mystical, and universal elements of the Messianic era were inextricably blended together, and that different phases of this powerful complex of hope, faith, and fancy achieved prominence at different times, dependent on the changing fortunes of Israel.

CHAPTER THREE

HELLENISTIC JUDAISM

I N their fateful encounter with the cultural world of Hellas, the Jews of Alexandria first came face to face with paganism at its highest level. Heretofore, monotheism had flowered and matured while the Jewish people lived in virtual isolation from their neighbors, cognizant only of the outer forms and expressions of heathendom. The prophets of the First Commonwealth directed their barbs of bitter invective against the desiccated remnants of paganism and idolatry, without taking specific account of the mythological ideas which purported to justify the elaborate rites at the pagan shrines. To Isaiah, idolatry was simply and purely fetishism; that is, the actual worship of "the stock of a tree."[1] To Ezekiel, the nations of the world appeared to be worshipers of lifeless idols of wood and stones, not devotees of gods that "dwelt" in certain images.[2] Yet we know from the Ugarithic tablets that the Canaanites in particular and the Near Eastern peoples in general had developed magnificent mythological systems, purporting to account for the rhythms of nature and the destiny of man.

A deepened awareness of the higher reaches of pagan thought is evident in postexilic Judaism. It was then that the vision of a mission unto all the children of man dawned upon the Jewish mind. To be sure, the Jews absorbed some popular conceptions, such as the doctrine of the angels and of the resurrection, but, on the whole, Judaism confronted the intellectual world of Babylonia and Persia with implacable opposition. The awareness of divine unity was sharpened by the challenge of Zoroastrian dualism, and the reality of man's freedom was asserted against the Babylonian belief in astrological determinism. Judaism insisted that the Lord was at once the fashioner of light and the creator of darkness, He Who sits upon the heavens and He Who looks upon the poor and the lowly in spirit.[3] Even in Babylonia, however, the contact between Judaism and paganism remained largely peripheral, ceremony being matched against ceremony, a tabu against a *mizvah*, a myth against a Biblical tale, with no common method and no common fund of ideas to provide a meeting ground for the exchange and clarification of ideas.

The Hellenic world offered a form of paganism that was esthetically attractive, purged of the crude savageries of the Near Eastern faiths. In addition, a quasi-secular culture had developed in the Hellenistic world, embracing literature, art, philosophy, and entertainment. Greek philosophy provided not only a number of lofty ideals, but, what is more, a pattern of reasoning and a method of attempting to assay the truth of any conjecture. Greek art appealed to the universal sense of beauty and form, quite independently of any mythological illusions. Judaism confronted the challenge, therefore, not so much of an alien faith in Zeus, Athena, and Apollo, as of a semi-independent secular world, with standards of judgment and fields of expression that were generally human and not specifically pagan. Yet there was just enough of a bond between the philosophic, esthetic, and civic disciplines of Hellenism and the ceremonies of Greek religion to make the pious Jew feel that he trod on dangerous ground. On the folk level, the athletic exercises, the games and tournaments presented the predominant challenge, while, on the intellectual level, the various schools of Greek philosophy brought into question the basic convictions of Judaism concerning God and the good life. Whereas in all previous history, Judaism had been sheltered from the influence of alien faiths by a double barrier of dogmatic exclusion, erected in part by itself and in part by the surrounding native creeds, it was now confronted with an open secular field, in which cultural values were largely based upon universal human foundations, and in which it became increasingly more difficult to maintain the validity of its self-imposed barriers.

The conquests of Alexander and the consequent mass migrations and resettlements in the Mediterranean world induced an attitude of tolerance to differing religious practices, resulting in various degrees of syncretism in the huge metropolitan centers of the ancient world. Gods were freely exchanged and identified with one another. The people came to feel that the different religious faiths were like so many languages, conveying the same thoughts in various idioms. This commingling of gods and faiths in the great centers of the ancient world was aided by the progress of philosophy, which regarded all outer forms of religious ceremonialism as being of no particular consequence.

In the first centuries of the Hellenistic era, the Stoic movement became the strongest ally of decaying paganism in its varied forms. The Stoic teachers projected the idea of the world soul, under the aspect of the gods popular in every country, interpreting the myths and rites in every locality as being allegorical or symbolical representations of the universal truths of Stoicism.[4] While Stoicism, as an ethical philosophy of life, had many points of contact with Judaism, its teachers did not scruple to effect alliances with hoary superstitions and barbaric rites, lending the mantle of philosophy to cover the worship of Baal and Astarte in Syria and Isis and Osiris in Egypt. Paganism thus came to function in the Hellenistic world on two planes, the upper, rarefied plane of philosophy and the lower, popular plane of primitive religion. And between the two planes there was frequently no stronger bond than the tortuous rhetoric of occasional Stoic preachers. While in Judaism the twin lights of intelligence and conscience were fused with the fires of patriotism and the dark passions of mysticism to form one lambent flame, in Hellenic civilization the three elements diverged. Man's intellect and moral sense were elaborated in the philosophic schools; the loyalties of patriotism were celebrated in the rites of the official or " civic " religions, and the protean yearnings for mystical union with the divine were articulated in the so-called " mystery " religions.

Side by side with the intellectual " melting pot " of the Hellenistic world, there came to be an actual biological commingling of nations and races, first in the Hellenic world, later in the Roman Empire. The Stoic movement assisted in the popularization of the concepts of humanity and reason, leading to the gradual deprecation of the value of local differences. The ancient barriers between Greek, Syrian, and Egyptian religions crumbled steadily through the successive generations of Hellas until, for most enlightened people, they came to be only local memories and provincial peculiarities. The proper and decent thing to do was to accept the prevailing rites and customs in every region and to consider them to be of no real importance. Humanity, its fundamental aspirations, were the same the world over. Hence, all peoples living together in one locality must learn to worship together, imploring "the gods" for the common good. Accordingly, the so-called "civic religions" developed; these were semi-religious and semipatriotic in character, and all residents were expected to participate in them. The spirit of intolerance shifted its hold from the ancient faiths to the new synthetic ceremonies, which only a "stiff-necked people" refused to accept.

The most important form of "civic religion" was the deification of kings and emperors. Based upon the belief that men can rise to the status of gods, the Ptolemys of Egypt, the Seleucid monarchs of Syria, and later the emperors of Rome assumed the dignity and title of gods, demanding that sacrifices be brought to their images. Characteristic of this trend of thought was the reply of Caius Caligula to Philo's argument that sacrifices are brought daily in the Holy Temple for his welfare, "This may be true, you sacrifice, but to one other than myself. Of what good is it to me if you don't sacrifice to me?"[5]

In sum, the Jew faced the challenge of an esthetically appealing paganism, allied with a universal cosmopolitan attitude that was all-pervasive, and loosely associated with the free and inquiring spirit of philosophy as it was taught in the contemporary Greek schools.

While on the popular level Hellenism made powerful inroads against the Jewish community in Palestine (as is evidenced by the eagerness of the Hellenizing priests in Jerusalem to import Greek institutions, launching a series of events which culminated in the institution of the festival of Hanukkah, 165 B.C.E.), on the intellectual level, Judaism was on the offensive from the very beginning. The early Jewish writers in Greek aimed to convert the pagan world to Judaism so as to bring about the realization of the prophetic dream of Messianic perfection. In the century preceding the Christian era, Judaism made impressive headway in gaining full-fledged converts and in the dissemination of its ideas and practices among millions of sympathetic Gentiles "who feared the Lord."[6] Accordingly, it did not then seem unreasonable to look for the speedy attainment of Isaiah's vision of Judaism triumphant, with all the nations walking up to Mount Zion to "learn of His ways and walk in His paths."[7]

The Septuagint translation of the Bible was intended not only for the use of the Greek-speaking Jews, but also for the general reader of Greek literature. The famous letter of Aristeas represents the translation as a miraculous event, having been carried out with divine guidance by seventy-two sages, under the leadership of the high priest Eleazar. One of the early Hellenistic Jewish philosophers, Aristobulus, who probably lived during the generation of the Maccabean revolt, followed up the Septuagint with a commentary in which the philosophic import of the Torah is expounded. Such Biblical phrases as "the hand of the Lord" and the references in Scriptures to the descent of God to behold the actions of men, to His resting on the Sabbath, His coming down upon the mountain of Sinai and His sounding of the *shofar* when the Ten Commandments were proclaimed, these and similar anthropomorphic allusions were interpreted by Aristobulus as symbols or human analogies for the inexpressible and ineffable nature of God. So persuaded was Aristobulus of the essential congruity of philosophy and the Holy Scriptures that he sought to prove that Pythagoras, Plato, and Aristotle derived their doctrines from the Hebrew prophets, launching speculations concerning the Jewish inspiration of Greek philosophy that were elaborated upon in diverse ways by many ancient and medieval scholars. Writing in the last third of the first century of the common era, the historian Josephus asserted, "Our earliest imitators were the Greek philosophers, who, though ostensibly observing the laws of their own countries, yet in their conduct and philosophy were Moses' disciples, holding similar views about God."[8] In general, the exponents of Judaism in the Hellenistic world approved the teachings of the philosophers, combated vigorously the moral and ritualistic expressions of paganism and maintained that the purveyors of "mystery rites" were fakers and charlatans, for only the rites of Judaism were God-given.

A powerful missionary message is contained in the Jewish Sibylline Oracles. A Jewish author or group of authors framed these impressive messages to the pagan world in the form of poetic verses, supposedly uttered by a pagan prophetess or sibyl.

Mixing prediction with instruction, the Sibylline Books present "Jewish propaganda under the guise of paganism." In biting satire, the author rebukes the Gentiles for their worship of demons, ghosts, snakes and cats, idols of stone and wood. In language that is reminiscent of the thunder of Isaiah, the sibyl contrasts the glory and majesty of the one God with the folly of idolatry, threatening those who will not repent of their pagan ways with the fires of hell, and promising for the righteous a share in the "green paradise," where they will "eat sweet bread that will descend from the star-studded heavens."[9] Nor is the rebuke of the Jewish preacher concerned with theological matters only. In the manner of the Biblical prophets, he castigates the Greeks and Egyptians for the looseness of their morals, the faithlessness of their women and the helplessness of their poor, contrasting these failings with the social idealism and humane legislation of the "children of Abraham." "For He who dwells in heaven fashioned the earth for all men to dwell in it together."[10] In time to come, the author declares, the Hellenes will recognize the stupidity and sin of idolatry and will join in the worship of the Supreme Deity. Following a world-shaking catastrophe, the survivors of mankind will join Israel in the worship of the one God.[11] The burden of the Sibylline Oracles, therefore, is propaganda for conversion to Judaism, or at least for the acceptance of its spiritual-ethical message and the acceptance of the worship in the Holy Temple of Jerusalem.

The association of ethical virtues with the Jewish religion and the vices of immorality and callousness to human suffering with paganism were underlined by the then polar contrast between the actual lives of the hedonistic Greeks and the puritanical Jews. Thus, Ernest Renan writes: "But the best arguments for Jewish propaganda were the lives of the plain, Jewish folk: They were happy, content with their lot, even in difficult circumstances, satisfied with very little; at the same time, they were truly wise, philosophers in their own peculiar way. Without fear, and with confident innocence, they rebuked the Greeks and the Egyptians for their impudent baseness and their low vices."[12]

Josephus, too, in his defense of Judaism, points out that the ideals of the Jewish religion implied a commitment to virtuous living and were not merely beautiful abstractions, designed to delight a logician.

" Even among the pagan masses there is considerable zeal for our worship. There is no city in the lands of the Hellenes and the barbarians, or in the world generally, where our observances have not been disseminated—such as the observance of the Sabbath, the keeping of the fast [Yom Kippur], the lighting of the candles and many dietary observances. They too strive to emulate the spirit of brotherhood that prevails among us, our deeds of benevolence, our love of work, our patience to endure the decrees against us. How wonderful it is that all these achievements are effected by the appeal of the Torah itself, apart from any external inducements or sensual attractions. And as the Lord fills the universe, so does the Torah permeate all of mankind."[13]

The author of the *Wisdom of Solomon* is concerned with the problem posed by the occasional prosperity of the wicked and the sufferings of the righteous. This perennial dilemma of ethical monotheism is resolved by means of the doctrine of immortality, for " the righteous live forever," whereas the wicked one is as a " guest who has come for one day."[14] The author personifies wisdom and affirms it to be a partner of the Almighty " sitting with Him upon His throne." While earthly wisdom is accessible to all men, it is but a pale shadow of true wisdom, pure and incorruptible, which dwells eternally in heaven. Because of its high origin, " wisdom does not come to an evil soul and does not dwell in a body given over to sin."[15] The author rebukes the Greeks for their worship of images, explaining the origin of the errors of idolatry in a rationalistic manner.[16] He heaps scorn upon the Egyptians for their worship of animals and maintains that paganism is to blame for the evils of homosexuality and immorality generally. The vice of homosexuality was particularly widespread in the Hellenistic world. St. Paul regards it as a Greek vice.[17] In spite of his contemptuous judgment of Greek life, the author freely employs some concepts of Greek philosophy, the assumption of a hylic matter as the raw material of creation and the description of wisdom as a quasi-independent force, responsible for rational thought and ethical feeling as well as the inspiration of the prophets and the performance of the miracles.[18]

It was in the writings of Philo Judaeus that Hellenistic Judaism attained its highest development. In his voluminous works, Philo dealt with every aspect of the conflict between Judaism and Greek thought, arriving at a philosophy that, in its essentials, set the pattern for the next sixteen centuries of European thought among

Jews, Moslems and Christians. In the Philonic synthesis, philosophy begins "with a preamble of faith," but the final substance of faith is philosophy. Two worlds of thought are brought together and intermingled so thoroughly as to seem all of one piece. Accordingly, both Hellenic philosophy and Hebraic faith are modified fundamentally, and a new spiritual creation emerges, philosophical Judaism, in which mystical fervor, intellectual analysis, and loyalty to tradition are blended together. The piety of Philo lacks the simplicity and naïvete of the Palestinian rabbis, but it is many-sided and beautiful, poetic and profound, partaking both of the rationalism of modernists and the mysticism of saints.[19]

Philo (circa 20 B.C.E.-40 C.E.) devoted himself from earliest youth to the pursuit of learning and the attainment of the highest goals of piety. Scion of a wealthy and aristocratic family, he sought, not pleasure, glory, and power, but virtue, wisdom, and a mystic union with the Supreme Being. At first he was convinced that these goals could only be approached through the avenues of asceticism and retreat from the world. In his maturer years, he discovered the futility of the ascetic pathway, and he determined to find God by working for the betterment of society, pursuing a career of teaching and preaching in the synagogue.

" I often left my kindred and friends and fatherland," he wrote, "and went into a solitary place, in order that I might have knowledge of things worthy of contemplation, but I profited nothing: for my mind was sore tempted by desire and turned to opposite things. But now, sometimes even when I am in a multitude of men, my mind is tranquil, and God scatters aside all unworthy desires, teaching me that it is not differences of place which affect the welfare of the soul, but God alone, who knows and directs its activity howsoever he pleases."[20]

In his fifties, the greatly beloved teacher was compelled to interrupt his tranquil meditations and to undertake a hazardous journey to Rome, in defense of the rights of the Alexandrine Jews and the right of Jewish people in Palestine to refuse to worship the image of Caius Caligula. On this occasion Philo was forced to engage in a running debate with anti-Semitic detractors in the attempt to win the favor of a petulant and psychopathic tyrant. Philo's report on his mission is the first recorded account of a formal defense of Judaism against its defamers. As it happened, Caligula died, and his successor, Claudius, largely exonerated the Jews of Alexandria, restored their rights, punished their attackers and relieved the threat to Jerusalem.[21]

The Alexandrian community was well advised to choose Philo to defend the Jewish faith, since he represented a form of Judaism that was universalistic and in accord with the best thought of the Hellenistic world, even while it remained staunchly loyal to tradition and to the sentiments of the masses. The major sin of Judaism, from the pagan point of view, was its separatism. The pagan masses interpreted the Jewish refusal to participate in the exercises of "civic religion" as being due to "misanthropy," Jewish hatred of all Gentiles. In their ignorance of the rabbinic motivations for the laws of Judaism, they attributed the "peculiarity" of Jewish laws and the remarkable tenacity of Jewish people to inordinate racial pride, religious exclusiveness, and bigoted contempt for their neighbors.[22] This opinion was fortified by the popular philosophers of the Roman world who regarded all external ceremonies as being of no intrinsic significance. Few indeed were the men who were able to see Judaism from within as the faith of a people that was dedicated to the redemption of all mankind, determined to guard its purity and integrity in order the better to fulfill its role in the human drama. It was in behalf of all men that the healing faith of monotheism was to be preserved and advanced, but this task could not be achieved if the people to whom it was entrusted were to succumb weakly to the lures and pressures of their environment. Judaism was arraigned before the Hellenistic masses and the Roman government on the score of its misanthropy. What more fitting therefore than the selection of a champion who expounded Judaism to the Hellenistic world in terms of its loftiest concepts and its universal ideals?

The most profound difference between Judaism and paganism was centered around the idea of God. Yet the views of the philosophers were essentially in a class by themselves, since they interpreted the gods of the Homeric pantheon as so many figures of speech; occasionally, too, they wrote of God as one. To Philo, the philosophic teachings in their purity constituted an " inferior form " of the Jewish faith. But the views of the philosophers could not possibly be treated as a homogeneous body of doctrine. Philo rejected the Aristotelian concept of the Deity as the unmoved mover, since it implied the eternity of the world and denied the miracle of creation. Similarly, Philo repudiated the Stoic view of God as a material principle, immanent in physical nature, revealed in reason and expressed in the laws which govern all events in the universe. The Stoics believed the fundamental energy of the universe to be a quasi-rational logos, conscious, inflexible, and benevolent. In addition, they thought of seminal logoi as being sparks of rationality, diffused through the universe and accounting for the enduring pattern of things and their ebullient vital energy. Philo could not accept a material conception of the Deity, since Scripture emphasizes the spiritual character of God's being and His difference from the material world. Thus, the most popular philosophy in the contemporary pagan world was as unacceptable to Philo as paganism itself.

In addition, the pride of the Stoic, arising from his belief that his human reason, when freed from its bondage, is essentially identical with the divine logos, was sheer abomination to Philo, who felt that God can only be known in utter humility. Philo would have agreed wholeheartedly with the rabbinic dictum that the Lord says of the arrogant one, " He and I cannot dwell in one domain."[23] To Philo, all knowledge was a direct gift from God, involving the active participation of divine energy. It is not by his own reason that man apprehends God, but by the goodness of God, Who grants to the man He favors flashes of insight. " Through God, God is known, for He is His own light."[24] Man's mind is an open tablet, which contains no knowledge of its own, but which acquires knowledge either through the senses or through a quickening act of God.[25]

Philo agrees with Plato that God is not only " The Good," Who is the source of all humanly perceived values, but also the creator of the universe. In his *Timaeus*, Plato pictures God as implanting a " world soul " into the universe, which thereupon begins to function as the all-embracing dynamic force of the world. In this concept, God Himself remains aloof from the goings-on of all mundane existence. Creation was due to His power, but He does not stand in direct, immediate relationship to His creatures. Such a view would naturally be incompatible with the teachings of Judaism and hardly conducive to the worshipful mood, the feeling of total dependence or the sense of nearness of God, which is the essence of monotheistic piety. Accordingly, Philo introduces a "correction" of the Platonic system. The "world soul" is not simply an objective entity which stands between God and the world. Rather, the logos, taking the place of the "world soul," unites God with the world, for it remains in permanent attachment to God even while it enters into the world as its dynamic and creative force.[26] While God is spirit, exalted above the visible universe and different from it, He is in constant contact with the world through the logos, which wells out from Him as from a bottomless fountain and overflows into the universe. Consequently He is both transcendent to the universe in His inner being and immanent in it as its dynamic essence. He is, at once, far and near.

Philo's conception of the logos can best be understood by the analogy of speech. In the Holy Scriptures, God, the invisible, is pictured as communing with men through the agency of speech. The rabbinic contemporaries of Philo assumed that prophecy was extinct in their generation, yet they still believed in the divine origin of a voice, a *Bath Kol*, which could be heard at crucial moments.[27] God's voice or speech was conceived as the manner whereby the will of the Deity was revealed in the actual world. In speech the unity of thought is translated into an ordered multitude of diverse sounds, i.e., the *one* of spirit is translated into the many of matter. In Philo's writings, the term "logos" means reason, or wisdom, or speech, or word. It is a process which begins with God, where it is one and spirit, and culminates in the multifarious phenomena of the universe where it is many, concrete, and material. In the mind of man, this direction of the logos may be reversed and its pristine unity recaptured. Philo writes, "God speaks not words, but things."[28] His creative energy flows down from above as a mighty river, which branches out as it descends "and overflows and gladdens all things."[29] This stream of creative energy inspires men to lofty undertakings, fills them with noble thoughts and, on occasion, it may transport them to the rapturous heights of ecstasy. On the human plane, the logos is divided into many logoi, which stimulate the human imagination, both in their descent from God and in their ascent back to their source.

Up and down through the whole soul, the logoi of God move without end: when they ascend, drawing it up with them, and severing it from the mortal part, and showing only the vision of ideal things; and when they descend, not casting it down, but descending with it from humanity or compassion toward our race, so as to give assistance and help, in order that, inspiring what is noble, they may revive the soul which is borne along on the stream of the body.

The logos is more than the quickening principle of divine intelligence; it is also the flow of His love and redeeming grace. The qualities which appear separate in human experience are one in their source. It is at once an emanation of divine qualities and an instrument of His power by means of which He continually controls the course of events on earth. Philo believed in the reality of divine miracles, though he also interpreted some of the Biblical miracles allegorically. As a rule, in Philo's thinking God maintains uniform laws on earth by means of His logos, but on occasion He intervenes in behalf of the righteous by means of the same instrument.[30]

The net philosophic content of Philo's thinking may be summarized as follows: (1) God in Himself is transcendent to the universe and to all the qualities which man's mind is capable of conceiving. He is "superior to virtue, superior to knowledge, superior to the good itself and the beautiful itself";[31] (2) God created the ideas as the "patterns" and "powers" of all existing things and the logos as the all-embracing instrument containing them, operating them, and modifying them at will; (3) God, through the Logos, rules the world, changing the laws of nature at will. "Like a charioteer, grasping the reins, or a pilot the tiller, He guides all things in whatsoever direction He pleases, as law and right demand. . . ."

Philo's concept of God is a reassertion of Biblical monotheism against the challenge of logical-mechanical thought that is implicit in much of Greek philosophy. The God of monotheism is a projection unto the infinite of the concept of personality, and personality cannot be fully comprehended in the meshes of a mechanistic universe. Therefore philosophers who base their speculations about Deity upon the analysis of physical nature either deny both God and personality by reducing them to a necessitous mechanism, or else they remove both concepts to a totally "other" world. Neither alternative is truly congruent with the psychological reality of religious faith, though both have served at one time or another as its rationalistic façade. Philo refused to accept the first or Stoic alternative, but neither was he content with a God who had abdicated His freedom to a "world soul." Instead he retained the Biblical concept and he resolved all contradictions by pointing to the inscrutable and unknowable nature of God. The human mind can ascend the spiritual ladder of the logos, but it can never comprehend the character of God in Himself, save in the recognition, on the highest levels of insight, that He is one. Philo wrote that God "presents to the mind which has vision the appearance of one, sometimes of three; of one, when the mind is highly purified. . . ."[32] Polytheism, which assumes a pluralistic universe in which all forces operate as semi-independent entities, is true to nature as it appears to the dry and sober contemplation of the uninspired observer. But as the mind quickened by the Divine spirit grows in intuitive understanding, it glimpses at last the truth that God is one, though how and why opposites cohere in Him, it cannot tell.

Philo believed implicitly that the laws of Moses were divinely revealed, but his problem was not to prove the inspiration of the Scriptures so much as the uniqueness of that inspiration. Divine revelation was a cheap commodity in the ancient world. The word "enthusiasm" means "to be in God," but the motley breed of enthusiasts in Greece and Egypt did not earn the high regard of the educated people. Plato distinguished among four different types of ecstatic "frenzy"—the kind which results in divining the future; the devotional enthusiasm of the priest; the transporting "muse" of the poets; or finally the only type superior to sense-perception and reason, the philosophic frenzy in which ideas are apprehended in their ideal purity.[33] Philo points out that the prophetic state is a synthesis of the four categories of "frenzy" assumed by Plato; it is prediction and piety, poetry and philosophy blended. The greatness of prophecy consists in its many-sidedness, for, like virtue, it depends on the perfection of the intellect, the imagination, and the emotions. The prophet is therefore superior to the philosopher, especially when his conscious faculties are stimulated, not blotted out by "frenzy," and he receives his message through a divine voice. Indeed, the gift of prophecy of this high order is confined to the Jewish people, not because of racial qualifications, but on account of their habitual dedication to the service of God.[34] The fact is, Philo would say that nowhere else than in Israel did majestic personalities comparable to the Hebrew prophets arise. Hence the uniqueness and authority of Torah.

Lower degrees of prophecy, however, are available to all men and women who seek God. Thus, the gift of the divine spirit, *Ruah hakodesh,* may come to all who are endowed with a rational soul, and the Lord may choose to send messages by angels to those who are intellectually undistinguished. But while divine inspiration is a general phenomenon, Philo seems to say, prophecy in its normative sense, resulting in the revelation of a body of laws, is restricted to Jews alone. Philo believed that the Ten Commandments " were spoken by God in His own person,"[35] apparently through the agency of a miraculously created voice, " by a voice which, strange paradox, was visible,"[36] so that, as Scripture puts it, " all the people saw the voices."[37] But, while Philo accepted the divine origin of the Torah, he did not rest content with this dogma, for nearly all codes of law were in ancient times claimed to be divine. He needed to prove that the inspiration of the Scriptures was indeed many-sided, embracing the intellectual standards of the philosopher as well as those of the poet, the statesman, and the priest. If he could not do so, he would have had to agree that the Torah, even if of divine inspiration, was inferior to the teachings of the philosophers. Accordingly, his chief emphasis is on the intrinsic merit of Jewish laws. They are to be observed not because they are of divine origin but, he continually asserts, they are to be accounted divine because they conform perfectly to the laws of nature.[38]

While the highest form of prophetic teaching was granted only to Jews, the law is of universal applicability and even of cosmic significance. Moses prefaced his account of the laws with the story of creation in order to show " that the world is in harmony with the law, and the law with the world, and that the man who observes the law is constituted thereby a loyal citizen of the world, regulating his doings by the purpose and will of nature, in accordance with which the entire world itself is administered."[39] The Stoics admonished their disciples to live " in accordance with nature" and thereby to earn the designation, " citizen of the world." Philo adapts the concepts of the Stoics to his purpose.

Nature is not a self-contained reality; it is governed from above by the logos, and the law derives from the logos. The law is compatible with the spirit that rules nature, and the human soul apprehends this governing spirit in rare and beautiful moments. For it is man's noblest aspiration "to become like God, as far as this is possible; and to become like Him is to become holy, just, and wise." Philo refers again and again to this ideal of *imitatio dei*, for which he found ample backing both in the writings of Plato and in the oral tradition of the rabbis.[40]

In Greek philosophy, the good life is defined as the life of virtue, with different schools emphasizing different aspects of virtue. Philo accepted the prevailing virtues, the Stoic aim of freeing man's will and reason from the turbulence of the passions and the Aristotelian standard of the golden mean; but he insisted that "piety" is the "queen" or "leader" of all the other virtues, for man is not self-sufficient and alone but utterly dependent both morally and physically upon God. In turn, piety or "faith in God" is expressed in the reverent study of the law, in prayer and in the constant, humble awareness of man's need for repentance. With this "correction" of Greek thought, Philo changed the focus of ethical thought from "man in himself" to "man before God." With this modification of the hierarchy of virtues, Philo was able to assert that the laws of Moses are identical in purpose and function with the ideal laws of the philosophers, since the laws of Moses are intended to train men in the acquisition of all the virtues.

Philo classifies all the precepts of Judaism according to ten categories, corresponding to the Ten Commandments. In the discussion of each legal category he shows how it contributes to the life of virtue, concluding that the laws of Moses, "separately and all in common incite and exhort us to wisdom and justice and godliness and the rest of the company of virtues."[41] This overall purpose is the "soul" of the law, even as external observance is the body.[42] Naturally, the law fulfills its moral purpose only when it is performed with the right intent and in the spirit of piety. "Right actions that spring from forethought are of greater worth than those that are involuntary."[43]

Since man is not complete save when he turns in obedience and humility to God, Philo concludes that worship must be included among the virtues. Prayer was, in Philo's mind, of far greater worth than the offering of sacrifices in the Holy Temple of Jerusalem, since it is through prayer that man opens his soul to God. He inquires, "What house shall be prepared for God, the King of Kings? . . . Shall it be of stone or wooden material? " In answer, he declares, " Away with the thought, the very words are impious. . . . One worthy house there is—the soul that is fitted to receive Him."[44] Philo did not oppose the institution of sacrifices at the temple, and he journeyed at least once to Jerusalem in order to offer a sacrifice.[45] But his emphasis was on the inwardness of piety.

In common with the philosophers and the rabbis, Philo declares virtue to be its own reward, for its exercise trains a person to be independent of fortuitous external events and to be ever joyous. At the same time, Philo is not willing to forego or forget the blessings which were promised for the righteous in the Holy Scriptures. He looked forward to the restoration of the Jewish power and earthly bliss, through the advent of a Messiah; he believed that the gift of divine grace, resulting in the rare joy of mystic piety, was likely to be the portion of the righteous on earth, and he did not doubt that the joys of immortality were reserved for those who feared the Lord and walked in His ways.

Philo regarded the separation of humanity into Jews and Gentiles as a temporary phenomenon, to be ended with the speedy advent of the Messianic age. The "misanthropy" or "inhospitality" toward non-Jews which some contemporary writers found in Jewish law, Philo dismissed as a delusion, deriving from the pagan love of carnal pleasures. Anti-Semitism is essentially a revolt against the necessary disciplines of the higher life. It is due to the dislike of the laws of Judaism, "which are necessarily grave and severe, because they inculcate the highest standard of virtue; but gravity is austere, and austerity is held in aversion by the great mass of men because they favor pleasure."[46] Jewish law does not induce a lack of patriotism or instill an attitude of intolerance toward non-Jews. On the contrary, proselytes are welcomed into the fold with open arms and they are regarded as part of the covenant-people, bound by "kinships of greater dignity and sanctity " than the ties of blood.

With the advent of the Messiah, the barrier between Jew and

Gentile will be leveled and "each nation will abandon its peculiar ways, and, throwing overboard their ancestral customs, turn to honoring our laws alone, for when the brightness of their shining is accompanied by national prosperity, they will darken the light of the others, as the risen sun darkens the stars."[47] The Gentiles will not only become "God-fearers," as is predicted in the Sibylline Oracles, but they will also accept Jewish law in its entirety, for their reluctance to recognize the sublimity of the Torah is due in large part to the misery and wretchedness of the Jewish people.[48] The Messiah will cause the status of Jewry to be uplifted; and exiled communities will return to their land in glory, "guided by some vision, more divine than is compatible with its being of the nature of man, invisible indeed to everyone else, but manifest only to those who were saved."[49] It is not quite clear whether the reference is to a personal Messiah or to the logos, or to the *Shechinah*.[50] There will follow a reign of peace and prosperity for Israel, along with diverse punishments for the unrepentant enemies of Israel. This revolution of the wheel of fortune in favor of Israel will be sufficient to bring about the wholehearted conversion of the majority of mankind.

If "the laws" of Judaism interpose in practice a barrier of hate and bitterness between Jews and Gentiles, might it not be wise to abolish these laws, while retaining the general principles which they embody? This suicidal solution of the Jewish problem was advocated in Philo's day by influential people, including Philo's own nephew, Tiberius Julius Alexander, who rose to eminence as a Roman general and did not scruple to turn his legions against his own people. The assimilationists of the Hellenistic period were motivated decisively by a "practical" argument, such as the following: "Let us go out and make a covenant with the nations that are round about us, for since we separated ourselves from them many evils have come upon us."[51] This substitution of a covenant with the nations for the ancient covenant with the Lord implied the total abrogation of all the laws and customs through which the Jewish faith was expressed, and the acceptance in their stead of corresponding pagan and Hellenistic observances. The "practical" advantages of accepting this counsel were supplemented by the philosophic argument that particular laws and ceremonies are not essential to true religion. The philosopher can serve God by silent meditation, and, if he must join in public forms of worship, it is quite immaterial to him what shape or form the ceremonies assume. To justify his faith, Philo had to contend against the arguments of both the "philosophical" assimilationists and the "practical" realists.

Philo was particularly hard-pressed to oppose the "philosophers" in their ambition to abolish the ceremonial law, since he agreed with them in the need to "allegorize" the laws and to discover their universal meaning. If the external observance of the law be the inedible shell, while its meaning is the luscious seed, why keep the shell, especially when it is so terribly troublesome, after you have already digested the seed? To this argument, Philo replied that the observance of ancestral customs was itself an important virtue, since such practices served to maintain the community. "For customs are unwritten laws, decrees of men of old, not carved indeed upon pillars and inscribed upon parchment, but engraved upon the soul of the generations who through the ages maintain the chosen community."[52] It is the community, not the individual, that is the bearer of a living religious tradition, transmitting spiritual wealth from generation to generation. And customs constitute the warp and woof of communal life.

> For they ought to give heed to both—to the accurate investigation of the unseen meaning, but also to the blameless observance of the visible letter. But, not as if they were living by themselves in a desert, and were souls without bodies, and knew nothing of city or village or house or intercourse with men, they despise all that seems valuable to the many, and search for bare and naked truth, as it is in itself. . . . We should have to neglect the service of the temple, and a thousand other things, if we were to restrict ourselves only to the allegorical or symbolic sense. That sense resembles the soul, the other sense the body. Just as we must be careful of the body, as the house of the soul, so must we give heed to the letter of the written laws. For only when these are faithfully observed, will the inner meaning, of which they are the symbols, become more clearly realized, and, at the same time, the blame and accusation of the multitude will be avoided.[53]

As to the realists, Philo's retort was in effect the insistence that the Diaspora was only a temporary phenomenon. Israel was not designed to be mere dirt under the feet of impudent oppressors for ever. Soon the Messiah would arrive, punish all unrepentant Gentiles and re-establish Israel at the summit of the mountains ". . . all the prosperity of their fathers and ancestors will seem a tiny fragment, so lavish will be the abundant riches in their possession, which flowing from the gracious bounties of God as from a perennial fountain will bring to each individually and to all in common a deep stream of prosperity leaving no room for envy."[54] The resurgent national prosperity of Israel will be accompanied by the catastrophic downfall of its enemies. " Everything will suddenly be reversed, God will turn His curses against the enemies of these penitents, the enemies who rejoiced in the misfortunes of the nation and mocked and railed at them. . . ."[55]

Proceeding to interpret the inner meaning of specific institutions and precepts, Philo arranges all the precepts of Judaism in categories corresponding to the Ten Commandments, with the first five Commandments expressing the ideal of the love of God and the second five that of the love of man. " He who loves God but does not show love toward his own kind has but the half of virtue." Philo interprets the Sabbatical year and the Jubilee year in terms of their social significance, elaborating upon the principles of justice and the dignity of every human being, be he free or slave. The Sabbath institution he describes as the recurring symbol of man's participation in the dignity of the divine nature and his prerogative to emulate the perfection of the Supreme Being. Since contemplation is a divine activity—to Aristotle, the only divine activity—man must leave room in his life for the practice of contemplation. " Let us never neglect the example of the best life, the combination of action and thought, but keeping a clear vision of it before our minds, as far as human nature will permit, let us liken ourselves to immortal God by word and deed."[56] As a rule, Philo speaks of the purpose of the laws in human rather than specifically Jewish terms, interpreting the Sabbath, for example, as a covenant between God and humanity, not God and Israel. For this reason, he does not mention the Commandment to annihilate the Canaanites, nor does he ever make use of the prophetic metaphor of the people of Israel as a woman that is betrothed to her Lord.[57]

In listing the several festivals in the Jewish calendar, Philo displays a fondness for numbers that recalls the Pythagoreans. Regarding the number ten as the symbol of perfection, he asserted that the festivals were ten in number. To make up this arbitrarily chosen figure, Philo counted among the festivals each day taken as a day of dedication; also, the new moon; and he broke up the festival of Passover into three celebrations. In each case, Philo emphasized the natural or human quality of the holiday. Passover was not only the anniversary of the Exodus; it was also a spring festival, a memorial of creation and it was expressive of the determination to pass over from a life of the senses to a life of yearning for God, the unleavened bread serving as the symbol of the simple life, unspoiled by the effete craving for luxuries. Similarly, the *sukkah* was not so much a commemoration of God's concern for the Israelites in the desert as it was a symbol of the equality of all men and of the obligation of man to recall with due gratitude the troubles of his past. Philo did not list the festivals of Hanukkah and Purim, possibly because he regarded them as national feasts, not festivals of Judaism. In all his interpretations the basic theme was the struggle of the human soul for self-mastery, not the struggle of the Jewish people for the attainment of the good society.

True to his method, Philo expounded the dietary laws as disciplines intended to train man in the control of his emotions and appetites. In the late Hellenistic period, Jewish apologists were very sensitive on the score of these laws, which the Greeks ridiculed and reviled. The author of the *Letter of Aristeas,* who lived prior to the Maccabean revolt, did not scruple to state that the laws governing food and ritual purity were primarily intended to separate the Jews from other nations, though they also possessed symbolic significance.

"Therefore, in order that we may not mingle with others and stray from the righteous path by joining the corrupt, he [the legislator] set fences around us through laws of purity in food, drink, touching, hearing and seeing."[58] In keeping with his universal approach, Philo rarely stressed the isolationist aspects of Judaism. He also shunned the easy rationalization that the forbidden foods were somehow unhealthy, declaring, on the contrary, that pork and shellfish constituted the tastiest kinds of food. Unclean foods were forbidden precisely because they are so delectable to human taste as to symbolize the sensual life, which the man of piety and virtue is pledged to overcome and to discipline.

In many stirring passages Philo echoed the wrath of the prophets against those who were insensitive to the spirit of the ritual. Of him "who defiles his mind while he cleanses his body" Philo wrote, "For he has wandered far from the path of religion, mistaking ritual for holiness, and attempting to bribe the Incorruptible, and to flatter Him whom none can flatter. God welcomes genuine service, and that is the service of a soul that offers the bare and simple sacrifice of truth, but from false service, the mere display of material wealth, he turns away."[59] Hence, a knowledge of the intent of the law is all-important, for " the words of God may be compared to shadows whereas their inner significance is like the real objects."

While the numerous precepts of Judaism are so many aids to the attainment of the good life, their highest purpose is to lift up the human soul to the stage of ecstatic unity with the logos, ultimately with God Himself. At this point we note the central motif of mysticism which Philo introduced into Jewish piety. The Biblical poets and prophets did not seek to achieve ecstatic unity with the Supreme Being. The Hebrew term *ledovko*, " to cleave," has no mystical connotations in the Scriptures, denoting simply the perfection of loyalty and of obedience. For the prophets, every revelation was directed to practical ends. Unlike mystics, the prophets do not speak of the glories of rapt contemplation; as prophets, they are messengers of the Lord—no more. Philo identified the goal of mystical ecstasy with the gift of prophecy which is the special endowment of Israel. No earthly pleasures can compare with the delights of heaven-sent ecstasy, which floods the senses and overpowers consciousness. " When the divine light shines upon the mortal soul, the mortal light sinks, and our reason is driven out at the approach of the Divine Spirit."[60] Those who experience this union with the One live with the abiding assurance of even greater bliss in the hereafter, when the soul is liberated from its bodily prison.

Immortality was, to Philo, a gift from God, granted as a reward to the righteous. After death the souls of the righteous abide in heaven, while the wicked perish in both body and soul. On earth the punishment of the wicked is a tortured conscience, reflecting the anguish of a stunted soul.[61] Since Philo believed in the existence of incorporeal spirits, or angels, he found no difficulty in imagining the continued existence of the human soul, after death, in the form of an angel. To Philo, angels " are consecrated and devoted to the service of the Father and Creator whose wont is to employ them as ministers and helpers, to have charge and care of mortal man."[62] It is not clear why Philo prefers to allegorize purgatory or Hades out of existence, when he had ample precedent in both Plato and rabbinic tradition for the conception of hell as a real place of incredibly cruel punishment for the wicked. Plato, assuming an indestructible soul, was led to postulate a purgatory for the cleansing of the soul of the wicked and to suggest the possibility of a chain of reincarnation of human souls into beasts.[63] Philo, however, seems to have taken the belief in the goodness of God too seriously to glory in hell-fire and eternal or even temporary damnation. To be sure, Philo does not specifically deny the punishment of sin after death; nor does he repudiate in specific terms the doctrine of the resurrection of the soul, which the Palestinian rabbis had accepted as a fundamental dogma. It appears certain, however, that Philo did not believe in the literal resurrection of the body, preferring to interpret this dogma of Pharisaic Judaism in terms of the immortality of the souls of the righteous.[64]

The thinking of Philo is complex, many-sided, susceptible of a variety of conflicting interpretations. While in essentials Philo may be regarded as an authentic sage of Judaism employing the weapons of philosophy in defense of his faith, there are also shimmering surfaces to the vast sea of Philonic writings that reflect a totally different approach. He employs the language of the "mystery religions" current in his day to the point where he sometimes appears to interpret the rites of Judaism as preliminary steps in the long ascent of man toward the ecstasy of union with the Absolute. In the ancient world, two mystical ways were popular—the Persian type in which the worshiper identified himself by degrees with the powers of God, and the Egyptian type in which a female principle played the decisive role. In mysticism, unity with God is the goal, ritual practices are imagined to be effective sacraments leading to this goal, either because they are symbolic expressions of cosmic truths or because they magically exert cosmic and psychic effects, and there is a clear dichotomy between the common folk who simply practise the rites and the initiates who undertake to reach the ultimate goal. In rabbinic Judaism, the goal is not ecstatic unity with God, but the meriting of His favor; the laws are not "garments of truths" or rites charged with cosmic correspondences but ways of expressing obedience to the Almighty, and all children of the covenant are equally subject to the law.

In Philo, overtones of the mystical approach are powerful and abundant. The allegories of Philo are not merely sermonic devices, based on the principle that divine words will be edifying howsoever they are interpreted; his allegories are consistent, on the whole, and based upon an honored tradition. He was not merely following the rabbinic analogy of a hammer upon the rock, scattering sparks of instruction in all directions, but he believed that, in his commentaries for the initiates, he unfolded the inner meaning of the Mosaic law.[65] The ritual in its totality represented the "mystery of Aaron," in which the initiate rose by degrees to the point of achieving contact with metaphysical entities, worshiping the one God along with the forces governing the universe, while the "mystery of Moses" was reserved for those who prepared themselves for mystical ecstasy.[66]

The mystical approach gradually lifts its heroes beyond the pale of mortals and renders hazy the boundary between saints and divine powers. Thus, Philo writes of the high priest: ". . . because I think he has had indestructible and most pure parents, God as his father, who is also the father of all things, and Sophia for his mother, through whom all things were born."[67]

Similarly, the patriarchs are described as attaining the point of union with one or another of God's Powers.[68] It is through them that God's grace is channeled. Of Moses he writes: "Was he then God? I would not like to say, for the archprophet Moses was actually given this title as his lot when he was called the God of Pharaoh. At least, he was not man, but had a share of each extreme as though one were the pedestal, the other the head."[69]

Nor does Philo's exposition lack overtones of the type of mysticism that was associated with the Egyptian worship of Isis; namely, the saints' advance to perfection by way of union with the female principle.[70] Also, the supposition of two truths, the one of the mystical illuminates and the other of the common worshipers, prepared the groundwork for the emergence in later centuries of the paradoxes of Christian dogma. Commenting on the appearance of the three angels to Abraham who accosted them as the one Lord, Philo wrote: "So, truly and properly said, the measure of all things, intelligible as well as sensible, is the one

God who, though a unity in Himself, appears as a trinity because of the weakness of observers."[71]

In brief, Philo's commentaries postulate an inner organic unity for that secret teaching that is related to the written Torah as the soul is to the body. And this inner structure of ideas may appear in paradoxical guise to the eyes of the multitude. Thus, the Hellenistic Jews were not unprepared for a message that would oppose the spirit to the letter.[72]

It is not possible to assay at this time how much of Philo's Hellenism and mysticism was only verbal veneer and how much of it was intended in its full meaning. The fact remains that the ambiguities in Philo's language and thought served admirably as bridges of transition for those who sought to travel from the monotheistic world of Judaism to the secular and pagan realms of philosophy, and vice versa. Through the efforts of Philo and his associates, an intermediate realm of discourse was brought into being, extending between the warring worlds of Judaism and Hellenism. Within this syncretistic domain, the soil was prepared for the emergence of a new faith that would reflect its twofold origin in every facet of its expression. While Christianity arose among the masses of Galilean Jewry, its message found ready acceptance and able preachers among the philosophers of Hellenistic Judaism. There is hardly a dogma of Christian theology that does not reflect the labors of Philo and his predecessors.[73]

Fortuitously, or by the design of the Palestinian sages, Philo's works were not embraced among those sacred writings that the Jewish people cherished and preserved in the course of their long travail. Along with the rest of Jewish writings in Greek, Philo's commentaries were completely ignored. However, through subterranean channels, the basic ideas of Philo were echoed in scattered passages in the Talmud and Midrash. Possibly they were taught orally to gifted pupils, as similar secret doctrines were taught in contemporary Palestine.[74] In any case, we see them reappear though in deeply modified forms in the works of proto-Qabbalah and Qabbalah in later centuries. But it was in the intellectual halls of the Christian world that the words of Philo reverberated with undiminished resonance for a millennium and a half, expounding the fundamental assumptions of a religious philosophy of life.

CHAPTER FOUR

THE SECESSION OF CHRISTIANITY

THE historical origins of any faith are significant threads in the fabric of its enduring structure. To Christians the emergence of their faith out of the ferment of ideas in Judaism is the fundamental theme of their Holy Scriptures. The New Testament, as they see it, tells how the hopes and aspirations of the Old Testament were "fulfilled." Since the development of Judaism in the European world was conditioned for many centuries upon a keen awareness of the Christian challenge, Jewish thinkers were confronted with the need of understanding the process whereby the Christian religion arose within Judaism and then diverged ever more decisively from the parent faith.

During the dark centuries of superstition and fanaticism, the Jewish interpretation of the origin of the Christian faith could be stated only within severe limitations and in the context of bitter polemics. The modern period made possible an objective and scientific approach to the understanding of the early history of the Christian faith, a story that belongs inevitably within the ken of a student of the evolution of modern Judaism. As a spiritual citizen of the Western world, an American Jew can hardly understand the development and dynamic impetus of his faith without learning how the mighty branch of Christianity grew out of the ancient stem of Judaism.

Judaism was never a monolithic faith. While the high court in Jerusalem was theoretically endowed with the authority to pass upon heresies and to impose the death penalty upon those who defied its verdicts, there were few periods in the history of the Second Commonwealth when this authority could have been enforced. Up to the destruction of Jerusalem (69 C.E.), the Sanhedrin was frequently controlled by the Sadducees, who disbelieved in the Oral Law and in the Resurrection. Apart from

102

dissidents in the Hellenistic Diaspora, many different sects flourished within Palestine in the first century. While the Pharisaic group predominated both in numbers and influence, the Sadducees wielded considerable power, since they recruited their followers chiefly from among the temple priests and the governing classes.

Disdaining the authority of both Pharisees and Sadducees, the Essenes withdrew from the synagogue and the market place to dwell in communal settlements of their own, which they established on the fringes of towns and along the forbidding terrain of the Judean desert. Imposing austere disciplines upon their followers, the Essenic teachers cultivated an esoteric, theosophic lore, consisting of an allegorical interpretation of the Scriptures in accord with certain secret doctrines. While little is known of the Essenic philosophy, we know enough of their life to appreciate the lofty idealism which animated their mysterious gatherings. The Essenes scorned the normal activities of human society which centered around the acquisition of money and the raising of a family. Man's purpose on earth, they postulated, is to refine his soul, keeping it pure from the taints of greed, lust and worldly ambition. Theirs was a society of spiritual athletes, wrestling against the multiple weaknesses of humanity. In their settlements, everybody worked according to his ability and received from the common purse whatever he needed for his support. Yet their society was based on distrust and despair, not trust in God's goodness and man's potentialities, for they believed that divine wrath would overtake the masses of mankind and the vast majority of the Jewish people. Only the dedicated few would be saved. They concerned themselves but little with the political and national affairs of their day, since all human efforts were doomed to failure. It is God Who is the author of history, and temporary triumphs of the wicked may well be part of His plan. Hence, the principle of some of their teachers, "Resist not evil." However, in the final agony of embattled Jerusalem, some of them fought in the front ranks of the rebel forces, astonishing the Romans by their capacity to endure horrible torture without flinching.

The Essenic societies were organized on the basis of a graded system of membership, with complicated laws of purity attaching to every grade. The Essenes of the highest grade were "defiled" by contact with lower grade Essenes, let alone the touch of a non-

Essene. They observed the Sabbath with extreme rigor and emphasized the importance of baptism (*tevilah*) in their ritual. The common meals of the Essenes were solemn affairs, marked by periods of silence, elaborate ceremonies, prayer and study.

The Essene societies were in all likelihood not uniform, either in their practices or in their doctrines. We do not know of any central governing body for all the Essene societies, and we possess abundant evidence of the existence of different types of societies. Some groups consisted only of celibates, while others included married couples. Also, the societies in Alexandria appear to have stressed the allegoric meaning of the laws, rather than their literal observances.

The discovery of the Dead Sea Scrolls in recent years has added to our knowledge of the variety of dissident sects in the generation preceding the destruction of Jerusalem. At this writing, the exact relationship of the Qumran community to the other groupings in contemporary Judaism is still unclear. Nevertheless, the scrolls deepen our impression of the extent of diversity within the Jewish community. In addition, we possess a series of apocalyptic works, such as Baruch, IV Esdras, and Enoch, which reflected imaginatively and individualistically the popular hopes and visions of redemption.

To understand the genesis and growth of Christianity, we need to bear in mind the rich variety of opinion and practice in Judaism at the time when Jesus began his public career. The popular impression of Judaism as a monochromatic faith, with a single answer to every problem in life, is the source of much of the confusion which has bedeviled and beclouded the relationship of Judaism and Christianity throughout the ages.

In this chapter, we shall concern ourselves primarily with the following questions:

(a) What were the distinguishing ideas of Jesus and the early Christian community, of St. Paul and the rising Gentile church?

(b) What was it in Christianity that all groups in Judaism rejected?

(c) What were the elements in Christian teaching that enabled it to triumph over the pagan world and to win decisively from Judaism the race for new converts?

In answer to the first question, we note to begin with that Jesus lived and died as a Jew. He recognized the Pharisaic masters as the rightful authorities in Judaism, saying that "they sit in the seat of Moses; all things, therefore, whatsoever they bid you, these do and observe."[1] He believed in the resurrection of the dead and he moved generally within the spiritual world of the Pharisaic tradition. To be sure, he did not belong to the Pharisaic schools, which were centered in Jerusalem, so that he occasionally took the position of an outsider and an opponent when he disputed with some Pharisaic scholars. The Pharisaic teachers were not organized as a tightly knit hierarchy, guarding a rigid dogma and enjoying certain definite prerogatives. Theirs was a loose association, permitting wide divergencies of opinion, and consisting of small schools which centered round certain teachers. The people generally followed the teaching of the leading Pharisaic masters, but not without occasional protests and grumbling. The Pharisaic sages imposed upon themselves a series of "purity rituals," which necessitated their guarding against any physical contact with the common people. Though any pious Jew could join the Pharisaic society and undertake to abide by their "purity" regulations, the masses of the people, *am haarez*, doubtless resented the apparent exclusiveness of their teachers.[2]

Jesus was a teacher in the Pharisaic tradition, though he did not belong to the Pharisaic society and he did not associate himself with the Judean schools. In his exhortations he gave expression from time to time to the smoldering resentment of the masses against excessive severities in the ritualistic laws of the Pharisees, and against the occasional abuses of the Pharisaic regimen of piety. This paradoxical mixture of reverence and hatred for the scholars of the law, who at once guard and usurp the pathway to heaven, was illustrated many centuries later in the history of the Hasidic movement, which derived its social impetus at least in part from the dissatisfaction of the proletarian masses with the leadership of the rabbis. Jesus stood within the general Jewish tradition, of which the Pharisaic scholars were the official interpreters; but he was primarily a popular teacher with little or no attachment to the great Jerusalem schools of Pharisaic lore and law.

In his disputes with the Pharisaic scholars Jesus argued as one who shared their basic premises; he employed their methods of reasoning to justify his individual message of reform. For instance, the disciples of Jesus did not wash their hands before they ate bread. To wash one's hands was a rabbinic ordinance, which some authorities declared to be not mandatory; nevertheless, its habitual performance constituted a symbolic acceptance of "the words of the sages."[3] Apparently, too, this practice was then part of the entire complex of laws relating to ritual purity, though in Judaism today no such relation obtains.[4] A defiant refusal to wash one's hands could be construed as a public repudiation of the authority of the sages and a challenge of the policy to extend the laws of "purity" from the Holy Temple to everyday life.[5]

It is within the tradition, too, that Jesus' argument concerning vows belongs.[6] The Torah affirms that every vow is sacred. What if a person vows that his parents shall not benefit from his possessions? The sanctity of the vow conflicts in this case with the obligation to honor one's parents. At the time of Jesus, this question was apparently an unsolved issue. In the Talmud the vow is valid, but the duty devolves upon the son to appear before a court for the purpose of formally annulling the vow. Rabbinic legislation in this domain is described in the Talmud itself as "suspended in midair."[7]

It is within the Pharisaic framework, too, that we can understand Jesus' insistence that divorce was immoral. His claim that the Mosaic ordinance concerning a bill of divorcement "was written for the hardness of your hearts," is paralleled by the Shammaite principle that divorce was lawful only in the case of adultery. We find, too, that the Damascene sect, which opposed the institution of polygamy, cited in proof of their position the verse from Genesis that Jesus later quoted, "and the two shall become one flesh." In Matthew's version of the incident, the phrase is added, "Whosoever shall put away his wife except for fornication, and shall marry another, committeth adultery." Thus Jesus' position does not rule out divorce in cases of infidelity and is actually identical with that of the Shammaites. The very expression, "for the hardness of your hearts" corresponds to the Talmudic expression, "The Torah spoke only in opposition to the evil desire."[8]

Jesus' selection of the greatest commandments as being the love of God and the love of man is endorsed by the rabbis of the Talmud.[9] His reply to the Sadducees, who ridiculed the belief in resurrection, is typically Pharisaic and is indeed found in the Talmud; to wit, if God is the God of the living and He is referred to as the God of Abraham, Isaac and Jacob, then the patriarchs must be alive.[10] The wholesale indictment of the Pharisees, contained in the twenty-third chapter of Matthew, was probably directed against a degenerative tendency within the movement, which other teachers also castigated; namely, the human temptation to substitute the external trivia of ritual for the growth of inner piety. This temptation is inherent in all organized religions. The classical prophets had already inveighed against it.

In addition to these legalistic differences, Jesus defied the Pharisaic scholars by the conclusions which he drew from his own concept of the nature of his being. As we shall see later, Jesus became convinced that he was a "heavenly being" incarnate, the "son of man" predicted in Daniel or in the Book of Enoch. From this conviction he drew certain inferences which ran counter to the teachings of the Pharisaic scholars, since they did not recognize his "true" being. His disciples plucked ears of corn on the Sabbath; when rebuked by the Pharisees for this act of his disciples, Jesus replied that the Sabbath laws did not prevent the regular sacrifices in the temple and the priestly regulations did not stand in David's way when he needed the showbreads to feed his men. But, he continued, he was "greater than David," "greater than the temple." Was he not the "son of man," foreseen by Daniel? And the "son of man is lord of the Sabbath." So the real issue between the Pharisees and Jesus was neither the institution of the Sabbath nor the extent to which it was "lawful to do good on the Sabbath."[11] The Pharisees conceded the merit of healing on the Sabbath, by word of mouth, if it could be done, and they subscribed to the principle, "The Sabbath is given over to you, not you to the Sabbath."[12] But the Pharisees disputed Jesus' claim to be the Son of Man, demanding a "sign"; that is, incontrovertible proof. Since no "sign" satisfactory to their judgment was given, they refused to recognize Jesus as the Messiah.

Jesus and his followers also thought in terms of miracles as signs of his mission; the question at issue was whether such signs had indeed been given. Repudiated by the leaders of his people,

Jesus pondered on the strange paradox of the Messiah coming down to earth and finding himself accepted by "women and children," but rejected by those who should know best. Many of his words of criticism were directed at the Pharisaic teachers, because they would not recognize that "the kingdom of God," or the Messiah, who is its dynamic focus, was among them. As his disappointment deepened, his criticism of "those who sit in Moses' seat" grew steadily harsher, more impassioned and less discriminating, beholding as he thought he did, "an inverted world," with those who should be first being last, and those who should be last being first.

The recognition on the part of the people that Jesus taught not as a scribe but as "one who had authority," and the opposition of the Pharisaic teachers, were both based not on a question of principle, but on one of identification. If he was indeed the hoped-for Messiah, he could heal and, by implication, win for people the forgiveness of sins, since diseases were supposed to be the effects of divine punishment for sins.[13] The Pharisees would have conceded the propriety of indulging in celebration, instead of fasts, if only they had been persuaded that "the bridegroom" was indeed with them.

The main burden of Jesus' teaching was a call to repentance, to the practice of "righteousness exceeding that of the scribes or of the prophets" and to "follow him," in the sense of recognizing him as the hoped-for redeemer of Israel. His demand was therefore a direct corollary of the belief that redemption was at hand. If the Messiah was already here, waiting only for the right time to be "revealed," by ascending to heaven and descending from the clouds, as the ruler of the earth, then the sober, everyday pattern of rabbinic piety could be expected to yield to a mood of unworldly, mystical enthusiasm. On the threshold of the Messianic era and "the world to come" it is not unreasonable to cease worrying over food and clothes, leaving it to the Father that is in heaven to provide for such needs, even as He does supply pretty petals to the "lilies in the field" and a home for the foxes. If the "kingdom of heaven" is at hand, why worry over the petty details of mundane existence? On this assumption, the rebellious mood of the Zealots is unjustified, and a return to the basic fundamentals of religion is called for.

The ethical teachings of Jesus in the Sermon on the Mount, were " un-Jewish " only in the sense that they did not correspond to the everyday pattern of piety, echoing as they did the spirit of the generation that believed itself to stand on the threshold of the " end of the world." Jesus taught his disciples not only to observe all the Commandments, but to go beyond them in their quest for ideal piety. Thus, he extends the principle of murder to include the acts of insulting and showing anger; he requests that forgiveness of men should be sought prior to the seeking of forgiveness from God; he extends the prohibition of adultery to the least experience of the feelings of lust; he forbids divorce, save on the ground of adultery; he forbids swearing in any circumstances; he asks that his disciples return not evil for evil, but that they turn the other cheek; he extends the principle, to love your neighbor, so as to include one's enemies; he enjoins that charity be done in secret and not for show, and that people judge not others that they be not judged; he pleads that prayer be uttered from the heart, not with clamor and show, avoiding " vain repetitions, as the Gentiles do." In addition to these ethical principles of conduct, he calls upon his disciples not to be anxious about food and shelter, but to have faith and to pray for their needs. " Be not therefore anxious, saying what shall we eat? or, what shall we drink? or, wherewith shall we be clothed? For after all these things do the Gentiles seek; for your heavenly Father knoweth that ye have need of all these things. But seek ye first his kingdom and his righteousness."[14]

These teachings are of lofty nobility, even if unworldly, but they are not without multiple parallels and even identical expressions in the multicolored strand of Talmud and Midrash. Neither in its own time nor in any of the later phases of authentic Jewish thought could any of these sayings have been regarded as in any sense incompatible with the genius of Judaism.

Nor was the historical Jesus more universalistic than the rabbis, as some Christian scholars have erroneously maintained, viewing him as they did in the light of the subsequent developments of Christianity. If anything, Jesus, as described in the Gospels, was more narrowly nationalistic than the Hillelite school of the Pharisees. For example, he rebuked the Pharisees for their eagerness to spread the message of Judaism to distant lands in order to obtain proselytes.[15] He refused at first to extend the benefits of his healing powers to a non-Jewish woman, for the reason that the "bread" that was meant for the children should not be cast to the "dogs."[16] For this reason, too, he commanded his disciples not to go to the cities of the Gentiles or even to the settlement of the Samaritans, but only to Jewish towns.[17] Doubtless this contempt for the Gentile world reflected the prevailing sentiments of the masses, but the Talmudic sages more often than not transcended these natural prejudices of an embattled people. They affirmed that even the vilest of people can repent and return unto the Lord.[18]

Jesus did not set out to proclaim a new faith, but he stressed the prophetic core within the teaching of rabbinic Judaism. As the prophets protested against the popular belief in the efficacy of sacrifices, he protested against the tendency to equate the massive rituals of his day with true piety. At the same time, he warned of the imminence of the Messianic era. The bliss of "the world to come" was supposed to be the special reward of the Jewish people for their long martyrdom. How, then, could the Gentiles be expected to share it, on an equal basis, entering as they do in the eleventh hour? To be sure, many publicans and sinners seemed to be among the elect, but then this apparent "inversion" of the moral order could be understood as a case of one hour's repentance achieving more than a lifetime of punctilious piety, a possibility which the rabbis acknowledged.[19] However, this rare occurrence can hardly be expected to serve as a general rule. Jesus himself restricted his message to the Jews, and his disciples extended it very hesitantly beyond the confines of the Jewish people. Clearly, then, Jesus was not more "universalistic" than the rabbis of his day. However, he contributed to the subsequent extension of the gospel outside the Jewish world in several ways; principally by his explanation of the hard fact that the masters of the law and the leaders of the people repudiated him, while the naïve, the women, and the children followed him. Forced as he was to rank the simple believers in his mission above the learned sages of the Sanhedrin, he suggested a new standard for the identification of the "remnant that is saved," thus setting the stage for the eventual substitution of belief in him for the observance of the Torah.

But what did Jesus believe himself to be? Some modernist

Christian historians maintain that Jesus did not fancy himself to be the Messiah at all. This impression is refuted by all the sources, both Jewish and Christian. Thus, John the Baptist sent word from prison, through his disciples, inquiring whether Jesus was indeed " he that cometh," or " look we for another? "[20] Jesus' reply was that his divine nature was attested by the fact that miracles were being performed, indicating the operation of the Holy Spirit. " The blind receive their sight and the lame walk, the lepers are cleansed and the deaf hear, and the dead are raised up, and the poor have good tidings preached unto them."[21] The proof of Jesus' divine nature and mission is here the very " sign " which the Pharisaic masters demanded. On many occasions, Jesus referred to himself as the " son of man," a term which was then applied in some visionary circles to the hoped-for heavenly redeemer.[22] In his view, John the Baptist, who preached the speedy advent of the kingdom of God, was Elijah, while he was the Messiah, and the miracles which he performed were proof of his triumph over Satan.[23] " But, if I by the Spirit of God cast out demons, then is the kingdom of God come upon you."[24] When he appointed twelve apostles, he instructed them to tell the " good men " of the coming of the kingdom, certifying their mission by giving them "authority over unclean spirits, to cast them out, and to heal all manner of disease and all manner of sickness."[25]

Apparently his purpose in going up to Jerusalem was to demand that he be recognized as " the king that cometh in the name of the Lord."[26] Doubtless he expected that he would indeed be revealed in his " true " heavenly character if the heads of the nation accorded him his due. His disciples expected this consummation, and even began to wrangle among themselves as to who should be first in the kingdom of God. Jerusalem was the spiritual center of the people. There, in the Holy Temple, if anywhere, the Messiah was to be revealed.[27] Indeed, the authorities in the temple challenged him to declare his source of authority. In answer, he cited the baptism of John as the preparation for his coming as the Messiah, and, in a parable, he intimated that while the prophets were the servants of the Lord, he, Jesus, was His " beloved son."[28]

That the Messiah would make his first appearance before the high court in Jerusalem is specifically stated in the Talmud.[29]

The new era, it is assumed, would begin as soon as the high court or Sanhedrin attested to the authenticity of the Messiah.

The concept of the Messiah was too complex and many-sided to be defined by any one rigid formula. Nor was it unaffected in any single period by the changing fortunes of the Jewish people. As the vital "hope of Israel," drawing to itself the resentment, wrath, and protest of the people against the miseries of their lot as well as their fondest pictures of a perfect world, the Messianic hope was like a glittering star in the heavens, scintillating with the richness of its lights, presenting vibrantly varying phases of its being to different people at different times. In the Talmud the conception of the Messiah is still fluid and undefined, with one authority going so far as to declare that "there is no Messiah for Israel, since he was already consumed in the days of Hezekiah."[30] Varying opinions are recorded as to the "name of the Messiah," with the Mishnah declaring that the "name of the Messiah was one of the things created before the world was brought into being." Professor Wolfson maintains correctly that the "name of the Messiah" refers to the incorporeal form of the Messiah, not merely the name.[31] Consistently and invariably, the dominant facet of the Messianic concept reflected the historical travail of the Jewish people, serving as the counterpoise to earthly events, the consolation for their wretchedness and the consummation of their hopes.

Broadly speaking, the Messiah presented a double aspect, that of a conquering hero and that of an especially created heavenly being, most favored by God, who will subdue the wicked angels and usher in a new age. In the apocalyptic literature, especially the Book of Enoch, the latter image prevails. It is natural to assume that the masses of the people did not clearly distinguish between the two types of Messiah. In their hopes, the two aspects were generally fused together in the image of a mystically favored, divinely chosen person, who would free Israel from its political shackles and usher in an unparalleled era of well-being for all men. The Messiah would end the "dominion of evil," as embodied in the Roman Empire, precisely because of the spirit of God that would rest upon him. Conversely, a successful Jewish military leader could always lay claim to being the Messiah, since the actual work of the Messiah was being achieved by him.

Nevertheless, it is possible to distinguish two types of Messianic concept, deriving from the thought of that period—the one stressing the "earthy" qualities of the Messiah, the other his divine, or superhuman qualities. In the dialogue of St. Justin, Rabbi Tarfon (Tryphon) is quoted as saying, "We Jews all hope that the Messiah will come as a human being, among human beings."[32] While the references to the personality of the Messiah in Tannaitic literature are extremely few, the best evidence for the continuing appeal to Palestinian Jews of the earthy type of Messiah is to be found in the circumstance that Bar Kochba, leader of the revolt against Hadrian (131-135 C.E.), was acclaimed by Rabbi Akiba as the Messiah.

In later Talmudic literature, Bar Kochba is described as arrogant and impious. He is supposed to have exclaimed, "Lord, don't help us and don't spoil it for us." Another passage portrays Bar Kochba as appearing before the Sanhedrin with the claim, "I am the Messiah." The rabbis reply that the Messiah will be endowed with the divine gift of rendering judgment instinctively. They tested him, and, discovering that he lacked this capacity, they ordered him to be killed.[33] Thus it is clear that the Messiah had to possess a mystical, miraculous character.[34] Parallels between this fanciful trial and the real trials of Jesus are obvious. From a cryptic comment by the founder of the Academy in Jabneh, Rabbi Johanan ben Zakkai, it appears that King Hezekiah was regarded by many as the prototype of the Messiah: just, pious, penitent and victorious, not through clever strategy or martial heroism, but through a miraculous intervention by God. Before his death, Rabbi Johanan ben Zakkai asked that a "chair be prepared for Hezekiah, King of Judah."[35]

References to the mystical character of the Messiah abound in the Midrashic collections of the Talmudic and post-Talmudic period. These passages may well echo long-smoldering sentiment. We read of the prior existence of the Messiah in paradise, along with Elijah and others who entered paradise bodily.[36] Elijah and the Messiah write down in a heavenly book the merits of Israel.[37] Particularly interesting is the contention of the anonymous majority of the sages that "Elijah comes, not to push away and not to bring near, but to make peace in the world."[38] Elijah was of course a human being, but at the same time more than human, since he was translated bodily into heaven. He is also supposed to have been the incarnation of Phineas, grandson of Aaron, and of Melchizedek.[39] If Elijah, precursor of the Messiah, is a superhuman figure, the Messiah may likewise have been pictured in similar fashion, as being endowed with suprahuman or angelic qualities.

As a matter of fact, the apocryphal books, which were doubtless highly influential in the time of Jesus, continued to develop Daniel's vision of the "son of man" along mystical lines. The Book of Enoch, in its oldest sections, contains descriptions of the Day of Judgment and of the fires of hell that await the wicked—passages that are quite reminiscent of the threatening tenor of the gospels. Following the Day of Judgment the temple will be removed, and the Master of the Sheep will bring down from heaven a new temple in its place—a promise attributed to Jesus in the gospels.[40] Along with the Jews, vast masses of Gentiles are to be gathered in the house of the Lord, with the Messiah being the first one to enter the new world, while " all the nations fear him and implore him constantly." The Messiah will sit on a throne, judging the people and determining their proper place.[41] The dead will come to life, and the barrier between the human and angelic worlds will disappear. The sinners will be punished, unless they repent in good time. Those who have denied the Lord and His Messiah will be burned in a hellish fire.[42] The divine drama of redemption is acted out in terms of the universal co-ordinates of good and evil, belief and unbelief, not in terms of the national fortunes and political realities of Israel. Here, then, we encounter a quietist variant of the Messianic hope, affording little justification for any spontaneous acts of rebellion against Roman authority as the means of ushering in the Messianic period.

In the *Wisdom of Solomon*, the Messiah is portrayed primarily as the righteous judge, made strong by " the Holy Spirit," relying on the Lord for protection, not on military might. Nevertheless, the Messiah is not completely devoid of national concerns, since it is still his function to gather the exiles together, reunite the "holy people" and extirpate iniquity from their midst. The nations will recognize his supremacy of their own free will, since the cosmic spirit of evil will have been overcome on a global scale.[43]

In the Syriac Baruch, the troubles preceding the triumph of the Messiah are portrayed in great detail. The Messiah bursts upon the horizon in dazzling splendor as " brilliant lightning," ending this wretched epoch of tribulation, and settling all accounts with the enemies of Israel; ushering in a golden era of universal prosperity, joy and peace, which in turn will lead to the emergence of a new world. In another work the Messiah is portrayed as " an eagle rising from the sea " and as " the son of man " rising from the sea. Existing from before the creation of the world and guarded by God until the time of his revelation, the Messiah is frequently called " my son " by God. This endearing title is used in the sense of adoption, not of procreation, as in God's promise to David, " He will be unto me a son and I shall be unto him a father."[44] At the same time, the " son of man," the favored " son " of God will be a son of David, as in this passage: " This is the anointed one, whom the most High hath kept unto the end [of days, who shall spring up out of the seed of David, and he shall come and speak] unto them and reprove them for their wickedness and their unrighteousness, and shall heap up before them their contemptuous dealings."[45] The Messiah is then a prophet and a preacher. He subdues the army of the wicked, but not with physical force. " He neither lifted up his hand, nor held spear, nor any instrument of war," but out of his mouth there issued a flame and a storm which consumed the multitude. Jesus' rejection of Zealot pressure to lead a rebellion has here its counterpart, if not its source. In the interpretation which follows the dream, this consuming flame is described as " the law, which is likened unto fire."[46]

From all these references, it appears that there existed a popular literature and tradition concerning a mystical Messiah, who would consummate the moralizing and spiritualizing labors of the ancient prophets. This Messiah would still be the " son of David," restoring dominion to Israel, but his efforts would be directed mainly toward the conquest of Satan, or the spirit of evil. It is out of the circles that cultivated these apocalyptic works mentioned above that Jesus gathered the raw material for his own fiery message, in which he figured as the incarnate " son of man."

Contemplating the career of Jesus as a whole, we find that he moved completely within the mental world of Judaism, but that he opposed each of the organized groups in his day. He repudiated the Sadducees, who denied the validity of the Oral Law and the doctrine of the Resurrection. His driving of the " money-changers out of the temple,"[47] whose legitimate function it was to exchange the coins of the various realms brought to Jerusalem from every corner of the Mediterranean, was a direct affront to the Sadducees who were in charge of the management of the Holy Temple. The Parable of the Good Samaritan was in all likelihood also directed primarily against the pure-bred aristocratic Sadducees, jealous of their ancient pedigrees and fearful of ritualistic contamination by the touch of a dead body.[48] He also opposed the Zealots, who were particularly powerful in his native Galilee, by directing the struggle for redemption away from the realm of revolution and into the channels of piety and penitence. The battle against the " dominion of evil " will not be won by the sword, but " by rendering unto the Lord what is the Lord's." In this policy, he concurred with the quietist party among the Pharisees.[49] Again, he opposed not the Pharisaic movement, but the Pharisaic teachers, principally for their refusal to recognize him as the " Son of Man," derivatively for their coolness to his message of repentance and their complacent reliance on sheer observance of the law, and partly, as a teacher, because of his objection to some of the principles evolved in the schools—in particular, the laws of vows, of the Sabbath, of divorce, and of the complex " purity " regulations. As to the Essenes and such sectarian groups as are reflected in the Dead Sea Scrolls, he appears to have been influenced by their teachings in regard to dispensing with money, in offering no resistance to evil, and in attempting to exceed the " righteousness " of the Pharisees. He regarded the apocalyptic preacher, John the Baptist, as Elijah, and John's followers appear to have drifted into the Christian camp.

None of the ideas of Jesus would have led either the Pharisees or the Sadducees to seek his death, providing ideas could have been kept free from involvement in the turmoil of political life. But around him a Messianic movement formed, which aimed at speedy release from the yoke of Rome, even if not immediate rebellion. Mass ideas, like the Messianic conception, are amorphous and protean, assuming different shapes in the minds of different people and varying in response to the changing pressures of life. The finely cut logical concepts of philosophers may be rigidly fixed by calm analysis, but not the ideas of the people, which are heavily laden with the weight of sentiment and powerfully impelled by unconscious forces. The high priests were genuinely afraid of the effects of the slightest ripple of Messianic excitement, knowing that the Roman authorities would have drowned it in the blood of the pilgrims first, following up the pogroms with a post-mortem investigation.[50]

Of course, if the priestly high court had been convinced that Jesus was indeed the Messiah, they would have protected him with their very lives. In spite of a superficial worldliness, they were fanatically pious and intensely patriotic. It was indeed their function to interrogate all claimants to the dignity of the Messiahship or the authority of prophecy. If the high court was not convinced of the authenticity of the Messianic claim, then the claimant was automatically designated as a false prophet, in the Deuteronomic sense, or as a "sorcerer," since his "signs" were in that event attributed to witchcraft. It is reasonable to suppose that many of the members of the high court as well as of the crowd which demanded the penalty of death for Jesus were eagerly waiting for a "sign," by which the passionately awaited Messiah would be revealed at last. Even while they called for his death, they hoped for his triumph, thus forcing the hand of Providence, as it were, and presenting the unknown preacher from Galilee with the inescapable choice of proving himself or departing from the scene. In the same way, many Jews, sixteen centuries later, looked forward with mingled emotions of hope and fear to the forthcoming encounter between Sabbatai Zevi and the Sultan of Turkey. The intense excitement and mass hysteria aroused by the appearance of a would-be Messiah was almost unbearable, and the attempt to resolve it, in one way or the other, was historically inevitable.

After the death of Jesus, the report of the Resurrection, first envisioned by the feverish imagination of Mary Magdalene, from whom "seven demons have been cast out," served to reawaken the faith of the scattered and disillusioned disciples and to set into motion a new wave of hysterical excitement. The disciples of Jesus believed they were efficacious in driving out demons with the name of their master, and that the "spirit of holiness" (*Ruah hakodesh*) was manifested in their assemblies. The contagion of mass babbling, known as "speaking in tongues," was to them proof of the outpouring of the divine spirit, as described by the prophet, and the attestation of the imminent reappearance of the Messiah.[51]

The little band of disciples in Jerusalem lived and thought as Jews, praying in the temple and observing all the Commandments, with James, the brother of Jesus, attaining an uncommon reputation for piety, because of his kneeling on the floor of the temple for many hours at a time. However, they added to their Jewish heritage the following convictions: the belief that they had seen and known the Messiah; a certain body of precepts and parables taught by him, stressing the inwardness of piety and cautioning against excessive preoccupation with the niceties of ritual; the assurance that " the spirit of holiness " descends upon those who pray and heal in his name; the conviction that it is most important to recognize his Messiahship; the hard fact that he whom they believed to be the Messiah was rejected by the leaders of the people, so that the leaders and the way they taught were somehow fundamentally wrong; an unworldly, communal way of living, which could not endure permanently, but which provided a firm core of dedicated celibate missionaries, untrammeled by the burden of financial responsibility and the dead weight of settled life.

The followers of Jesus were in no sense more universalistic than the Pharisaic schools, but in shifting the focus of emphasis from the knowledge of the Torah and the observance of the Commandments to the belief in Jesus, they created a standard of piety which was new to Jews as well as to the Gentiles. In terms of this new requirement, Gentiles could enter the charmed circle of believers as easily as the Jews. For the new dispensation, the past was no barrier. By their inveterate insistence that the excitement of " speaking in tongues " was proof positive of the appearance of the Spirit of Holiness, they were also adopting as a measure of holiness a psychical phenomenon which, as they soon discovered, is not confined to Jews. Peter's historic act of converting Cornelius and his household is justified by him as follows: " And they of the circumcision that believed were amazed, as many as came with Peter, because that on the Gentiles also was poured out the gift of the Holy Spirit. For they heard them speak with tongues and magnify God. Then answered Peter, can any man forbid the water that these men should not be baptized, who have received the Holy Spirit as well as we? "[52]

The conversion of Cornelius opened the door to the preaching of the "good tidings" to the large masses of "semiconverted" Gentiles who abounded in Palestine and throughout the Diaspora. The vague consciousness of a new dispensation and the keen expectation of the imminent return of the Messiah provided fresh impetus for the drive to preach the Gospel among the Gentiles. In turn, the admission of uncircumcised and nonobservant Gentiles in ever greater numbers into the band of the faithful served to heighten the sense of a break with the past. The inexorable logic of facts insensibly transmutes the inner logic of ideas.

A fundamental decision, made by the infant church after long hesitation, proved to be of momentous historical significance. Should they insist on the rite of circumcision before admitting Gentiles into the fold? Jewish tradition was not yet clearly defined at that time. The seven Noachide principles, the observance of which was required of all Gentiles, did not include the rite of circumcision. Hence, Gentiles could presumably share in the bliss of the Messianic days, as being *haside ummoth haolam*, without submitting to the rite of circumcision. We read in Josephus that the ruler of the Adiabene kingdom was converted to Judaism and advised by a certain Hananiah that circumcision was not demanded of him.[53] Later, however, a visiting Jewish scholar persuaded him to be circumcized. It was certainly considered a meritorious act, on the part of a Gentile, to be circumcized so as to be able to share in the privilege of eating the Paschal lamb and so as to feel completely and unreservedly part of the congregation of Israel. In the Jabneh Academy, following the destruction of Jerusalem, we find Rabbi Joshua ben Hananyah, liberal spokesman of the generally dominant wing, declaring that baptism without circumcision renders one a proselyte.[54] In this case, however, the view of Rabbi Joshua did not prevail, and Judaism continued to insist on the performance of the rite which is so extremely difficult and dangerous for grown men.

In the early Christian community the issue of whether circumcision should be required of Gentile converts was for a long time undecided, though there was no question of its indispensability among the Jewish believers. Many of the Christian followers in Jerusalem reasoned that a Gentile could not be fully accepted into the congregation of the elect if he did not undergo this rite. "Except ye be circumcized after the custom of Moses, ye cannot be saved."[55] Peter appears to have been undecided on this issue, while Paul insisted that to require circumcision of Gentiles amounted to the admission that faith in the Messiah is not in itself sufficient for salvation.[56] Paul's opinion prevailed, aided as it was by the success of his missionary activities and the rapid growth of Gentile churches. James decided that Gentiles should be required only to avoid idolatry, refrain from eating strangled creatures and drinking blood—roughly the seven Noachide principles.[57] With the removal of the barrier of circumcision, the conversion of large masses to Christianity became possible, and the new religion was launched, beyond the confines of the congregation of Israel.

Characteristic is the remark of Peter, "Now, therefore, why make ye trial of God, that ye should put a yoke upon the neck of the disciples which neither our fathers nor we were able to bear?"[58] Circumcision was important not only in itself but also for its associations, for it symbolized the barrier of laws and customs between Jews and Gentiles, a barrier which constituted a tremendous obstacle to the process of converting the Gentiles.

The Christian movement began among the Galilean peasants, who were removed psychologically as well as geographically from the centers of Pharisaic learning in Jerusalem, but it appealed very largely, even in its earliest days, to the Hellenistic Jews, who dwelt in Jerusalem permanently or who had journeyed there as pilgrims. This development is apparent in the report that the Hellenistic believers were given representation in the management of the infant church, in the very first years of its organization.[59] It was out of the colony of Greek-speaking Jews, that the first Christian martyr, Stephen, emerged, meeting his fate in the course of an argument with other Jews, who hailed also from the Hellenistic Diaspora.[60] Saul of Tarsus, who later became the famed apostle to the Gentiles, took part in the condemnation and stoning of his countryman, Stephen.

The Hellenistic Jews were predisposed to sympathize with the ideas of the Nazarene's followers. In the first place, they were not as habituated as the Jews of Palestine in the meticulous observance of the law. Living in the midst of a Gentile majority, the observance of the law was exceedingly difficult for them. If salvation was to be achieved solely through loyalty to the Torah, then their chances were, to put it mildly, very slim. For rabbinic Judaism had not yet developed, at that time, an ordered body of religious rituals that was considered adequate to take the place of the sacrificial cult in the Holy Temple. A Talmudic comment reflects a judgment which must have been keenly felt by the countrymen of Paul: " He who dwells outside the Holy Land is as one who has no God."[61] Furthermore, the very soil outside Palestine was declared " unclean " by the Pharisaic sages. Hence, all the Jews of the Diaspora were unable to share in the Palestinian pattern of piety which placed so much emphasis on the laws of " purity." Accordingly, these Greek-speaking Jews were eager for a message that would open up a pathway of salvation other than that of the punctilious observance of every tittle of the law.

Secondly, the Greek-speaking Jews were prepared, by the commentaries popular among them, to consider the law as an instrument for the spiritual life, not as a supreme goal in itself. Though Philo insisted on the need of observing the law, he did not esteem obedience in itself as the epitome of virtue, and he pointed to allegorical and esoteric meanings of the law as the real values of faith. Philo tells of teachers in Alexandria who intimated that once the spiritual import of the law was understood, it was no longer important whether or not one abided by its literal denotation. While Philo's repudiation of these opinions may have reflected the feeling of the majority of Alexandrian Jewry, even his loyal disciples were no longer content to regard the immediate and unquestioning acceptance of the law itself as the essential content and basic import of God's will. Accordingly, they were prepared to think in terms of a possible contrast between the spirit and the letter of the law, to sympathize with any revivalistic movement which called for a return to the basic elements of faith, to question and even to repudiate the legalistic refinements of the Palestinian schools.

Third, while the concept of the Messiah which prevailed in the feverish and rebellious atmosphere of Palestine was weighted largely with nationalistic and political elements, the Messiah appeared in the vision of Hellenistic Jews as a heavenly, mystical redeemer. Living outside the land of Israel, they were accustomed to think of Rome as largely a benevolent force, protecting them against the wiles and pressures of the Greek and native population. To be sure, Rome was occasionally harsh and uncomprehending, especially in its dealings with the Jews of Palestine, but it was no more representative of the cosmic forces of evil than humanity itself, with which the Roman Empire was sometimes identified; so they were not disposed to think of the Messiah as the leader of a revolt against Rome. Also, being subjected to the influence of the various pagan faiths, which included the myth of a savior-god, dying and rising again to life, they were easily tempted to mold the image of the Messiah after the pagan patterns with which they were familiar.

And, finally, the Jews of the Hellenistic Diaspora did not possess the authentic teaching of the Pharisaic schools in any tangible and authoritative form. They had the Bible in Greek translation, but none of the compilations of the Oral Law, which existed then in the form of memorized oral traditions, were available in translation. The Greek-speaking Jews were entirely dependent on the occasional visits of scholars from Jerusalem, who came to solicit their help in behalf of special causes. Kept in line by these tenuous threads, the Jewish communities in the Hellenistic Diaspora were an easy target for a determined missionary society that spoke to them in terms of the " fulfillment of the law and the Prophets " and pointed out to them the way whereby the irritating barrier might be removed between " Jew and Gentile, Greek and barbarian."

It was through the activity and philosophy of Paul that Christianity departed completely from the faith of Judaism and from the pattern of loyalties that prevailed among the Jewish people. The faith that evolved out of his peculiar psychical experiences contained an impassioned bias against the vital core of Jewish life. At the same time, his marked success in organizing largely Gentile Christian churches created a *de facto* situation, in which the bearers of the new faith, the majority of the " saved," were no longer Jewish people. In turn, this situation could not but engender a series of new developments, whereby pagan patterns of thought and action would penetrate ever more deeply into the spiritual atmosphere of the new faith. Paul was the principal historical instrument through which the monotheistic message of Judaism was separated from the Jewish people and incorporated into the life of a Gentile church.

Paul began his life as a Jew, and the discrete elements out of which he built the theology of the Christian church are Jewish, one and all. But the extremism of his nature, the impassioned dogmatism of his preaching and the impetus of the forces let loose by him were such as to carry his influence out of the confines of Judaism and into the broad expanse of the Gentile world. A Hellenistic Jew who studied in Jerusalem under Rabban Gamaliel and there identified himself with the Pharisaic party, he carried certain basically Jewish ideas far beyond their normative limits in Judaism and thereby evolved a new faith. The small Nazarene sect of believers in the Messiahship of Jesus could have functioned as an integral part of the variegated panorama of Judaism. The scholars Geiger, Graetz, and Klausner agree that "there is not one ethical teaching in the Gospels which is not paralleled by similar statements in the Talmud."[62] Indeed, according to Josephus, the Pharisees protested vehemently when James, the brother of Jesus, was executed by the Romans, and, according to "The Acts," Rabban Gamaliel, head of the Hillelite school of the Pharisees, opposed the persecution of the infant sect.[63] In the whirlpool of sectarian currents and cross-currents of first-century Judaism, there need not have been any particular objection to a group that criticized the Pharisaic overemphasis on ritual, that believed it knew the "name" of the Messiah and that hopefully awaited his return. But in the mind of Paul the doctrines of the Nazarenes were fused into a new pattern of sentiments and beliefs, which was as un-Jewish in theory as it was in consequence.

We may begin by noting that Paul's concept of the Messiah was more distinctly nonearthly, nonpolitical and nonnational than that of Jesus or that of the original Judeo-Christian church. He was indifferent to the teachings and career of the person Jesus, his message of penitence and piety, his disputations and doctrines. It has been remarked that he quoted Jesus but rarely, concerned as he was only with the "risen Messiah." In one of his letters he declares that his all-absorbing loyalty is directed to the transformed Jesus, after he had risen from the dead, not to the earthly Jesus who lived "in the flesh."[64] He does not argue for the Davidic ancestry of Jesus, nor for his supposed birth from a virgin, nor does he construct his argument upon the thesis that the life of Jesus and his career on earth fitted the prophetic description of the Messiah.

To Paul, Jesus was the son of God, the instrument of divine redemption, the one through whom Satan will be conquered and the dominion of God's grace ushered in. The Messianic era, when Israel would be exalted and its national hopes fulfilled, is, in his mind, elbowed aside by the eschatological doctrine of the " world to come," the new world in which human existence would take on an angelic character. " For the kingdom of God is not eating and drinking, but righteousness, peace and joy in the Holy Spirit."[65] The rabbis described the " world to come " in similar terms, declaring that it offered none of the fleshly enjoyments, but that in it " the righteous sit with their crowns upon their heads, enjoying the radiance of the divine presence."[66]

But the rabbis also believed in a Messianic era, of varying duration, when life here on earth, in all its mundane materiality, would be ennobled through the abolition of war and the achievement of a perfect society.[67] Paul entirely eliminated from his vision this intermediate period of earthly bliss, perhaps unconsciously because of his contempt for the body and all the impulses of " the flesh," perhaps consciously because the Messianic era implied the realization of the Jewish hopes for national resurgence and the overthrow of the Roman Empire. As a member of the Syrian branch of Diaspora Jewry, Paul did not share the violent hatred of the Romans so characteristic of the mentality of his Palestinian brothers. He was rather proud of his Roman citizenship. Manifestly, the elimination of the dream of national triumph from " the hope of Israel " removed at one stroke the embarrassing entanglements of early Christianity with the ethnic and political ambitions of the Jewish people. At the same time, this Pauline transformation of the Messianic hope deflected into unworldly channels the prophetic passion for the improvement of this world and the amelioration of evil here on earth. The fashion was thus set for the bifurcation of the religious ideal, leaving the physical world to its devilish devices and reserving all " religious " aspirations for the " kingdom of God " to the domain of prayer and pious meditation. The prophetic passion for uncompromising righteousness and absolute justice in society was imbedded in the law which, according to Paul, had ended its usefulness when the kingdom of love dawned upon the horizon.

"Servant," Paul admonished, "be obedient unto them that, according to the flesh, are your masters, with fear and trembling, in singleness of your heart, as unto Christ."[68] This sanctification of the *status quo* in the earthly world proved to be of ominous consequence in the later development of Christianity. "Let every soul be subject unto the higher powers. For there is no power but of God; the powers that be are ordained of God. Whosoever therefore resisteth the power, resisteth the ordinance of God; and they that resist shall receive to themselves damnation. . . . Wherefore ye must needs be subject, not only for wrath, but also for conscience sake."[69] From this sanctification of political authority, there is but a slight step to Luther's preachment fifteen centuries later of the supreme virtue of "obedience," which became so deep a part of the heritage and character of the German people. "I, Martin Luther, have slain the peasants who died during this rebellion, for I goaded authority to the slaughter. Their blood be on my head."[70]

To Paul the Messiah, or Christ, was the heavenly being standing next to God and between Him and the world. While he does not refer to Christ as the logos, he thinks of Christ as the intermediary between the Creator and His creatures. He writes of the "kingdom of the son of his love, in whom we have our redemption, the forgiveness of our sins, who is the image of the invisible God, the firstborn of creation."[71] Now in later Midrashic collections, there are references to Metatron, "Whose name is the same as that of his Master,"[72] and Jacob was believed to have had his image engraved on the divine "throne of glory."[73] Mention is even made of one fanciful interpretation according to which Jacob is called a god.[74] These and many similar expressions were never meant to be taken literally and were employed generally in a rhetorical and hyperbolic sense. Paul made use of rabbinic homilies and imagery in the approved Pharisaic fashion. Thus, for example, he contrasted the state of the Christian believers with their former position as Gentiles, maintaining that they were previously "servants," but as Christians they were "sons."[75] However, Paul had a way of endowing old words with new meanings and turning a stylistic simile into a literal, theological dogma. He takes the "sonship" of the Messiah to be that of a real relationship between God, the remote, transcendent Father, and

the near, immanent "son," representing at once an anthropomorphic being and a cosmic force. At that time there abounded
in the Eastern Mediterranean world, proto-Gnostic doctrines
concerning angels and "spheres," which later found expression
in the writings of the Gnostics, the teachers of the mysteries of
divine knowledge. Standing on the boundary line between the
Judeo-Christian world and that of paganism, the Gnostics pene-
trated only the periphery of Judaism, laying the conceptual
groundwork for the fantasies of Qabbalah. But they bequeathed
much of their theosophic speculations to the early Christian and
Manichean philosophies. While Paul opposed every form of pride
in esoteric "knowledge," he thought of the Messiah in theosophic
terminology and he spoke of the "mystery" of God that he taught
in the churches.[76]

To become a Christian meant, for Paul, not merely to know
the truth regarding the Messiah, but also to become one of the
elect and the saved. In this respect, too, he carried a Jewish
doctrine to extreme lengths. The Jews, being the chosen people,
would be saved, for the most part, on the Day of Judgment, when
their enemies would be vanquished. But the Talmudic sages were
divided on the question of whether or not "the pious of the
nations have a share in the world to come."[77] The liberal rabbis
were broadminded enough to recognize that the pagans of their
day were not really idol worshipers, that they were merely keeping up the practices of their ancestors.[78]
Paul was impelled in his missionary efforts by the logic and
pathos of the doctrine of exclusive salvation which formed only
a subsidiary trend in the mainstream of Judaism. He preached
that only those who believed in the gospel as he expounded it
would be saved from the dire punishments of hell.[79] Addressing
the congregations which he founded, he wrote, "God chose you
from the beginning unto salvation."[80] And speaking of the final
judgment, he described it as "rendering vengeance to them that
know not God, and to them that obey not the gospel of our Lord,
Jesus."[81] He mourned over the disbelief of the Jewish people in
the divinity of Jesus, believing that this denial of the Messiahship of Jesus doomed his brethren, "according to the flesh," to
everlasting perdition.[82] Yet his love for his people was strong
enough for him not to make peace with the thought of Israel's

rejection. He prayed that he himself "might be anathema" for his people's sake, and he revealed to his Gentile converts the "mystery," that Israel's rejection was only temporary. It was providentially designed that Israel should reject the gospel, in order that "by their fall, salvation is come unto the Gentiles."[83] Driving home the thought of Israel's eventual acceptance of the gospel, he wrote, "A hardening in part hath befallen Israel until the fullness of the Gentiles be come in, and all Israel shall be saved."[84] This sentence proved to be of great protective value to Jewish people in the Middle Ages, since it described the Jews as certain to be converted in the course of time, and thus exempted them from the penalty of extermination which was meted out to other nonbelievers and nonconformists.

The impassioned fanaticism of Paul which consented to the condemnation of the vast majority of mankind that did not believe in Christ was due in large measure to his burning belief in the imminence of the "second coming" of the Saviour. Expecting the transformation of this world momentarily, he could not take a long and tolerant view of people. "We shall not sleep, but we shall be changed," he wrote to the Corinthian church.[85] Since he believed that the end of the world was near, he exhorted his followers, "and make not provision for the flesh."[86] The decisive proof of conversion, to him, was the hysterical excitement of "tongues" and "prophesying" previously described, which he interpreted as baptism in the Holy Spirit, though the proof of living in grace was selfless devotion, the spirit of love and fraternity. Belief in Jesus was to him not merely an intellectual assent, since the belief is so contrary to reason and experience, but evidence of belonging to the company of the elect. The very absurdity of "Christ crucified," which is "foolishness to the Greeks, a stumbling block to the Jews," makes it the acid test of the "chosen," for "no man can say Jesus is the Lord but in the Holy Spirit."[87] Human wisdom is of no avail. For man to be saved, "Let him become a fool that he may be wise."[88]

This antirationalism of Paul's led him to accept the doctrine of predestination and the corresponding principle of the helplessness of the human will. Those who believe were predestined from the beginning of time for salvation, while those who rely upon their wisdom and refuse to accept the gospel were marked out for perdition before they were born. Writing to the Ephesian church, he declares, ". . . even as he chose us in him before the foundation of the world, that we should be holy and without blemish before him in love. . . ."[89] This doctrine is in striking contrast to the Jewish principle of the freedom of the will. Before birth, the sages declare, it is determined whether one shall be rich or poor, strong or weak, etc., but it is not determined whether one shall be righteous or wicked.[90] For a human being remains morally the master over himself, responsible for his deeds. As Rabbi Akiba phrased it, "All is foreseen, but the choice is given."[91]

Associated with the principle of predestination is the belief in the powerlessness of the human will. Paul bequeathed to Christianity the fervent conviction that man could not possibly be saved by his own effort. "For the good which I would I do not, but the evil which I would not, that I practise."[92] The law of Judaism, which makes salvation dependent upon good works, is of no avail to weak-willed humanity. The law makes us conscious of sin, but according to Paul, the power to overcome sin is not given to mankind. (The Talmud does not minimize the potency of man's evil impulse, *yezer hora*, but man can seek and obtain God's help in overcoming it. Interesting in this connection is the rabbinic conception of the Torah as a "spice" transforming the evil impulse.)[93]

The rabbis also spoke of the impossibility of observing the entire law, but they insisted that the reward of each commandment is infinite in scope, and that the power of repentance is able to overcome and outweigh all sins. "In the place where the repentant stand, perfect saints cannot stand."[94] The belief in repentance was so fondly cherished by the rabbis that they fancifully portrayed some of the great sinners of history as penitents.[95] Paul appears to ignore completely the principle of repentance in Judaism—a striking fact in one who studied "at the feet of Rabban Gamaliel." Perhaps he thought of repentance as an irrational and profound psychical upheaval, such as was involved in his own conversion, and not as a calm and reasoned effort to change one's ways.

Convinced that salvation through the observance of law is impossible, Paul pleaded for the repudiation of the law. In the Christian era, belief is substituted for action. The dominion of love superseded the dominion of the law, "for if righteousness is through the law, then Christ died for naught."[96] It was the purpose of Jesus' death to atone for man's sins, and those who join themselves to him by an act of belief are liberated from sin, since they become "new creatures." "We were buried therefore with him through baptism into death . . . likeness of death, so also in the likeness of life. . . ."[97]

The repudiation of the law was possibly the most potent factor in the separation of Christianity from Judaism. The other Christian apostles allowed that the rite of circumcision might be waived, but they still accounted it a mark of piety to observe the whole law. In the normal course of the progressive intensification of piety, Jewish rituals and ceremonies would have been accepted ever more widely. But Paul regarded the law as the counterpoise to the dominion of love: "If ye receive circumcision, Christ profiteth you nothing."[98] The new dispensation is not superimposed upon the old, but set over against it as its bitter enemy. To be sure, only the ritual of the law was rejected, not its ethical and spiritual content. For Paul was an intensely moralistic preacher. Every Christian was to regard his person as a "temple of God," which may not be defiled, and he was to let all his actions spring out of the fountain of love and faith in his heart. The fundamental principle of love was thus set in direct antithesis to the principle of justice in the law.

The Talmudic sages regarded the ideal of love as essential to the good life and as the vital core of the divine scheme of things. "The Torah begins and ends with the ideal of loving kindness," they said. Rabbi Akiba declared that the commandment "And thou shalt love thy neighbor as thyself" is the most fundamental rule in the Torah.[99] But love, to the rabbis, was not a substitute for the quest of justice, but a supplementary principle. How well they knew the emotionalism, irrationalism and capriciousness of love, when it is not tempered with the sober, rational, universal principles of justice.

To Paul, the world was seen in the form of a drama, in which the Lord first offered to save men by giving them the law, but when the law failed, the Lord decided to inaugurate the dominion of love, by offering His son as a sacrifice of atonement. The rabbis, by contrast, spoke of the two attitudes of the Lord toward the world—*midath hadin*, "the policy of law," and *midath horahmim*, "the attitude of mercy or love." But these two attitudes are not mutually exclusive in God. When the Lord created the world, He saw that it could not exist if He insisted on judging all His creatures in strict justice. Therefore, " He associated with it the attitude of mercy."[100] In the rabbinic view, God is thus the perfect embodiment of both justice and love, while in Paul's mind, His justice and His love are opposites, belonging to different periods of time.

Another concept which Paul expanded far beyond its bounds in Judaism is that of sacrifice. We noted in a previous chapter the tension between the rational and the mystical elements of Judaism in regard to the institution of sacrifices. On the one hand, we encounter liberal views, such as the following:

The Lord ordained the complex regimen of animal sacrifices not because He needs or desires or approves of it, but because He wanted to wean the Israelites away from the worship of demons and idols.[101] Hence, the institution was only an educational device, suitable for a primitive stage in the evolution of the Jewish faith. So long as people were not mature enough to worship God by prayer, study and deeds of love, they had to worship God by the naïve and primitive methods of animal sacrifices.[102] In an interesting passage, the inquiry is posed, " A sinner, what is his punishment? Wisdom declares that evil pursues sin, prophecy decrees the death of the sinner. Torah prescribes the offering of a sacrifice as the means of atonement. But the Lord Himself asserts, ' Let him repent and he shall be forgiven.' "[103] Accordingly, when the Holy Temple was burned by the Romans, a system of regular prayers was instituted to take the place of the sacrificial rites. When a messenger announced to Rabbi Johanan ben Zakkai that the Holy Temple was razed to the ground, the great sage replied, " Fear not, my child, we have a rite equally effective, that of loving kindness."[104] In other passages, the study of the law is described as an adequate substitute for the ritual of sacrifice.

On the other hand, these rationalistic views were balanced in Judaism by mystical and occult ideas. Some rabbis asserted that the rites of the Holy Temple were powerful devices for the attainment of the remission of sins.[105] The fact is that pious Jews continued to pray for the restoration of the regimen of animal sacrifices and the rebuilding of the Holy Temple. And a large portion of the Talmud consists of discussions of minutiae of the prescribed sacrifices. Doubtless primitive notions of ritual were not completely overcome in the pattern of piety that is reflected in the Talmud, though occasional rationalistic glimpses are encountered in abundance.

Paul reverted to the powerful residue of mysticism and mythology in Judaism, interpreting the institution of sacrifice as an occult, cosmic phenomenon of tremendous efficacy, operating within the inner substance of the universe. If through animal sacrifices men were forgiven for their sins, how much more effectively should forgiveness be achieved through the sacrifice of the son of God? The " blood of the lamb," he insisted, is capable of washing away all sins. But a rationalist would inquire, " If God desired to forgive men and to love them, why could He not do so without a sacrifice? " Here we encounter the substratum of mythological belief in the effectiveness of sacrifice, long outgrown in the liberal, rationalistic trends of Judaism. " There is no forgiveness save by blood," a Talmudic tradition asserts. Some rabbis taught that " the death of saints is forgiveness for the world,"[106] and there is even a statement to the effect that the angel Michael stands in the midst of the heavens and sacrifices the souls of the saints.[107] But this insight into the vicarious suffering which saints take upon themselves is still far from the principle of individual salvation achieved by faith in the son of God. While Paul defends his belief with casuistic devices reminiscent of those employed occasionally by the rabbis, it is probable that the real source of his ideas is to be found in the pagan mysteries of Osiris, Dionysus and Adonis (Thamus) in which those who share in the ritual of the god's death and rebirth rise along with him to renewed life.[108]

Paul's mind was a strange combination of the mystical and the practical, the speculative and the statesmanlike. Along with a bizarre complex of theosophical concepts, a profound ethical philosophy and a sublime vision of God's attribute of love, Paul was moved, consciously or unconsciously, by the laudable ambition of breaking down the wall between Jews and Greeks. The generation in which he lived was not unfamiliar with the peculiar madness of anti-Semitism, deriving from the sharp line of division in belief and practices that separated the Jews from their Gentile neighbors. Riots verging on civil wars were common occurrences from Cyrenaica to the eastern boundaries of Syria. The initial success of Paul in converting numerous Gentiles led him to recognize in the new faith the providential instrument whereby the Jews might be liberated from the burden of hatred, which weighed so heavily upon them and which did in fact lead to their decimation in Egypt and Libya in the civil war of 111-113 C.E. "For he is our peace, who made both one, and broke down the wall of partition, having abolished in his flesh the enmity, even the law of commandments contained in ordinances."[109] This vision of a reconciliation between the two great peoples of antiquity was even then an ideal so devoutly to be sought that it appeared again and again in Paul's thought as a powerful undercurrent, determining the fundamental directions of his evolving theology. For he was paradoxically statesman as well as mystic. As we have pointed out he saw a "mystery" of Providence in the repudiation of the gospel by the Jews, inferring as the reason for this disappointing development the possibility that the Gentiles might be saved. "But by their fall, salvation is come unto the Gentiles."[110] The Jews would enter the community of the saved, as soon as the "fullness" of Gentiles was acquired. Apparently he felt that the smoldering hostility toward Jews in his day was so powerful that large masses of Gentiles could not be expected to join the true faith, no matter how strongly it appealed to them, so long as it was the peculiar treasure of the Jews. The separation of the Christian faith from the fate and destiny of the Jewish people was a necessary condition for its widespread dissemination.

In summarizing the rise of Christianity and its gradual departure from Judaism, we focus attention especially upon some oft-cited questions. First, "Why was Jesus rejected by the leaders of the Jewish people?" This question is asked by enlightened and modern-thinking Christians, who suppose that Jesus was rejected because of his ideas—his critique of the excess of ritualism, his championing of the moral essence of religion, his preaching of the principles of "peace on earth, good will toward men." No longer accepting Jesus as a divinity, modernists revere him for his vision of the good life and they tend to portray his contemporary opponents in such a manner as to form a suitable foil for his "liberal, humanistic" message. On the other hand, Jewish nationalist historians, like Klausner, strive to discover in the gospels a peculiarly " un-Jewish " philosophy, such as the " negation of life" or "the negation of Jewish nationalism." Both Christian modernism and Jewish nationalism turn history into propaganda.

It is obvious from the above that, in his teachings, Jesus did not differ markedly from the other Pharisaic masters of his day. His ideas on human conduct find parallels in the vast homiletic literature of the Midrash and the Talmud. What his disciples accepted and the majority of Jews repudiated was not the moral-legal teaching of Jesus, but his conviction that he was the son of man, the hoped-for Messiah. His fate was therefore that of a pseudo-Messiah in Israel, of whom there were many. While Jewish scholars are not agreed on the question whether Jesus would have been executed by Jewish authorities if they possessed at that time the right to inflict the death penalty, the fact is that the priestly and Pharisaic leaders were not then free to follow the laws of Judaism. In the circumstances in which they lived, any Messianic pretension, no matter how "spiritual," involved the stirring up of revolutionary excitement among the people against their Roman oppressors. The common people cannot appreciate the fine semantic distinctions in the concept of the Messiah that modern scholars are able to discern. The priestly and political leaders of the people were generally held personally and collectively accountable for every revolutionary disturbance. The story of Pilate washing his hands to prove his innocence, when he was known to execute in cold blood thousands of innocent people on the slightest pretext, is a later attempt to remove the guilt of deicide, in the *Divine Comedy*, from the Romans and to place it upon the Jews. To reinforce this transfer of guilt, the Jews are made to say, " His blood be upon us and upon our children."[111] This guilt-transference has resulted in the murder of millions of people through the ages, and the cup of sorrow is not yet filled. From the Jewish point of view, Jesus was "rejected," by the leading Pharisees only in the sense that his claim to Messiahship was repudiated, since the Messianic age of glory was not ushered in by him. And the Sadducaic priestly hierarchy was not continued in Judaism, as it was rejected in Christianity.

Another question of major concern is, " Why was Christianity rejected by the masses of the Jewish people? " In answer, we note that large numbers of Jews did embrace Christianity. After the lapse of one generation, the majority of Christian converts were no longer of Jewish but rather of pagan ancestry, though the vital nucleus of leadership was drawn from among the Jews. Among the Jewish adherents to the movement, Greek-speaking Jews from the Diaspora soon became the most active expounders of the faith, while "the fearers of the Lord," the Gentile semiconverts to Judaism, became the source of the rapidly growing Christian community. Many large settlements in the Jewish Diaspora dwindled in numbers, as a result of the aggressive propaganda and tremendous activity of the "new Israel." Like Paul, many of them, especially in Alexandria, were accustomed to the acceptance of the law, "in spirit," not according to the letter. Many, too, must have been moved by the prospect of breaking down "the wall" that separated the Jews from the Greeks, turning them into hostile rivals. This motive was undoubtedly intensified following the destruction of Jerusalem, when many Jews in the Diaspora resented the zealot and anti-Roman tendencies of Palestinian Jewry. The Jews of the Diaspora were divided into two camps according to their attitudes toward the Roman government and the pagan population. While the metropolitan masses generally sympathized with the program of the Palestinian Zealots, the leaders sought to establish bonds of mutual understanding with the pagans. In the course of time, the reasonable policies of the leaders gave way to the mass hysteria of the Jewish population, incited as it was by the hordes of refugees from the Palestinian holocaust. Eventually, the Jewish Diaspora in the Roman Empire was almost entirely annihilated as a consequence of a succession of rebellions led by Zealot elements. On the other hand, the pro-Roman population may have joined the Christian congregations which were known to be opposed to the policies and methods of the Jewish nationalists.

Paul's ambition to remove the barrier of hate between the Jews and their neighbors in the Diaspora was undoubtedly shared by many enlightened and far-seeing Jewish leaders in his own generation and in the century following his death.

Virtual civil war between Jews and Greeks in Caesaria, Palestine, set off the Great Rebellion of 66-69 C.E., which resulted in the burning of Jerusalem and the desolation of Judea. Both in Palestine and in the Diaspora the upper levels of Jewish society endeavored to allay the zealotry of inflamed masses, but without success. As the refugees from the Palestinian holocaust fanned out into the Diaspora, the Zealot mentality obtained the ascendency in province after province, leading to civil riots and the virtual extermination of Jewish people in the lands of Cyprus, Cyrenaica, and in portions of Egypt and Syria. The great upheavals in the years 111-113 and 131-135 C.E. resulted in the decimation of the Jewish population in the Eastern portion of the Roman Empire. During these intermittent civil wars, the Jews of the far-flung Diaspora were torn between the desire to allay the mutual hatreds and to achieve a genuine fellowship of spirit with their neighbors, and the self-isolating tendency of the Zealots. Paul's bold policy of effecting one community of " Israel after the spirit " out of the embattled groups in the ancient world must have found ready support among those Jewish leaders who looked for a realistic *modus vivendi* with their Gentile neighbors. Great numbers of Jews must have joined the "new Israel" during the riots and wars, from 66 C.E. to 135 C.E. In Palestine itself the Ebionites and other Jewish Christians functioned as independent sects for several centuries.

Nevertheless, while the solid base of the Christian movement was in the beginning Jewish and semi-Jewish, the greater number of Jews did not accept the faith of Christianity which made such rapid gains among the general population. The question before us is, therefore, what was it in Christianity that made it a decisive force in the pagan world, while it remained a sectarian and fringe-community in Israel? What historical function did Christianity fulfill in the Roman world that it could not fulfill for the Jewish people?

The answer to this question is fairly clear. In the pagan world, Christianity became the vehicle of ethical monotheism. Through it, the God of Israel was brought into every corner of the Roman world, shattering the ancient idols in the hearts of men. Basically, the same course of development was set in motion in the Roman Empire that in an earlier age had eliminated idolatry, and with it the entire mentality of paganism, from the spiritual life of Israel. Many centuries later we encounter the same phenomenon in the rise and rapid triumph of the Moslem faith. Just as the Hellenic civilization contained certain universal values endowing it with a deathless appeal for all mankind, Jewish ethical monotheism constituted an invaluable stage in the maturation of man's spiritual nature, so that its ultimate triumph was historically inevitable.

None of the pagan gods was capable of rivaling the God of Israel in the appeal to man's fundamental needs and his higher spiritual nature. Paganism was highly developed in the first centuries of our era, having built up profound and systematic philosophies, multiple rites and magnificent temples. But precisely because of its high state of development it could not move onto another spiritual track. Its gods were personifications of forces, real or imaginary, which were limited in their scope, power, or interest, arising out of primeval chaos and ultimately dependent on its impersonal, occult power. Such gods could not evoke from the spirit of man the feeling of absolute devotion that comes only with the realization of standing before the living heart of the universe. All the pagan gods, no matter how exalted, such as Mithra of the Persian pantheon, were still subject to the dark forces of fate which encompassed the world, with the result that they could be worshiped after the fashion in which "saints" or angels are implored, but not in the same mood of total devotion, total self-surrender and total commitment with which the God of Israel is approached.

In pagan philosophy, thoroughly refined concepts of the Deity were available since both Neo-Platonism and Stoicism made peace with the pagan priests, allowing room in their own metaphysical systems for the gods that were popularly worshiped, and interpreting the crude myths in allegorical fashion as symbols of metaphysical truths. But the "high God" of the philosophers and the low gods of the populace were artificially held together by unconvincing stratagems and intellectual *tours-de-force*. The philosophical God was not emotionally stirring and the popular gods were no longer convincing, while the marriage between them was too obviously one of expediency.

In Jewish monotheism, God is unique both in the absoluteness of His power and in the ethical perfection of His attributes. He stands outside the world, "unique" in being different from all created objects in the majesty of His thought, in the certainty of His concern for all men. He is both far and near, eluding the grasp of the subtlest metaphysical thinking, closer even than the closest friend to him that is lowly of spirit. So magnificent a conception, stirring in its timeless truth and compelling in its noble beauty, will never cease to appeal to the mind of man.

Christianity triumphed in the Roman world principally because it functioned as the vehicle of the deathless truth of Jewish monotheism. More specifically, it was not the complicated theology of Christianity centering around the person of the son, but the pure and simple monotheism of " God the Father " that won the hearts of the Greeks and Romans. Legends of gods dying and rising again, dramatizing the perennial mystery of nature, were to be found in abundance in the classical world. But no god ever died in the pagan pantheon as part of a scheme of salvation in the mind of the one God Who loves men, rebukes them ceaselessly, judges them fairly and helps free them from bondage to evil and sin. The legends of the Messiah, as they came to be reworked in the Christian imagination of later years, occasionally took on the tone and color of ancient pagan myths. However, monotheism remained the core and substance of Christianity, the dynamic idea which lent it the driving power to spread over the entire ancient world, endowing the ways of man with the divine aura of faith and love and shattering all the idols and their temples in its path. The earthly career of Jesus provided for the Gentile world a dramatic commentary on the ethical implications of monotheism.

Manifestly, Christianity could not fulfill in the Jewish world the functions which it carried out in the Greco-Roman world since Jewish people were monotheistic already. Among the Jews, it could only argue the thesis that the Messiah, as predicted by the prophets, had already arrived and that in him the Scriptures were fulfilled. This argument regarding the intent of the Scriptures placed upon the Christian challenger the burden of proof. No reasonable person could possibly blame the Jews for remaining unconvinced and refusing to suppress the truth, as they saw it, for the sake of any earthly gains.

Furthermore, as Christianity developed, pagan conceptions came to color its thoughts ever more noticeably, leading to the doctrines of the virgin birth, the trinity, transubstantiation, and the adoration of saints and images. As time went on, Judaism and Christianity deviated even more decisively, until they became mutually incommunicable, with their respective proponents unable to discover any common ground in their disputations.

The great Nahmanides, champion of the Jewish faith in the famous disputation at Barcelona in 1263, asserted:

> The core of the true dispute among us is not the concept of the Messiah . . . but the crux of the issue and the reason for the argument between Jews and Christians is the fact that you impute to the Deity things which are exceedingly repugnant. . . . For what you state, and this is the essence of your faith, reason cannot accept, nature does not permit, and the prophets never implied. Also, the belief in miracles cannot be extended to cover such a phenomenon . . . that the creator of heaven and earth and all their hosts should go through the womb of one Jewess, grow in it nine months, etc. . . . The thought of a Jew and a man cannot tolerate such a belief, hence you argue for naught and your words are wasted, for this is the essence of our dispute.[112]

So, to the pagan world, inured to the myths and mysteries of dying gods, Christianity presented the aspect of an ethically monotheistic faith, constituting a long advance in the spiritual history of mankind. On the other hand, to the puristic monotheistic Jews, Christianity could only add a confusing medley of myths and legends. In their ceaseless criticism of Christian dogma, the Jews represented a rationalistic and humanistic leaven which was certainly a powerful factor in preventing the dark mythology of Christianity from triumphing over the genuinely spiritual heritage it derived from Judaism—the luminous core of ethical monotheism.

At this point, we must face a truly penetrating question: If it was the Jewish element in Christianity that led to its triumph, why did not Judaism itself succeed in converting the Hellenistic world? Doubtless many factors account for this. Some scholars, chiefly Christian, attribute this failure to the so-called " clannishness " of the Jews and the " narrowness " of their faith. In their view, the great ethical principles of Judaism were, in their application, confined to the Jewish people. The non-Jewish world did not count, and the Jewish leaders were not interested in " saving " them. Converts were taken into the fold of the faith, but only after they had become part of the " nation " of the Jews, through circumcision.

This view is tragically erroneous and grossly misleading. The liberal trend within the Jewish religion extended the love and providence of God to all men, though it did not set the observance of the law as a condition for salvation. In theory, the observance of the "seven Noachide principles" was, for Gentiles, sufficient for salvation. Nevertheless, the Hellenistic Jews conducted an active missionary campaign, which was remarkably effective even if it was not centrally organized. Some scholars maintain that in the first century of our era, there were approximately three million Jews in the Diaspora of the Roman Empire and some five million semiconverted "fearers of the Lord."[113] The gospels quote Jesus' criticism of the zeal of the Pharisees in pursuing their missionary efforts to the ends of the earth.[114] Naturally, all Jewish people were not of one opinion as regards the advisability of seeking converts. In the second century of the common era, two leading rabbis debated this issue, whether the acceptance of converts is good or bad, since some of them were known to relapse again into paganism.[115] The liberal rabbis affirmed that if a Gentile acceded to the truth of ethical monotheism and lived by its precepts, he was "saved," even if he did not take the step of full conversion to the faith of Israel. However, a complete conversion, involving the observance of all the *mizvoth* was, even for the liberals, a meritorious act.[116]

The rabbinic insistence on the commandment of circumcision bore no relationship at all to any "national" requirements. Circumcision was a religious ceremony, ordained by Abraham as a sign of the covenant, obligatory upon all who enter into the fold of the covenant-people. Once a Gentile was circumcized and baptized, he was subject to the law, in all respects, as Jews were.

It was not, therefore, through lack of interest or lack of zeal that Judaism failed to win the Mediterranean world. In the first place, the ceremony of circumcision was a formidable obstacle. The fact that there were so many "fearers of the Lord," who did not consent to take the next logical step of circumcision, is itself evidence of the difficulty of that step. Furthermore, circumcision as the final act of conversion was prohibited by the Roman emperors, with the Emperor Domitian going so far as to engage spies with whose aid he "extracted large fines from poor persons convicted of becoming proselytes, and executed wealthy ones in order to confiscate their property."[117] But more potent than the pain of circumcision was the liberalism of Jewish doctrine. So long as, according to liberal Jewish thought, God-fearing Gentiles were not denied the blessings of salvation in the "world to come," why should they forsake family and friends, risking death on the charge of "atheism," merely in order to gain additional merits? The very liberalism of the Jewish faith blunted the edge of its missionary efforts and discouraged any concerted endeavor to organize permanent missionary societies. Hence, only a small proportion of the vast masses that felt the influence of Judaism actually joined its ranks. Liberal faiths are not particularly successful in converting large masses, precisely on account of their liberalism. Furthermore, the liberal and humanistic elements in Judaism were in part neutralized by their tension with opposing forces. The antiliberal trends in ancient Judaism were indeed isolationist and imbued with the spirit of zealotry, either for the law or for the temporal triumph of the Jewish people. They neither sought nor welcomed converts to the faith.

In addition, there militated against large-scale conversions to Judaism the circumstance of Jewish defeat and dispersion. The Jewish faith and the Jewish people were indissolubly one. How could large masses of Gentiles be convinced that God had chosen Israel when they saw the Roman eagle thrusting its claws ever deeper into the flesh of the lion of Judah? We had occasion to note in the previous chapter that Philo believed the national triumph of Israel in the days of the Messiah would of itself be sufficient to convert all the people of the world to the faith of Judaism. The Psalmist too felt that the low estate of Israel prevented its faith from winning the hearts of men. "Not for us, O Lord, not for us, but for Thy name, give glory, for Thy mercy and for Thy truth's sake. Wherefore should the nations taunt us, saying: 'Where, then, is their God?'"[118]

To be sure, the early Christian community was recruited mainly from the proletarian masses of the population. The Christians, however, had no national stigmata of defeat to live down. In the first generations they looked forward to the immediate return of the Christ, accounting all the suffering they encountered in this world as trials of faith and marks of favor, signifying the assurance of greater rewards in the future. Whatever the personal fate of individual Christians may have been, the Christian church as such was not involved in the military and political struggle of nations for a place in the sun. In contrast to the Jewish people who battled heroically for freedom and lost, the kingdom, for Christians, was not of this world. The destruction of Jerusalem and the burning of the Holy Temple were the collective catastrophes of the Jewish faith, while the occasional persecution of individual Christians did not connote a similar defeat for the church as a whole. By the time St. Augustine felt impelled to defend the Church against the charge of bringing about the downfall of Rome, the triumph of Christianity was assured.

It is important also to note that " the barbarian proletariat," to use Toynbee's phrase, generally chooses a heretical form of the faith of the nuclear, cultural center. Religiously, the Jews were the nuclear community in the Roman world, and the Christian Church was the dynamic heresy within Judaism. A heresy embodies for new converts both their admiration and their hatred for the nuclear group. Thus the pagan acceptance of Christianity was paralleled by the Persian acceptance of Shiite Islam, the Burmese acceptance of Buddhism, the Gothic conversion to the Aryan heresy.

It remains but to outline briefly the steps whereby Christianity and Judaism separated. In the Roman Empire, Judaism was a "legal faith" with its followers enjoying certain privileges that exempted them from all communal functions which involved idolatrous practices. The early Christians, both Gentiles and Jews, constituted part of the legally recognized unit of the synagogue. But while it was legal for Jews to practise their faith, it was expressly prohibited for them to proselytize Gentiles. For this reason Jews were expelled from Rome in the reigns of Tiberius and Claudius, while Jewish proselytes were subject to the death penalty on the charge of " atheism." So the threat of expulsion hung over the heads of the Jews of the Diaspora, by reason of the activities of Paul and the other Christian missionaries.[119]

Up to the destruction of the temple in Jerusalem in the year 69 c.e., Jews and Christians constituted part of one community, though the pagan world was beginning to take cognizance of the difference between them. Nero singled out the Christians for persecution, leaving the Jews of Rome alone, possibly through the influence of his wife, Poppaea. On the other hand, Titus fully expected to deal the death blow to both Judaism and Christianity by the conquest and destruction of Jerusalem.[120]

In Palestine, prior to the year 69 c.e., differences in regard to the observance of the law and the formulation of Messianic doctrine were tolerated for centuries. The Sadducees, who repudiated the Pharisaic Oral Law in its totality, controlled the proceedings in the temple, and dominated the Sanhedrin of Jerusalem, the highest tribunal of Judaism, during the major period of its existence. In view of such radical divergence of opinion, the peculiar beliefs of the Christian sect, observant in the Pharisaic sense as most of them were, could not have caused a decisive break with Judaism. It is significant that the Greek-speaking Jews in Jerusalem were responsible for the stoning of Stephen.

In the great uprising against Roman rule in the year 65 c.e., the Christians withdrew from the national effort, retiring to the city of Pella on the eastern side of the Jordan. Later the Roman Emperor Nerva exempted Christians from the payment of the punitive tax that was imposed on all Jews in his realm, the *fiscus Judaicus*. The rabbis shared the suffering of their people, though they advised against rebellion, and under the leadership of Rabbi Johanan ben Zakkai they assembled in the city of Jabneh. Following the great catastrophe, the character of the Jewish community was transformed from top to bottom. The Sadducees, the Zealots, the Essenes, and even the minority Pharisaic party of Shammaites were reduced to insignificance, disappearing completely from Jewish life in a generation or two. The bonds of political unity and national life, which supplemented the ties of religion in previous centuries, were now shattered into hopeless fragments. It became all the more necessary, in the judgment of the rabbis at Jabneh, to standardize the theory and practice of Judaism, so that the Torah might function as the one unifying factor in Jewish life, taking the place of the Temple, the priestly hierarchy and the Sanhedrin. It would be misleading to apply the modern terms " religion " and " nationalism " to the revolution which took place in Judaism during the latter part of the first century, but it is important to note that in the transition effected at Jabneh the multiplicity of loyalties and parties gave way to a high degree of uniformity secured by a rigid adherence to the law, as defined and formulated in the Central Academy. Reduced to helplessness in its own homeland and scattered through the distant provinces of the Roman Empire, the Jewish community sought to find its enduring rock of unity and strength in the Torah. The law became the purpose and instrument of survival, the spiritual and indestructible homeland of a defeated and dispersed people.

In addition, the Jewish communities in the Diaspora were

greatly disheartened by the destruction of the temple and by the triumphant propaganda of the Christians. If Judaism was to live, it had to have firmness of structure, definiteness of doctrine and clarity of purpose. The rabbis at Jabneh, faced with the task of reconstituting a broken people around the emergent synagogue, could not evade the task of dealing with the Christian sect in Judaism.

Under the leadership of Rabban Gamaliel of Jabneh, a prayer (the *birchath haminin*) invoking the aid of God for the confounding of heretics was inserted in the standard set of Eighteen Benedictions. Since Jewish Christians could not repeat this formula, they were compelled to leave this synagogue. Through the messengers which the patriarch sent to the communities of the Diaspora, this policy was extended to every synagogue, compelling the Christians to forego the protecting shelter of the Jewish community. This formal separation took place at about the year 100 C.E. A leading historian writes, "The generation of Jews and Christians which followed the destruction of Jerusalem, not the generation which first heard the preaching of Christ, is responsible for the separation which follows."[121] The Bar Kochba rebellion, in which the bulk of Palestinian Jewry followed the lead of Rabbi Akiba and acknowledged Bar Kochba as the Messiah, further widened the breach between Jews and Jewish Christians. During the Hadrianic repression which followed, circumcision was declared a capital crime even for Jews. Later, the Antonine emperors relaxed the prohibition, but only so far as Jews were concerned. Thus, Jewish missionary efforts were virtually prohibited, while Christian propaganda was allowed free rein, save for brief intervals.

On the Christian side, the growing separation between Jews and Christians led to an increasingly more violent hatred of Judaism. Not content with Paul's judgment of the law as the temporary "schoolmaster," Jerome went so far as to say that God deliberately contrived the law in order to deceive the Jewish people and to deny them His salvation.[122] The Patristic writers were caught on the horns of a dilemma. On the one hand, they had to maintain the bond with the Old Testament, in order to overcome the extremism of the Gnostics, to prevent their people from identifying Jesus with any one of the half-dozen deities which popular mythology represented as having died and risen again, and in order to endow the Christian faith with the then highly-prized aura of antiquity. On the other hand, they had to denounce the attempt to live in accord with the words of the Scriptures and to defame the people that continued so to live.

They solved this dilemma by turning the entire Old Testament into a symbolic narration of the coming of Christ, finding a reference to their Saviour in every other verse. Thereupon they proclaimed themselves and the members of their churches to be the true "heirs of the promise," applying every favorable reference and blessing to themselves and every rebuke or curse to the Jews. This fantastic travesty was followed by an official version of Jewish history, which portrayed the Jews as the followers, not of Moses, Aaron, David, Samuel, Jeremiah and Isaiah, but of Dathan and Abiram, Ahab and Manasseh. The New Testament passages, dating from the second century, speak of the Jews "as being of their father, the devil" and represent all Jewish people as saying, "may his blood rest upon us and upon our children."

The separation had become complete. The new faith to which Judaism gave birth was afflicted from infancy with a pathological Oedipus complex. Summarizing this development, James Parkes concludes: "No people has ever paid so high a price for the greatness of its own religious leaders."

The cherished words of the prophets were taken by the Christian zealots to be so much damning testimony against the Jewish people. A wall of misunderstanding and hate was erected by the narrow zealotries of the two faiths. And in the turbulence of passion, the light of either faith became invisible to those whose eyes were accustomed from childhood to the illumination of the other. In the darkness of the medieval period only the philosophers were aware of the unity of the Judeo-Christian tradition that underlies the diversity of creed and ritual.

CHAPTER FIVE

THE QARAITIC OFFSHOOT: THE PROTEST OF RELIGIOUS INDIVIDUALISM

THE progressive crystallization of Judaism into a massive structure of laws and institutions, governed by an authoritative hierarchy, was completed in the early Gaonic period of the seventh and eighth centuries. While the Palestinian centers of learning deteriorated steadily, under the harsh rule of the Byzantine Empire, the Jews of Babylonia and adjacent centers enjoyed a high degree of autonomy. The Palestinian Talmud was left in its comparatively unfinished form at about the year 350 C.E., when many teachers and students migrated to the academies in Babylonia. There the Babylonian Talmud continued to be developed for several more generations, until it attained its present form, in the school of Rovina, at about the year 500 C.E.

Thereafter, only minor emendations were made in the text by the Saburoi; i.e. the Expounders. The Mohammedan Conquest of Babylonia opened up a new era of security and prosperity for the entire Middle East, with almost complete autonomy for the religious minorities in the vast area of the Califate. Recognized as the official heads of the Jewish community, the Exilarch and the Geonim were authorized to levy taxes upon and collect "gifts" from all the Jews of the Moslem dominion.

Their religious authority augmented by secular power, the Exilarch and the Geonim, together with the scholars (*alufim*) in the front ranks of the hierarchy, exercised undisputed sway over the people, save when the tensions among these leaders erupted into an open struggle. In a general way, the Exilarch represented Jewish secular autonomy and the Geonim constituted the supreme fount of religious authority, but this distinction was only vaguely glimpsed in the ancient Moslem world, with the result that clashes between the heads of the academies and the "head of the community in exile" were frequent. For the most part, the highest offices in the academies and in the judicial system run by them belonged by tradition to certain families, though occasionally an outsider, such as Saadia, succeeded by the sheer impetus of rare genius in breaking into the inner circles of leadership.

The Geonim declared the Babylonian Talmud to be the sole source of authority, relegating the Palestinian Talmud to a subordinate position.[1] At the same time the one academy of Sura, or the two academies of Sura and Pumbeditha, were at different times constituted as the highest tribunal in Judaism, *bimkom sanhedrin gedolah,* "in place of the great Sanhedrin."[2] Their legal decisions were accepted as final by all the Jewish communities in the Diaspora.[3] In the course of time, the Gaonic hierarchy, humanly enough, acquired pride as well as prestige and power, identifying its opinions with the living word of God. Thus, a famous responsum from an eighth-century Gaon reads:

> There are among you disciples who dispute the decisions of the Geonim, the pillars of the world, saying, "Whence do they derive this thing?"— pointing to passages in their books. But they do not understand the work of God and the labor of His hands. They do not even comprehend a little of that which was known by the disciples of the disciples of the smallest among the Geonim.
>
> How, then, do foxes that have not seen the light dare to cast reflection upon God and His portion? Their [the Geonim] wisdom and their dialectic is the word which the Lord commanded to Moses. Even though they say, "So it is," failing to cite evidence from any place, one must not doubt their word, whether it refers to great or to small things. A man who dares dispute any decision of theirs is like unto one who rebels against God and His Torah.[4]

The combination of an entrenched and proud hierarchy with a divinely inspired, canonized Talmud left hardly any room for freedom of interpretation and research. Resentment against the arrogance of the ruling hierarchy led to a radical reaction against the entire tradition of the Oral Law. A modern scholar points out that the "Geonim raised the Talmud to the level of the Holy Scriptures."[5] Actually, the canonization of the Talmud was a gradual process, since the discussion in the academies presumably reflected the cultural and social forces operative within Babylonian Jewry. But when the authority and power of the religious hierarchy in the Mohammedan period was added to the dogmatic canonization of the Talmud, all dissidents in theory or in practice found themselves hard-pressed, forced to submit to a rigid, unyielding law.

After being suppressed for several generations, this mounting resentment found expression in the Qaraite revolt.[6] In the eighth century Anan, a rejected candidate for the post of Exilarch, became the spearhead of a rebellion against the Talmud and against the autocratic authority of the Geonim. Under his leadership, Qaraism erupted into the open, after smoldering in the dark for several generations.

In this chapter we shall be mainly concerned with the ideas which the Qaraitic movement evolved, leaving the study of the early origins and the complex socio-economic causes of this great schism to the historians of general Jewish life.

Ideologically, Qaraism does not reflect one mood or system of thought, but like an oriental tapestry it is woven out of many strands. The ideology which Anan, or Benjamin Nahavendi, or later theoreticians supplied was superimposed upon an existing anti-Talmudic tradition, antedating the movement by many generations. Accordingly, much of the inner dialectic of Qaraism, especially in regard to the new laws introduced by them, appears strangely forced and artificial. Nevertheless, certain basic ideas stand out in bold relief.

The fundamental principle of Qaraism is the direct responsibility of the individual to God. Every Jew is in duty bound to study the Scriptures for himself and to follow the inferences which appear to him to be justified. Rabbinic Judaism enjoined upon every individual the duty of studying the Torah, but it left the prerogative of rendering final decisions and authoritative interpretations at first to the prophets, then to the Sanhedrin, later to the scholars of the academies headed by the Geonim. The Qaraites pushed the principle of individual study and contemplation to its logical conclusion. No body of intermediaries should be allowed to stand between God and the individual, neither a hereditary priesthood performing mystic ceremonies for him, nor a hierarchy of well-born scholars arrogating to itself the sole right to expound and to apply the divine revelation. It is entirely sufficient for a person to know that the Scriptures contain God's revealed word, addressed to him and intended for his felicity and salvation. Can it be logically supposed that God would choose an inadequate instrument for human guidance? Manifestly, then, the teaching of the written Torah must be assumed to be altogether sufficient for salvation, if it be studied in the light of another God-given gift, the power of reason. Every human being is granted the power of understanding and judgment, as a personal endowment to guide his individual decisions. In matters of faith as in all other domains of life, he is expected to employ his own judgment, interpreting the Scriptures in the light of his own understanding. If two persons differ in their interpretations of any one law, both will be accounted praiseworthy in the sight of God if they will follow their own respective interpretations. To search the Scriptures diligently, to consult one's conscience rigorously, to rely on one's own painfully acquired judgments— these are the basic precepts of what may be described as the Jewish Protestant movement.

Some of the expressions of this rigorous individualism are of enduring interest. Anan expressed the genius of his movement in the counsel that he addressed to his followers: "Search ye well in the Torah, and do not rely on my opinion."[7] The second great exponent of the movement, Benjamin Nahavendi, declared at the end of his book:

> I, Benjamin, am but one out of a million and a hundred million. I am neither a prophet, nor the son of a prophet. . . . Thus, too, every Qaraitic scholar follows the same procedure, writing down the results of his reflection, in accord with the duty to analyze and penetrate to the essence of things. Thus it may happen that two brothers may follow two different interpretations, or a son may challenge the opinion of his father, without the father being allowed to rebuke him as follows: "Why did you change my word?" The same situation may develop as between a disciple and his master. In this manner, we fulfill our obligations and attain salvation in the sight of God, though there may be mistakes in some of our words and books. The reward of the author is great in that his efforts enlighten the understanding of people.[8]

This principle imposed a severe obligation upon the individual Jew, removing from him the social prop of conformity and making it mandatory for him to be a lifelong student and searcher. As Anan put it:

> Thus, Scripture employs the term "his God," not simply "God," for if a person believes a certain practice to be a *mizvah*, even if it is not a *mizvah*, he is judged for its violation, since, in his view, it is a *mizvah*. But, if he knows it is not a *mizvah*, or if a person who studies the Torah

tells him it is not a *mizvah* and he does not forsake it, then he is a false witness, and the Merciful One will destroy him.[9]

It is now believed that the Qaraites preserved remnants of an ancient, non-Talmudic tradition. Inevitably, too, with the passage of time their movement acquired distinctive practices and customs, forming a definite tradition of their own, but their reliance on the individual's own interpretation of the law made them in principle antitraditionalists. A tenth-century Qaraite writer pleaded:

> Know, my brothers, the children of Israel, that everyone must depend upon himself. Our God will not accept the apology of the one who says, " Thus did my masters conduct themselves. . . ." Also, there is no such obligation as to follow the customs of the fathers in all instances. On the contrary, it is for us to examine their ways and to compare their actions and judgment with the words of the Torah, to see if they are compatible. . . .
>
> And do not say, " What can we do, seeing the Qaraites too don't agree among themselves—whom shall we follow? " For the Qaraites don't claim to be leaders, ordaining laws for the people according to their will. But they search and seek in the Torah of Moses and in the words of the prophets, examining as well the opinions of scholars of earlier times. Thus, they say to their brothers, the sons of Jacob: " Learn and interpret, search, examine, and act according to the conclusions that appear to you to be fully attested by solid evidence."
>
> And do not say, " How can such a situation make sense? " The answer is that this is the will of God from us. It is for us to do the *mizvah* which our understanding declares to be fully justified, not that which we might ourselves desire. What, then, if divisions arise among us? When the righteous Redeemer arrives, he will settle all differences. But if a man should say, " How can the *mizvoth* be dependent on the wisdom of one's heart? " we say to him, " How can it be otherwise? " Shall we merely follow the path of the many, when the Torah declares " Thou shalt not follow the many for evil "? Let the many pursue it [knowledge] and understanding will increase.[10]
>
> And if one should say, " What is the ignorant man to do who knows nothing? " we shall reply, " It is his duty to study and to acquire knowledge, to observe and then to do . . . for he who merely performs rites without understanding them is no different from a donkey carrying a burden."[11]

Another Qaraite scholar of the eleventh century pointed out that the first duty of man is to learn. " The Lord, blessed be He, imposed upon us the obligation of learning Torah and retaining it in our hearts. . . . And if one forsakes this commandment and does not learn the Torah of God and the nature of His unity, which is the obligation of all rational beings, then he has no excuse at all. . . ."[12]

This principle of religious individualism was balanced in Qaraism by inherited dogmas, the naïveté of the times, and a singularly sad and somber mood of ascetic piety. Nevertheless, the emphasis on individualism was certain to promote in time the growth of a rationalistic spirit. Taught to rely upon their own interpretations, the Qaraites could not but accord to human reason the most decisive influence in the formulation of their own thought. We find them on occasion stepping beyond the bounds of literalism to inquire into the reasons for the *mizvoth*. They abolished the ceremony of *halizah* along with the entire institution of levirate marriage because, they felt, it was designed for the purpose of safeguarding family property, in a tribal-patriarchal society which no longer existed in their day.[13]

Some of their scholars explained the reason for the sacrifice of the Paschal lamb as a demonstration of the repudiation of Egyptian totemism. for the Egyptians regarded the lamb as a sacred animal. In the same spirit, they cited historical circumstances in explanation of the rites of Yom Kippur and the other holidays.[14] One of the later Qaraites laid it down as a firm principle that, " if a person cannot understand a precept, he should not accept it."[15] For this reason, too, they abolished the practices of affixing a *mezuzah* on the doorpost and of putting on *tefillin* for the morning prayers, maintaining that the verses which call for the cherishing of the words of the Torah " between thine eyes " and " on the doorposts of thy house " were not to be taken literally.[16]

The rationalistic spirit, inherent in their position, led the Qaraites to ridicule the many legends in the Talmud which reflect an anthropomorphic concept of the Deity. In this repudiation of the naïve lore, folk-magic, and superstition which is occasionally interspersed among the legalistic passages of the Talmud, the Qaraites displayed a rationalistic approach to religion which provided a powerful impetus for the subsequent development of religious philosophy by rabbinic Jews. However, in the eighth and ninth centuries, philosophy was a forgotten discipline among both Qaraites and Rabbinites. Instead, a crude pattern of theosophic speculation and quasi-magical devices attained considerable popularity and authority among the masses of Talmud-true Jewry.

In the Gaonic period, there appeared many collections of naïve, theosophical homilies and fanciful, mystical formulae, which were especially vulnerable to the rationalistic criticism of the Qaraites. The letter-mysticism of *Sefer Yezirah* and the fantastic visions of the heavenly "palaces" described by the *Haikholoth* school of visionaries form what may be called proto-Qabbalistic literature, a body of esoteric learning and occult practice which the Geonim did not dare endorse completely or repudiate altogether. The Qaraites took advantage of the embarrassment of the Geonim concerning these lush outcroppings of Jewish mysticism, citing the productions of theosophy and superstition as unmistakable stigmata of the corruption of rabbinic Judaism.[17]

In the same rationalistic spirit they criticized the practice of distributing amulets to the sick, decried the popular practice of praying on the graves of saints and protested against the widespread custom of lighting candles, offering incense, making vows, and arranging celebrations on the sacred spots.[18] To the credit of their incipient rationalism, we may also cite their decision to equalize the status of the woman with that of the man in regard to divorce, their protest against the contemptuous attitude of the schools in the Talmud toward the ignorant masses, their opposition to the deeply rooted dogma affirming the resurrection of the dead, and their reinterpretation in naturalistic fashion of the commonly accepted Biblical tale that Elijah ascended bodily to heaven.[19] Some of the Qaraites, at least, acknowledged explicitly the relative truth of the Mohammedan and Christian faiths, believing that both Jesus and Mohammed were true prophets who brought authentic messages of redemption to millions of pagan people.

Anan's injunction against the study of astronomy was probably based upon the close association between astronomy and astrology in his day.[20] The basic belief of astrology—to wit, the assertion that man's fate is determined by the stars—was obnoxious to the Qaraitic teachers, since it implied the belief that man was not morally free. Indeed, the belief that man was designed to be utterly free, standing completely on his own before God, was one of the most fundamental convictions of Qaraism. Man's fate was not determined by the stars, nor even by inexorably functioning laws of nature, but by the direct operation of the will of God. This firmly held principle of an immediate contact between God and man led some Qaraitic teachers to the conclusion that the advice of physicians must not be sought in the event of illness, except for such wounds as are caused by human or external agencies.[21] The followers of Anan assumed that diseases are the marks of divine wrath and that every individual must rely upon his own prayers and good deeds to win divine favor and His healing. Suffering is a road to repentance.

The passionate insistence of the Qaraites upon human freedom is appreciated the more keenly when it is seen against the background of the first theoretical controversy in Islam, between the "Kadariya" and the "Jabariya." The latter party was so impressed with the principle of God's omnipotence that it declared all events to be directly determined by God, leaving no domain for the automatic operation of laws of nature, nor any room at all for human initiative. The deeds of each person were determined by the divine will, as well as the rewards and punishments appertaining to them. The former party revolted against these morbid teachings, which seemed to agree with the literal meaning of the Koran and with the fatalistic mood of Orthodox Moslems. To the "Kadariya" the quality of divine justice was pre-eminent. How could the just God punish people for acts which they did not freely choose? The Qaraites favored the liberal, humanistic approach of the "Kadariya," developing the implications of the principle of individual freedom with relentless determination and frequently with misguided logic.

The emphasis placed by the Qaraites on the range and effectiveness of human freedom is evidenced in their renewed Messianic fervor. The founder of the Qaraitic sect was closely associated with the sorrowing sectarians, the "Mourners for Zion" (*Abalai Zion*), who did not drink wine nor eat meat, "groaning and moaning" for the destruction of Jerusalem. The early Qaraites dressed in black garments and consciously cultivated the somber spirit of melancholia in order that they might be numbered among the "moaners and groaners" foreseen by the prophet Ezekiel (9:4). This penitential and sorrowful mood was by no means a natural reaction to an unforgettable tragedy of the distant past, but a deliberate endeavor to hasten the advent of the Redeemer. Already in the Talmud an intimate association between mourning and redemption was assumed. "He who mourns over Jerusalem will be privileged to see its rebuilding."[22] To keep the longing for redemption fresh and strong, Anan changed the formula of the *Berochoth* from the traditional " Blessed art Thou, O Lord, our God, King of the universe . . ." to " Blessed is the Lord, out of Zion." To give concrete expression to their longing for redemption, the Qaraites launched a sustained and widespread agitation among their followers to migrate to Jerusalem, or at least to make it possible for some members of their communities to live and pray in Jerusalem. An early Qaraite manifesto reads:

> And know that the wicked in Israel say one to another, " It is not for us to come to Jerusalem, until He shall gather us in as He had scattered us." But these are the words of fools, who anger the Lord. For even if it were not a divine commandment to come to Jerusalem in bitter mourning, we should have understood it, with our rational faculties, that the rebuked should come penitently to plead and pray before the gates of Him who rebuked them. . . . Before the ingathering of the exiles, come to Jerusalem and stand before the Lord, changing guards of prayer day and night. . . . It is for you, our brethren, the children of Israel, to go out of all countries, you who fear the Lord, ere troubles and vicissitudes overtake all lands. . . . You who seek the Lord should now leave, to precede the many that will follow, as the rams precede the sheep.
>
> But if you will not come, because you are hustling and bustling in your business, then send from every city five men, together with their sustenance, that we might be one society to pray before the Lord constantly on the mountains of Jerusalem. . . .[23]

Believing that the deeds of man determine his fate, the Qaraites could not resign themselves to the thought that the hour of redemption was predetermined; that the long painful exile was decreed inexorably, regardless of penitence and piety. Did not even the Talmudic rabbis declare that penitence could bring about immediate redemption?[24] If, then, Jewish redemption was withheld in spite of persistent abasement and endless penitence, might it not be that the teaching of the rabbis was at fault? Perhaps, then, Jewish piety was misdirected by the Geonim, who taught the people to accept the authority of the Talmudic sages instead of the rule of His written word and the living message of a pious conscience. Accordingly, the Qaraites were convinced that only a radical return to pure Judaism, such as they championed, could result in the consummation which rabbinic Judaism had failed to achieve, and hasten the advent of the Messiah.

A tenth-century Qaraite writes: "And know that it is our obligation to warn our brothers, the children of Israel, and to rebuke them. For the kingdom of the house of David has not yet appeared, nor will it arrive unless we repent and bring Israel back to God."[25]

The emphasis of the Qaraites on rationality, conscience and freedom was potentially capable of evoking a thoroughly liberal movement in Judaism. However, the objective situation of the Jewish people was so weak and precarious as to stifle the full flowering of a liberal faith. Scattered through many lands, as the Jews then were, subject everywhere to the double operation of debilitating, ruthless pressures on the one hand, and seductive enticements to conversion on the other, they could ill afford the luxury of untrammeled individualism in the field of religion. The Jewish will to live, aroused and overstimulated by the persistent awareness of living on the brink of disaster, could not but direct the tenacious loyalties of the people toward the established institutions of collective authority. In the exigencies of a battle, the virtues of discipline and obedience prevail over those of freedom and thought. The Qaraites, too, found it impossible to order the life of their followers entirely on the basis of individual freedom, and, for the sake of communal harmony, they reintroduced the principle of *Sebel Hayerushah*, "the burden of inheritance," utilizing a variant of the rabbinic ban, to achieve a measure of discipline in their ranks.

Furthermore, the need of providing powerful motivation for Jewish living imposed a definite limit upon the extent of rationalism and universal tolerance that Judaism could teach without inviting complete disintegration. Manifestly, a thorough rationalism, exclusively esteeming the universal principles of conscience, reason and piety, might have led to the detached philosophical conviction that the difference between Judaism and other faiths was relatively unimportant, since all Judaic religions fostered the living kernel of faith and differed only in symbols and rites. In the straitened circumstances of the Jewish people, such an attitude might have produced a veritable flood of conversions to the dominant faith. If all religions of monotheism are substantially the same, why sacrifice the wide horizons of the prevailing religion and risk even life and limb for the sake of Jewish symbolism?

So the tolerance of Qaraism toward other faiths was forcibly stunted and prevented from attaining full development. The Qaraites came to insist on the principle of segregation from the Gentiles to an even greater extent than the rabbinic Jews, prohibiting the food which was in any manner touched or prepared by non-Jews. The Talmudic ban applied only to food which was completely cooked or baked by non-Jews.[26]

Because of the same unyielding pressure of circumstances, the early Qaraite teachers opposed the study of secular branches of learning. Moved by the inflexible zealotry of single-minded piety, they begrudged the time students would use in the study of secular subjects, since that time could be spent so much more profitably in the learning of the word of God. But in addition to their jealous zeal for the study of Torah, they feared the destructive effects upon their followers of the extension of their rationalistic attitude into the domain of secular culture. Once reason and conscience are recognized as basic principles of conduct, the foundation is laid for the development of cultural values that can be shared alike by Jews and non-Jews. But such a neutral domain of culture would expand of its own momentum, preparing the ground for Jewish assimilation and disintegration. In the eighth century, the Jews in the Moslem world were hardly prepared for the blandishments of the secular world. Rationalists are prone to a progressive restriction of the sphere of faith, reducing its hold to the point where contact between Jews and Gentiles would grow apace while the cohesive power needed for the maintenance of the Jewish community would steadily diminish. Sensing this danger, the Qaraites were forced in practice to restrict the domain of free inquiry, even while in theory they extolled the role of the individual's private judgment.

The rationalistic spirit inherent in Qaraism was also counteracted by the literalism and the ascetic pietism of the sect. Repudiating the Talmud along with its Gaonic interpreters, the Qaraites lavished all their love and devotion upon the literal meaning of the Scriptures, in utter neglect of the need for religious development and the progressive adaptation of rituals to life. In their attempt to turn back centuries of Jewish history and return to the original, the unspoiled faith, they developed puritan attitudes and rigid laws which were all but unlivable. The ascetic quality of their piety, deriving from the duty to mourn over the destruction of the Holy Temple, was superimposed upon the old, rigorous practices which the Talmud abolished, and combined with a letter-bound philosophy of interpretation which multiplied the austerities and self-mortifying rites of religion. The result was a virtual proliferation of dolorous ordinances, obedience to which gave these sectarians the aspect of lifelong mourners. They prohibited the lighting of candles for the Sabbath and the holidays, the eating of veal and mutton, the drinking of wine, the indulgence of conjugal love on the nights of the Sabbath and the festivals. These prohibitions were later relaxed, especially among the European Qaraites, through the efforts of scholars who lived in Constantinople. Nevertheless, the ordinance of Qaraite assemblies in Luck and Troki, of Poland and Lithuania, in the seventeenth and eighteenth centuries reaffirm such restrictions as not to promenade on the Sabbath and the festivals, not to permit the children to play in the streets, not to ask a Gentile to kindle the fire in the stove on the Sabbath.[27] In addition, they enjoined a number of fasts and special prayers, going so far as to ordain a seventy-day period of fasting, a three-day fast on Purim and a midnight service of lamentation on the night of the Sabbath. They introduced symbolic reminders of the destruction of Jerusalem in the course of the performance of the circumcision ceremony and in the midst of the celebration of a wedding. Before the performance of the rite of circumcision, the *Hakham* reminds the gathering of the " destruction and desolation of the Holy Temple."[28] In the course of the wedding, they would sprinkle the bride and groom with ashes and recite, " If I forget thee, Jerusalem. . . ."[29]

They frequently reckoned time according to the date of the first or the second destruction of Jerusalem.[30] For many centuries their followers could be distinguished from a distance by their dark attire and emaciated appearance. It was only by slow stages that the Qaraites outgrew the severe rigorism of the first centuries of the movement. But even in the late medieval and modern period, their Sabbaths remained joyless and cheerless, with the European Qaraites approximating most closely the practice among rabbinic Jews, and the Oriental Qaraites clinging to the gloomy customs of earlier years. Their synagogues were crippled, in addition, by the revival of the obsolete laws of ritual purity, for both men and women, which made it impossible on any one day for a large proportion of their people to enter the sacred precincts of the synagogue.

Nevertheless, in spite of their severity the Qaraites constituted a leaven of rationalism and criticism in the Jewish world of the medieval era. Their very presence necessitated an unceasing re-examination of the laws of Judaism, and a continuous scrutiny of the historical sources of the Jewish faith. Their persistent criticism of the legendary lore in the Talmud helped to prevent the expressions of naïve folk piety from being congealed into dogmas. While rabbinic mystics continued to spin their fantastic speculations to those initiated in the mysteries, the collections of Aggadah, within the Talmud and outside of it, did not receive the unqualified and authoritative endorsement of the Geonim. Compelled as they were to defend the veracity of the chain of tradition and the illustrious character of the Talmudic sages, the Geonim solved their dilemma by neither sanctioning nor repudiating the legends of the Talmud in a forthright manner. Those Geonim who were philosophic-minded attempted to read new meanings into the old naïve words.[31] The resonant call of the Qaraites for a return to the Holy Scriptures led to the revival of the use of the Hebrew language and of the study of its grammar. The rabbinic Jews were compelled to follow their opponents in these studies in order to be able to counter the aggressive propaganda of these Jewish protestants. In their zeal for the purity of Jewish monotheism, the Qaraites also turned the attention of their contemporaries to the study of the philosophy of the Jewish religion. Early Jewish rationalism, reaching its climax in the philosophy of Saadia Gaon of the tenth century, owes its origin to the bold criticism of the intrepid sectarians. The propaganda of the Qaraites attained the apex of its effectiveness in the tenth century, when the institutions of the Gaonite and the Exilarchate began to decline. But, though they did not succeed in winning more than a small minority to their cause, they managed not only to survive but also to produce valiant writers and erudite scholars down to modern times. The Qaraites ventured into the field of philosophical speculations, in advance of their rabbinic brethren, identifying themselves completely with the Mutazilite school of thought among the Arabs. In common with the Moslem theologians, they elaborated a rationalistic theology, which emphasized the principles of God's unity, incorporeality, man's freedom and

God's justice. Like their liberal Moslem confrères they insisted that man's concept of the rational and the good is a valid clue to an understanding of the divine will. In contradiction to the Orthodox Moslem teaching that whatever the Lord commands is good, they declared that the Lord commands only that which is good. So strongly were the views of the Qaraites and the Mutazilites identified that the works of one group could easily be credited to the other.[32]

Nevertheless. as we shall see in the next chapter, it was not a Qaraitic scholar but a rabbinic philosopher, Saadia Gaon, who produced the greatest philosophical work of this school in Judaism.

CHAPTER SIX

THE RISE OF JEWISH RATIONALISM

THE rationalistic movement in Jewish philosophy found its first great exponent in Saadia Gaon, who was born in Egypt at the end of the ninth century (882-942 C.E.), By the sheer brilliance of rare genius he achieved so unique a reputation for erudition that the Exilarch of Babylonian Jewry chose him for the highest post of religious authority, that of the Gaonate of Sura. Though he did not belong to one of the Gaonic families and did not acquire his learning in either one of the two Babylonian Academies, Saadia attained this commanding position in rabbinic Judaism at an early age. Through his efforts the authority of the Babylonian Gaonate was upheld against the pretensions of the Palestinian scholars, who promulgated a calendar that differed, in respect to the dates set for the various festivals, from the official calendar of the Babylonian Gaonate. Saadia, too, combated the Qaraites most vehemently, as well as other heresies which flourished in his time. Of special interest is Saadia's effort to answer the two hundred strictures against the Bible, which a non-Orthodox scholar by the name of Chivi Ha-Balchi propounded. Chivi's naturalistic critique was so successful that a number of Persian communities employed his anthology of approved Biblical selections as a textbook for the instruction of their young.

SAADIA GAON

In Saadia, rabbinic Judaism acquired an unexcelled and indefatigable champion who reasserted its basic insights in clear and ringing terms. Saadia's rationalism is of particular interest because it is at once thoroughgoing and dogmatic, uncompromising in its sincere reliance upon rational thought and yet essentially uncritical and narrowly circumscribed. In his fundamental hypothesis, affirming the capacity of reason to explore the nature of the universe and to discover the meaning of God and of revelation, he ranges himself on the side of the rationalists and declares:

> I state it as a rule, that all which may be found in the books and words authored by one of us, who believe in One God, speaking of Our Creator and His deeds in language which true speculation contradicts, we may be absolutely certain that the expressions are used figuratively. Those who search for their true meaning will find it. . . .[1]

On the other hand, Saadia wrote a commentary to *Sefer Yezirah*, the classic text of proto-Qabbalah, which is an expression of the anti-intellectualist, mystical trend in Judaism. As we shall see in the sequel, Saadia lived in an age of "primitive rationalism," when the content of rational thought was extremely meager and circumscribed.

As an enthusiastic believer in the adequacy of the human intellect for the quest of metaphysics, Saadia was puzzled by the multifarious follies of mankind. Patiently he set to work to discover the sources of error and to classify them. Basically, religious truth is as demonstrable as the solution of a mathematical problem. The fear that rational reflection might lead to atheism is justified only in the case of the common untutored masses, who are steeped in myths and superstitions. The Lord revealed His Word, through His prophets, not because it was inaccessible to human reason, but on account of the slow and gradational process of human speculation. Sustained reflection cannot but lead to truth. But the flesh is weak. Hence the dangers deriving from laziness, especially the failure to follow the dialectic effort to its logical end. Knowing that the human race is rational only by starts and spurts, the Lord revealed the Torah in order that people might not be "without a faith" before they have successfully reasoned things out for themselves.

> Because He knew, in His Wisdom, that the goals of the dialectical process cannot be reached save in a considerable measure of time. . . . Thus, women and young people and those who do not know how to reason will still have a perfect faith.

He takes issue with all who doubt the capacity of reason to achieve full and absolute certainty, singling out for special criticism those who believe that rational knowledge comes in lightning-like flashes of insight—a principle which Maimonides later embraced. Manifestly, intuitions of this type can be corroborated only by their recurrence, not by the processes of logical analysis in the broad light of day. Saadia recognizes that "their creaturely nature makes people subject to doubt and error,"[2] but the power of reason, if sustained and methodically carried out, cannot but lead to the final and absolute truths of revelation.

> For the disciples, when they have completed their studies, will find no dispute or confusion whatsoever. . . .
>
> The Lord informed us that complete clarification will come to us if we search and reason in every phase of the revelation which he gave us through His prophet, and He assured us that the disbelievers will find no argument in the Torah against us and that there is no valid evidence for those who doubt our faith.[3]

After the fashion of the prevailing liberal wing in Moslem thought (the Mutazilites, believers in the unity and justice of God), Saadia begins his demonstration of the existence and nature of God, by pointing out the obvious "creaturely" character of the physical universe. Everything that we apprehend with our senses is in a state of perpetual flux. But change involves the double process of ceasing to be and coming into being. Hence the cosmos in all its complex and ceaselessly varying phases is an ever-dying and ever-newly emerging universe. The power of permanence cannot inhere in it, otherwise it would resist changes, in at least one or another aspect. Therefore the ultimate cause of this perceived universe is to be found outside the flux of existence—in a Supreme Being, Who is not of the world and Who is not subject to the all-pervasive process of change.

God is outside this changing universe, transcending even the dimensions of space and time, for these dimensions are in reality qualities of physical nature. Can we envision time or space without relating them to actual things, as they change in the flux of existence? But God is eternal, outside the flow of time, noncorporeal, beyond the reach of spatial dimensions, without biography. Since we derived the existence of God from the variability of every phase of physical existence, it follows that God is unchanging, "for if any one change were possible in regard to him, all changes of this world would likewise be rendered possible."[4] He would no longer be the unconditioned ground of all existence.

Though God is unlike the material world and everything of which we have any knowledge, we may nevertheless assert that "He is one, living, all-powerful and all-wise, with no thing or action being comparable to Him."[5]

These qualities are implied in the concept of a Creator. He is one because multiplicity assumes spatial barriers. Furthermore, if one Creator is logically sufficient, why assume more? By the same token, He is all-powerful and all-wise, since the effect of His power and His wisdom are manifested in the intricate design and orderly functioning of nature. He is living, we know, for He governs the events of every moment in relation to the totality of His design, combining power over the physical universe with reason, will, and purpose. As human beings, we think of the quality of life as involving the perpetual process of change, but life is conceivable apart from a body as a spirit relating all events to His purpose.

The Scriptures speak of the Deity as if He were corporeal, referring to His "right hand," His "eyes," His "face," His "feet," but such expressions are not to be taken literally. They are attempts to express the qualities and powers of the Deity in terms that are humanly comprehensible; that is, by analogy to physical objects. Since we think in physical terms, we are compelled to refer to Him in words which, in their strict sense, do not apply to Him. How else express His ineffable nature?

> If we were to speak of Him in true language, we should have to forego and reject such assertions as the following—that He hears and sees, that He loves and wills, with the result that we should be left with nothing but His existence alone. . . .[6]

As a believing Jew, Saadia was certain not only of God's existence, but also of His having revealed His will through Moses. According to the Torah, some things and some actions are hateful to the Deity, while some things and some actions are pleasing to Him. But how can we speak of the one who is not subject to any qualifications as either loving or hating? Are not love and hate emotional qualities, involving changes in the nature of their subject? Saadia's reply is as follows:

> The fact that we find it said that He loves or hates things is to be understood in the sense that everything commanded by Him is called "loved" by Him and every action enjoined and prohibited by him is called "hated," in regard to Him.[7]

Saadia does not inquire whether the expressions of God's will through the medium of prophets who lived at various times are not themselves temporal modifications of His being. We might ask, did not a change take place in His nature when He emerged from the stillness of eternity to pronounce the deathless words at Sinai? Saadia would answer this question in the negative because God is essential activity, the source of all activity. He is the source of all change, but unchangeable through outside efforts and influence. Saadia thought of all the energy in the universe as manifesting the ceaseless activity of the will of God, since, in his day, nature was regarded as so much passive matter, moved every moment by a fresh impulse of the Divine will. Unknown in his day was the reasoning in Aristotle's treatise on physics, namely the analogy comparing nature to a self-perpetuating machine, acting in accord with laws that inhere in its very being. Saadia, along with the contemporary Mutazilite thinkers, assumed that the motive power for all the changing events in nature derived directly from God. Activity in time is, therefore, of the essence of the Supreme Being and not inconsistent with the time-space transcendence of the divine nature.

However, Saadia was disturbed by the fact that the prophets speak occasionally of visions of the Deity. These visions cannot be regarded merely as the vagaries of poetic fancy or as the fantasies of an excited imagination. For if it be admitted that the uncertain faculty of imagination is involved in the visions of the prophets, how can we tell where imagination stops and true vision begins? Therefore Saadia assumes that the visions seen by the prophets refer to an especially created pattern of light and glory, " superior to the angels,"[8] which God fashioned for the purpose of verifying His Word to His prophets. This mythical creation of unearthly radiance and splendor is called in Scripture " the glory of God," *Kevod Adonai,* and the sages refer to it as *Shechinah.* It is a mark of honor for a prophet to hear the divine command issuing out of this brilliant effulgence, which may or may not appear in human form. Saadia appears uncertain whether Moses saw only this vision, since Scripture affirms that he spoke with God " face to face,"[9] but in his commentary to Exodus 33, he interprets the vision of Moses in the cleft of the rock as referring to this " created light " (or *Nivra*).

Referring to Moses' plea that he behold the glory of God and the divine response that Moses may see God's back, but not His front, Saadia explains the passage as follows:

> I wish to say in explanation of this entire passage that the Creator possesses an effulgence which He created and showed to the prophets in order that they might be convinced that the words they hear are indeed from the Creator. When one of them sees it, he declares, " I have seen the glory of God." Some, too, speaking figuratively, say, " I saw God ". . . . But when they perceive this light, they cannot endure contemplating it, because of its tremendous potency and splendor. Their physical constitution might disintegrate and the spirit might depart from him who looks at it, as it is said, " lest they burst toward God to see, and many of them will fall."[10]

Therefore, Moses, our teacher, requested that the Creator might strengthen him, so that he might be enabled to contemplate that light. He was told that this effulgence is exceedingly potent when it first appears, and that it is not possible for him to see and contemplate it without dying. But when he is protected by a cloud, or by something like it, until the first radiance of that light passes, as it was said, " and I shall put my hand over it until I pass," it becomes possible for him to endure this overwhelming experience. Thus, when the initial radiance of that light passed, He removed the covering thing from Moses, and he looked at the latter part of it, as it was said, " And I shall remove My hand, and you will see My back." But it is false to assume that any prophet could see the Creator Himself.

This concept of *Kavod Nivra*, a created aura or effulgence, the one end of which is too exalted to be seen even by Moses and the other end being accessible to the vision of the inspired, was destined to undergo a long and complex development in the literature of Qabbalah. For Saadia, this concept, the seed which is already assumed in the Targumim, constituted the bridge between philosophic speculation and popular religion, making possible the retention of the time-space transcendence of the Deity, while allowing for the literal truth of prophetic inspiration and the assumption of the holiness of special places.

> It cannot be maintained that the Creator occupies space. . . . Only things that are material occupy space. . . . When the prophets speak of Him as being in the sky, they intend to point to His greatness and glory, because the heavens are to them loftier than anything else. . . . The expression, " and the Lord dwells in Zion," is used in a figurative sense, for the pur-

pose of magnifying the importance and nature of that place. Also, it was
there that His created light was revealed, which we mentioned earlier and
which is called " *Shechinah* " and glory. . . .[11]

As a full-blooded optimist, Saadia boldly asserts that life is
good and that the goodness of God's nature is the reason for His
decision to create the universe. But His goodness being infinite,
can we assume that He designed for man only the limited measure
of happiness that is attainable in this world? To Saadia this
assumption was unthinkable. Hence he derived the doctrine of
revelation as well as creation from the belief in divine goodness.
In His infinite love for His human creatures, God gave them
precepts and commandments so that they might merit "final bliss
and perfect happiness" in the hereafter. Was it not possible for
God to award so happy a fate for man without subjecting him to
a special set of ordinances? The possibility cannot be gainsaid,
but would it be just or rational? As Saadia saw it, the enjoyment
of a reward is doubled when it is truly deserved.

> Reason decrees that in the enjoyment of aught that is good, the portion
> of those who work and deserve their reward should be double that of those
> who have not done a thing to merit divine favor, but the Lord was simply
> kind to them.[12] Reason does not allow that the two should be placed on
> an equal footing. Since this is so, our Creator inclined, in our case, to the
> better part, allowing for our advantage twice the reward that would have
> been our due if we had not performed any deeds. . . ."

Revelation, therefore, is an expression of divine solicitude for
human welfare. Saadia, accordingly, assumed a series of revelations that came to mankind prior to the advent of Moses, since
the good God could not possibly have left mankind for any
length of time without a knowledge of His will.[13]

It is interesting to note that the difference between those who
lead a good life, apart from any revelation, and those who, in
addition, abide by the revealed Commandments is that the latter
receive a double reward. The multitudes without the law are not
condemned to eternal perdition or to the fires of purgatory or
even to the desolate shadows of Sheol. For them, as for the people
of revelation, the good God had designed a radiant destiny, but
"reason demands" that those who perform additional religious
deeds should receive a double share of heavenly bliss.

The Commandments of the Lord fall into two parts: "rational

commandments," the validity of which all rational beings are compelled to recognize, and "traditional commandments," which cannot be justified altogether by the canons of reason. It is the *mizvoth* of the latter category which were designed for the purpose of increasing the reward of the pious. Thus Saadia writes:

> And the second category consists of commandments which reason does not decree to be either inherently good or inherently evil. By His command and exhortation, the Lord added them for our benefit, to increase our reward and bliss on their account. . . . Nevertheless, when we examine them carefully, we shall find advantages and rational values, at least in part. . . .[14]

In addition to the many opportunities they afford for earning additional rewards in the hereafter, the *mizvoth* fulfill an educational function here on earth. Thus, the dietary laws serve to counteract totemism, or the worship of animals. Hailing from Egypt, Saadia was keenly aware of the danger of ascribing sanctity to animals. The fact that the meat of some animals is permitted militates against the tendency to endow any animal with the magic of taboos; the animals that may not be eaten are declared to be unclean, and the unclean cannot possibly be identified with the sacred.[15] One reason for animal sacrifices is to impress upon the sinner the dread consequence of sin, for the slaughtering and dismembering that is administered to the body of the animal should, but for the grace and forgiveness of God, have been done to the one who brings the sin-offering.[16] The scapegoat, taken to "Azazel" and cast down from a desolate rock in the wilderness, was not a grudging gift to Satan, but a sacrifice in behalf of the Israelites as the goat marked "for God" was evidently sacrificed in behalf of the priests.[17]

If revelation is not entirely subject to rational criticism, how is the true revelation to be recognized? We have already stated that to the agent of revelation, the prophet, a special sign was given, authenticating the message he heard. "Thus, a sign was shown unto them, which would begin with the opening of the verbal message and end at its close; such as a pillar of smoke or of fire or a bright light. . . ."[18]

But how are the people to tell whether the testimony of any prophet was true or false?

When the prophet presents himself for the first time to the people, he must offer a sign, for the Creator, blessed be He, does not transform the substance of things before He informs the people of His intention, in order that His act might lead men to believe in prophecies.[19]

When such a "sign" is given, the people are obliged to "declare the prophet to be holy and to believe in him." To be sure, sects here and there might be misled by false prophets, but "in the great community, opinions will not differ."[20] Saadia thus enunciates the principle of confident reliance on the general consensus of the loyal community. Consciously or not, he embraces the Orthodox Moslem principle of *Ijma,* based on a saying of Mohammed: "My people will never agree to accept that which is false."

Remembering the many pseudo prophets and pseudo Messiahs in Babylonia, two centuries before his time, Saadia asserts that the gift of prophecy is confined to the land of Israel.[21] He further maintains that the Torah cannot change, since the will of God, of which it is the expression, is not subject to change. Furthermore, Scripture declares Israel to be eternal, but "our people is a people only through its Torah."[22] In turn, the Torah is authenticated by the tradition of great miracles, performed through Moses, especially the miracle of manna in the desert, than which no evidence could be more compelling.[23]

However, if miracles authenticate a prophet, may not other faiths lay claim to similar certification? Indeed, whatever qualities other religions may lack, they always ascend the stage of history with an impressive assemblage of claimed miracles. At this point Saadia hedges somewhat, reverting to his rationalistic thesis that every faith must approve itself primarily in the light of reason.

"For the reason we believe in Moses is not alone the account of the signs and wonders that he performed, but our reason for believing in him or any other prophet is that he exhorts us to do that which is right. . . ." No, we shall reject him if he calls upon us "to follow that which is contrary to our reason, which teaches that justice is good and falsehood is abominable."[24] So the final decision rests with our faculty of rational judgment. To Saadia, reason was not merely a faculty of logic, but a source of moral judgment; intelligence and conscience were inseparable, different facets of the one God-given power. No succeeding revelation could possibly contradict the prior revelations of Torah and conscience.

Since our sense of justice is a reflection of the clear and immutable principles of divine reason, we are justified in inferring that God cannot act unjustly. It follows that man's power to choose between good and evil must be completely free from any interference. Not having assumed the operation of inexorable laws in physical nature, Saadia is not worried by any interference with man's freedom of will that might derive from his physical nature. But he is at great pains to prove that the Creator does not prejudge the actions of men and does not predetermine their lives. "For the Creator exerts no leadership in the actions of people, and does not compel them either to serve Him or to disobey Him."[25] Man's freedom provides the central motif in the Divine drama of creation. For its sake, evil is intermingled with good, and many opportunities are provided for the foolish and the wicked to go astray.

Saadia poses the ancient paradox of divine foreknowledge and human freedom. If God knows in advance what men will do and if, as we must presume, His wisdom cannot fail, how can we assert that men are free to choose? The answer is that God's knowledge is as that of a wise spectator, who assesses the probabilities of a series of events, achieving a perfect score, time after time, without interfering physically in the actual process, which remains a matter of chance. Hence, conceivably God's foreknowledge could be refuted by human acts. Saadia was not aware of the deeper levels of this problem; the fact that man is inwardly determined by the play of physical forces within his heart, leaving no room for inner freedom.

To Saadia the whole universe was the stage for the operation of human freedom. He was certain that, as the earth is the center of the universe, so man is the center and focus of all creation. Man's littleness in comparison with the majestic vastness of the sun and the stars is no proof of his insignificance.

> For even though his body be small, his soul is wider than the heavens and earth, since his knowledge embraces everything that is in them, rising to an apprehension of what is above them, and of that in which they have their being; namely, the Creator, may He be blessed. . . .[26]

The counterpart of man's freedom is divine reward and punish-

ment. In order to make possible a measure of genuine freedom, it was necessary for God to arrange matters so that the wicked would not be fully punished for their sins in this world nor the righteous automatically rewarded. Else people would choose righteousness not for its own sake, but because of the rewards attendant upon it. Therefore God ordered matters so that the wicked are frequently rewarded in this life for the few good deeds they occasionally perform, in order that, following their death, they might go straight to hell. Similarly, the righteous may suffer on earth in punishment for those minor sins, which are virtually unavoidable, even for saints, in order to increase their heavenly reward for their patience and forbearance. "With all this, He does not forsake His servants in this world, without rewarding them for their good deeds and punishing them for their evil actions."[27]

The effect of good and evil deeds upon the soul is immediate and automatic, though the results may not be apparent in the sight of human eyes.

> We affirmed that the soul is a pure rational substance, purer than the substance of the stars and the spheres. . . . After this, it became clear to me that as the soul acquires merits it becomes still purer and more luminous . . . and that, as its sins accumulate, it becomes opaque and dark. . . .[28]

These sins and merits refer to deeds, since thoughts are not punishable. Man is not saved by dogma, or condemned for deviations in belief. Saadia's liberalism, however, stops short of tolerance for atheism. "Among all the things for which man is punishable, there is no precept relating to matters of thought or conscience, save the denial of the Creator, for this is a sin that man can reach only through his thought. . . ."[29]

But, though a person is permitted to speculate concerning all matters of faith, he must not allow his fancy to entertain interpretations of the commandments that deviate from the established norms, lest he fall into the dark errors of Qaraism. "And he who speculates about the commandments, generating doubts concerning the law, belongs in the category of the false prophets. . . ."[30]

With a few exceptions all sins may be wiped away by an act of sincere repentance. Saadia is extremely liberal in his conception of repentance, requiring neither ascetic exercises for the mortification of the flesh, nor a total inner transformation of the sinner:

And I desire to explain further that when a person consents whole-heartedly, at the time of his repentance, not to repeat a sin, then his repentance is acceptable. And if his lust should lead him thereafter to repeat his sin, his repentance is not negated, but all the sins which he committed, before repenting, are forgiven to him.[31]

This definition may be contrasted with that of the Talmud which states that repentance is achieved, when, upon the recurrence of the same temptation, the sinful act is not repeated.[32] This test is generalized in the statement of Maimonides that repentance is achieved " when the Creator, Who knows all secrets, testifies " that the person will not sin again in similar circumstances.[33]

BAHYA BEN JOSEPH

The philosophy of Saadia was enriched and deepened by the profound overtones of piety in the popular classic, *Duties of the Heart*, written between 1100 and 1156 C.E. Little is known of the author of this gem of pietistic literature, save that he lived in Mohammedan Spain and held the office of *Dayyan*, or judge of the Jewish community. Bahya ben Joseph Ibn Pakuda composed his major opus in the first half of the twelfth century, when the full impact of Aristotelianism was not yet felt and when the climate of philosophical thought did not differ markedly from that of the time of Saadia.

Bahya is as optimistic about the aid which religion might receive from rational reflection as his illustrious predecessor, if not more so. He recommends the constant study of Saadia's book, elaborating and refining the latter's proofs for the existence of God. However, his chief concern is not the exposition of a system of thought, but the detailed application of religious and philosophical thought to the actual problems of living. The *Duties of the Heart* is a classic example of the *mussar* literature, which flourished in almost every period and which translated the abstract teachings of the philosophers and the Qabbalists into concrete maxims for the guidance of the individual. The *mussar* books deal with ideas as springs of action, examining not so much their mutual consistency as their import for the vocation and destiny of man. They are popular works, not in the sense of superficiality or lightness of exposition, but because their orientation and content are life-centered.

Bahya's main purpose is to direct attention to the "inner service" that man owes to God, exposing to view the emotional and intellectual components of piety, without which the mechanical observance of the Commandments is meaningless. In his introduction, he summarizes these "commandments of the heart" as follows:

> That we believe in a Creator who formed the world out of nothing, who is incomparable; that we recognize the meaning of His unity; that we serve Him in our hearts; that we reflect on the wonder of His creations so that they might be signs for us, pointing to Him; that we trust Him, yield to Him and fear Him; that we tremble and feel shame in the recognition of His scrutiny of our inner and outer deeds; that we yearn to do His will; that we devote all our deeds to the hallowing of His name; that we love Him and love those who love Him, in order that we might come nigh unto Him, that we hate His enemies. . . .

The author realized that the depths of the soul cannot be fully plumbed, but he hoped that each person would continue the task of self-examination and self-purification, once the method is pointed out to him.

> It may be compared to an astrologer who entered the house of a friend and sensed that a treasure was in it. He searched for it, and, upon finding it, discovered that the silver had turned black, because it was tarnished with rust. Thereupon, he took a small part of it, washed it well with salt and vinegar and then wiped it neatly, until the silver regained its sheen, beauty and splendor. Then the master asked him to clean the rest of it. . . .[34]

The unity of God is not a phrase that one may utter with the lips in prayer, only to forget about it the next moment. Merely to follow tradition, to mouth the prescribed formulae, is not enough; God must be served with the mind, which is His greatest gift to mankind. God's unity means His uniqueness, His difference from all material things and the absence in Him of any attributes and dimensions of matter. Therefore the study of metaphysics is required for the genuine service of the Lord.

> Truly did the philosopher speak when he said that the Cause of causes and the Beginning of all beginnings can be served only by the one who is by nature the prophet of the generation or by the genuine philosopher, on account of his acquired wisdom, but all other people worship one who is not God, because they do not understand an existent, save it be composite. . . .[35]

It follows that God can be worshiped truly only by the one who understands the full import of His unity, "knowing the proofs for His existence and being capable of arriving at the true conception of His unity by the way of dialectic and the right rational argument. . . ."[36] The pursuit of philosophical speculation is thus an integral element of piety, "for we cannot be certain that those who accept His unity on the ground of tradition will not associate others to Him in worship."[37]

In his proofs for the existence and unity of God, Bahya follows the methods of Saadia, but his exposition is direct and popular. He points out that if time had no beginning, it could have no finite parts; if the present moment be thought of as a pencil marking a line on a moving roll of paper, which is the process of time, then if the roll is infinite in length, the present moment could not have been reached. It follows that the world had a beginning; that is, that it was created.[38]

Bahya is especially impressed with the design and intelligence that is evident in every sphere of existence, devoting a whole chapter to detailing the wonders of creation.

> Do you not see that if a person spills ink suddenly on blank paper, it is impossible that the splotch assume the pattern of ordered writing and readable lines, as is done by a pen? And if a man had brought to us a paper with ordered writing on it, such as cannot be done without the employment of a pen, and had said that this pattern of writing was formed by itself, we should have denied it to his face, for it is impossible without the intention of a designer. . . . How much more is it inadmissible to assume in the case of the universe that is infinitely vast, profound and intricate, that it came about without the prevision, wisdom and power of a being that is all-wise and all-powerful?[39]

By these and by similar approved philosophical reflections, Bahya arrives at the concept of a nonmaterial Deity that is the first cause of all existence. He quotes approvingly Aristotle's generalization, "The negative attributes are more true in regard to God than the positive attributes."[40] We can say of God *that He is* and *what He is not*, but not *what He is*.

> Some sages were asked concerning the Creator, "What is He?" They answered, "He is One." Said the questioner, "How is He?" Replied the sages, "He is a great king." Continued the questioner, "And where is He?" The reply was, "In the intuition." But, persisted the questioner, "You did not answer my questions." Replied the sages, "You asked us in words which imply references to creatures, not the Creator, but we indi-

cated to you the qualities which our understanding imputes to Him. Other qualities cannot be applied to Him."

Thus, some sages would say in their prayers, "My God, where can I find Thee? And where cannot I find Thee? Thou art hidden and unseen, but all is filled with Thee. . . ."[41]

Indeed, some forms of speculation in regard to the Deity are worthy, and even obligatory, while uncritical questions are self-stultifying and hazardous, like the attempt to understand the sun by fixing one's unprotected eyes upon it.

Bahya finds no difficulty in reconciling his abstract concept of the Deity with the concrete and personal descriptions of God in the Scriptures. Religion is philosophy brought down to the understanding of the masses. For this purpose God needs to be spoken of in corporeal terms so that all people, the vulgar as well as the sophisticated, might be moved to worship Him.

> The man of heart and understanding will seek to remove the shells of the words and their materiality from the subject and lift it high in his thought, step by step, until he will achieve as much of the truth of the subject as he is able. But the fool thinks of God as He appears to him out of his literal understanding of the idioms of the language. . . . For the expression which seems to convey a corporeal quality does not hurt the understanding person, since he recognizes its true import, but it is useful for the unsophisticated in that it moves his heart and mind to accept the thought of the existence of a Creator, Whom he is obligated to serve.
>
> We may compare the situation to a person who came to visit one of his wealthy friends, bringing with him some cattle. The host, desiring to feed his guest, sent him a great deal of oats and fodder for his cattle, and a little food for himself. Thus the sacred language of the books of our prophets and sages employs many corporeal experiences, in accord with the understanding of the masses . . . but the books contain also a few hints of spiritual ideas for the benefit of the sensitive and thinking people. . . .[42]

Though Bahya seems to accept a purely abstract concept of God, he writes constantly out of a deep awareness of the nearness of the Supreme Being and he does not permit his keen dialectic to interfere with the sentiments and intuitions of his saintly piety. The last nine chapters of his book deal with the various phases of the religious consciousness, as if the first chapter, which expounds the existence and nature of God, had not been written. Indeed, popular pietistic societies among European Jews, down to modern times, would generally omit the first chapter, concentrating all their zeal and enthusiasm upon the study of the rest of the book. Bahya, however, was not consciously inconsistent. In his day a reasoned concept of the Deity did not imply indifference to the fate of individual human beings, nor did it connote the inflexibility of the divine will. Like Saadia, he does not assume the existence of any laws of nature, operating inexorably and uniformly, dealing alike with the righteous and the wicked. Bahya sees the intricate wisdom of the direct intervention of the Deity in all the complex phenomena of nature. In a beautiful passage he compares the innate intelligences observable in living creatures to the rainbow colors which result when the all-inclusive light of the sun strikes a prism of glass.[43] The reflected intelligence of the Deity is especially noticeable in the human personality which is in a real sense a "small universe" or microcosmos.[44] But this intelligence is not an inherent and distinct force in nature, independent of the Creator, but a direct and continuous expression of the divine will. Divine intelligence is the heavenly counterpart of the body of knowledge that we on earth call Torah.

Bahya's intellectualism is directed toward the spiritualization of the Jewish faith. Mere observance of the Commandments is, to him, only the introduction to piety, not its essence nor even its expression.

> Because the service which is in accord with the Torah is as a corridor to the service which is demanded by reason. For piety is as the seed that is planted, and the Torah is as the cultivation of the soil, its plowing and weeding, and the aid from God as the rain which waters it, but the final fruit is the emergence in one's heart of the desire to serve God, for His name's sake, not because of hope of reward or fear of punishment. . . . Also, that the number of the *mizvoth* in the Torah is finite, 613 to be exact, but the *mizvoth* of reason are virtually infinite in number, for as man's knowledge deepens, so does his piety. . . . Thus it was said of some pietists that they were always penitent, for as they grew in the cognition of God, they were constantly made aware of the insufficiency of their prior service. . . .[45]

Reason was, to Bahya, more than an aid to the understanding of the true meaning of the Torah. In the impassioned quest of man's intellect for the fullness of truth Bahya recognized a response of the human soul to the call of God. By searching for truth with unrelenting zeal a man opens his soul to the flow of divine grace. So reason leads man's spirit to that which is beyond all human understanding.

Bahya describes in figurative language a conversation between reason and the soul, in which the former guides the latter toward ever deeper levels of religious truth. Of special interest is the following passage:

> Said the soul, "And what is the good that will come to me when I renounce [all unnecessary pleasures, 'the love of corporeal enjoyments,' 'the love of dominion, pride and jealousy,' 'refinements in speech and the desire to curry the favor of men'] and what is the evil that will come to me if I cling to them?"
>
> Replied reason, "The good is peace of soul and its freedom from the dark gloom of the world, the pleasures of which are mingled with pain and the lusts of which are ephemeral. . . ."

The quest of reason is to subordinate every expression of human life to the service of the Lord.

> He should not think save in remembrance of Him, not look but in His ways, not listen but to His Words, not eat but that which He gives to him, not speculate but concerning His greatness, not serve but through that which He desires, not rejoice but in His service, not seek but His will, not to run but in His mission, not to stop but from going counter to His will, not to sit but in His house, not to get up but in His faith, not to read but His books, not to put on but the garment of His fear, not to sleep but on the bed of His love . . . and so in all his movements, he should not lift a foot or move an eyebrow but so as to fulfill the will of his Master in regard to them.[46]

As reason thus trains man to devote every movement of his body and every tremor of his spirit to God, it assures him that he can rely completely upon the solicitude and concern of His Master. "For no creature is capable of helping or hurting him, save with the permission of the Creator."[47] This assurance leads man to put his entire trust in God, so that all the events and vicissitudes of existence assume a reassuring aspect for him. "In the peace of his soul, the scope of his understanding and the littleness of his worry concerning the problems of this world, he may be compared to a master of alchemy who knows how to turn silver to gold, copper and nickel to silver. . . ."[48]

The pietist will work for a living, but he will not enslave himself for its sake, or be over anxious concerning it, knowing that the Lord will see to his wants. Bahya illustrates this thought with the story of a pietist who undertook an extremely hazardous journey for commercial reasons. In a distant land he met a pagan sage who pointed out to him the contradiction between his exertions in his travels and his faith in God. " If your faith were really sincere, wouldn't you believe that God could supply your necessities in your own city? Why, then, did you undertake to travel to so remote a place? " The pietist found no answer to this query. Returning to his country, he determined never to leave it. . . .[49]

Faith in God leads the pious to work hard for their sustenance, for hard and consistent work is itself a *mizvah*, but they labor without panic or hysteria, in the spirit of trust and devotion. Most people, on the other hand, embitter their lives by their very anxiety for its sustenance:

> They may be compared to a man in the desert who, being very thirsty, came upon a pit of brackish waters, rejoiced greatly with it and drank his fill of it. But, as he rose from the pit, he espied a fountain of sweet waters. Naturally, he regretted his haste in drinking the bitter waters.

Bahya speaks frequently of the virtue of solitude. He does not ask his readers to divorce themselves completely from the affairs of this world, though he upholds the monastic ideal as fitting for the " chosen few."

> It is, therefore, proper that among the people of the Torah there should be individuals who represent this special pattern of piety and who accept all its disciplines, in order that they might serve the people of Torah, by turning them away from the beastly passions of the evil desire. Thus, they minister as spiritual physicians to the souls of men. . . .[50]

As a general rule, Jewish piety requires active participation in the life of the family and the community. Nevertheless, every person should set aside hours, at regular intervals, when he can retreat in thought from the world and let his mind dwell on " the accounting of his soul," and on the love of God.

In the " accounting of the soul," the credit side consists of all actions done for the love of God and the debit side of every other action and inner sentiment. All is evil that is not motivated by the feelings of piety; yes, even the innocent pastimes of life. " For the great enemy which you have in the world is the fund of desire which is poured into the faculties of your soul and which is mingled into the disposition of your spirit."[51] The purpose of all the strategies of piety is " to make reason superior to the passions of the soul and the master of them."[52]

Bahya elaborates on the tactics of piety, especially the lifelong battle against pride and the endless quest for humility. He calls his readers to undertake daily some menial and degrading tasks so that they might become indifferent to the praise and blame of men. He cautions especially against the abuse of the power of speech, citing in illustration the punishment of one who spoke evil of "a dead dog."

> Said one of the pious, " Many people will come to the day of accounting, and when their good deeds are shown to them they will find there merits which they did not earn. They will say, ' We have not done these deeds.' They will then be told, ' One who spoke evil of you earned those merits and they were placed to your account. . . .' "[53]

Humility is the key to all the virtues.

> Said one of the saints to his disciples, " If you did not have any sin I should have feared for you because of that which is greater than sin." The disciples inquired, " What is that which is greater than sin? " Said he, " Pride and hypocrisy."[54]

Lofty as are the demands of Bahya, he does not raise the ideals of piety above the reach of the common people. On the contrary, he makes every effort to persuade his readers that through the power of repentance, the practice of contemplation, and the supreme virtue of humility, they might all attain to the loftiest degrees of spirituality. Conceiving of repentance not as a complete inner transformation but as a yielding of the individual to the divine will, which is followed by a divine act of grace and forgiveness, Bahya brings the opportunity for repentance down to the level of all men.

Repentance is immediately effective and the noblest peaks of piety are surely attainable, because the Creator helps man to rise above himself. If man does all within his power, subjecting his impulses to the service of the Lord, then the Lord " helps him to attain the virtues which are beyond his capacity in the fields of knowledge, service of the heart, and sincerity of conscience."

Constant striving is rewarded with divine teaching, " so lofty and ineffable that it may almost be compared to divine prophecy." The student who strives for wisdom finds in his heart a superior spiritual treasure, which no man could possibly give him. " Man must cultivate the soil and plant the seed of piety, but it is the

Lord who waters the plant and endows it with the power of growth."[55]

Bahya speaks of an infinite number of Commandments, because the practical precepts of Judaism are to him only the beginning of the true service of the Lord. "For the most important purpose of the commandments which relate to the actions of the body is to stimulate awareness of the commandments which are in the heart and conscience, since they are the focal point of divine service and the root of the Torah."[56]

The demands of the Torah are only preliminary exercises, preparing a Jew for the higher degrees of divine service, which transpire within his soul. The inner service of the heart was all-important to Bahya. He was not antinomian. The scrupulous performance of the *mizvoth* was essential, but they were only the first steps in the adventure of piety. And the inner path of worship is infinite, even as the distance from man to God.

> When the believer engages in their observance with heart and conscience, achieving spirituality through them, as much as he is able, the Lord will open for him the gate of spiritual degrees, so that he might attain through them to levels that are above his capacity. . . .[57]

The *mizvoth* are the preliminary steps in the great and arduous task of "polishing the mirror of the soul" that it might behold truly the wisdom of the Lord and His Love.[58]

The final goal of piety is to acquire the pure and unadulterated love of God. When this stage of piety is reached, all the passions of the soul pale; people then "cease to prefer one thing rather than another, trusting in the Creator, that He will select for them that which is good and right. . . . Their own merits appear small in their eyes because of their desire and longing to do the will of the Creator." Occasionally they retreat from the society of men in order to be alone with the memory of God, even as all lovers seek to express their love in solitude.[59]

> But what is the love of God? It is the yearning of the soul and its inclination of its own accord to its Creator, in order to cleave to His superior light . . . when the soul senses that light is added to its substance and power to its spirit, it inclines its desire to Him, fastening its thought and yearning upon Him. . . .[60]

But though the love of God is the end of all strivings of the pious, it is not the beginning of them. "For it is impossible for the love of the Creator to be settled in our hearts if the love of the world is there."[61] It is easy enough to love God superficially, or even occasionally, but in its true form love is the climax in the path of piety, coming, as it were, automatically, after a lifetime of self-discipline and self-examination.

> You will not be able, following all these preparations, to refrain from inclining toward Him, in your heart and conscience, in pure sincerity and perfect faith, yielding your soul to His love and relying upon his pity and the greatness of His mercy; you will not at that time associate the love of anything else to the love of Him. . . . He will be your company in solitude, sitting with you in the deserts; a place full of people will be in your eyes as if it were empty and an empty place as if it were full; you will not be bored by their presence or worried by their absence; you will be always happy with your God, your Creator, delighting in His will and yearning to meet Him. . . .[62]

Bahya's emphasis is consistently on the inwardness of piety. Though he favors occasional retreats into solitude, he rejects the practice of asceticism and the extremism of lifelong hermits, " who are so enamored with the love of the Creator that they cease to think of the love of people. . . . This class of people is furthest removed from the even balance of the Torah, because they forsake the concerns of the world altogether. It is not in keeping with the law of the Torah to retreat completely from the society of men." Somewhat closer to the spirit of the Torah are those who continue to live among people, but who renounce all luxuries and all activities, even those of speech and thought, that do not contribute directly to the cultivation of the love of God.

The one kind of retreat from the world which is always desirable is the one which takes place within the heart of man.

> To withdraw from the world in heart and conscience, but to associate physically with the people of the world, in all the arts of civilization . . . despising this world and its wealth, and yearning for the world to come . . . .
> The pious man shows his joy in his face, but he hides his sorrow in his heart; his sympathy is all-embracing, but his ambition is very weak; he does not remember hatred, nor does he covet, or speak evil of any man; contemptuous of office and despising power; he gives, when asked, and forgives, if robbed . . . softer than butter and sweeter than honey . . . his troubles are many, but his complaints few; when he sees good, he remembers; when he sees evil, he covers up . . . the deeds of others appear to him purer than his own, and every soul is in his eyes nobler than his own; knowing his faults, remembering his sin, loving God . . . associating with the poor, loving the righteous . . . a father to the orphan. . . .[63]

In this total design of piety, every *mizvah* is a reflection of an inner reality. The *mizvoth* of Judaism are outer expressions of the inner "duties of the heart," though the relationship between action and intention is not always apparent. The dietary laws, for instance, were intended to train the Jew in the virtue of self-discipline and to remind him of the duty to serve God. Every forbidden act symbolizes immoral acts that the observant Jew learns to loathe. Likewise, the positive ritual commands of the Torah were designed to recall to us the obligation to dedicate all our waking moments to His service. The *mizvoth* are perpetual reminders of His will.[64] At the same time, the *mizvoth* are popular substitutes for the genuine service of the Lord. In His goodness, God consented to accept ritual acts of devotion, since most people are incapable of attaining true spirituality. He helps the humble worshipers to reach levels of piety that are beyond their strength.[65] And in "the world to come" He grants the purified souls the privilege of "adhering" unto Him and delighting in His supreme light.[66]

MOSES MAIMONIDES

In the philosophy of Moses Maimonides, Jewish rationalism received its classic formulation. Concerned as we are with the evolution of Jewish thought, not the achievements of Jewish philosophers, we need hardly take account of the works of men like Abraham Ibn Daud, who represented the same general approach. So comprehensive was Maimonides' treatment and so overwhelming was his authority that the medieval philosophers who followed him may be considered as commentators upon one or more sections of his monumental *Guide to the Perplexed*. Time and again the zealous champions of Orthodox piety fought doggedly against his influence, but without success. No one who aspired to expound the world view of Judaism found it possible to by-pass the mighty edifice of thought he had erected in the declining years of his life.

Born in Cordova, Spain, on March 30, 1135, Moses Maimonides was scarcely thirteen years of age when he joined his family in flight from fanatical Moslem invaders. For five years or more he and his family had to live outwardly as Moslems while they sought eagerly for a secure refuge, where they could return to Judaism.

After many years of wandering, Moses and his family finally settled in Cairo, Egypt, where his reputation as a physician grew apace. In time he became the court physician of the Sultan Saladin and later of his son, Al-Afdhal. Though he now enjoyed widespread fame as the outstanding physician of his generation, he nevertheless found time to write the most comprehensive and systematic compendium of Jewish law. The Cairo Jewish community acknowledged him as its spiritual leader soon after he settled there. He wrote his philosophic treatise, the *Guide*, in the form of a letter to a beloved disciple, Joseph Ibn Aknin, who later achieved distinction as the *Nagid* (leader) of the Syrian Jewish community. When he died in 1204, his authority and fame were so great that the Yemenite community included his name in the Kaddish, and, throughout the Jewish world, this saying became current: "From Moses to Moses, there was none like Moses."

Though Maimonides pushed the quest of reason further and more resolutely than all of his predecessors, he nevertheless was far less naïvely optimistic about the power of reason to comprehend the mysterious depths of being. In opposition to Saadia, he conceived of the art of thinking as an endless adventure, marked by prophetic flashes of insight which illuminate the darkness of existence for brief moments. The light of reason is not the steady, all-pervading light of day, but the brilliant, uncertain flash of lightning in the darkness of the night. Reason is more than a series of plainly proven propositions; beyond its limited, luminous core there extends a vast and shifting penumbra, broken by occasional and sudden shafts of light. Extending toward the Infinite, reason merges into intuition or prophecy, or shades into its opposite, the dubious limbo of myth and imagination.

You must not think that these powerful secrets are known unto their final essence to any one of us. Not so, but the truth appears to us at times clearly, like the light of day, and then our habits and the course of nature obscure it again so that the dark night of ignorance envelops us, almost as before. We may be compared to one who sees the flash of lightning time after time in the midst of a very dark night. And there was one among us to whom the lightning appeared time and again, with brief intervals between them, so that he was in a steady light, with the night turned into day—this was the level of the greatest of the prophets. . . . But there are also some who have not seen the light at all, even on one day, and they continue to grope in the dark . . . they are the masses of the people. . . .[67]

The learned men and thinkers move unsteadily between the dark night of the masses and the dazzling steady light of Moses.

But even if the quest of reason is beclouded with uncertainties, it is still the chief vocation of man to pursue this quest, to the limit of his capacity, for he gives expression to the essential core of his being when he engages in sustained and rational thinking. The image of God in man is not man's freedom of will, as Philo taught, but the capacity to think objectively and logically. Human reason is capable of ascending far beyond the range of utilitarian purpose, concerning itself with the essence of things. Man becomes steadily more divine, hence more human, as he liberates his mind from the concerns of the moment and contemplates the hierarchy of essences in the universe, which rise to the highest mysteries of God. Thus Maimonides accepts Aristotle's definition of man as a "rational animal" and the corollary which follows from this definition; namely, that the highest vocation of man is the contemplation of the noblest truths of existence. It is true that "human reason has doubtless a border, beyond which it cannot go. . . ."[68] Nevertheless, it is for man to walk the pathway of reason to the utmost limit of his powers.

Rabbinic Judaism, as it is crystallized in the discursive discussions of legalistic problems in the Talmud, ranks Torah-learning as perhaps the noblest activity in life. But the Talmudic concept of learning is strictly delimited, revolving around the intricacies of the law, as it was revealed at Sinai, shunning the free questioning of the human mind and avoiding the dangerous ground of metaphysics. Maimonides considered the casuistic excursions of the Talmud to be of no intrinsic value, save as they led to the determination of the laws governing the life of the Jew. For the sages of the Talmud, the noblest activity in life was to engage in the dialectic of legalistic discussions, even if no useful purpose was served by this sterile bandying of stock arguments. Since the law was God's Word and man was fashioned for the purpose of serving God, what else but the "study of Torah for its own sake" should be considered as man's highest effort? To Maimonides, however, the universe was bigger than the Torah and life was bigger than the law. Hence, legalistic casuistry was not a religious exercise in itself, but only a tool in the service of piety. One must study the Talmud in order to learn the laws of Judaism that are needed for guidance in daily living, but, once these laws are formulated and clarified, it becomes the business of the Jew to turn his mind to the study and contemplation of the basic truths of life.

To make it possible for most people to extricate themselves quickly from the labyrinthine maze of the Talmud so as to be prepared for the open horizons of philosophy, Maimonides labored for ten years on the task of systematizing the laws of the Talmud. He believed that, in its well-ordered form, the law could be mastered with ease, leaving time and mental energy for the contemplation of the secrets of the universe. Maimonides' great code, *Yad Hahazakah,* was more than another book on Jewish Law. It was intended to shatter the self-imposed barriers of the Jewish mind and to redirect the intellectual energy of Jewish people from Talmudic casuistry to science and philosophy. What he proposed, therefore, was in reality a radical revision of the Jewish hierarchy of values, and the opening of fresh vistas. Had his proposals been widely adopted, the characteristic patterns of Jewish thought and practice would have been fundamentally transformed. Not only did he dare to rank the faculty of reason, which is the same in all men, as the highest expression of the divine in human nature, but he also implied that rabbinic learning with all its intricacies was of only subsidiary value in the spiritual economy of life and that the proper vocation of the Jew was to join with the noble scholars of all faiths in the study of generally human disciplines, which culminate in philosophy and metaphysics. This transvaluation of Jewish values is best expressed in the fifty-first chapter of the *Guide,* a chapter which elicited the shocked response of many rabbis: "This chapter was not written by the Master, and, even if he wrote it, it should still be burned."[69]

Comparing the relation of God and humanity to a king sitting in the midst of a big and mighty palace, with his subjects roaming hither and thither in search of him, Maimonides declared:

Those who desire to enter the house of the king but have never seen the house at all are the majority of the people of the Torah, the ignorant people who can only perform *mizvoth.* And those who have reached the house but walk around it are the Talmudists who believe the true doctrines which they have received from tradition and learn the ways of serving Him, but are not trained in the understanding of the roots of the Torah and do not engage in the attempt to prove their faith by reason. But those who have trained themselves to speculate concerning the principles of the faith have already entered the vestibule . . . and he who has come to know the proof of that which can be proven and has learned from the divine attributes that which it is possible to know, and has come close to the understanding of that which can only be approached but never known, has already entered into the palace with the king. Know, then, my son, that so long as you engage in the studies of mathematics and logic, you are of those who walk round the house to seek the gate . . . and when you understand the studies of natural phenomena, you enter the hallway of the house. And when you complete the studies of nature and understand divine things, then you have entered the King's house, and you are with Him, in the inner court. . . .[70]

In thus ranking the exercise of reason as the noblest task of man and the pathway to God, Maimonides did not conceive the problem of theology to be the conquest of reason by faith, but the determination of the proper domains for the functioning of each faculty. In its own sphere of operation, reason is essentially jealous, brooking no rivals in the finality of its analysis and judgment. One cannot drive bargains and patch up compromises with reason, but having determined the field extending beyond its reach, we may allow the postulates of faith to prevail in that area of indetermination. In effect, Maimonides argued for the " right to believe " in regard to matters that are not subject to rational proof or disproof. He did not set out to refute the philosophers by proving that reason is fallible in the domain of metaphysics; on the contrary, he followed reason as far as it goes and expressed the opinion current in the philosophical circles of his day when he declared, " But there is, without doubt, a limit to human reason, beyond which it cannot go. . . ."[71] If we attempt to go beyond this limit, we must still be guided by the balance of probabilities, " believing that which poses the least number of difficulties." But in the twilight realm of doubt, when several equally tenable propositions are presented, the testimony of tradition may be allowed its due weight.

What is it that Maimonides subsumed under the heading of reason? Manifestly, the postulates of human reason differ from age to age. Between the time of the early rationalists, Saadia and Bahya, and the period of Maimonides, the great commentaries on Aristotle by Ibn Roshd and Avicenna had appeared; and at the same time, Aristotle's own work on physics became known. The world view which Aristotle projected emphasized the recognition of the inherent laws of nature which unfailingly regulate the phenomena of the physical universe. The succession of events in nature is not dependent on the arbitrary will of God, but is simply the unfolding of a chain of cause and effect, as rational as the principles of mathematics, as inexorable as the iron laws of logic. It is this discovery of the self-determination of physical nature that transforms for Maimonides the basic problems of the philosophy of religion.

> One rule I must state to you; to wit, as Themistius said, existence does not accommodate itself to ideas, but the true ideas must emerge out of the world as it exists. As I examined the books of the Kalam thinkers and the books of the philosophers (Aristotelians) to the best of my ability, I found that the former thinkers followed one basic line of reasoning, differing only in details. The assumption upon which all their thought hinges is that existence is not inherently rational, but that it follows simply the customary pattern of change. In reason, a different succession is possible. . . . There is no permanent nature to things to all. . . . Many times, they identify imagination with reason. . . . But I seek to prove the existence of God without disputing the nature of existence, and I shall not differ with Aristotle, in matters for which there are proofs. . . .[72]

Like Aristotle, then, Maimonides proceeded to prove the existence of God by pointing to the universality of the law of cause and effect. If all phenomena of the present moment are necessarily caused by other phenomena, which in turn are the effects of still other events, we have an endless chain of causes. It takes an infinite length of time to contain an infinite series of events; hence, the present moment and its events could not ever be reached if the past were infinite. The reality of the present means that the final cause is outside the wheel of time. In the Aristotelian system, the events of the physical universe are caused ultimately by the active reason, which in turn is moved by higher, more ethereal spheres, with all these forces finding their ultimate source in God, the unmoved mover, Who is beyond either time or motion. Each link becomes more spiritual and less physical, more abstract and less mobile, as the chain of causation rises from earth to God. The spheres are kept in motion by the power of love, the love of God, a much subtler force than any that prevails on earth. The differences in the position and motion of the spheres are due to their respective degrees of comprehension of the Deity, but the Deity is absolutely unmoved, thinking only of Himself.

The sphere loves that which it conceives of as the most beloved object, which is the Lord, may His name be exalted. In this sense, it is said that the Lord moves the sphere; that is, since the sphere seeks to attain that which it has conceived. . . .[73]

And know that all the philosophers agree that the management of this lower world is carried out by powers which flow upon it from the spheres as we have mentioned, and that these spheres understand and know that which they effect. . . .[74]

The rotating spheres were conceived of as intelligent beings, endowed with subtle, ethereal bodies, kept in their circular motion by their love and their adoration of the divine nature and purpose.

Do not think that these spheres or intelligences are like the other physical forces, which operate by nature without comprehending the effect of their work, but the spheres and intelligences understand their work, choose and lead . . . they possess will and choice.[75]

Maimonides, then, operated with the concept of an inflexible causal law inherent in nature, but his world was not the sheer soulless machine of modern materialists. Mechanical necessity was the lowest force in a universe where knowledge and love jointly constituted the ultimate source of power. The spheres of heaven were conceived as spiritual beings, endowed with will, purpose, and thought. Out of their ceaseless rotation flowed all forms of earthly energy. And the higher the level of an existent in the scale of being, the greater was the role of the spirit in its makeup. Thus intelligence was the central focus of reality in the divine economy of the universe.

Maimonides accepted the medieval version of the Aristotelian system, going so far as to declare that " everything which Aristotle maintained concerning all that exists from the lunar sphere to the center of the earth is true, without doubt."[76] Nevertheless, he insisted on disagreeing with his master concerning the most basic of all philosophical issues; namely, whether the world was created by God or whether it is eternal. Maimonides pointed out that Aristotle did not really prove the eternity of the universe, contenting himself with the extension of the present observable chain of causality into the timeless past. But the eternity or the creation of the universe is a question that cannot be resolved by reason alone. Either assumption takes us beyond the physical world and its dimensions of space and time to the boundary of the great unknown, where reason cannot penetrate. If we assume eternity, we face the mystery of the nontemporality of God, Who stands outside the chain of causality; if we assume creation, we assume a time when the incomprehensible act of the emergence of being out of nothingness took place. In either case, we move into a transrational realm, where our rules of logic fail us. Maimonides decided in favor of creation first on the ground of the balance of probabilities, and second because the doctrine of creation "makes the Torah possible."

The religious view of life posits the supremacy and dominance of God, the source of all noble values, over nature, the complex of physical forces in the universe; hence, it must insist on the doctrine of creation, as the reflection in time of this fundamental conviction. By the same token the principle of the eternity of the universe implies that God and physical nature are somehow coeval, that the things of God have their place in the total scheme, but not in a decisive, absolute manner. The doctrine of creation makes the Torah possible in a more specific sense: accepting it, one can assume that the world was designed from the beginning as a fitting arena for the concretization of the ideals of the Torah. The physical laws of the universe were designed by the Creator to assure the ultimate achievement of human perfection in the Messianic era, and the specific miracles of the Bible were pre-arranged, set into the causal chain of events at the beginning and so timed as to occur at crucial, decisive moments. It is therefore possible to accept the inner necessity and inexorability of natural law and at the same time to believe that the reported miracles of the Bible did really take place.

To be sure, Maimonides allegorized some of the miraculous tales of the Bible, especially those relating to the early history of mankind. Nevertheless, he declared that such miraculous events as the splitting of the Red Sea did in fact occur, without controverting the laws of nature, since God had fitted these miracles from the beginning into the structure of nature and history. But it is also His will that the course of nature, as He set it in the six days of creation, shall not be changed. "We shall thus concede to Aristotle one-half of his opinion, in that we believe that all existence is firmly and eternally fixed in its nature, in accord with the design of God. . . ."[77] All the miracles of the

Bible have been previsioned by God and made part of the un-folding course of nature, but neither the will of God nor the process of nature is ever changed.

The corollary of divine perfection is unchangeability since in the Aristotelian system all change is due to the presence of matter while God is pure form. We have seen that the process whereby the existence of God is inferred is one that implies a source of all motion. Hence, the ultimate cause must be free from motion. Furthermore, we think of God as the perfect being, but if He be perfect, any change in Him is bound to diminish His perfection. Again, we arrive at the idea of the one God by noting the inter-dependence of all things and their interaction. It follows that God cannot be dependent, or subject to being acted upon by any of His creatures; nor can we assume that His will is subject to change in accord with the changing actions of men.

This principle of perfect divine imperturbability conflicted fundamentally with the popular psychology of religious belief and practice. In prayer, man addresses God as if He were a per-son, whose will might be affected by prayer and contrition. But, if God be self-enclosed and unchangeable, what sense is there in prayer? We shall presently describe Maimonides' concept of prayer; at this moment, we must stress that the principle of divine perfection was fully and unflinchingly accepted by Maimonides in spite of its extreme difficulties.

Manifestly, every activity with which we are familiar involves some form of change. Hence, every divine attribute must be inter-preted as applying to God in a different fashion from its applica-tion to all other beings. Removing all anthropomorphic qualities from our concept of God, we must still think of Him as being "alive, wise, willing and potent," in infinite perfection. But we must not think of these divine attributes as being identical with the corresponding qualities in created objects, where they are inextricably bound up with matter. Maimonides had nothing but contempt for the pseudo philosophers who, disavowing popular anthropomorphism, imagine that they meet the demands of logic when they remove only gross corporeality from the divine being, but continue to attribute to Him the psychical qualities of per-sonality which imply change and materiality.[78] He insisted that the four qualities of life, wisdom, will and power apply to God "only as homonyms, not in any other respect"; i.e., there is a correspondence but not an identity between the meanings of these earthly qualities and their divine connotations.[79]

So he wrote of the Deity as " existing but not in existence, living but not in life, knowing but not in knowledge, powerful but not with power, wise but not in wisdom . . . one but not in unity. . . ."[80] The net meanings of these paradoxes is the negation of negatives of these qualities; to wit, God is not nonexistent, nor dead, nor ignorant, nor powerless, nor multiple. It follows that we may describe God only in negative terms, indicating what He is not. But this *via negativa*, this way of knowing God by recognizing all that He is not, must not be despised, for it is endless in extent and many-sided. As we ascend the ladder of speculation, we come to perceive more and more concepts and abstractions that cannot be applied to Him. Simple-minded people attribute all the qualities of personality to God; it takes strenuous intellectual discipline to realize that our most subtle concepts, including, of course, space and time, do not apply to God, Who is beyond these categories of existence. We grow in the knowledge of God as we perceive His "difference" from all things, how all the instruments of our thought fail to grasp His essence. "We understand Him in the measure in which we grasp His final incomprehensibility."[81]

But if we can only know what God is not, what shall we make of the usual attributes by which God is known in Judaism? Thus, we speak of God as all-merciful; is He then affected by our sorrows or moved by our tears? Maimonides declares that God is "merciful . . . but not in the sense of being affected or being changed. . . . But He, may He be exalted, has brought us into being and continually provides for those who have no claim upon Him. Therefore He is called merciful. . . ." The quality of mercy is applied to Him in the sense that actions of mercy abound in the world created and directed by His will. The thirteen attributes which Moses applied to God are therefore to be taken as a description of the state of affairs in God's universe, not as qualities of His being. These qualities were selected by Moses because they might serve as ideal goals for rulers. When we speak of God as "kind," "vengeful," "jealous," "merciful," we mean, first, that actions emanating from Him sometimes correspond to these human categories and, second, that these qualities should serve as norms of conduct for human rulers. "As He is merciful, so be you merciful; as He is kind, so be you kind," etc.[82]

The qualities of mercy and kindness, which imply an emotional reaction, cannot be applied to the Deity, but neither can those of justice or rulership, since it is impossible to postulate any relation between God and His creatures, every relation positing a plane of reality common to the objects related. "How, then, can we envisage a relation between us and Him, Who possesses no phase of being in common with that which is outside of Him?"[83]

If no common plane, hence no relationship, between the Deity and His creatures can be assumed, how does the Torah portray God as communicating verbally with Moses and other prophets? According to Maimonides, the act of speaking involves physical connotations which cannot be attributed to the Deity. While previous philosophers were content to assume a miraculous "created voice" which echoed the thoughts of God, Maimonides was consistent enough to disavow any such artificial contrivance, save as a hallucination in the imagination of the prophet. When the Torah describes God as speaking, it refers to "the changeless will and desire" of the Deity, "comparing His manner of expression to ours." But in strictness, "It must be made clear to you that the quality of speech is inapplicable to Him."[84]

By the same token, the tablets of stone which Moses brought down from the mountain were written not by "the finger of the Lord" but by Moses. The Torah speaks of the "writing of God" in a figurative sense, reminding us that all literary efforts, including the art of writing itself, are divinely inspired in varying degrees.[85]

When the Jewish people stood at the foot of Mount Sinai and heard the Ten Commandments recited by Moses, they were so deeply moved that in their imagination they heard voices and beheld wondrous sights. But the account of the revelation at Sinai must not be taken literally. Though Maimonides granted the possibility of "created lights" having been placed at Sinai by God at the time of creation for the purpose of impressing the multitude, he hinted that such "sights" were present only in the imagination of the people. However, he saw no harm in believing that a "created light" marked the presence of the *Shechinah* at Sinai and in the Sanctuary.[86]

The important point to bear in mind is that, according to

Maimonides, the account of the Sinaitic revelation in the Book of Exodus should be read as a parable (*moshol*) and that, in general, "the inner meaning of the words of the Torah are the gems while the literal parables are no more than illustration."[87]

A prophetic vision is always accompanied by symbolic sights and sounds, the products of a feverish human imagination. The divine voice at Sinai was accordingly "not an actual voice, but a simple, rational, prophetic comprehension."[88] We should not be surprised at the "sounds" which the people heard at Sinai, for these were simply effects of the Active Reason playing upon the imagination of the people.[89]

Does this mean that prophecy itself is a matter of human imagination? Not altogether. We must remember that the Greek philosophers, too, allowed the truth and value of "prophetic frenzy," though they insisted that the grains of truth in it were frequently overlaid with mountains of chaff. Maimonides himself declared "that even those who believe in the eternity of the universe do not negate the possibility of prophecy."[90] The prevailing concept of the universe was a combination of Aristotelianism and Neo-Platonism, postulating a continuous flow of reason and inspiration from God, through the agency of the spheres, down to the Active Reason and thence to the mind of man. The more a person disciplined and refined the powers of his imagination and reason, the better he prepared himself for the reception of this "flow" of the Active Reason.

Maimonides pointed out that the common people imagine prophecy to be a purely divine phenomenon, with the prophet serving only in a passive capacity. It is God who bestows His grace upon whomsoever He chooses; hence, a person can neither prepare himself for prophecy nor can he resist the Word when it comes. The "philosophers," on the other hand, maintained that prophecy was purely an art which could be cultivated by man, through the progressive refinement of his faculties. He himself believed that prophecy was a joint activity of both God and man. He concurred with the philosophers in assuming the need for mental and emotional preparation, but he maintained that the flow of prophetic inspiration was not automatic with the Deity. Even when a person is fully prepared for the prophetic gift, God may withhold it from him. For in the being of God freedom as well as necessity are one and inseparable. Prophecy is thus compounded of both human wisdom and divine inspiration.

The important prerequisite for prophecy is self-discipline, especially the control of the emotions. Maimonides took special pains to stress the imperative need of controlling the sexual impulse, doubtless in order to controvert Mohammed's claim to prophecy, since the latter's love life became extraordinarily exuberant after he became a "prophet." To Maimonides, as to Aristotle, the "sense of touch" generally and sexual pleasure in particular was a "shame" for the human race.[91] He was convinced that it was impossible for man to be a lover of woman and a seeker of God at the same time.[92] Prophecy represents the highest possible perfection of the human personality, the perfection of the imagination as well as of the senses and the intellectual faculty. Hence, it is inconceivable without prior preparation. "Even at Mount Sinai, though all the people saw the great fires and heard the wondrously frightening sounds, only those who were properly prepared attained levels of prophecy, and in accord with their degrees of preparation. . . ."[93]

It follows that the "divine flow" derives from God, in accordance with His will, like lightning from a cloud, assuming a variety of forms and expressions as it crystallizes in prophecy; for the prophet contributes his own character and imagination to the luminous core of his inspired vision. Since the "divine flow" is essentially a forward thrust, aiming at the perfection of human society, it may be incorporated in a variety of inspired actions, as well as in a verbal message. Great creative achievements in almost every field of endeavor are prophetic in origin and quality or, more correctly, "protoprophetic." The feats of Samson are described in the Bible as due to "the spirit of God." Divine inspiration may come in dreams, enveloped in the picturesque garments of fantasy. Only among the greatest prophets does prophecy appear in daytime visions of varying degrees of rational clarity. Accordingly, Maimonides described eleven degrees of prophecy, projecting a unique and unparalleled category for the prophecy of Moses.

Maimonides asserted on the authority of Scripture that the visions of Moses were devoid of mediating elements, perfect, and uncontaminated by the vagaries of imagination. While prophecy in general is a humanly attainable goal in the process of self-improvement, the prophecy of Moses was a unique and perfect expression of the divine will. At this point Maimonides lapsed, consciously or unconsciously, into the realm of dogma. As we shall see presently, he believed that some dogmas were needed in order to establish one "Torah-community" for philosophers and the common people.

If prophecy is a consummation that is humanly attainable, how can we account for its absence in contemporary Jewish life? Why has it been extinct since the completion of the Bible? To be sure, from time to time false prophets appeared to claim the allegiance of the people. Maimonides himself took part in the arduous task of exposing a Yemenite false prophet. But if prophecy is for the most part a human achievement and if the good God is not likely to withhold His grace from those who deserve it, why are there no prophets in the contemporary world?

Maimonides' answer is characteristic both of his logical consistency and his lack of pragmatic realism. Our evil and distraught times, he claimed, fail to provide the physical conditions that are needed for serenity and peace of mind. A perfect, prophetic personality can only thrive in a perfect, peaceful and happy society. (As if the Biblical prophets lived in an age of peace and serenity!) The Jewish people, in particular, Maimonides declared, driven and distressed as they are in every corner of the globe, can hardly be expected to produce perfectly balanced personalities. "This, then, is doubtless the essential and immediate reason for the cutting off of prophecy in the time of exile; to wit, the sorrow and heaviness of heart which beset us."[94]

Some scholars believe that Maimonides considered prophecy a possible attainment for the people of his generation. There is reason to assume that he himself believed he had reached the heights of prophecy. Believing in the imminent advent of the Messiah, he naturally looked forward to the revival of prophecy in his generation, for the true prophet must precede the arrival of the Messiah.[95]

Having established the validity of the general belief in prophecy, Maimonides proceeded to reassert the Orthodox dogma that only the Torah of Moses could be regarded as true revelation. Many Jewish sectarians, including the Qaraites, had accepted the belief that both Jesus and Mohammed were "true prophets." Unwilling to risk the dangers of complete tolerance, Maimonides insisted that Christianity was only one step above idolatry, and Mohammed was just "insane." How could one pretend to be a prophet who has not even learned to despise the pleasures of the senses? "Holiness is the repudiation of sexual relations."[96]

Nevertheless, both Christianity and Islam were, according to Maimonides, divinely ordained "preparations" for the ultimate establishment of the kingdom of God. In other words, they tended to lead mankind toward the truths of monotheism, though they were not absolutely true in themselves.

Just as it is impossible to assign a valid purpose to every phenomenon in life, though the existence of inner purposiveness within living things is obvious, so too we can find the radiance of purpose in many portions of the Torah, though not in every verse and every detail. However, we cannot but affirm that there is a general purpose for the precepts of the Torah and that this fundamental purpose is "the improvement of the body and the soul" of men. Rationality is the noblest quality of human beings. Could God be conceived then as less rational than men? Without attempting to account for every detail of the law, we must discover God's purpose at least in the most important precepts and *mizvoth*.

Maimonides divided the *mizvoth* of the Torah into fourteen categories, assigning some rational motivation for each of them. In general, he declared, rituals and ceremonies are related to ideals and sentiments in several diverse ways—as practical guidance is to good intentions, as a concrete illustration is to an abstract doctrine, as a shell is to a kernel, as the body is to the soul. "For ideas without deeds which affirm and fortify them cannot continue to be effective among the people."[97]

The attainment of perfection in piety is dependent upon the establishment of ideal physical conditions for the individual and a just order in society. Spiritual perfection is intellectual greatness superimposed upon ideal moral qualities, which are in their turn dependent on a just and equitable order in society. Consequently we arrive at a threefold goal as the ultimate purpose of the Torah:

> Our final conclusion emerging out of all these postulates is that every commandment, be it positive or negative, has as its purpose to correct injustice or to instill such ethical qualities as are needed for the good of society; or to teach opinions that are true or ideas that are needed for the prevention of evil, or the training in good virtues. . . .[98]

It is interesting to note that Maimonides referred to two classes of beliefs, those that were true in themselves and those that needed to be affirmed as true for the sake of an ideal, stable society. Like Plato in *The Republic,* he was keenly conscious of the need for cementing a society by means of affirmations that were not strictly true, but were suited to the needs of that particular society. Like Aristotle, he frequently affirmed that "man is by nature a political being." It is impossible for great men to attain their full spiritual stature in isolation. A just and perfectly ordered society is needed as the matrix, for the emergence of a small number of chosen souls who will attain the perfection of "cleaving unto the Active Reason." This select group of saintly philosophers will understand and continually contemplate the abstract conception of the Deity, outlined above. But the large masses of the people cannot be expected either to comprehend so subtle a concept or to rest content with a God idea that is completely stripped of all the elements that they associate with personality. A façade of opinions or dogmas is needed, Maimonides believed, in order to provide a foundation of ideological unity for the Jewish community. For this reason the Torah enjoined the belief in certain humanlike qualities of the Deity, such as His hearing and seeing, His pitying, loving, and avenging. These qualities are not true, in the strict sense of the word, but they must be affirmed *as if* they were true, since they are "necessary" for the maintenance of the community of Israel. These "necessary" ideas, considered strictly as social instruments and armored with the unyielding rigidity of dogma, do not conflict with the logical truths of philosophy; on the contrary, the dogmas of the Torah-community provide a moral atmosphere and a congenial social environment for the emergence and growth of philosophical and saintly souls. At the same time, these "necessary" ideas do not violate the philosopher's passion for truth, since for his own meditations he will know how to interpret them in accord with the axioms of reason.

Understand what we said in regard to beliefs: at times the commandment contains a true belief, which is true in itself, not in its relation to some other purpose, like the belief in the unity of God, His eternity and incorporeality. But at times a belief is enjoined which is necessary for the removal of iniquity or for the acquisition of good qualities, like the belief that the Lord, may He be exalted, becomes angry at the one who robs, as it is written, " And my wrath shall be kindled and I shall kill," or the belief that He, may He be exalted, will hear the cry of those that are wronged and oppressed and will save them, as it is written, " And it shall be, when he will cry unto me, I shall hear, for I am merciful. . . ."[99]

Some beliefs tend to authenticate themselves by the actions that they inspire:

It is clear that the belief in the possibility of a sinner's return belongs in the category of the beliefs which are indispensable for the existence of the Torah-community, for it is impossible for man not to err or sin . . . and if he believes that he will never be able to atone for his sin, he will continue in his error, possibly even intensifying his rebelliousness to the point of becoming irretrievable. But thanks to this belief in repentance, he will mend his ways and return to the practice of good virtues, becoming possibly even more perfect than before his sin. . . .[100]

In another connection, Maimonides defines repentance as the attainment of that psychical level which in the judgment of God would make the erstwhile sinner reject the temptation to sin, if the identical opportunity were again presented to him. In other words, repentance is not success in winning an act of pardon from the Almighty, but the mending of one's character, by dint of persistent effort. But to people generally who are beset with the feelings of guilt and helplessness the practices of prayer and repentance must be represented not as so many exercises in self-purification, but as petitions for the grace and favor of the Almighty King and compassionate Father. The belief in divine forgiveness is the example of a " necessary " idea that becomes true if accepted in all sincerity.

This twofold meaning of the same act, one for the philosopher and one for the masses, is not self-contradictory, since every society is inevitably an organic whole. The ultimate purpose of the Torah is fulfilled in the lives of the few philosophical saints, but these giants of the spirit can thrive only in a concrete, many-sided community and for its sake. As one commentator put it : [101]

And it is necessary that the mass-man should believe that God is moved by human petitions and rituals of propitiation. Though this belief is false, strictly speaking, it is necessary for the existence of society. Therefore these beliefs are called necessary, not true. The wise man will understand that these beliefs are said in accord with the maxim, " The Torah spoke in the language of men. . . ."[102]

Along with ideas true and " necessary " the Torah enjoined the observance of many commandments, which were designed for the purpose of maintaining an ideal, justly ordered society. This overarching purpose was the central motivation of all the laws regulating relations " between man and man."

As to ritual observances, Maimonides noted that the Torah was given in the midst of certain historical circumstances and that the significance of each rite can be seen only when it is viewed against the background of the prevailing pagan practices in the time of Moses.

The complex laws, regulating the sacrifices in the sanctuary and temple, were designed for the purpose of weaning the people away from the worship of pagan deities. In the days of Moses the people were not yet ready for more elevated forms of worship. They could not conceive of serving the Almighty in any other way than by bringing offerings into the temple. Hence, it was necessary for Moses to adapt his teaching to the primitive habits of his contemporaries.

> Moses' predicament may be compared to the appearance of a prophet in our day who would call to the service of God in the following manner: " The Lord commanded you not to pray to Him and not to fast and not to seek His help in time of trouble, but to let your service consist in thought only, without deeds."[103]

Such a message would be in keeping with the inner truth of faith, but it would hardly be accepted by the people of our day. In the same way, Moses was compelled to take account of the habits, rites and ideas which prevailed in his generation. He could not antagonize the people by rejecting ways of thinking and acting that were dear to them. He could only regulate and spiritualize their customs, so as to lead them by degrees in the right direction, and he had to begin at the people's actual point of spiritual development.

Maimonides was familiar with some pagan practices from quotations and descriptions which he found in contemporary Moslem literature. Though he was clearly aware of the paucity and inaccuracy of the information available to him concerning the rituals of the heathen, he felt justified in propounding the general rule that Judaism evolved in the course of an arduous struggle against the follies and rites of the pagan world. All the quasi-magical rites in Judaism were ultimately due to the strategy employed by Moses and his successors in their relentless efforts to combat the inroads of the pagan mentality. Many a time the architects of the Jewish faith had to stoop in order to conquer.

The essence of paganism is the worship of the creature, rather than of the Creator; i.e., the attribution of independent dominion to stars, mountains, rivers, names of angels, etc. For this reason Maimonides considered astrology and the juggling of mysterious "names" by the proto-Qabbalists of his day to be at once sheer stupidity and unalloyed paganism. Judaism is, in essence, a continual protest against the pagan worship of the creature and against magical reliance on the manipulation of occult forces. It is at the point where magic and naïve superstition end that Judaism begins.

> The knowledge of these [pagan] ideas and rites is a very important gateway leading to the comprehension of the reasons for the commandments, for the root of our entire Torah and the axis upon which it turns is the determination to erase these ideas from the hearts of men and to eliminate them from the world . . . it is the primary, general intention of the whole Torah. . . .[104]

With the limited information of the history of religions at his disposal, Maimonides endeavored stoutly to explain the rites of Judaism as being primarily so many acts of symbolic repudiation of the ways of heathendom. Occasionally, too, a magical practice had to be included within the Torah, as an unavoidable concession to the ingrained primitive habits of the people of Israel at the time of Moses. For, as Maimonides put it, " It is impossible for human nature to go suddenly from one extreme to the other."[105]

The Torah, for example, prohibited the eating of the fruit of a tree in its first three years of growth (*Arla*). This prohibition was a silent protest against the policy of the pagans to dedicate such fruit to the use of their temples. The Torah ordained the bringing of the fruit of the fourth year to the Holy Temple; the purpose of this commandment was to make certain that the people will not bring the fruit to the pagan altars. It will be noted that Maimonides was not dismayed by the fact that two opposing strategies were employed by the Torah to counteract the same pagan custom. Maimonides also pointed out that the bringing of fruits to pagan temples was occasionally accompanied by immoral and orgiastic fertility rites which were intended to hasten the growth of the trees. After four years, there was no longer any danger of such practices.

The Torah prohibited the practice of grafting the branch of one tree upon the stem of another because the pagans would indulge in unnatural sexual acts in connection with this work (*Kilaim*). Similarly, the planting of grains in a vineyard was prohibited so that the Israelites would be removed as far as possible from the temptation to indulge in the immoral, magical rites that were frequently performed in connection with these practices. The prohibition of interweaving threads of flax and wool (*Shatnez*) is based on similar reasoning; namely, the fact that pagan priests made it a point to wear garments made from cloth that was woven in this manner.[106]

In the Holy Temple, the tablets of the law were placed in the Ark, within the Holy of Holies, not because there was any holiness or divinity in the tablets themselves, but simply to indicate that the words of the prophets constituted the basis of the covenant between God and Israel. Since prophets derived their inspiration from angels (the Active Reason), the belief in angels had to be reinforced by the representation of the cherubim. The rite of burning incense in the Holy Temple was designed for the purpose of eliminating the noxious odors resulting from the burning of the sacrifices on the altars, not to offer a pleasing fragrance to the Almighty. The sacrifices offered in the temple consisted of cattle, goats and sheep, for these were sacred " totem " animals to many of the pagan nations, and in slaughtering them the Jews demonstrated their disbelief in the sanctities of the pagan world. The pagans would bring leavened and sweetened offerings to their gods, but not salt. This is why the opposite practice was enjoined in the Torah; i.e., leavened and sweetened foods were prohibited, but salt was to be sprinkled on all offerings upon the altar.[107]

The drinking of blood was prohibited "for blood was very unclean in the eyes of the Sabeans [Near Eastern pagans], who nevertheless would drink it on special occasions, believing blood to be the peculiar drink of the demons, so that when they partook of it, they thought they entered into partnership with the demons and learned the future from them."[108] It is for a similar reason that the eating of meat was prohibited altogether, so long as the Israelites dwelled in the desert of Sinai, for the worship of demons is very widespread in the desert. Later, when they entered into the land of Israel, where such practices were almost unknown, the prohibition on meat was rescinded.

In the Torah we find a detailed description of sacrifices that were to be brought daily, on the Sabbath or in honor of the new moon. The new moon sacrifices are of special interest to us, since they appear to be the residue of moon worship. Manifestly, the sacrifices described in the Torah were in effect long before the Torah was accepted by the Israelites. The Torah simply allowed the established practice to continue since the Israelites were powerfully addicted to it, specifying, however, that the offerings were to be brought to God, not to the moon. In this manner the danger of moon worship was averted. But as to "the offering of wine," Maimonides wrote, "I am disturbed about it up to this day. Why should it be commanded, seeing the pagans also offered wine to their gods?"[109] For that matter, Maimonides also confessed his inability to find a good reason for the table in the sanctuary and the showbreads that were placed upon it.[110]

As to the laws of ritual uncleanliness, which seem so cumbersome and unnecessary, Moses' general aim was to soften the harsh and complicated regulations of the pagan nations, but he could not shock the sensibilities of the people and defy their ingrained prejudice. "For this Torah of God . . . came to lighten the burden of existing rites, and if some of them appear to you to involve a great deal of trouble and annoyance, it is so only because you do not know the customs and ideas which prevailed at that time. . . ."[111]

Thus the laws of ritual defilement were designed in part for the purpose of discouraging people from coming into the Holy Temple too frequently. Insofar as the masses are concerned, familiarity breeds contempt. The more the common people were kept away from the Holy Temple, the more they were likely to revere it. Accordingly, the laws of defilement were so designed that, at any one time, "You will find very few people that are clean." Another motive for these precepts is to induce people to stay away from that which is ugly or disgusting. Third, "The Torah had to accommodate itself to the accepted customs of the time, for the Sabeans lavished a great deal of energy upon such matters as ritual uncleanliness."[112]

A good illustration of the primitive obsession with rites of purification is the law governing the periodic "uncleanliness" of women and the complex ritual of lustration in specially designed baths (*mikvah*). Among some primitive people, "the menstruating woman had to be locked in a house all by herself, the places upon which she walked were burned and whoever spoke to her became unclean. . . ." If you compare these stringencies with the comparative mildness of the regulations in the Torah, Maimonides concluded, you will note the spirit of moderation that governed the laws of Moses.

As to the dietary laws, most of the requirements of Judaism are simply sanitary regulations. "The best part of the meat is permitted for us." The flesh of the pig was prohibited because of the unclean habits of this particular animal. "And if the eating of pork were permitted, the streets and the houses would be as dirty as latrines, even as are the countries of the Franks [Europeans] in our day." This is what the famed physician of Egypt thought of the Christian lands of Europe. *Mutatis mutandis!*

Blood and *trefa* (non-kosher) meat are bad for digestion. As to the mixing of meat with milk, "it appears probable to me that there was about it an odor of pagan worship. It is possible that they boiled meat with milk in the course of one or another of their celebrations."[113]

The laws of marriage and divorce constitute the basis of a justly ordered society. The law concerning the "bitter waters" to be given to the woman suspected of adultery, establishing an ordeal for the discovery of sexual sins, was designed to discourage marital infidelity by scaring the superstitious women and embarrassing the understanding ones.[114]

The law of levirate marriage existed long before the covenant at Sinai. Since the people could not be weaned away from this primitive custom all at once, the Torah modified the law by the introduction of the ceremony of *Halitza*.[115]

The law of circumcision established a sign which is common to all Jewish people. At the same time,

One of the reasons for circumcision, to my mind, is to lessen the enjoyment of sexual intercourse and to weaken this organ as much as possible. . . . That circumcision lessens this organ's capacity for conjugal relations and sometimes removes the pleasure associated with it, I have no doubt.[116]

The major portion of the Torah was devoted to the ordering of an ideal society, so designed as to encourage at least some people to devote themselves to the cultivation of the noble qualities of the soul. As to the *lex talionis*, the principle of "an eye for an eye," it was, to Maimonides, simply an application of the principle of absolute justice.

> And he who lost a limb through the actions of an assailant, then the same limb should be removed from the assailant, "as he put a blemish in a man, so a blemish shall be put in him." Though we today substitute money for this punishment, do not be disturbed, for our intention is here to explain the reasons of the verses in Scripture, not the words of the Talmud.[117]

Sufficient illustrations have been cited to indicate the rigorous and even ruthless logic which Maimonides brought to the analysis of the Jewish faith. The essence of Judaism is the belief in the one incorporeal Deity and the determination to cleave unto Him. But the Jewish faith developed in distinct historical circumstances; therefore, it adopted and preserved in its passage through history some irrational rites, vestiges of the ancient struggle against paganism. For the most part, these rituals possess no intrinsic significance, save insofar as they are needed for the maintenance of the Torah-community.

Maimonides himself did not draw any conclusion as to the superfluity or obsolescence of the rituals, but his system of thought was bound to lead to this consideration. And, in spite of his silence, he did not doubt for a moment the rightness of following the inner logic of his ideas to its ultimate conclusions. For, as he saw it, reason is virtually identical with the will of God. Indeed, it is the one quality which derives directly from God, being the inherent law of His being. Scriptural language at times attributed all natural phenomena to the Deity, since He was the source of all power and the laws of nature were designed and fixed by Him.[118] But while the forces of nature were established by God, they did not represent His will in the same sense as the light of reason, deriving automatically from God, through the agency of the Active Intellect. Sin and failure are due to matter; the direct action of the Deity is reason. And reason is at all times good.

"For through the knowledge of truth, all hatred and quarrels are eliminated, and people cease to injure one another."[119] We must not compromise with the strict dictates of the intellect in interpreting the Torah, "for only the truth is acceptable to Him, and only falsehood does He hate."[120]

We have seen before that the qualities of compassion and anger are attributable to the Deity only as "necessary" ideas. Does it mean then that God is completely uninterested in the affairs of men? Is religion entirely a one-sided affair, recording man's search for God, but not the corresponding concern of God for man? To Aristotle, God is indeed completely self-enclosed, thinking perpetually only of the noblest possible object, Himself. But Maimonides operated within a Neo-Platonic modification of Aristotelianism, which assumed a continuous "flow" of divine power down through the successive spheres and by means of the Active Reason. This divine "flow" from God to man consists of a volitional phase, an element of guidance or providence, as well as the gifts of reason and prophecy. It follows that those who cleave to the Active Reason, and in the measure to which they do so, are lifted up to a realm in direct contact with the Deity, sharing in the luminosity of His reason and the serenity of His will. Like the stars and the spheres, their life is raised above the accidents of matter here on earth and drawn into an ethereal circle resplendent with the light and peace of Providence.

While most Aristotelians maintained that the Providence of God extended only to the unchanging species of mankind, not to the transient lives of individual human beings, Maimonides enlarged the domain of immediate divine Providence to include those rare souls who achieved a mystic union with the Active Reason.

Affirming the absolute freedom of the human will, he maintained that it is possible for man to attain a measure of citizenship in the domain of spiritual purity that is subject to divine Providence.

Divine Providence, as I see it, follows upon the divine flow. . . . For I do not believe that God is ignorant of aught or powerless in any sense, but I believe that Providence is associated with reason, deriving from it. . . . Hence, concerning all who are affected by this flow it may be said that they are governed by Providence to the extent to which they have attained of reason. . . .[121]

It follows that divine Providence is not extended to all human beings in equal measure, but that the extent of Providence is directly proportionate to the varying increments of perfection among men. Thus, too, we may infer that His Providence is very powerful in the case of the prophets and in accord with their prophetic level. . . .[122]

The closer we come, by study and devotion, to the dominion of divine Providence, the more removed we are from the evil accidents of this material world. Only good qualities flow from the divine source, while the manifold evils of life proliferate in direct proportion to our distance from the divine realm of the spirit. This is true in a twofold sense.

First, the individual, protected by divine Providence, is shielded from the ruthless operation of natural law, at least so long as he is united in thought with the divine Being.

Therefore it seems to me that when one of the prophets or perfect saints is afflicted with any of the evils of the world, the misfortune could occur only at a time when he had temporarily forgotten his noble thoughts. And the extent of his misfortune is related to the length of that period of forgetfulness and to the quality of the matter which engaged his attention. Thus we allay the great doubt of the philosophers, who negated individual Providence when they saw the occasional misfortunes of the pious and the saintly. . . . Now this mystery has been explained. . . .

Secondly, the prophets and dedicated philosophers know that the one true and perfect good in the world is not health or wealth or fame, but simply the knowledge and love of God. These goals are attainable by man, and when the saints know themselves to be in possession of ultimate truth, their happiness cannot be disturbed by any of the blows of fate. They are at one with God in their lifetime and even the final disaster of death cannot remove them from their home in the divine realm of eternity.[123]

It appears doubtful that Maimonides assumed the continued separate existence of souls after death. Since it is matter that breaks the one up into the many, the souls of the righteous may be expected to merge into the Active Reason, each to the extent of its mastery of metaphysical truth.

It follows that the souls of common people are not at all immortal, that immortality is not a gift bestowed by the Almighty as a reward but is an achievement of the person on earth. Man is born with the capacity to acquire immortality by mastering the impulses of his flesh, training and disciplining his mind, learning the truths of existence and cleaving in love to the Deity. " For the souls which are left after death are not the same as when they were born, since at birth the soul is only a potential power, while upon its separation from the body following death, it is an actual thing. . . ."[124]

It follows from all the above that man's one opportunity to acquire perfection, happiness and immortality lies in an austere pursuit of rational reflection and metaphysical knowledge. Yet reason is not an isolated phenomenon, distinct from the other powers of personality. If reason is good, goodness is rational; hence, all the virtues of the good life are indispensable for the healthy functioning of the rational faculty. And the development of these moral virtues is made possible in turn by a revealed Torah, which establishes a perfectly ordered society, guarding against the infiltration of erroneous beliefs and evil practices. Thus, at its source, reason is dependent upon the achievement of balanced virtues, and virtue is the fruit of life in accordance with Torah.

In the same manner, reason in its loftiest reaches does not function in the isolation of sheer abstraction. To Maimonides, reason and pious devotion go hand in hand. Contemplation and love merge at their peaks; it is there that man concentrates all the powers of his soul upon the achievement of unity with the divine source of life. To know God is to love Him, even as the Hebrew verb, *Yo-dea* means both to know and to reach the ecstasy of love.

> Thus I have explained to you that the stream of reason which flows toward us from the Lord, may He be exalted, is the bond which unites us with Him, and the possibility is afforded to you to fortify this bond, and you may also, if you wish, act so as to weaken and finally to sever this bond. But it is strengthened only if it is used with the love of God. . . . This is the love that is deepended to the point where attention cannot deal with any other thought. . . . For as the powers of the body are progressively weakened and the fires of lust are extinguished, the reasoning faculty is strengthened, its light is intensified, its understanding clarified and man's joy with the object of his understanding is deepened . . . until the soul is separated from the body through the intensity of that joy. . . . This phenomenon is known as " death by a kiss "; it is thus that Moses, Aaron and Miriam departed from this world. . . .[125]

In the *Guide to the Perplexed* Judaism attained the very apex of its development as the faith of reason. Only the great authority of Maimonides permitted the *Guide* to be tolerated by the exponents of tradition. Even so, it was severely criticized, occasionally banned, more frequently permitted only for those over thirty. It was not included in the curriculum of study in the great *yeshivoth,* but the adventurous souls who dared to think for themselves regarded the *Guide* as their Bible. For centuries storms of controversy centered about it, with the rationalists and the antirationalists abating their polemical fury only when the menacing clouds of hatred from without threatened both camps. Translated into Latin within a decade of the author's death, this masterpiece of the physician-rabbi of Cairo soon became one of the chief source books of Christian scholasticism, favored especially by St. Thomas, the master builder of official Catholic theology.

ISAAC ALBALAG

The heroic course of Jewish rationalism was not ended by the death of Maimonides. Many hundreds of authors of lesser stature wrote books in the spirit of the *Guide,* which they described as *tif-ereth galuthenu,* "the glory of our exile." A flood of creative energy was opened up by the encouragement of unfettered reasoning and free research. However, the vast majority of these rationalistic commentators did not materially change the system of their master, contenting themselves with expositions of the implications of his thought for the varying problems of Jewish life.

The ambiguous passages in the *Guide,* designedly vague and equivocal in order that the average reader might not be offended by their revolutionary import, were gradually clarified by a host of commentators. Of special interest is the contribution of Isaac Albalag, who elaborated Maimonides' distinction between "true" and "necessary" ideas into a theory of "twofold truth." The truths of philosophy and theology were assigned to different domains of life, so that what was true in one discipline could be false in the other.[126]

This doctrine was favored by the contemporary Paris school of Christian theology, but it had no real roots in Judaism since dogmas or beliefs assumed to be indispensable for salvation never loomed large in the total pattern of Jewish faith.

But atypical as Albalag's views were in this total pattern of

Jewish thought, they were not unrepresentative of the period in which he lived. Like Maimonides, he believed in two systems of ideas, one designed for the common people, the other for the philosophers in every generation; but unlike his master, he drew a rigid and impassable line between the two domains. " In the Torah, every verse has a double meaning—the first for the common people and the second for the thoughtful and the understanding."[127]

Between the two meanings there can be no reconciliation, for the truths of philosophy and religion are mutually contradictory. Albalag rejected Maimonides' attempt to achieve a synthesis between reason and faith. For instance, he declared that the eternity of the world could not be gainsaid. Philosophers may accept the doctrine of divine creation in its " perfect " sense— that is, connoting the continuous creative activity of God—but they cannot identify their cosmological teachings with those of tradition. " I point out herein that it is possible so to interpret the first chapter of Genesis as to leave no contradiction between it and philosophy, but I myself do not accept this interpretation."[128]

Recognizing the absolute gulf between philosophy and faith, Albalag advised that each be accepted as valid within its own domain. Within the organic unity of personality there is room both for the reason of the philosopher and the faith of the traditionalist. The compassionate God of religion and the self-enclosed Deity of philosophy serve different functions in the total pattern of life. The philosophic concept is the answer to the quest of our intellect, the religious a response to the yearnings of our emotional life. Both concepts, in their purity, are needed by all of us at different times. The philosopher is sometimes in need of the consolation afforded by the rites and symbols of religion; and no believer is completely immune to moments of philosophical speculation. Of course neither the philosopher nor the traditionalist comprehends the fullness of truth. The prophet and the philosopher apprehend different sides of truth, for the latter " sees the abstract concept in the concrete object, while the former sees the abstract concept as a concrete reality." The prophet institutes symbols, which are profoundly significant even if he does not completely understand them, while the understanding of the philosopher reflects a phase, but only a phase, of the mysterious fullness of reality.

The strain of skepticism in Albalag's thought gave way gradually
to an increasing faith in mystical intuition. Pursuing the inner
logic of mysticism, he arrived at the belief that God stood in need
of man even as man needed God, since the universe, with man as
its conscious expression, was itself the expression of the Deity.
God attained self-consciousness in man! This bold assertion of
modern humanistic pantheism was anticipated by Albalag, whose
own personality combined the strains of ultrarationalism and
theosophic mysticism. He translated the works of the famed
Arabic mystic, Al Ghazali and, in his later writings, favored the
views of the emergent Qabbalistic school, which postulated an
intimate correspondence between God, man, the world, and the
Torah. In fact, in his spiritual odyssey from the synthetic,
Maimonidean philosophy to the recognition of the mutual incompatibility of reason and faith, thence to the possibility of the
"twofold truth," and finally to a sympathetic hearing for the
rising movement of Qabbalistic mysticism, Albalag faithfully
reflected the development of Jewish thought from Maimonides,
the rationalist, to Cordovero, the speculative mystic.

No man could long live with such views as the following,
though they are inevitable in an age of transition:

> In this manner, you will find my opinion in many respects opposed to my
> faith, for I know by proof that one proposition is true by nature, and I
> believe in the words of the prophets that its opposite is true in a miraculous
> way.
>
> For just as the intentions of a philosopher can only be understood by a
> philosopher, so the intentions of a prophet can only be understood by a
> prophet. . . . Therefore, it is not fitting to set the one in contradiction to
> the other, but the wise man will accept the one on the basis of a rational
> proof and he will accept the other on simple faith. . . .

The philosopher and the prophet each see only one phase of
reality. So it can be shown that God acts neither by natural necessity nor yet by the caprice of will. Tradition pictures God in
the latter guise, philosophy in the former. " But the existence of
this kind of action is not understood by the common people, nor
do the philosophers understand its character. This is why the
Torah did not write it, leaving room for the conceptions of the
populace. . . ."[129]

RALBAG

The paradoxical and bold opinions of Albalag could well serve as an illustration of the uneasy transition between the age of reason and the epoch of Qabbalah. Yet, in the next generation, the synthetic philosophy of rationalistic Judaism was to rise to still another apex of achievement in the works of the encyclopedic genius, Rabbi Levi ben Gershon, known as Ralbag.

Ralbag's great theological treatise, *Milhamoth Hashem*, appeared in the south of France one century and a half after the *Guide*. Gershon, or Gersonides, was an outstanding Talmudist, physician, mathematician, and astronomer. His father was also a renowned scientist and he had grown up in the favored milieu of Provence, where philosophical Judaism was still assiduously cultivated. Four years after his death in 1344, the unparalleled bloody massacres which accompanied the ravages of the Black Death razed to the ground more than three hundred Jewish communities in France and Germany. The fanatical populace of Western Europe vented its blind rage and its fear-crazed hysteria, which came to be known as the "red laughter," upon the hapless Jews in their midst, accusing them of poisoning the wells. When the riots subsided in 1350, the survivors of Jewry in France and Germany were physically broken and spiritually fatigued and depressed, unequal to the task of rethinking the intellectual presuppositions of their faith.

Living on the eve of this black night of disaster, Gersonides boldly carried forward the rationalistic adventure of Maimonides. Like his master, he believed in the duty of seeking truth at all costs. "For the Torah is not a law which compels us to accept falsehoods, but its purpose is to direct us to the attainment of truth, insofar as this is possible."[130] Insisting that nothing in the Torah can be contrary to reason, Gersonides had no difficulty in explaining, even at times in explaining away, the nonphilosophic passages of the Bible. For instance, the account of creation in the first chapter of Genesis, he declared, really assumed the timeless existence of uncreated primal matter; Joshua's stopping of the progress of the sun in the heavens was to be understood as a rhetorical gesture; Jacob's wrestling with the angel was only a dream of Jacob's. Gersonides sought and found a philosophic and universal purpose in every chapter of the Torah.[131]

At one with Maimonides in the passion for rational consistency, Gersonides criticized and elucidated several important details in the faith of reason. In the first place, he denied the sufficiency of the cosmological proof for the existence of God, which maintained that the motion of the heavenly spheres implied the existence of an Unmoved Mover. Instead, he favored the teleological proof, which derived from the manifest existence of order and purposiveness in the world. He was particularly impressed with the marvelous intricacy of design that is manifested in the instincts of insects and animals. He thought of God chiefly as the great designer of the universe, its Architect and Master.

In line with this concept, he did not follow Maimonides in the belief that the world was created out of the absolute naught. Impressed with the extent of unnecessary evil in the world, with the considerable range of the contingent and the unplanned, Gersonides argued in behalf of the eternity of primal matter, the source of the accidental, the chaotic and the frustrating. In his philosophy, the two primal poles of reality were not being and naught, but design and chaos. Through the divine act of creation, God's design was imposed upon the potential matter, producing a world which, after all these years, is still not altogether perfect, a world consisting of both design and chaos, beneficent purpose and blind chance. All that is good and beautiful in the world is due to the imposition of form by the Supreme Being; all that is evil and painful is due to the obstinate resistance of uncreated matter, its lack of plasticity and malleability. Purposiveness is found in the world, but the whole universe does not serve one grand purpose. The marks of divine purposiveness are evident in every aspect of life, but especially in the instinctive reactions of animals, in which millions of minute reactions are co-ordinated in behalf of the life of the organism as a whole, especially in behalf of the life of the species.

Elaborating upon Maimonides' concept of Providence as proportional to a person's attainment of pure and adequate metaphysical ideas, Gersonides inquired as to the manner in which this divine concern was expressed. Ruling out the notion of the unity of divine will and reason, he maintained that the divine concern with the thinking individual was limited to the gift of insight. The favored philosopher is granted neither worldly goods nor protection from physical ills, but only the light of understanding. Just as the operation of Providence in the case of animals is shown in their being endowed with instinctive forms of knowledge and action, so the especially favored individual is endowed with the gift of intuition, over and above his rational knowledge—intuitions concerning the affairs of this world as well as insight into abstract truths.

It is thus evident that His Providence operates among the individuals of the human race through the information that He bestows upon them concerning the good or the evil that might come to them. This knowledge comes from Him in varying ways, depending upon the relative achievements of people—their nearness to or distance from the Active Reason. Thus, the men who are powerfully united with the Active Reason receive this information in a perfect manner which is the way of prophecy. . . . Others, who have not attained this degree of perfection, are guided by the Lord in that they receive from Him intuitive hints directed toward ends which they do not understand . . . or they get sudden impulses of fear, causing them to move away from the evil which has been prepared for them by the order of the heavenly bodies. . . . And this way of informing is sometimes very weak. . . .[132]

Restricting the activity of God in this world, Gersonides repudiated the easy compromise of Maimonides in regard to the riddle posed by God's foreknowledge and man's freedom of choice. If God knows in advance what man will do, then the freedom of man is only apparent, for he cannot act in any other way than that which has been foreseen by his Maker. Maimonides sought to evade the horns of this dilemma by insisting that God's knowledge was utterly different from man's knowledge, the two forms of cognition having indeed nothing in common but the term "knowing." In human terms, the contradiction between foreknowledge and freedom is real and inescapable. But since divine knowledge is a unique, humanly incomprehensible category, there need be no contradiction. Gersonides rightly rejected this dubious equivocation. If there is any sharing at all between man and God it is in the field of knowledge. There is no comparison in extent between a finite intelligence and an Infinite Mind, but their identity in kind cannot be questioned. Else how could logic have any meaning? Gersonides concluded that God knows the contingent as being contingent, not the results that will issue from it. Man's freedom is real, and God's knowledge of things human is therefore limited.

It is clear then that the phase which He knows is that in which all things are ordered and limited, as is the case in the Active Reason, for it has been explained that in this sense the term " knowing " is applicable, and the phase which is not known to Him is the one in which events are not strictly ordered, being only possible and contingent, for in this sense, knowledge is not possible. . . .[133]

Man's chance to share in the divine intelligence immanent in the universe is his one opportunity to achieve the final bliss of immortality. For insofar as man is made of flesh and blood and an animal soul, he is part of the restless and transitory world of matter. But man may also attain the knowledge of clear concepts and eternal principles as they inhere in the Active Reason, thus uniting his mind with the ruling mind of the physical universe. This " acquired reason " of man is the immortal part of the human personality.

It is thus perfectly clear that the acquired reason is eternal of necessity, for the acquired reason is nonmaterial [nonhylic] and that which is not material does not possess in itself the cause of its own disappearance. . . .[134]

In this manner, the level of the fortunate immortals varies greatly, and the more one's understanding of the systematic unity of concepts approaches that of the Active Reason, the more intense is his bliss, and the joy and delight in his conceptions is the more thrilling. . . . The sweetness of the concepts is related to their perfection. . . . That is why our sages agreed that there were different levels for the righteous in paradise. . . . When they said, " All Israelites have a share in the world to come," they meant that through the guidance of the Torah, many Israelites are bound to attain some knowledge of correct metaphysical concepts, whether much or little. Still, when they say, " all Israelites " they mean " most Israelites."[135]

This last is so stated since not all Israelites could possibly attain sufficient unity with the Active Reason to become immortal in any significant sense.

Though Gersonides occasionally repeated the pious formula that the inferences of reasoned speculation must be discountenanced when they contradict the clear teachings of tradition, he nevertheless hewed rigidly to the line of philosophical truth. as he understood it. With Maimonides, he accepted the authenticity of the prophetic phenomenon but as to its content, he allowed reason full scope for investigation and judgment. The Torah and its *mizvoth* were to him so many aids for the achievement of a perfect contemplative life. He believed in the coming of the Messiah and even calculated the date of his advent, but he clung firmly to the conviction that "understanding is life," and that religion could not possibly set itself against the truths of philosophy.

In Gersonides' *Wars of the Lord*, the faith of reason attained an even clearer and more radical formulation than in Maimonides' *Guide*, revealing both the genius and the danger of rationalism. For a long line of succeeding thinkers, Gersonides became the *bête noire* of Jewish philosophy. His *magnum opus* was contemptuously referred to as *Wars Against the Lord*, though his popular commentary on the Torah was widely accepted and read since it enriched the Scriptural verses with additional meaning and uncovered the "spiritual utility" of each of the chapters of the Pentateuch.

CHAPTER SEVEN

THE DECLINE OF RATIONALISM

HISDAI CRESCAS

HISDAI CRESCAS (1340-1410) represents the great turning point in the rationalist movement in medieval Judaism. He still lived and labored within the great philosophical tradition of the intelligentsia of Spanish Jewry, but he it was who did most to undermine its liberal spirit and its faith in reason. Scion of one of the most prominent Jewish families in Spain, he combined deep Talmudic learning with an encyclopedic comprehension of the general thought of his time. For a while he served as adviser to the King of Aragon and on numerous occasions he was challenged to defend his ancestral faith against the strictures of Christian theologians. Famed masters of Talmudic law, such as Rabbi Isaac ben Shesheth, referred to him with great deference, while a circle of philosophy-minded friends and disciples gathered about him in his native city. Acclaimed by his many admirers as "head of the philosophers," he boldly turned the weapons of logic against the rationalists. The tragedy of martyrdom in his own family shattered his faith in the rationality of man and deepened his faith in God. In the great pogrom wave of 1391, his beloved son chose to die "for the sanctification of the name" rather than to follow the many prominent rationalistic Jews who, in the hour of trial, deserted their faith and embraced the protection of the Cross.

Thoroughly acquainted with the New Testament, Crescas, in defending his faith, frequently took the offensive and criticized the Biblical foundations of Christianity with merciless rigor. In his criticism of Christian theology, he concentrated his fire especially upon the doctrine of vicarious atonement for human sins, pointing out the paradox of God redeeming the world from His own law and will by the sacrifice of His son. Unbroken by pain and sorrow, Crescas retained his firm faith to the end and the luminosity of his thought served to guide and comfort several generations of perplexed and harried Jews.

All that was left of the prosperity and glory of the golden age of Spanish Jewry faded rapidly in his lifetime, giving way to hopeless misery and despair. The way of reason, for all its chaste nobility, offered no comfort in a dark and unreasoning world. Crescas led his despairing, disillusioned, and penitent disciples down from the high pinnacles of reason to the traditional, secluded valley of naïve faith with its secure, darkly shadowed ramparts. But such is the paradox of human thought that Crescas, the bitter foe of Aristotelian rationalism and the fervent defender of unquestioning faith, became unwittingly one of the intellectual precursors of Spinoza's reassertion of an antireligious rationalism [1]

In his main work, *Or Adonoi (The Light of the Lord)*, Crescas refuted the twenty-five basic propositions of medieval Aristotelianism, as they were formulated by Maimonides. Of special significance was his contention that the infinite could be real, a contention which reappeared in European philosophy at the dawn of the age of reason in the systems of Bruno, Descartes and Spinoza. To Crescas, however, the infinity of the world was proof of the essential incomprehensibility of reality. In regard to the ultimate secrets of the universe, "the gates of speculation are closed," a mournful phrase which recurred with monotonous consistency throughout his philosophical system. With pitiless logic he demolished the well-worn clichés of medieval philosophy; to wit, that "the thinker, thought and the object of thought are one." At this point, too, the net effect of his argument was to emphasize the nonintelligibility of existence. Thought is an arrow which pierces the universe, but does not encompass it; in their essence, God and the universe remain elusive.

Crescas was willing to accept from philosophy the concept of God as the prime mover. The ultimate source of all activity, God transcended all humanly known motions and appearances. However, he contended, the philosophers ventured far beyond their depth when they presumed to determine with logical precision the exact nature of God's attributes. Indeed, the pretentious definitions of the rationalists were neither more logical nor more relevant than the naïve anthropomorphisms of the populace. Since the Deity is unknown, the "negative" attributes of philosophy may suggest to our minds a totally inadequate awareness of "the Lord, who sought to dwell in darkness." May not the negations of the rationalists err as much on the side of spiritual emptiness as the affirmations of the anthropomorphists err on the side of materialistic fullness? "If we negate an attribute of His that should not be negated, we may err in the direction of rebelliousness and denial and possibly repudiate His divinity."[2]

Knowing that He is not body, we may affirm with certainty His absolute unity and immateriality. But beyond this point we may not go. How then shall we understand the manner whereby He is in constant contact with creation, and especially with mankind? In the Aristotelian universe, reason as pure activity is the basic analogy for the comprehension of the nature of the divine being. God is absolute thought, thinking Himself, and man approaches God by the avenue of sustained logical contemplation. Having denied the power of reason to grasp the essence of things, Crescas is left with the concept of God as transrational, elusive and mysterious—more akin to the soul, as in Plato, than the intellect, as in Aristotle. Is God then simply the unknowable? Is pure skepticism the final fruit of philosophy? Crescas shied away from the treacherous shoals of skepticism and pointed out a causal analogy for the understanding of God's nature. From His acts we infer the quality of His being. True, we do not and cannot know the essence of God, but the world in all its beauty is here, pointing to a being Who expresses His nature through the bestowal of existence, life and kindness. Hence, He is a creative soul and love belongs somehow to the essence of His being.

Jewish tradition concurs with Aristotelian philosophy in attributing the perfection of joy to the Deity. But the philosophers assumed joy to be a concomitant of the activity of pure thought. They understood the ineffable joy of immortality to be the union in death of the finite intellect of man with the infinite intellect of God. Actually, Crescas pointed out, joy and sorrow belong to will and feeling, not to rational thought. Is it not logical to assume that joy is a concomitant of love, not of thought? The Lord rejoices in His ceaseless creativity, "renewing His primal works day by day," and those who cleave to Him in love are similarly imbued with the joy that is divine. The broad and popular avenue of the love of God leads to joy both in this world and in the hereafter, not the narrow and aristocratic path of the intellect.

> Since He bestows of His goodness and perfection with will and purpose, it follows that the love of goodness and continuous creation belongs to His being. Is not this true joy, as it is written, " The Lord rejoices in His deeds "? . . . Hence, the perfect good that can come to man is to cleave unto Him, and this achievement is the secret of genuine prayer. . . .[3]

Crescas substituted love for thought, with the saint taking the place of the philosopher at the head of the queue seeking the " nearness of God." Human perfection is attained not through the progressive refinement of speculation, but through the cultivation of the love of God. The prophet, who by definition stands nearest to God, is therefore the favored saint who seeks Him by way of evergrowing devotion, not the speculative philosopher, who sharpens his intellect by the subtleties of logic.

> It is therefore clear that only he is prepared for this perfection of prophecy who cleaves to Him and removes himself from the society of men in order to concentrate upon this service. . . . The more the saint binds himself in love to God, the higher he rises on the ladder leading to the consummation of prophecy. And if he persists in clinging unto God with all the devotion of his being and in single-minded concentration, it cannot be doubted that the divine flow of inspiration will come to him. . . .[4]

Though he contested Maimonides' concept of the intellectual character of prophecy, Crescas accepted the great rationalist's belief that prophecy is a permanent possibility, for the voice of God is not silenced. Only " the troubles of the time " make the needed degree of loving concentration unattainable in the lands of exile. Prophecy is more a human attainment than a divine gift, more the progressive sharpening of man's intuition than a sudden act of revelation on the part of God, " for it derives of necessity from the perfection of the love of God and of a man's cleaving unto Him, these activities constituting the essential cause of prophecy."[5]

Involved as he was in continuous controversy with Christian theologians, Crescas wrestled with the question, " Why did not the Hebrew prophets attempt to call the other nations to the service of the Lord, that they too might rest under the wings of His *Shechinah*? Should not the Hebrew prophets have undertaken missionary journeys to the Gentiles? "

Convinced that the content of prophecy was simply divine love, he was compelled to conclude that the greatness of a prophet could be measured by the outpouring of his love for mankind and the ardor of his labors for the redemption of human souls; hence, by the intensity and scope of his missionary endeavors. But this principle seemed to afford aid and comfort to the Christian claim that Jesus was the "greatest of all the prophets." Was it not through the impact of His message that the magnificent missions of Christianity were undertaken? If we should judge the fervor and genuineness of any prophet by the number of people that were affected by his message, directly and indirectly, the accidents of history would be allowed to distort the truths of faith. In particular, the truth of Judaism would be obscured, for how could the meagerness of Jewish missionary success be stacked against the magnificent triumphs of its rival faiths? Still, the question remains, why did not the Hebrew prophets, out of the superabundance of their love for God and man, undertake preaching missions to the Gentiles?

In answer to this challenge, Crescas contended first that the Gentiles of Biblical times were not ready for any monotheistic teachings. It would therefore have been utterly useless for the prophets to preach to them. Nor were the pagans really responsible for their pagan ways, since the character of a people, and the nature of its historical culture, was determined by the stars and by their ancestry. "The heavenly bodies direct the affairs of this lowly world, and all gifts come to men in relation to their ancestry. . . . Thus, the proselytes from the other nations were then like a malignant growth upon the people of Israel, since the Gentiles were not yet ready for this perfection."

The second argument of Crescas is relevant even today. Judaism, he asserted, did not send individual missionaries because the entire people of Israel was one massive missionary society, preaching the truths of monotheism by the sheer weight of its existence. The many-sided life of a whole people sounds a message more unmistakable and effective than that of any number of individual preachers.

> For it is through our being exiled and scattered among the nations that His name is proclaimed among all men and the message of the prophets is articulated. . . . And when the truth is revealed in time, all the nations will come to serve Him, shoulder to shoulder. . . .[6]

Thus, while the ultimate design of God is "to bring about the perfection of the entire human race, through piety and good works," the Jewish people constitute His chosen instrument for this purpose. And the Jews fulfill this assignment by their very existence in all the lands of their dispersion.

This concept of the Jewish "mission" is based upon Crescas' interpretation of the nature of Israel's superiority in the domain of spiritual life. In this phase of his thought, Christian influence and the subconsciously felt need of countering Christian claims are most apparent.

Owing to Adam's sin in eating the forbidden fruit, the "corruption of the serpent" entered into the soul of mankind. Nahmanides, the great precursor of Qabbalistic thinking, had restricted the effect of "original sin" to the incidence of death. Were it not for Adam's sin, man's body might have continued to be immortal, but no man is accounted a sinner in the sight of God because of Adam's sin.[7] Crescas remained true to this Jewish insistence on divine justice and man's individual responsibility, but he contended that Adam's sin left in the hearts of men a heritage of "concupiscence," "a powerful impress of materialistic inclinations, so that the entire race of mankind became predisposed to degeneration and oblivion." God does not prejudge man on account of this "primal sin," but, Crescas asserted, the non-Jewish portion of mankind is nevertheless so fashioned, in consequence of Adam's sin, as to be unable to achieve the perfection of divine love.

Abraham stood "at the opposite pole" from Adam. When he was circumcised, he became a "new man," and whenever the covenant of Abraham is performed, it is "as if a sacrifice of blood and flesh" is given to the Almighty, atoning for Adam's sin, and reinstating man's original nature. Circumcision is more than a one-time act; in reality it constitutes a continuous sacrifice, since, through it, "man's lust is weakened." Also, Abraham's sacrifice of his only son, Isaac, was accepted by God as full atonement for Adam's sin in behalf of all the seed of Abraham and all who enter into the covenant to the end of time. "Behold, thus He brought the children of Israel to His service, removing them from the laws which direct the affairs of all men, because of this sacrifice which embraces the totality of the nation; that is, the binding of

Isaac upon the altar. . . ."[8] In the Talmud, it is claimed that the
"corruption" which the serpent injected into Eve, and through
her into all mankind, was removed from the children of Israel
when they accepted the Torah at Sinai.[9] Crescas, apparently
under the influence of Christian theology, preferred to rely on
the redemptive potency of the sacrifice of Isaac. Possibly, too,
Crescas had in mind an old tradition to the effect that Isaac
was actually slaughtered on the altar, burned to ashes and then
revived.[10]

Through the life and achievements of the patriarchs, the
Jewish people, said Crescas, became biologically conditioned for
life in accordance with the high standards of the Torah. They
were endowed with a constitution that is free from those compulsions of lust and instinct that enter into the making of non-
Jewish humanity. As we have seen, the pathway to perfection
consists in the cultivation and refinement of piety or the love of
God, and the central goal of the Torah is the development of
"true reverence for and love of God." In turn, this ultimate
purpose is achieved through the perfection of the qualities of
character and by the attainment of right ideas. In all their ramifications these goals explain the *mizvoth* of Judaism. The complex
ceremonies serve to emphasize God's meticulous concern with the
Jewish way of life and to impress upon Jews the need of yielding
all we have and are for the love of Him. Torah and *mizvoth* prepare the Jew for the ordeal of martyrdom, the final proof of the
perfect love of God.

> From the Torah it becomes clear that His Providence is very exacting in
> our case, which realization reminds us continually of His lofty greatness
> and of our infinite littleness, so that we are led to cling unto Him, may
> His name be blessed, though we are infinitely removed from Him. . . .
> Since beliefs are instilled into the soul through the repetition of actions,
> Providence saw fit to instill righteous faith into our souls, through the
> ritual of the sacrifices. For by bringing our offerings into the Temple,
> we acknowledge that all the goods of life and the objects of the senses
> derive from Him and His beneficent concern. . . .[11]

The dietary laws have been designed to guard us from foods
which cause "dullness of the mind, or evil qualities of character,
or unhealthy lusts." In addition, their very complexity reminds
the Jew of the extreme concern of God for the way in which he

conducts his life; for this reason, the Jew is moved to respond with love and perfect devotion.

Because of their heritage of patriarchal merit and their loyalty to the Torah, the Jewish people constitute an object of special divine concern, set apart from the forces of nature. "The stars" govern the affairs of mankind generally, but the Jews are ruled directly by God.

> For it is proper that Providence should be extended in greater measure to those that are higher in perfection. So divine Providence is incomparably stronger in the case of the human race than in regard to all other animal species. For the same reason, it is to be expected that the people which has moved furthest along the road to perfection should be favored with heightened divine concern. . . .

Crescas agreed with Maimonides that Divine Providence extended only to the small group of men who lifted themselves above the level of the masses. But while the great rationalist made intellectual attainment the measure of man's ascent toward the sphere of divine concern and rule, Crescas regarded the cultivation of inner love and piety as the touchstone of nearness to God. "For he who is more beloved by Him is more guarded by His Providence." And the Jewish people as a whole are lifted above natural law and subjected to the special rigors as well as the peculiar kindness of His direct rule.

But if the Jewish people are thus especially favored, how can we account for their pitiful wretchedness and seemingly interminable agonies? It took unparalleled tenacity of spirit to affirm the favored status of Israel in the divine plan of historical development at a time when a series of cruel disasters almost decimated the Jewish communities of Western Europe. Yet Crescas could not retreat from this position without forfeiting all claims in behalf of his people.

His replies to this question emerge out of the total argument of his book:

(1) Since God is good and loving, the evil that we find in the world can only be understood as a form of unknown good. Perhaps its purpose is to rebuke the sinner and cause him to return, or it may be designed to intensify the love of the righteous. But evil is the prelude to good. "Before we were presented with the test, He did not know that we loved Him. For the truth is that

we did not love Him before the test as much as we did after the test."

In this case Crescas was able to write from sad experience. His great personal tragedy deepened his piety and intensified His love for God. Thus, the agonies of Israel may be designed "to subdue our hearts to the limit of the possible or to add future kindnesses to our lot."

(2) "True reward and punishment is of the soul." Our career upon earth is only the testing ground of our spirit. In the final accounting it will appear that each individual was justly treated.

(3) "We know it from true tradition that the world is judged in accord with the majority of each generation." If the majority is found culpable, the minority must suffer in this physical universe, with all individual accounts being settled in the world to come.

The true saint, Jewish or not, may well suffer on occasion, "when he is not so deserving as to cause the established order to be changed on his account. Such an eventuality does not constitute a deviation from the justice of God. For these universal variations of reward and punishment are ordered generally by the heavenly bodies."[12]

(4) In the wisdom of God, it may be necessary for Israel to endure extreme horrors and agonies, not only for the sake of its purification but also in order to aid in the progress of mankind. Many of the troubles of our people are traceable in the last resort to our uprootedness from our homeland. By the inscrutable decree of God, we were exiled among the nations, "in order that we might be prepared to draw them to the service of the Lord in the end of days. Also, that they might benefit from the merit of this nation."[13] All the tragic travail of our people will be more than justified if, in our capacity as missionaries unto mankind, we help to usher in "the kingdom of heaven" on earth.

It is indeed remarkable that Crescas was able to think in terms of a Jewish "mission" in behalf of the Christian world, even when that world, in its benighted fury, robbed Him of His beloved son. In his own case, the dogmatic formula proved effective: the greater man's suffering, the greater his power to love.

If the purpose of the Torah is the cultivation of the love of God, and piety, cannot the same end be achieved by other faiths? Why then should a Jew lay himself open to divine punishment if he yields to the pressures and blandishments of the dominant faith?

In Crescas' time, the Jewish rationalists had come to accept the principle that a person's faith is not dependent upon his will. Hence, in justice, a person may not be punished for his beliefs. This liberating principle of modern democracy was charged with dangerous implications for the Jewish community. Why brave the horrors of the Inquisition and the ceaseless malice of fanaticism if dogmas are only instruments of piety, while the universal values of ethics and religion are alone inherently significant? To combat the massive trend toward baptism, especially among the intellectuals of his generation, Crescas felt called upon to point out the limitations of this doctrine.

True, he said, a person may not be blamed for his sincere beliefs, since the human mind is and ought to be a free instrument. But a Jew who serves God with utmost devotion derives so much joy from the practice of his faith that he cannot possibly bring himself to abandon it. His belief then becomes so tenacious that he willingly chooses death in preference to baptism. If any individual Jew fails to acquire this perfect unity of faith and feeling, his character is somehow defective. And for this failure to cement his faith by love and joy, a person may be justly punished.[14]

From this argument, it follows that an insensitive and indifferent Jew who practises his faith in a cold and perfunctory manner commits no additional crime in converting to another religion. He merely proves his laxness by his foul act of desertion.

We have seen that Crescas believed reason was incapable of comprehending the will of God. A pious man will therefore eschew the philosophical pathway of negations, lest he be tempted to deny one of the powers of the Lord. Following this line of reasoning, Crescas found fault with the manner in which the well-known contradiction between God's knowledge and man's freedom was solved by his predecessors. Carrying the principle of divine knowledge to its ultimate conclusion, Crescas argued that no limit could be set to the infinite attributes of the Deity. No thing or event is outside the scope of divine power. In every phase of life we behold the operation of inexorable necessity, in accord with the laws of nature which derive from God, without any trace of indetermination, freedom, or contingency. How, then, is man's freedom to choose between good and evil to be understood?

Crescas advanced the principle that " the contingent is found in things in regard to their own status, but not in regard to their causes." In other words, man feels free to choose, and his choice may be determined by laudable or culpable motives, but this felt freedom of action, which is quite sufficient for moral purposes, in no way contradicts the actual chain of necessitous cause and effect by which his action was determined. In effect, Crescas denied the principle of human freedom, though he was deeply conscious of the demoralizing tendencies of the mood of determinism.[15] A learned contemporary of his, bearing the Jewish name of Abner, accepted baptism, offering as his apology Crescas' teaching that all the actions of man are determined in any event.

Substituting the pathway of love for that of metaphysical speculation, Crescas found no difficulty in justifying other forms of existence in the hereafter, such as are postulated in the doctrines of heaven and hell. He assumed that after death, the tendencies which the soul had acquired in life continued to affect it, even while it was surrounded by the perfect ideas prevailing in the world of truth. If the soul, while on earth, acquired the supreme idea of the love of God, the intensity of its joy attains unimaginable heights when it beholds the truth of its earthly orientation. If, however, it acquired an inner coldness and indifference to the things of God, then the soul feels itself pulled apart in the hereafter by opposing forces.

> When the soul of the devout, after separating from the body, enjoys the radiance of the *Shechinah*, it obtains infinite delight, since it longs by its nature to unite with the spiritual . . . but the degrees of this delight differ in accord with the measure of the love and devotion acquired on earth.
> Since the knowledge of opposites is one, when a soul used to materialistic pleasures does not obtain that for which it longs, it endures such agony as may be compared to the pain of burning. . . .[16]

Having established the principle that "the gates of speculation are closed" in regard to the ultimate mysteries of existence, Crescas reaffirmed the belief in the resurrection of the dead. Furthermore, he saw in the resurrection not only an opportunity for righting the wrongs of this world, but a means of demonstrating the truth of Judaism. When the dead rise from their graves, all men will become convinced of the truth of the Torah. Thereafter all men and women will live forever, serving the one true God, "Whose name will be One."

On the same principle of *ignorabimus*, he considered it possible that prayer might be effective in changing the predetermined course of events. He did not assert this belief as a certainty, but he was positive of the error of the rationalists who turn their doubts into negative dogmas. By the same token, the power of repentance cannot be ruled out, since God, Who is the ABSOLUTE GOOD, could not have left erring man to his own devices without providing the safeguard of repentance. He did not even reject the belief in amulets, in demons, in the occult power of the names of God, or even the belief in metempsychosis.

"So long as the people who maintain these beliefs base their faith upon tradition, then the gates of speculation are closed on this question."[17] Weak as the testimony of tradition may be concerning these points, the cocksure denials of the rationalists were, to Crescas, weaker still.

The anti-intellectual refrain of Crescas is a fitting epitaph for his generation's "failure of nerve," the widespread mood of despair and disgust with all human pretensions which grew apace as the train of disasters continued to afflict the wretched survivors of Spanish Jewry. Yet the light of philosophy was not completely extinguished, and in the first part of the fifteenth century, it was represented by Joseph Albo, a disciple of Crescas, who was the leading exponent of Judaism in his generation.

JOSEPH ALBO

Like Crescas, Joseph Albo was occasionally called upon to defend the Jewish faith against the strictures of Christian theologians. Born in the province of Aragon in Spain, he was still a young man when he took part in the famous disputation in Tortosa (1413-14). The Jewish protagonists were called upon to prove, for the thousandth time, that their continued repudiation of the Christian substitute for Judaism was not due to sheer stubbornness. In his lifetime, Christian intolerance grew in intensity, while the hold of Judaism upon its devotees steadily weakened, through the spread of cynicism and despair. The golden age of Spanish Jewry was already but a dim memory, and the harsh aspects of fanaticism and superstition in the contemporary world were becoming ever more painfully apparent. Inevitably the unlovely spirit of the age weighed heavily upon the minds of men like Albo, making it difficult for them to liberate themselves completely from the oppressive intellectual atmosphere in which they lived. Taking into account the sad circumstances of his life, his retreat from the lofty pinnacle of rationalism is not as remarkable as the consistent sweetness of his temper and the unruffled tolerance of his views.

Laboring in the gathering fanaticism of fifteenth-century Spain, Albo projected the question, " Is only one religion true? " Deeply aware of the malignant consequences of the prevailing Catholic doctrine of exclusive salvation, Albo and his Jewish contemporaries felt that the good God Who rules mankind, in all its multifarious variations, could not possibly be guilty of so unfair an arrangement of conditions as would predispose by birth and education one portion of humanity for salvation and the rest for perdition. The perfection of divine goodness is inconsistent with the belief that any one group possesses the only true faith.[18]

Yet it was not possible for Albo to accept the philosophical position that all religions may be equally useful in training mankind to obedience. In the circumstances of their time, the Jews could not afford an attitude so liberal as to leave them no valid reason for the arduous labors and the continuous sacrifices that Jewish life entailed. Albo was impelled therefore to find a rational position between these two conflicting points of view, so as to justify the sacrifices demanded by Jewish loyalty, while outlining a basis for tolerance and understanding among different faiths.

Albo began his exposition (*Sefer Haikkarim*) with a description of the general principles of a religious faith, as distinct from an ethical code of conduct. His liberal approach is manifested in the very concept of " a religious faith," since the protagonists of " a one and only true religion " would never consent to the existence of any such category as religion in general. A religious faith, according to Albo, consists of three affirmations: that God exists; that His will is revealed; that He rewards and punishes people in accordance with their manner of living.

Albo accepted these three principles of universal religion as virtual axioms. If God is good, He could not have left mankind without some sort of statement as to the ways in which He is to be served.[19] To be sure, the twin lights of intelligence and conscience in human nature provide a measure of guidance, but only of a very vague and general type. Without the aid of divine guidance, even the keenest conscience can err. Could one conceive of a philosopher nobler in the endowments of mind and heart than Plato? Yet it was Plato who suggested that women be treated as the common possession of the community.[20] Plato's error in this regard illustrates the insufficiency of human reason for the attainment of the good life, the life that is approved in the sight of God.

Revelation is indispensable. But since religion is a human pattern of living, the content of revelation at any one time and in any one place is affected by the manifold factors which condition human reactions. God is one and the same, but human beings are many and varied. Hence, religions which lead men from their various situations to the one God should be as diverse as mankind in their ritual expressions, but one in their essential teachings. Why, then, should anyone insist on imposing one pattern of worship on all the different peoples of the earth? Religions may and indeed should differ, as languages and social mores do, reflecting in their variation the peculiar qualities of each ethnic group, in respect to character, endowment, and environment.

> For even when the Torah of Moses was made available to Israel, the Torah of the sons of Noah was valid for all the nations. . . . There is no doubt that the Gentiles could attain salvation by means of the Noachide faith, since it was God-given, though the degree of salvation thus achieved could not have been so high as that which Israel was enabled to acquire by means of the Torah of Moses. . . . It follows then that two divinely given Torahs may be valid at one and the same time for different nations.[20a]

In elucidation of the doctrine of the Noachide Torah, it is important to bear in mind that no specific rites, dogmas or practices are comprised in this term, so that many different forms of the Noachide faith could be valid at one and the same time. The

Noachide Torah in Albo's formulation is a generic name for all faiths that embody and subserve the principles of ethics and piety, possibly even those which associate other divine beings with the one God in their worship. (This is a moot point in *Hahalachah*. In some formulations " the seven precepts of Noah " retain dogmatic elements.)[21] Thus, for Albo, Christianity and Islam would qualify as authentic Noachide faiths, certain to bring salvation to their worshipers.

But if salvation is attainable by means of faiths other than Judaism, albeit to a lesser extent than through the Torah, why should the Jew cling with might and main to the special forms of worship of his people's tradition? If the spirit of piety is the sole intent of the divine will, and the detailed precepts of the law only historically conditioned expressions, why cannot the Jew serve God through the medium of the dominant faith, whatsoever it may be? To these questions Albo offered several replies:

First, the *mizvoth* of Judaism are intended to make the peaks of salvation easily attainable by the average Jew. The Torah is not a yoke, but an invaluable privilege, enabling its faithful followers to enter the loftiest halls of heaven. In comparison with the delights of heaven, all the pleasures of this earth pale into insignificance. How, then, can a Jew forego his advantage of " the eternal life," for the sake of a few miserable crumbs in " the world of the hour "? Albo lists as one of the six basic principles of the Jewish faith the belief that every single *mizvah* stores up for a person the blessing of eternal salvation. " We believe that the spiritual perfection of a human being can be attained by means of any one *mizvah*, out of all the commandments of Moses, our teacher, for if this principle is not accepted it would follow that the Torah of Moses, our teacher, made it more difficult for man to attain perfection." This latter conclusion cannot possibly be accepted, especially in view of the aforementioned statement that " through the Noachide Torah, people attained a certain level out of the many degrees of the world to come. As they said, ' The pious among the nations have a share in the world to come.' "[22]

In this insistence on the possibility of attaining salvation by means of one *mizvah*, Albo brought to the fore a new principle in Judaism, which was only vaguely foreshadowed in Talmud and Midrash. Maimonides first formulated this doctrine in his first great work, the commentary on the Mishnah, but he made no reference to it in his later works. Albo elevated this estimate of the sufficiency of every single *mizvah* to the rank of a central dogma, deliberately ignoring the possibility of punishment for the nonperformance of *mizvoth*.[23] Apparently he was driven to this conclusion by the arguments of his Christian interlocutors. Doubtless they plied him with many elaborations of the Pauline thesis that salvation " under the law " is so difficult as to be virtually impossible; that the multiple requirements of piety in the Mosaic law can only be reconciled with the doctrine of a good and loving God on the supposition that they were intended to serve as the educational and disciplinary measures of a " schoolmaster "; that the law was an expression of God's justice, while salvation by faith was made possible by a special act of divine grace. In Albo's interpretation, the law became an expression of divine grace, making the bliss of salvation available to the Jew on extremely easy terms, his performance in love and devotion of any one of a number of *mizvoth*, commandments which are easily fulfilled. Albo turned attention away from the many opportunities for sin inherent in the very concept of the law, thereby providing powerful support for the confident assurance of the Jew that he was the object of special divine favors.

Second, if the validity of every other faith could be questioned, Judaism alone towered serenely beyond the reach of the turbulent waves of doubt. " Everybody " (meaning Mohammedans and Christians) admits its truth.[24] " How could 600,000 men be wrong? " This number was especially designed by Providence, for, according to Qabbalah, there are 600,000 types of human personality. And all the Israelites at Sinai, numbering 600,000 male adults, witnessed the marvels of revelation and heard the voice of God speaking to Moses. " For all of them were prophets in that hour and heard the voice of God articulating the Ten Commandments, hearing also the voice saying to Moses, as follows, ' Go and say to them.' "[25]

Conscious of the irrational dogmatism implied in the assumption that all Jews, regardless of their educational and spiritual attainments, were raised suddenly to the highest pinnacle of prophetic insight, Albo nevertheless insisted on the truth of this dogma, citing the plain testimony of tradition and throwing all philosophical scruples to the wind.

Even though reason does not accept it, it is nevertheless entirely true, since it is authenticated by the experiences of our people and its tradition . . . for the tradition of one's parents is near in certainty to the evidence of our senses, evidence which we must trust, in spite of its repudiation by reason.[26]

Albo rejected the Maimonidean thesis that prophecy is in large part a natural phenomenon, being a degree of insight attained on rare occasions by those who train their characters and refine their faculties by the disciplines of philosophy. This insight is, according to Maimonides, primarily a human achievement supplemented by divine grace, which the Lord seldom withholds. To Albo, prophecy was an incalculable, astonishing miracle, an unpredictable incursion of divine grace. It is altogether an act of God. Why then, should we not assume that the gift of prophecy was granted at Sinai to the totality of Israel?

Albo challenged the Maimonidean thesis that prophecy was the climactic attainment of philosophers. " For we never find any philosopher or scholar attaining the level of prophecy. . . ." Not through the rigors of logic and the subtle speculations of metaphysics, but by way of humble submission to the divine will and the meticulous observance of His law do men attain that state of divine intoxication, " when clinging with all the power of their soul to God, they acquire the power to change the nature of existence, compelling the forces of nature to do their bidding and performing various signs and miracles. . . . Thus, you will find that the masters of faith perform miracles, not the great scholars and thinkers."[27] Far from questioning the miracles of the Bible, Albo was quite ready to accept fresh miracles from " masters of faith." Great indeed was the distance that philosophy had slid down the mountainside of reason from Maimonides to Albo.

Albo was satisfied by these arguments that a Jew could not possibly find a faith as authentic as his own. Hence, for a Jew, only his own religion is fully adequate. To be sure, the believing Jew will still confront unanswered questions and unresolved problems. He may continue to ask why God did not grant the fullness of revelation to non-Jews. But such questions will not undermine his basic convictions.

We may say that if all religions were in dispute with each other, maintaining each the nondivine character of the other, then indeed our doubt would have been very great, exceedingly difficult to remove, but since they all admit the authenticity of one [Judaism], claiming only that it was valid up to a certain time . . .[28]

Albo took up the challenge of Moslems and Christians that Judaism was superseded by their respective revelations. " Can these new faiths," he asked, "claim proofs of authenticity as powerful as those of Judaism?" Their faith was based altogether on the testimony of certain individuals, the apostles of Jesus and the companions of the Prophet respectively, not of a whole people numbering 600,000 adult men. Albo, like Halevi and Nahmanides, regarded it as utterly unthinkable for the tradition of a whole people to be erroneous.

In view of Albo's extreme traditionalism, did he believe that the laws of Judaism would remain unchanged for all time?

Heir to the rationalistic tradition of Maimonides, he could not but recognize that the historical motivations for some of the rituals of the faith were of dubious value for his own generation. If the forbidden foods were prohibited because they or the methods of preparing them had some sort of connection with pagan rites and practices, why should we continue to observe them at a time when paganism is no longer a living faith? In posing this question to himself, Albo was not primarily concerned with pressure from his own contemporaries for the abolition or the modification of the dietary laws, but with the intellectual need of justifying the *mizvoth* in terms valid for his day. Having noted the distinction between the seed of universal religion and its particularist shells in the case of the Noachide faiths, he was driven to apply this distinction in the case of Judaism as well. How can laws which arose out of certain historical circumstances be valid for all times?

In answer, Albo softened the dogmatic assertion of Maimonides that the Torah will never be changed. Offering an evolutional concept of Jewish law, he anticipated in some ways the historical approach of modern Judaism. The eternity of God, he maintained, does not necessarily imply the eternal validity of the law of God, for laws are related in their effects to human beings, even as they are related in their source to God. While the central truths of religion are eternally valid, precepts of law necessarily reflect a human factor since they need to take account of changing habits, conditions, and opinions. The formulation of Jewish law, at any one time, reflects both eternal principle and the human situation.

This observation, Albo believed, was amply supported by the facts of Jewish history. Contrary to popular belief, Jewish law did not remain static through the ages. Was not the *mazeba*, a stone erected as a symbol or seat of the Deity, "beloved in the days of the patriarchs," and later prohibited by the Torah? Similarly, before Noah, it was prohibited for human beings to eat meat; in the days of Noah, the prohibition was relaxed completely, and through Moses the laws governing the proper use of meat were instituted. By utilizing in this manner the evidences of development in Bible and Talmud, Albo arrived at the startlingly contemporary conclusion that "the divine faith changed the permitted into the prohibited and the prohibited into the permitted in accordance with the change of times."[29] For the truth of a divinely inspired faith is demonstrated precisely in its flexibility and adaptability to changed conditions. "It is proper for the faith to be modified in accord with the manner in which the receptivity of the people observing it is altered by the change in circumstances."[30]

One of the accusations which the Christian disputants leveled against the Jewish rabbis was the charge that the rabbis were actually modifying the original law of Moses by their interpretations and enactments. The Jews were not faithful to their own ancient heritage, the Christian critics contended. Albo accepted the charge, turning it neatly into a compliment. If the laws of Judaism were designed solely to please God, they could not change. But their intention was not to please a tyrannical autocrat but to edify humanity. And human beings are always subject to change. Hence the principle of development in religious life. God does not demand worship from human beings in keeping with His unchanging nature, but He allows His faith to be adjusted to the changing ways of mortal men. Accordingly, though Albo believed that the dietary laws were, in some instances, intended to guard the faithful from foods "which produce heaviness and corruption in the soul," he nevertheless envisaged the possibility of their modification, and even their partial abolition.

We too shall say that there is nothing to prevent us from maintaining that the divine faith will in the future relax some prohibitions, such as the heavy fats (*helev*), blood, and sacrifices brought outside the Holy Temple, which were prohibited originally following upon the exodus from Egypt because the people were then given to the worship of demons. . . . It is altogether possible that He will permit these foods for us again. This indeed is the opinion of some of our sages, who said, "The Lord releases those that are bound," and "The Lord will permit the prohibited."[31]

This prediction refers to the Messianic age. In the meantime Jewish law is kept flexible and adjustable by means of the powers of legislation bequeathed to the rabbis. According to Albo, the range of authority for rabbinic legislation and interpretation was vast even in the lands of the Diaspora and before the advent of the Messiah.

For it is impossible that the Torah of God should be so perfect as to suffice for all times, in view of the perennially emerging problems in the relations of people to each other. The range of possible contingencies in the application of the law are too great to be included in any one book. Therefore there were given to Moses at Sinai certain general rules, not stated in the Torah in so many words but only suggested by subtle hints, so that the scholars of every generation might apply them to changing circumstances.[31a]

Albo's conception of the Torah as divine love, applied, formulated, and crystallized into laws, enabled him not merely to fend off the attacks of Christian detractors, but also to soften the harsh and austere features of philosophical rationalism. Salvation, it will be recalled, was dependent, for Maimonides, on the attainment of high intellectual powers of abstraction and the sustained practice of loving contemplation of the Supreme Being. Obviously the vast majority of mankind could never expect to attain the blessing of divine Providence and personal immortality. Moved by the traditionally Jewish concern for the poor and the unfortunate, Albo dissented from this aristocratic view. Is it conceivable, he asked, that the kind Lord would deny to most of His creatures the very possibility of achieving the ultimate purpose of their life? And the mental equipment for contemplative saintliness is obviously not given to most people. Albo's sensitive conscience revolted at the suggestion that the heavenly bliss of immortality was confined to a few chosen souls. "It is clear that all or most of those who rightfully belong in the category of mankind must be able to achieve the goal set for human life."[32]

Since the pathway of abstract reasoning is too difficult for most people, we are driven to the conclusion that the emotional out-reaching of the soul, expressed in faith and reverence, is equally acceptable to the Almighty. "For divine justice demands that the faithful should attain the level of eternal life which is set by the Torah, since they trust in God and believe in His law, though they do not acquire rational concepts. . . . The destiny of eternal life is dependent on faith."[33]

While Maimonides declared that the art of systematic reflection growing out of a good life leads to God, and Crescas countered with the assertion that self-sacrificing love is the one bond between God and man, Albo suggested that simple faith is equally effec-tive. He agreed with the great rationalist that rational thought is an intimate bond between man and God, drawing the soul of the philosopher "naturally," as it were, toward the source of its being.[34] But he maintained that the goodness of God so predisposed matters at the time of creation as to make the bliss of eternal life possible for those who cannot undertake the vigorous exercise of the intellect and are unable to devote them-selves with single-minded attention to the cultivation of His love. "The Lord makes salvation accessible to man, providing an easy way of serving Him, by the observance of His laws and precepts."[35]

Albo did not, like Saadia, assume that the mere faithful per-formance of the *mizvoth* was sufficient for salvation. Imbued with the ways of thinking of the philosophical school, he considered a share in the world to come to be dependent upon some sort of transmutation taking place within the soul of the worshiper. So he insisted that mere obedience and humble performance of *mizvoth* is not enough. The rites of Judaism are effective only insofar as they are instrumental in cultivating the attitude of reverence and trust, for it is these qualities that relate man to his Maker. Reverence and trust are qualities of man's soul, and they can be cultivated by means of concrete actions of worship and service to the Lord. "For no material being attains the per-fection which is peculiar for him save through material acts."[36] The *mizvah* then is the candle; the psychical attitude generated and sustained by it is the light.[37] And the purpose of all the com-mandments is formulated by Albo as follows: "That there may be cultivated within the soul the faculty of trust in and fear of

God, for when this power is attained the soul is uplifted unto God to the point of acquiring the quality of eternal life."[38]

This "fear of God" is not to be confused with the common understanding of the word "fear." It certainly is not simply fear of punishment. Applied to God, the word "fear" takes on many unique overtones and undertones of meaning, such as trust and love, awe and reverence. It is in fact a unique, indefinable power and orientation of soul. The positive and negative valances of love and fear are commingled in it. Man's soul senses the goodness of God even while it perceives His overwhelming majesty; its joy and its fear are one. "The soul rejoices and delights even as it fears and trembles."[39] Love and fear merge into one, as both feelings rise to crescendos of intensity—in the awareness of God's nearness—"the love of God delights the soul and thrills it."

Having set the principle of divine love in the center of his system, Albo found no difficulty in explaining the Creator's choice of Israel as the people of revelation. Why did the Lord choose Israel as the recipient of His law and His message unto mankind? God's choice was an act of love, and love is notoriously inscrutable, unpredictable, arbitrary. Love, as we know it in our human experience, is the pale reflection of the infinite, divine power; hence, even in God it may be presumed to be an irrational fiat of will. By elevating love to the rank of a primary divine faculty, not merely an accompaniment of reason, Albo restored the quality of arbitrariness to the Supreme Being. "But the love, which is not evoked by the object, having its source in the will of the lover, is arbitrary, not compelled by any cause."[40]

Accordingly, Albo did not follow the liberals in rationalizing the concept of the "chosen people" out of existence, nor did he follow Halevi in assuming the Jewish people to be a specially endowed species of humanity, a kind of super-humanity, exalted by hereditary qualities of soul above the rest of mankind. To Albo, the choice of Israel was an act of divine love, but the ultimate purpose of that choice was the salvation of all mankind. And the divine choice does not inhere in the blood of the Jews but in their tradition and their historical situation. Every individual Jew shares in this chosenness only to the extent that he renders himself into a fitting instrument of God's will. The people of

Israel as a whole will attain its consummation in body and soul only with the advent of the Messiah, who will elevate all mankind to the sublime heights of perfection.

> For if this kindness which has been promised by oath to David—to wit, that the Messiah will come in order to perfect the human race and enable it to attain its goal—is not realized, then the entire race of mankind will have been created in vain. . . .[41]

The entire career of the Jewish people is a prelude to the achievement of Messianic perfection for the human race. Israel's sacrificial loyalty to the Torah engenders a redemptive force, which will one day bring salvation to all. In speaking of the collective destiny of the Jews, Albo moved from a rational universe of discourse to the realm of lyrical fantasy. He yielded not infrequently to the seductive fascination of Qabbalah, employing some of its terminology and identifying the astronomical spheres of the philosophers with the divine *sefiroth* of that esoteric lore.

> For the Intelligence which is formed through the Torah is a separate Intelligence, independent and permanent, exercising dominion over all material things, so that the prophets and the saints were able to fashion wonders and miracles by means of this Intelligence which was acquired through the Torah. It functions as a separate Intelligence, actuated by the Active Reason, which is the *sefirah*, called *Yesod* [foundation], or the Sabbath.[42]

Albo did not allow himself to doubt that saints and prophets are indeed able to perform miracles. In the mental atmosphere in which he lived and worked, miracles seemed to be part of the scientifically authenticated body of experience. How different the mood from that of Maimonides or Gersonides! Why doubt miracles, Albo exclaimed, "since experience has proven that nature is subject to the control of the saints and the pious and those who observe the commandments of the Torah!"[43] In another connection, he added, "He who doubts that the Lord will fulfill the will of the prophet or the saint who is deserving of it, is as one who doubts the Torah and a root of its roots. . . ."[44]

But if Israel was chosen to be the special object of divine concern, why is it of all peoples the most wretched and the least favored?

Albo's answer is that, in the first place, there is nothing which is good that does not involve an admixture of evil. In this mundane world, evil and good are correlatives, unthinkable apart from each other. Could one sense sweetness if one did not experience bitterness? Only in the heavenly delights of divine love is pure enjoyment possible, whereas, in the physical realm, "wherever goodness is encountered, an admixture of some evil is inevitable."[45] Accordingly, the earthly misfortunes of the Jewish people are no more than "the admixture of some evil" in the wondrous lot of a people favored above all nations by the consciousness of playing the central role in the drama of human salvation and the prospect of high heavenly rewards.

Second, Albo maintained that Israel's sad lot among the nations was only temporary, a brief and necessary step in the process of redemption.

> For the chick is not generated in the egg until after it has become rotten and the seed begins to sprout only when it has turned seemingly to mud. Thus, too, the salvation and bliss of the nation will be attained only after the nation had descended to the very depths of disintegration, resembling almost complete decay.[46]

It follows that the worse their situation became, the more they could look forward to speedy redemption. And in comparison with the glories and joys of the Messianic era, the miseries and agonies of their history will appear to be paltry and insignificant.

Admittedly, however, it is because of their sins that the Jewish people were driven from their native land. May it not be that these sins were indeed so vast as to invalidate the promises of redemption in the Holy Scriptures? May it not be that the Jews are now a rejected, no longer a chosen people? Albo conceded the possibility of Israel's sins having been numerous and grievous, but he contended that the infinite love of God is sufficient to overcome any possible failing on the part of Israel. In this way he neatly turned the Christian argument that the Lord has permanently rejected the people of Israel. If, as the Christians contended, God is infinite love, how could His forgiveness have proven insufficient to atone for the sins of Israel, no matter how offensive those sins may have been? Albo, speaking for Judaism, maintained that God dealt with mankind by means of the policy of love as well as the policy of law. In the case of Israel, God may be expected to rely on the policy of love almost exclusively, especially at the time that He set from the beginning for the coming of the Messiah. For the Messianic era is the time when His love prevails, and the Messiah is the bearer of His mercy.[47]

Albo's firm belief in the infinite goodness of God was evidenced also in his discussion of reward and punishment in the hereafter. At a time when, in the Christian world, the dogma of eternal damnation was scarcely questioned, he stressed the incompatibility of such a cruel doctrine with the concept of a merciful God. Only for twelve months does the soul of the sinner endure the excruciating pain of purgatory; thereafter it ascends the scales of beatitude toward ever higher peaks. And just as the agonies of hell are limited in their duration, the bliss of paradise is completely unlimited, for the love of God in infinite.

Yet the narrow and bigoted spirit of that age was so powerful and pervasive that even this sweet-tempered theologian could not bring himself to apply the principle of divine mercy

> to the heretics and to those who deny the Torah or doubt the resuscitation of the dead, and to the others mentioned by our sages in Mishna and B'raitha. For they, doubting the roots of the faith, in whole or part, or the conclusions deriving from them, ought to remain under the jurisdiction of the law, with their punishment enduring forever, since they have removed themselves from the totality of Israel and from the category of the seed of the lovers of God and the observers of His commandments. But those who admit the essentials of the Torah, though they may have committed some sins, are properly the recipients of the mercy that is extended to the observers of the covenant and to the seed of His lovers. . . .[48]

The pervasiveness of the superstitious spirit of the age is evidenced frequently in this beloved classic of Jewish thought. The belief that the resuscitation of the dead is made possible by the agony of the Messiah was affirmed by him without any rationalistic qualms as to the rightness of vicarious atonement. Nor was this belief for him merely a device for the righting of all the wrongs of existence. The resurrection was for him the time when man will come fully into his destiny, attaining everlasting bliss and spiritual perfection. Albo accepted the opinion of Nahmanides that " after the revival, the dead will live as long

as their nature permits; thereafter their bodies will become purified like that of Elijah and they will exist eternally in body and
soul. However, they will then no longer make use of the organs
of sense, they will not eat and will not drink, they will not die
but will live on endlessly."[49]

He interpreted many of the legends in the Talmud literally;
for instance, the story of Rabbi Judah the Prince, who, for many
days after his death, continued to visit his home every Friday
night and recite the *kiddush*.[50]

He believed in the efficacy of a blessing given by the saints,
especially when it is supplemented by the laying on of hands.

> And when the recipient is not himself prepared to receive the divine
> effulgence of grace, the benediction is effected through the agency of a
> prophet or a saint, who, in blessing, becomes an instrument for the bringing
> down of that divine effulgence—and this is the significance of the hands
> placed upon the recipient. . . .[51]

In contrast to Maimonides, who battled valiantly against these
superstitions, Albo succumbed to the fanaticism of his age and
embraced the belief in the real power of witchcraft.[52] He also
assumed the ubiquitous operation of malevolent demons. By the
same token, he followed the Qabbalists in the assumption that
diverse miracles could be performed through the permutation and
combination of the letters in the several names of God.

> For wonders could be performed through witchcraft or sorcery, as the
> magicians of Egypt did, or through one of the Holy Names, for the names
> are the instruments of God, as it were, since He endowed them with the
> power to perform miracles. He who employs the names in order to make
> known the will of God, like the prophets, or for the sake of vindicating
> God's honor, like the saints, is beloved above and below, and he does not
> die in the middle of his days. . . .[53]

ISAAC ARAME

Albo and his generation had moved a long way from the lofty
eminence of Maimonidean thought. They still proceeded bravely
to weigh their beliefs in the light of reason and conscience, but
the gathering pressures of their fanatical and ruthless environment broke their nerve and sullied their spirit, so that the com-

forting shadows of naïve faith appeared to them more desirable than the bright glare of cold reason. Yet Albo was still a sweet-tempered rationalist in comparison with the men who attained intellectual leadership in the generation following his—the generation which witnessed the terrible catastrophe of the expulsion from Spain. Perhaps no one represented the spirit of that unfortunate generation more faithfully than Isaac Arame, whose classic work, *Akaidath Yizhak,* was used down to our own day as the inexhaustible treasure house of philosophical sermons and as an introductory volume to the great works of medieval Jewish thought.

The major purpose of Arame was to hold in check the impulse for philosophical reflection. Armed with the logical weapons of philosophy, he sought to humble the pride of the rationalists and to demonstrate the superiority of faith over reason. In the vivid imagery of a preacher, he described a nightmarish vision, in which he beheld a faithless husband take a scheming servant girl into his house. The cunning maid speedily won her master's affections, so that he made her the mistress of the house in place of his faithful and loving wife. Philosophy, he insisted, must be regarded as the maid, seeking to usurp the place of faith, the rightful wife. In his view, many of his colleagues followed the lure of reason to the detriment of tradition, contorting their faith to suit the abstractions of philosophy and torturing the clear meaning of the Scriptures in order to serve the pride of intellect.

Not that Arame was a literalist. On the contrary, he employed the allegorical method of Scriptural interpretation, in the manner of Philo, expounding the first half of the Book of Genesis not as a saga of antediluvians and patriarchs but as a symbolical account of the growth of the human personality. However, Arame employed the allegorical method as a means of extolling the virtues of naïve faith and the perils of speculative reason, demonstrating the dangerous folly of intellectual pride. Adam's primary sin in the Garden of Eden consisted in his daring to reason about the divine command, trying to understand its motivations and implications, when he should have obeyed blindly and without question. Adam's sin was the more offensive because he had been warned to keep his rational faculties under strict control.[54] While Maimonides interpreted the verses of the Scriptures so as to make them accord with the truths of science and philosophy, Arame, writing for a disillusioned and disenchanted generation, insisted on the contrary procedure, picking and choosing out of the verses of Holy Scriptures whatever seemed to accord with the mood of anti-intellectualism, to encourage his contemporaries to forsake the seductive blandishments of philosophy and to rest content with the dogmas of naïve faith. " Philosophical speculation must not stir its hand or its foot, save with the permission of the inner logic of the Torah and the prophets."[55]

He praised the Christian theologians for their subordination of philosophy to dogma.

> For they favor their faith, defending each of its articles of belief and refusing to yield an inch to philosophy. Thus, they take liberties with philosophy as our wise men are doing with the Torah.[56]
>
> Woe is us, for we have been hurt by our scholars . . . who remove us from our sanctities and prolong our exile. How can we expect redemption from among the nations when we are moving away steadily from the true faith while they are moving ever closer to it?[57]

One of the most fundamental issues between the rationalists and the traditionalists was the interpretation of the attributes of the Deity. While the naïve believers envisioned the Almighty in terms of the vivid, anthropomorphic imagery of the Bible, the rationalists presented proofs for the proposition that God was without form, without body, unchanging and unchangeable. Robbed of all human features and denied the comforting overtones of Scriptural language, the Deity of the philosophers was conceived as an abstract being, dwelling in His isolated perfection, unmoved by human petitions, unaffected by human praise. Philosophers might attain glimpses of His nature, by sustained reasoning, but how can distraught and troubled men aspire to address themselves to Him or hope to obtain redress for their sufferings? When the concept of the Deity is denuded of vividness and deprived of warmth in order to satisfy the austere demands of reason, the feeling of the reality and nearness of a living God fades from the mind of man, leaving a cold and comfortless specter, which affords little solace to man's anxious and yearning heart.

Arame disputed the contentions of the philosophers, maintaining that the manlike vision of God assumed by naïve faith is essentially true. Of course God is not like man in any literal

241

sense, yet the vision of God assumed by simple believers corresponds somehow to His ultimate being. As a philosophical thinker, Arame felt bound to repudiate the ascription to the Deity of any "material quality, multiplicity or changeability"; nevertheless, he maintained, as a man of faith, that these qualities apply to the being of God "in a higher sense." The intent of the prayerful mood is true, in a mysterious and paradoxical way, even if the language of prayer is not literally applicable to the Infinite.

> We believe, with a perfect faith, that we must not deny to Him any attribute in its perfection which is adumbrated in the anthropomorphic language of faith that is employed in Scripture. This is what our sages meant by the expression, " The Torah spoke in the language of men. . . ." Doubtless divine Providence does not mind the error of the masses in the direction of materiality as much as it warns against the contrary tendency to limit His knowledge, restrict the area of His Providence or to deny one of His powers—a tendency which might lead to utter disbelief. . . .

To Arame, Providence was a real and effective force in the everyday living of the everyday man. Far from being a rare and ethereal effulgence attuned to the meditations of philosophical saints, Providence was a real and regular force, paralleling the natural order of physical cause and effect. In this concept of Providence as a kind of miraculous order, similar to the laws of nature, Arame followed the suggestion of Nahmanides. The inner logic of faith, Arame and Nahmanides declared, implied the operation of an "intelligent nature," as contrasted with physical nature, a supernatural sequence of events within the natural order, reflecting the divine will, in all concrete situations (*Hanhagah ni-sith* or *te-va ha-cham*). Both natural law and the miraculous order of Providence derive from the will of God— the former being symbolized in the name *Elo-him*, the Hebrew letters of which add up to the number of the letters in the word, *Te-va*, or nature, and the latter being designated by the Tetragrammaton *YHVH*, the name of love or mercy.

There is no contradiction between these two forms of divine activity, nor is it necessary to follow the Qabbalists in assuming that they reflect opposing tendencies in the nature of the Supreme Being. (In Qabbalah, *din* or "law" is opposed to *rahmim* or "mercy.") The impersonal order of nature is needed in order to provide a predictable order of events as a solid and impersonal background for man's freedom of will. Nature must operate according to impersonal, inexorable laws, so that those who choose good rather than evil shall do so out of the goodness of their hearts and not for the sake of any immediate rewards. If pious deeds were to lead directly to success and happiness, no genuine piety would be possible. On the other hand, the providential order is needed for special occasions and crucial turning points in the history of mankind. Together, the two co-ordinate forces make certain that human history shall follow a predestined course, allowing both for human freedom and divine destiny. It follows that miracles are not rare and isolated breaks in the physical chain of causation, but the public manifestations of an inherent but generally hidden providential power, continuous and all-pervasive. And this supernatural-natural order is evoked not only by important events, but also by important people, whose entire life may well be governed by the order of *YHVH*, rather than that of *Elohim*.

The emergence of great men and great deeds is a phenomenon which involves the providential order. In vain do we try to comprehend them in purely natural terms. As taut strings in one instrument vibrate in sympathy when the proper notes are struck in another musical instrument, though it be far away, so a direct and intimate relationship subsists between man, "the microcosmos," and the universe, "the macrocosmos."[58] But this inner resonance comes into play as part of the providential order only when man's whole personality finds expression in some concrete act. Selfish and unworthy actions involve only the satisfaction of an impulse or a drive, a specific passion or a particular appetite. Hence, they transpire completely within the natural order. On the other hand, goodness and piety are expressions of man's total personality, evoking the beneficent operation of the providential order.

By the assumption of an "intelligent nature," Arame justified the miracles recorded in the Bible and vindicated the perpetual expectancy of divine aid, which is the mark of the pious. However, in his reliance upon the wonders of the providential order, he did not go so far as the mystic Nahmanides, who urged sick people to repose their faith in God and not to seek the help of physicians. Nahmanides commented on the verse in Exodus, "and he shall surely cure . . . from here we learn that it is permitted for the physician to heal the patient, but it does not follow that a sick person is permitted to call upon a physician for help. He should rather hope unto the Lord."[59] Arame, however, believed in the duty of self-help and spurned the suggestion of sole reliance on the curative powers of faith.[60]

In the structure of Jewish piety, nationalism and mysticism are generally arrayed together against trust in reason and the universal love of mankind. Hence, every recession of the rationalist spirit implied a retreat from the universal values of humanity and a consequent exaltation of the ethnic character of the Jewish people. Harassed and hounded on all sides, the Jewish people could scarcely live without an overwhelming confidence in the supreme value of their nation's existence. And the intensity of this defensive self-exaltation varied in direct ratio to the horrors of oppression. Writing on the eve of the expulsion from Spain, Arame affirmed the unique cosmic position of Israel, in terms which were designed to soothe and comfort his sorely tried contemporaries: "All was created and everything exists because of this nation."[61] In the hierarchy of creation, mankind is the "goal" of the plant and animal kingdoms, while Israel is the "goal" of mankind; i.e., Jewry is a kind of superhumanity. In turn, the saints are the "goals of the Jewish people." The highest purpose of God in creating the world was to bring forth saints, all creatures in the lower scales of existence being intended to serve those in a higher scale, so that there might emerge from time to time "spiritual supermen," men truly fashioned "in the image of God."[62]

Arame insisted that it is through the genus Israel that the "miraculous order of events" affects the lives of other nations, the entire people of Israel in all its empirical variations serving as the mythical *merkabah*—the heavenly chariot which functions as the mediating channel of divine grace. It is for this reason that God is designated as "the God of Israel."[63]

This assurance of being part of an especially favored people was not an abstract theory to Arame and to his unfortunate contemporaries who lived through one of the most harrowing catastrophes in history—the expulsion of the Jews from Spain. The consciousness of election was then virtually a felt experience, mingling with and softening the impact of every crucial event in their lives. Arame declared that the difference between Israel's nearness to God and that of the other nations is the difference between a woman's intimate knowledge of her husband when he lives with her and a woman who is assured by her lawyers that she has a husband.[64] The phenomenon of prophecy is an indication of the nearness of God to His people. It follows that "prophecy is as impossible for Gentiles as philosophy is for horses."[65]

The unparalleled age-old misery of Israel, which attained a disastrous crescendo in Arame's own lifetime, served only to heighten his sense of being part of the "chosen people." Facing the harassed refugees who seemed to be God-forsaken, this redoubtable preacher turned the tables on the apparent logic of events and used the very misery of his listeners as proof of their divine election. A man is jealous only of his wife. When he sees other women flirting with strangers, how does it concern him? Israel is the wife of the Lord, as it were; therefore He chastises His people for the slightest infraction of His disciplines.

> For the union of God with the people of Israel is as the union of man and wife in the bond of wedlock. . . .
> But the heathens, whom He did not sanctify for Himself and did not set aside, are not subject to His jealousy. What does He have to do with them? It has never concerned the Almighty that other nations worshiped strange gods. . . . On the contrary, the heavenly bodies were assigned to them for worship. . . .[66]

Yet, even in the overwhelming power of His wrath, the Lord had not forsaken His people. The Jews were dispersed among Christians and Mohammedans rather than among pagans in order that their monotheistic faith might not be subverted. Their bodies might be chastised but their spirits will not be broken. At a time when the horrors of the Inquisition and the flames of the *auto-da-fé* dominated the horizon, Arame esteemed spiritual benefits so far above mere material welfare that he could bring himself to thank God for scattering His people among intolerant Christians rather than among tolerant pagans.[67]

With all the fervor of his crusade against rationalism, Arame retained many of the typical features of philosophic thought. The *mizvoth* are not ends in themselves but instruments of piety. They were designed to help men attain ethical perfection through the cultivation of the qualities of humility and reverence.[68] The purpose of prayer is not to affect the divine will, but to render oneself capable of accepting His will. " In our prayers, we do not intend to relate our troubles to Him and to air them for His comprehension, but to improve our hearts and to resolve to do good deeds in His sight."[69] We pray in Hebrew because our use of the vernacular tongue would be proof of our laziness to learn the language of our faith.[70]

In keeping with the Jewish philosophical tradition, Arame defended the principle of human freedom. In debates with Christian theologians, he rejected the doctrine of predestination —that God's grace makes man live a good life and that God confers His grace upon whomsoever He wills. The principle of divine justice is incompatible with any such dogma, he maintained. Man as a rational being is utterly free, and the fall of Adam implies only the existence within human nature of propensities toward evil. But there is no inherited compulsion within us toward sin, and whosoever takes a step toward God receives immediately and almost automatically an accession of divine grace, which strengthens his resolve.[71]

Finally, in his conception of the people of Israel, he admitted occasionally, for fleeting moments only, that the term " Israel " referred to an ideal entity, the theoretical society of saints, which was truly international and by no means identical with the living people of Israel. He also looked forward to the time when the nations will admit their errors and accept the true faith, explaining Israel's dispersion as being designed for the consummation of this divine purpose.

> . . . because the reason for His having scattered the Jews among the nations is to give the peoples who rule over Israel the opportunity to hear the message of Judaism, learning of its ways and laws so that they will eventually accept it and love it. In this manner, Israel is destined to be the saving remnant of the nations. . . .[72]

JOSEPH YA-ABETZ

A younger contemporary of Arame's gave further impetus to the spirit of antirationalism, echoing the defeatist mood of the sadly distressed exiles from Spain. Rabbi Joseph Ya-abetz, one of the outstanding rabbis of hapless Spanish Jewry, led the battered but undefeated remnant of the once rich and proud community in the vain quest for a new refuge—a quest that ended tragically for the majority of the homeless and helpless emigrants. When, after many harrowing experiences, he finally found a post as the rabbi of Mantua in Italy, he set down his reflections on the failings of Spanish Judaism.

Spanish Jewry was the noblest branch of Israel; yet, upon it the wrath of God was poured, he reflected. May it not be that the very glory of Spanish Jewry was the cause of its undoing? The Jews of Spain were proud of their philosophers and their secular learning. Their piety was enlightened; their faith was, in comparison with the Jews of other lands, fairly liberal. Isn't the great catastrophe an expression of the divine disapproval of the course upon which the intellectuals of Spain had embarked for so many centuries?

Rabbi Ya-abetz was convinced that the love of philosophy was responsible at least in part for the awful punishment that overtook his countrymen. Israel sinned in forsaking the safe pathways of naïve piety for the vain pursuits of secular wisdom.

He rebuked his contemporaries for daring to probe into the secrets of the Torah so as to discover "the reasons for the commandments." So long as we have not acquired adequate knowledge "of the six orders of the Talmud," we are not permitted to "reflect on the secrets of the Torah, for then our sin would be comparable to that of Adam who was warned against eating of the tree of knowledge. . . . For the secrets of the Torah should be studied only by the great saints. . . ."[73]

The situation of the intellectuals might well be compared to that of a group of favored courtiers who were summoned by the king for an audience, along with the rest of the people. The courtiers were given beautiful horses to speed them on their way, while the plebeians walked on foot. But the courtiers were so enamored of their horses that they forgot about the king's summons, and dawdled their time away admiring the beautiful qualities of their mounts, while the common people, walking on foot, advanced far beyond them, coming into the presence of the king. The way of the *mizvoth* is slow and pedestrian, but safe and direct.

"In all my days, I saw only one out of a hundred of them [the

philosophers] occupied in the practice of the commandments. . . ."[74]

It was especially in the great trial of 1492 that the rationalists
failed to prove equal to the supreme trial of faith.

> To all of you, I address my plea: I am one of the exiles from Spain,
> driven out of that land on account of sin and failure. All who prided
> themselves on wisdom, or nearly all, forfeited their honor in that bitter day,
> while the women and the ignorant people willingly sacrificed their wealth
> and even their lives for the Holy Name of their Creator. . . .[75]

The overemphasis of the rationalists on the universal principles
of religion led them to become indifferent to the exclusive imperatives of Judaism. Indifferent to the ritual commands of Judaism,
they regarded conversion to Christianity or to Islam as the payment of a toll—a price not too high to pay for the precious gift of
life. The exigencies of Jewish survival required that unyielding
dogmatism and unflinching fanaticism be encouraged so as to
evoke that steely morale which alone could prove equal to the
needs of the time. We cannot afford to weigh dispassionately the
merits of other faiths.

> In the doctrine of creation we differ from the natural philosophers, but
> we are at one with Ishmael [Islam] and Edom [Christianity]. But in the
> doctrine concerning Mosaic prophecy and the divine origin of the Torah,
> we are separated from these peoples. . . . Certainly, since they repudiated
> the seven commandments which are obligatory for the sons of Noah, they
> are devoid of all merit . . . so that we, the community of Israel, are now
> the custodians of all the true doctrines. The existence of the nations is
> designed to provide servants for the people of Israel, following upon the
> advent of our Messiah. . . .[76]

Thus were the lofty doctrines of the Messianic redemption of
the entire race of mankind and Israel's role as the instrument of
human salvation meanly debased by the embittered rabbi into
the cheap coin of nationalistic pride. But how else, he wondered,
could Jewish morale be sustained?

The inquiring spirit of rationalism could not be simply dismissed as a dangerous luxury. The Spanish rabbis, led by the
encyclopedic Talmudist Rabbi Solomon Ibn Adret, had agreed
at one time to prohibit the study of philosophy for those who had
not yet reached the age of twenty-five. However, such measures

proved to be of dubious efficacy. The gateway of reasoning, once it was thrown wide open, could not be permanently shut. If the principles of Saadia and Maimonides were not to be regarded as fitting guideposts for speculation, whither should the inquiring Jewish mind turn for guidance? For in spite of the enveloping clouds of fanaticism and the violent storms of persecution, the Jewish intellect was not crushed, and the homeless, hounded wanderers continued to question ceaselessly: "Why believe in God?" "Why accept the Torah?" "Why practise the *mizvoth*?"

Sensing the resilient skepticism of his philosophic contemporaries, Ya-abetz pointed to the "hidden wisdom" of Qabbalah, which, he maintained, was fully in possession of all the secrets of creation. This occult wisdom is the ultimate source of all departments of knowledge and it is the distinctive heritage of the Jewish people, transmitted by a secret chain of tradition which goes back to the true prophets of the Bible.

The "reasons for the *mizvoth*," according to the Qabbalists, are not psychological, philosophical, and historical considerations, but the occult association of rites with the mystic powers that inhere in the name of God. It follows that those who perform the *mizvoth*, while they concentrate on the sacred name, achieve wonders in the invisible domain of the spirit.

> There is no man so foolish as to fail to understand that the knowledge of these names is the supreme purpose of the perfect and holy Torah which consists entirely of diverse combinations of the various names of the Holy One, blessed be He, as it is said, " I shall make him strong for he knows my name.[77]

However, the attainments of the masters of the secret wisdom are not purely magical, devoid of spiritual content. Ya-abetz stayed within the philosophical tradition to the extent of affirming that the soul of the worshiper is transformed by Qabbalistic meditations. The masters of the Name achieve lofty mystical states of "intense love of God and a mighty clinging unto Him," so that they even experience the bliss of immortality in this life.

But is not Qabbalah a "hidden wisdom," inaccessible to the masses of the people? Is the life of most people, then, devoid of purpose? We have seen that to the rationalists, the common people served to build and maintain the ideal Torah-society, which is the necessary matrix for the emergence of great and sainted men. Nevertheless, the traditionalists were dissatisfied with the limited measure of importance for the common man and inveighed frequently against the austerely aristocratic and haughtily exclusive faith of the philosophers. But is not Qabbalah similarly an esoteric science, limited to the chosen few?

In reply, Ya-abetz declared that all faithful and pious Jews were certain to share in the ineffable joy of the saints. If they do not attain the saving secrets of Qabbalah and mystical states of ecstasy during their lifetime, the opportunity for obtaining these blessings will be granted to them after death, when their souls will dwell in the lower levels of paradise, the so-called "earthly paradise," where learning and spiritual growth are still possible.

> For our Employer may be trusted to reveal the secrets of the Torah to the soul, following its separation from the body, which united itself in its lifetime to the learning of the commandments of the Torah and their practice. This is the meaning of the delights of the world to come that are described by our sages as follows: " The righteous sit, with crowns upon their heads, enjoying the radiance of the Presence." The crowns are the knowledge of the Torah and the *mizvoth*, while the enjoyment consists in the understanding of their deeper meanings. . . .[78]

"The reasons for the commandments" and the entire domain of religious beliefs and practices were lifted by Ya-abetz out of the sphere of human reflection and transposed to the dark limbo of theosophic dogma. In the incredibly harsh circumstances of their life at the turn of the sixteenth century, reasoned speculation was a daring adventure that the Jewish people could ill afford. Gradually but irresistibly, dogmatism came to replace rational thought and the "hidden wisdom" of Qabbalah, in all its imaginative grandeur and profound pathos, came to offer solace and consolation to the stricken Jewish soul, lulling the questioning mind into acquiescence by dreams and visions and tales of wonders.

Before we go on to examine the exotic realms of Qabbalah, in which genuine and penetrating insights are frequently commingled with popular fantasies and superstitions, we need to retrace our steps and return to twelfth-century Spain, where the romantic movement in Jewish thought found its noblest exponents. For Qabbalah, in one form or another, always accompanied and enveloped the trends of thought and sentiment that derived from the emotional and self-exalting phases of Judaism. Qabbalah is the traditional theology of romanticism; a comforting mantle of myths and symbols protecting the dreams and fancies of the Jewish people.

CHAPTER EIGHT

THE ROMANTIC MOVEMENT

IBN GABIROL AND HALEVI

THERE are only two fundamental ways of comprehending the mystery of existence. We may, like the rationalists, employ the weapons of the intellect and the principles of logic in interpreting the clues to an understanding of the universe. We may, like the romantic philosophers, assume that only our feelings correspond to the true nature of being. The romantics tend to view all intellectual problems as reflections of emotional and volitional tension. The conflict between faith and reason, between the rigidity of tradition and the restless querying of man's mind, is regarded by romantic thinkers principally as a psychological problem. If only an authentic attitude is assumed, the challenge of reason is certain to fade.

If feeling is deeper in the structure of reality than reason and if faith lies at the base of all thinking, then the "right" feeling and the "right" axioms are all-important. For the romantic philosophers, the victory is won at the beginning of the battle. It is the fundamental starting point that determines the conclusion. And the choice of the starting point is not within the competence of reason, but is an assertion of inner faith that underlies all thinking. We have to believe in order to understand.

Jewish romanticism is composed of two main schools, which might be designated as Individualist and Nationalist respectively. The Individualists postulate personal experience as essential to the acquiring of metaphysical truth, while the Nationalist school attributes special metaphysical qualities to the Jewish soul, rendering it, of itself, peculiarly suitable for divine inspiration. The romantic assumption of the Individualists that personal religious faith constitutes the avenue to metaphysical truth has been elaborated in Judaism chiefly by Solomon Ibn Gabirol, while the Nationalist assertion that the Jewish soul is so constituted as to be uniquely capable of receiving and recognizing divine truth is associated chiefly with the name of Yehudah Halevi.

Gabirol and Halevi were the leading poets of medieval Spanish Jewry, as well as its outstanding romantic philosophers. At one in foiling the thrust of incipient rationalism against the ceremonials of Judaism, they centered their attention, respectively, upon the universally human, and the uniquely Jewish, response. While Gabirol pointed to the supremacy of will over reason, faith over logic in both God and man, Halevi glorified the Jewish people as a kind of religious supernation, both thinkers thus endeavoring to insulate the precepts and practices of Jewish tradition against the corroding criticism of rationalist skepticism. Both philosopher-poets supplied the central pillars for the fantastic structure of speculative Qabbalah, which was unveiled with startling suddenness in the third quarter of the thirteenth-century.

Ibn Gabirol (1021–1058 or 1070) was probably the first Jewish philosopher on Spanish soil. He attained fame at an early age for his tender verses, written on both secular and sacred themes. His mystical philosophic poem, *Kether malkhuth*, has been included in the Sephardic liturgy for the Day of Atonement. By a strange conjunction of events, his philosophic work, *The Fountain of Life*, became a popular classic among Christian scholastics, who were unaware of the Jewish identity of the author, while only fragments of it were made available in a Hebrew translation. It was only in the nineteenth century that the great French-Jewish scholar, Solomon Munk, identified Avicebron, as he was known to the scholastics, as Ibn Gabirol, the foremost poet of Spanish Jewry.

The Fountain of Life is written in the form of a dialogue between a master and his disciple, the discussion centering exclusively on the metaphysical concepts of matter, form and will. So entirely free is the author from self-consciousness concerning his Jewish identity and faith, that the work could easily be taken as that of a Christian mystic. Indeed, some of the scholastics claimed to have found in it references to the Christian dogmas of the *logos*, Christ, and the Trinity. In any case, we now know that Gabirol's speculations were concerned with the task of charting the ideological map of Judaism and vindicating its distinctive patterns of piety. That his work could meet with such enthusiastic acceptance among Christian philosophers is proof of the essential similarity among the basic problems of theology.[1]

While *The Fountain of Life* is written in the form of a closely reasoned dialogue, the main theses of the author are really propounded as hypotheses. Gabirol describes the two principles of matter and form as being the two constituting factors of the spiritual realm as well as of the physical world. The ideas of the mind as well as the objects of the senses are composed of these two primal elements. With the Neo-Platonists, he assumed that all of existence was one continuous stream, flowing from the One Spirit, the source of all being. Hence, the coarse world of matter which our senses reveal to us is really spiritual in its origin, issuing out of the luminous source of all life, God. The multiplicity and the corruption of all earthly matter is due to its "remoteness" from the divine source. On the other hand, Gabirol insisted that the primal element, matter, was contained in the loftiest ideas of the mind, which cannot be completely separated from the data of the senses. All human ideas bear the marks of the senses so that only by a progressive process of abstraction is it possible for the mind to attain ever "purer" conceptions. An absolutely "pure" idea would consist of the primal element of form or, more correctly, pure form would be mirrored in it. For Gabirol, as for the Neo-Platonists, matter is the agent of plurality and primal form is the one. Hence, in the human mind, primal form is represented in the category of unity, which is present in everything that our mind comprehends. The mind sifts and classifies all sensual data by means of concepts; therefore, the unifying power of a concept inheres in all that is intelligible. But since every concept is in fact inseparable from the matter of sense-data, absolute unity is a goal which can be approached only by degrees, asymptotically, as the curve of a parabola approaches but never quite reaches the co-ordinates.

To the extent to which a man is cognizant of the inner unity of all existence, his soul approaches God, who is the One Source of all creation. This vision of an all-encompassing unity is only negatively attained through reason, insofar as it soars beyond the data of the senses and purges itself of multiplicity which is the mark of matter.

A positive approach to the One Source is also available to

man, for the human soul is capable of cleaving unto God by means of its will, which is a spark of the divine will. An act of will can grasp positively and at once the vision of unity which reason can achieve only negatively and by degrees. Gabirol conceives of the divine will as the force which drives forms into matter, operating as the dynamic principle of the universe and relating the shifting patterns of this earthly world to the eternal realm of ideas. Since the will is superior to reason in the scale of being, should we marvel at the fact that the volitional pathway sometimes succeeds in the quest of metaphysical truth, while the pathway of reason invariably encounters the revolving sword which bars this world from eternity? Indeed, it is possible for us to join ourselves directly unto the divine will, through a mystical experience of ecstatic union, and thereby attain life everlasting.

Gabirol appears to have regarded his theory of the divine will as an esoteric doctrine. At the end of *The Fountain of Life*, he refers to a work of his on the subject which, however, has never been found. We may presume that in his lost work he outlined the stages whereby the soul attains ever purer states of unity with the will of God. It is quite probable that he represented the *mizvoth* of Judaism as so many expressions of the divine will. Hence, every *mizvah* is an opportunity for an act of surrender to the divine will and a vision of His unity. The Torah as a whole is an infinite ladder, leading to unity with the divine will and deathless life.

With this general outline of Gabirol's thought, we are able to follow his exposition in the following excerpts from his main work (preceded by the present writer's abstracts):

(1) Every perception of our senses recalls to our minds the true image of things in the ideal world. This reaffirmation of Platonic doctrine is illustrated thus:

. . . the relation between the forms we perceive and the soul itself is exactly the same as the relation between a book and its reader; when it perceives the letters, the soul recalls the denotation of those letters and their true significance.[2]

(2) The character of things in the upper worlds can be understood by studying the structure of things here below, for in the universal chain of being there prevails a continuous correspondence, the material links representing the same interrelations which obtain in the higher links of the spirit.

Our purpose was to rise from the lowest point of all existents to the highest. We must regard what we find in the lowest levels as the symbol or the analogy of that which exists in the upper realms, for that which is below is a faithful representation of that which is above. . . .[3]

(3) The central difficulty in this hypothesis is the emergence of the category of space, which spiritual entities in their ultimate perfection do not possess, and which is the fundamental quality of all material things. The answer is that the descent of the chain of being is gradual, from its source in the thought of God to the material universe, leading from immaterial unity to divisibility, variety, and ultimately to extension.

How does the form of space flow from the upper Source to the lower world? The existence of all things is caused through nine levels. The first level is the existence of all objects in the knowledge of the Creator; below that, the existence of the general form in the general matter; below that, the existence of simple qualities in simple substances; below that the existence of simple substances within one another; below that, the existence of quantity in matter; below that, the existence of spatial dimensions, lines in space and points in line; below that, colors and shapes in space; below that, the interpenetration of parts in one body; below that, the existence of some objects in other objects—and this is place. Don't you see then that, in the extent to which a thing descends from the simple to the complex, it becomes more coarse and material, while as it rises it becomes more abstract and gentle?[4]

In the same manner as space serves as a base for colors, which are themselves nonspatial, so there is a kind of " spiritual space," a realm of being intermediate between spirit and space. In other words, the category of quality, in all its diverse forms, mediates between pure spirit and the category of quantity. The category of space which is the basic characteristic of matter is itself part of a continuous flux of being, corresponding to a certain quality of spirit, though spirit is nonspatial.

Space as it is seen here below is a representation of space as it is in the mysterious upper spheres.[5]

(4) The basic principle is continuity. A chain of existents extends from one pole of being to the other. Between every two objects there is a third mediating substance, so that there is no break whatever in the entire range of existence. Even soul and body are united by a mediating substance, called spirit.

Were it not for the spirit which mediates between soul and body, there would have been no contact between them.[6]

(5) In this chain of existents, we understand the higher links by means of the lower ones. However, as we advance to the very highest spheres, we are left with bare tangential determinations. The inner nature of true Being is impervious to the intellect.

I shall give you a comprehensive rule, according to which you will be able to judge the whole of existence. From the upper to the lower ends of creation, it is possible to distinguish four levels, by means of the following questions—if it is, what it is, how it is and why it is. The highest level is the one in regard to which we can only ask the question if it is, not what, how or why—this is the level of the Holy and Exalted One. Below this is the level in regard to which there is the question, what, not how or why. This is the level of reason. Below it, the level where we may ask, if, what and how, but not why. This is the level of the soul. Still lower is the level where, why, too may be asked. This is the level of nature and all that is derived from it.[7]

(6) In most theories of emanation, influence flows from the upper to the lower spheres automatically, but in Gabirol's system, it is the divine will that accounts for the dynamism of existence. Both form and matter are passive elements, and the will, which transcends reason, accounts for all creation and movement. While pure form is an aspect of God, primal matter is neither an opposing force nor a negation of His being. Gabirol sought to overcome the dualism inherent in Plato's system by identifying God with both pure form and pure will.

" For the will, which is the power of the Creator, extends and penetrates through all things. There is nothing outside of it, for from it the existence and continuance of all things is derived."[8]

At this point, we encounter the crux of Gabirol's difficulty. If God be pure form, dwelling in eternity, how can He also be will, operative in time? Pure form is eternal and at rest, while pure will is necessarily operative in time. This question is particularly pertinent since, according to Gabirol, the phase of will in God is distinguishable from the phase of form. In answer, Gabirol asserts that God's will is both eternal and operative in time. Eternal in itself, the divine will is reflected in the mirror of time. And the mirror of time in turn is brought into being by matter. The eternal will is, through the coarseness of matter, transformed into an impulse in space and in time. It is not clear whether Gabirol thought of the unifying principle, deriving from God and mediating between eternity and time, or whether he regarded the divine will as being God, inhering in eternity, but reflected and refracted in matter, space and time.

Disciple: Is not the will in itself rest? How, then, does it penetrate all things and become motion?

Master: This question does not concern us at this point, and it is the most difficult in the doctrine of the will. But what you have to know now is that the will penetrates all things without motion and operates in all things without time, because of the quality of its power and unity. If you wish to facilitate for yourself the understanding of this matter, consider the operation of reason in the soul, without motion and without time.[9]

The creation of all things by the Creator; that is, the emergence of the

form out of the first source, or the will, and its outpouring upon the
primal matter, is comparable to the outpouring of water from a fountain
and its continuous flow, in wave after wave. But, while the outpouring
of water is without pause and rest, the emergence of creation is without
motion and without time. And the impression of the form upon the
matter, which the will effects, is like the reflection of the image in the
mirror, which captures the form of the object without its matter. . . .[10]

We may compare creation to the word that a man articulates with his
mouth. In uttering a word, its form and understanding are felt in the
hearing of the auditor and in his reason. According to this example, we
say that the exalted and Holy Creator expressed the word, and its meaning was inscribed in the substance of matter. . . .[11]

In other words, the spoken word corresponds to the operation
of the divine will in time while the implied meaning corresponds
to the will in eternity.

But when the word leaves the speaker's mouth, it reverberates
in the air as a tremor of the air waves, no longer subject to the
volitional control of the speaker. Does not creation, by contrast,
contain the living impetus of the divine will? The paradoxical
nature of the will, in Gabirol's philosophy, defies the understanding, precisely because it was conceived as being closer to the
source than reason. The will, mysteriously partaking of both
time and eternity, can be understood not so much logically as by
an act of will, by man's decision to identify his own deeper self
with the divine Being. It is only thus that man truly feels that
he lives both in time and beyond it.

(7) We arrive, therefore, at the conclusion that the divine will is suprarational, and is the creative power in the world. Reason can help us to
understand that the will is the dynamic substratum of all that exists, but
beyond this knowledge reason itself is helpless. If we wish to pursue the
search for divine truth, we must leave the bedrock of reason and somehow
allow ourselves to be caught up by the divine current of will.

" But to reach the knowledge of this power, which is not merged either
with matter or with form, you must learn to bind your soul with this
power, insofar as it is blended with matter and form; and, by your gradual
ascent with this power, you will reach its beginning and source."

Disciple: What is the fruit that we obtain from this study?

Master: Liberation from death and attachment to the source of life.

Disciple: What is it which helps one to attain this lofty aspiration?

Master: To separate oneself, at the outset, from all things of the senses and
to concentrate one's entire soul on the things of reason, as well as to
cleave altogether to the giver of good. If you will do this, He will lift
His face unto you and favor you, in accord with His nature.

It follows then that Gabirol saw creation as an organic totality, in which the will of the Creator is the one dynamic force. The structure of the world, in all its gradations from the lowest to the highest links, is patterned after the structure of the human personality, in which reason rises above the senses and will towers above reason. The motion of all the lower parts of our personality is determined by the higher considerations of the spirit. From this analogy, it may be inferred that the way to God leads from the senses to reason, from reason to piety, from piety to mystical unity and the divine will. We begin with the cultivation of reason to free ourselves from the spell of material things. The life of reason disposes a person to appreciate the majesty of the divine will, as seen in all creation. Sustained reflection on the infinite chain of being generates the spirit of piety. Man begins to feel the desire to merge his will into the divine will to attain unity and bliss. Man's craving for mystical unity is thus an inversion of the process of creation, flowing from will to the forms of reason and from the forms of reason to material things. Man in his worshipful search for mystical unity with the supreme will is not a freak of nature but its representative and spokesman.

And I think that the functioning of the individual soul is patterned after the constitution and operation of the total universe, and this is the way to obtain perfect bliss and to reach that true delight for which we strive.[12]

The exalted piety of Ibn Gabirol, in which reflection proceeds from the mystery of the soul to the mystery of the divine being, and thence to the sinking of the human will in the all-embracing will of God, is best seen in his famous hymn, *Ke-ther Malchuth*:

Who can comprehend Thy power, when Thou didst create from the splendor of Thy glory a pure lustre? From the rock of rocks was it hewn, and dug from the hollow of the cave. Thou also didst bestow on it the spirit of wisdom, and didst call it soul. Thou didst form it hewn from the flames of intellectual fire, so that its spirit burneth as fire within it. Thou didst send it forth to the body to serve and guard it; it is as fire in the midst of it, and yet doth not consume it; for from the fire of the soul the body was created, and called into existence from nothing, because the Lord descended thereto in fire.

Yehudah Halevi was the classic poet and philosopher of the Jewish national soul. A rare and genuine mystic, he did not follow the mystic's usual pathway, in which the lonely individual seeks and finds unity with God. Instead he sought to find "God's nearness" by sinking his own self completely and without reservation into the living current of the "eternal people." Unlike most Jewish philosophers he did not look upon himself as primarily a rational being and secondly a Jew. On the contrary, his Jewish identity was to him the sole clue to metaphysical truth. As he faced the awesome challenge of the divine command, he felt that the truths which others sought in vain were contained within him, embedded firmly in his inmost essence and waiting to be uncovered. It was as a Jew that he experienced the wondrous paradox of mystical piety, the pride of being chosen out of all men to be summoned unto the presence of the Deity and the humble awareness of his human failure to respond in wholeness of soul to this persistent challenge.

In Halevi's philosophy, Jewish "peoplehood" is interpreted as the basic requirement for metaphysical insight and true piety. Although he lived and wrote centuries before the emergence of secular nationalism, the Jewish nationalists of the modern era were always able to make contact through his writings with the classic wellsprings of Jewish tradition. On the other hand, so many-sided is his influence that the Qabbalists, in all their other-worldly bias and fantastic dogmatism, may well be considered his spiritual heirs.

If through some cataclysmic catastrophe all Jewish books, from the Bible to the last Yiddish daily, were lost and only the *Book of the Kuzari* remained, it would still be possible for the historian to faithfully reconstruct the diverse strands of thought and sentiment which enter into the making of the traditional Jewish mentality. For Yehudah Halevi, the author of this volume, did not set out to defend the philosophy of the Jewish religion against the challenge of the metaphysicians and logicians of his day.[13] He began and ended his quest with the concerns and convictions of the living Jewish people, so that his volume represents a faithful reproduction of that cluster of ideas and feelings which rose to the surface of consciousness, whenever intelligent Jews reflected on the peculiar destiny of their people among the nations. Whereas other philosophers responded primarily to the challenge of the ideas of their day, Halevi was profoundly troubled by the unequal contest between the powerful globe-spanning dominant faiths, and the feeble, odium-laden faith of the living Jewish people. The ever-vibrant focus of his convictions and reflections was no abstract dogma or philosophical principle, but the sorry state of the divinely chosen and blessed people, a bitter paradox of which sensitive Jews were at all times profoundly aware.

One of the extant manuscripts of this volume carries on its frontispiece the heading, "In defense and proof of the Despised Faith," a phrase which reveals the polemical and defiant spirit of the author. Why did the true faith of Judaism command the loyalty of only a small, despised, and persecuted minority in every land, while its daughter-religions divided the western world among them? Did Judaism lack the power to appeal to the objective mind? If so, then the world consensus would seem to have indicated that Judaism as a faith need no longer be taken seriously.

Nor could it be maintained that Judaism was indifferent to the conversion of non-Jews, since it would then stand convicted of misanthropic clannishness and atavistic tribalism. To rationalistic thinkers, public approval or disapproval would appear to be of minor importance, since truth cannot be tested and proven by resort to a popular referendum. To an Aristotle or a Maimonides it was axiomatic that the capacity for true knowledge is limited to the chosen few. But Halevi, too much a man of the world to hold that world in contempt, was concerned with the concrete situation in which the Jewish faith, beginning with so impressive a head start over its rivals, nevertheless lagged so miserably behind them in its manifest appeal. He chose therefore as the setting for his work the one dramatic mass conquest by Judaism since the appearance of both Christianity and Islam, to indicate that in any fair contest Judaism could hold its own against the competition of other faiths and the attraction of secular philosophy.

The conversion of the King of the Khazars to Judaism is supposed to have taken place about the year 740, some four hundred years prior to the composition of Halevi's work (1130-1140). In Cordova, where the author lived and worked, the tale of the Khazars was a vivid reality, since a number of Jewish families in that city claimed descent from the Khazars. It was, therefore, quite natural for Halevi to relate his philosophy to the reputed triumph of the Jewish religion in the debate held at the court of Bulan, King of the Khazars.

The author begins his work by telling of a persistent dream which came to the just and enlightened King Bulan, in which the pagan seeker for truth and justice was admonished that " his intentions were acceptable, but his deeds were not." This heavenly warning, in Halevi's account, is the more significant in that the one document upon which it is based, the letter of Joseph, King of the Khazars, to Hasdai Ibn Shaprut, reports the heavenly voice as saying, " I see your ways and like your deeds." Halevi's alteration of this admonition reflects the basic tone of his entire exposition since the argument is shifted from a consideration of dogmas and principles to an analysis of the validity of the specific practices and rituals of each living faith. King Bulan's ideas and intentions may have been good, but it is the deed that counts, not the creed.

The metaphysical systems of Judaism, Christianity and Islam were beginning by this time to take on a degree of uniformity, making it possible for intellectuals to argue that God may be approached through the rites and ceremonies of any and all faiths, provided heart and mind are properly attuned to the love of truth. " Once you have achieved this exalted faith," says the philosopher, " do not be concerned with the question of which religion or faith or set of deeds and words you practice, or the language in which you pray. You may even invent a religion to serve your own special needs. . . . For the fundamental rule is to seek purity of heart in whichever way it may be attained, once the basic principles of philosophy are understood in truth."[14] Naturally, this lofty attitude militated most effectively against the continued adherence of Jewish people to their ancestral faith. If, to the enlightened, all paths lead to God, why continue to pay so high a price for loyalty to the practices and ceremonies of Judaism? As a matter of fact, we learn from the later history of Spanish Jewry that when the crucial test of persecution came, the philosophically trained Jews, with few exceptions, deserted the fold, while the naïve and unsophisticated believers retained the time-tested power of Judaism to live and to die for the sanctification of the Holy Name.

Halevi's reply to the challenge of rationalistic philosophy is offered in the principle that only God Himself can tell how He may be properly worshiped. As the nature of God may not be understood completely by man, so the things of God, the *mizvoth* of religion, cannot be man-made. If it be granted that the will of God is inscrutable, then it is logical to assume that He has His own ideas as to the manner in which He should be served. Manifestly, these metarational ideas, centered in the completely undetermined divine will, cannot be discovered by reason or speculation and can only be known through the direct act of revelation.

Relying on sheer speculation, one might maintain that God could best be served through the methods of the ascetic, who renounces the pleasures and comforts of the world for His sake. In reality, "The observance of the Sabbath brings one closer to the Creator than renunciation and asceticism," though it is a most pleasing observance. For religious observances must strike a balance between "fear, love, and joy." Indeed, "pure spiritual joy is the very acme of religious experience." And "if your joy becomes so intense as to pass into song and dance, then you have reached the height of service of and communion with the divine power."[15] In so complex a matter, rational speculation is therefore useless. Only through revelation can the proper pathway to God be known. Accordingly the argument descends from the ethereal heights of speculative philosophy to the earthly contest between the contending religions, each claiming to contain the one and only true revelation.

Insofar as Halevi was concerned, the claim of Judaism was challenged seriously only by the Christian and Moslem faiths. Since these two faiths admitted that Judaism had possessed true revelation in the past and maintained only that their own subsequent revelations superseded that of Judaism, it is obvious that the burden of proof rests upon the so-called daughter-religions. The presumption of truth is held by Judaism. The challenging faiths could prove their cases only by demonstrating that God had indeed declared Judaism invalid by an act of revelation as striking and certain as that by which He had made His will manifest to Israel in the first place. When the Torah was given to the Israelites at Sinai, God's revelation was made evident in the presence of 600,000 adult male observers, who saw the smoke and holy fire, and heard the thunder and the voice of God. Neither

Christianity nor Islam even so much as lay claim to a revelation given with so much *éclat* and in the presence of so many people as the original, admittedly true revelation at Sinai. Hence, their claims are discounted by the King of the Khazars, who undertakes thereupon to examine the faith of Judaism with great care and scrutiny.

In logical order, the author seeks first to prove the truth of Judaism as a living faith. Though he assumes the revelation at Sinai to be a universally accepted and therefore unquestioned fact, he nevertheless realizes that in the course of time even a divine treasure might be corrupted by uninspired human hands. Accordingly, he marshals evidences from the Bible and Talmud in proof of his contention that divine inspiration was withdrawn only slowly, and not entirely, from the Jewish people. He cites the rabbinic statement that the number of prophets in Israel was more than a million souls. When the gift of prophecy ceased to function, by virtue of the confiscation of the Holy Ark, the spirit of holiness in lesser forms continued to manifest itself in the life of saints and sages. The codification of the Mishnah, for instance, was a divinely inspired act, "for flesh and blood cannot compose such a treatise, save with the help of God."[16] All *takkanoth*, or rabbinic regulations, were similarly enacted with the aid of the felt divine presence.[17] Thus, in all the stages of its development, from Moses to the last *Responsa* of the Gaonic academies, Judaism was divinely inspired.

But how are Jewish people so certain of the unique truth and inspiration of their tradition? At this point, the author falls back upon the mystical experiences of his own soul, representing them to be the exclusive property of the Jewish people. The God of philosophy may be proved by arguments and disproved by the same means, but the personal God of Israel is directly apprehended by Jews. Endowed by a unique divine intuition, the Jewish people "taste" and "see" the holiness of God, so that they cannot possibly doubt His presence or permanently refuse to succumb to His will. "Thus, I understand the difference between the God of Abraham and the God of Aristotle, for to the former, souls are drawn by sight and taste, whereas the latter is the goal of dialectics. This direct apprehension of the divine leads those who experience it to surrender their souls voluntarily for their love of God, and even to die for Him."[18] Already, in the days of Halevi, the martyrdom of Israel for the sanctification of the Holy Name was an awe-inspiring and reverence-compelling reality, suggesting that there was something peculiarly intimate and unique in the relationship between the Jew and God. "And in truth, He is called the God of Israel because this perception of the divine is lacking among non-Jews."

Naturally, the King of the Khazars would not allow the doctrine of Israel's metaphysical superiority to go unchallenged. Why should the good God who loves all men single out one race for special distinction and endow them with an intuition for the divine? Halevi counters with the explanation that originally this intuition was the prerogative of all mankind, but that through the fall of Adam and the subsequent degeneration of his descendants, the special divine intuition came to be limited to the Jewish people. Even the righteous proselytes, like the King of the Khazars, cannot expect to attain this gift of intuition, since it is a hereditary quality of the race.[19] On the other hand, in propitious circumstances, the majority of Jewish people may expect to develop their inborn intuition virtually to the point of prophecy.[20] When this happens, "they are elevated above the human species, in the refinement of their souls and in their longing for the highest reaches of mystical communion with the divine in humility and purity. . . . Then their only longing is to return the soul to its divine state, when it is entirely separated from the senses, beholding the upper worlds, enjoying the perception of angelic light and listening to the divine speech."

To ask why this prophetic gift is not presently conferred upon all men is to question the wisdom of Providence in creating the many different species of this supremely variegated world, all governed by the laws of heredity. As well might one inquire why all creatures were not endowed with the gifts of speech and reason. All Jews are potentially prophets, and prophets constitute a suprahuman species in the scale of being, adapted for the perception of divine "lights" in a manner which cannot be understood by the rest of "fallen" mankind, even as the blind cannot understand the sense of sight.

Does it mean, then, that the Jewish people were designed by

God to be the "master race," lording it over the other nations? By no means. On the contrary, the proof of the election of Israel is the historical fact of its being immediately and ruthlessly punished for the slightest infraction of the law. While other nations are left to the dominion of natural law, the Jewish people are subject to the special Providence of God, Who rebukes "whomsoever He loveth." Halevi maintains that humanity forms a living whole and he asserts that Israel fulfills a special function in the organic society of mankind, directing all men to the path of true religion. Manifestly, "all the peoples of the world were groping in blindness before the appearance of the children of Israel." Through the revelation of God in the life of the Jewish people, "when the laws of nature were changed in their behalf," it was demonstrated that there is a "guardian and ruler of the universe." The hearts of all men were then directed toward the truth, to the point when today all the inhabitants of the world admit that the world is created, their proof being the historical experiences and career of the house of Israel."[21]

Israel has thus been designed to function as the "heart" of the nations, reacting to all the ailments in the body of mankind, while at the same time stimulating its conscience. Both Christianity and Islam derive from the fructifying power of Jewish genius, "constituting the necessary spiritual preparation for the expected Messiah." As the seed is put into the ground, really to rot there for a while, only to burgeon later into a tree with branches and leaves, with flowers that ultimately ripen into fruit containing the same seed, so Israel has been cast into exile, rotting there to all appearances, but continuing to produce and nourish in mysterious fashion the branches and leaves and flowers of Christianity and Islam. When these flowers will ripen into fruit, the seed of Judaism will be found in their core. In this manner, even the travail of Israel in exile is an instrument for the redemption of the world. "All the vicissitudes which come upon us have the effect of purifying the spirit of Torah which lives within us, purging us of all dross and refining the pure metal, so that through our purification and improvement, the divine power might cleave unto the world."[22]

From this interpretation of the spiritual effects of Jewish travail in exile one might gather the impression that Jewish people should resign themselves to their exilic existence, since it is their "mission" to influence and elevate the great non-Jewish world. Halevi, however, steers clear of this anti-nationalist pitfall. In his view, it is in mystical fashion, by their very existence, that the Jewish people affect the spiritual progress of the world, rather than by overt missionary efforts. Hence, they owe it to themselves and to the world to rehabilitate their existence on a healthy and creative basis, by reforging their bonds with the Holy Land. Jewish people can attain their full prophetic stature only in their own land, for that "divine intuition which is their special gift can flourish only in the land of Israel."[23] Even as certain plants are adapted only to certain climates, so is the power of prophecy, and the gift of intimacy with Providence which prophecy implies, capable of flourishing only in the chosen land, and only when that land is inhabited by the chosen people. While men of colossal spiritual attainments, like "Abraham, Moses and the Messiah," might achieve the level of prophecy outside the borders of the Holy Land, lesser Jews cannot hope for such a consummation save by migrating to the land of their fathers. Indeed, Abraham and Moses regarded it as their life's ambition to settle in the Promised Land, and the Messiah's function will be to bring all Jews back to their own land. Thus all prophecy is dependent on the Holy Land; those who live outside its borders can attain prophecy only by longing with all their might to dwell in it.

Since prophecy is the noble purpose for which the Jewish people was designed, it follows that Jews deny their own soul and mock their own reason for existence so long as they do not migrate to the chosen land, the air of which is "life for the soul." Indeed, Halevi is ready to concede that the Jews of his own day were in the category of the "dry bones" described by Ezekiel. But he argues, "We are not in the category of the dead, but in that of the tubercular patient, of whose recovery and life all the doctors have despaired, and who expects to be healed by a miracle which will controvert the laws of nature."[24]

Obviously, no patient can expect the help of God who does not himself strive and hope for recovery. Hence, it is the crucial sin of Israel to rest content with exilic existence and not to migrate to the land which is only one level removed from the Garden of

Eden (heaven). "Your love of Torah cannot be sincere if you do not make this place your goal, your home in life and death. Don't you say, 'Have mercy on Zion, for it is the home of our life' and believe that the *Shechinah* returns to it? And if it were only for the fact that the *Shechinah* dwelt in it approximately nine hundred years, noble souls should long for it in order that they might be purified in it, as is likely to happen in the places of prophets and saints, especially so since it is the gate of the heavens."[25]

Thus, Halevi begins by converting the Khazars to Judaism and ends by converting himself to personal Zionism. Step by step he was led inexorably to this conclusion through the unfolding inner logic of his faith. Judaism is the one true faith, as judged by the testimony of its own tradition, endorsed in a measure by the traditions of the two great related faiths. But the truth of tradition is itself endorsed by the testimony of personal experience, in which respect Judaism is pre-eminent, because every Jew is potentially a prophet, capable of seeing the "glory of God" and sensing the intimate presence of the Deity. And here is the rub. The potentiality of prophecy can only be realized in the Holy Land. The argument of the Jew *pro vita sua* remains, therefore, suspended in midair so long as he is in exile, deprived of the opportunity to "see" and "taste" the divine.

Never was a book so utterly a part of its author as the *Book of the Kuzari* was of Yehudah Halevi. The argument of the book led the author to undertake his famed journey to Zion, which was in truth an act of self-sacrifice, unique in the annals of mankind. Halevi undertook to go to the land then occupied by the Crusaders who had murdered all the Jews in Jerusalem, in order that he might "see" the "glory of God" and then die. The one moment of divine revelation would more than compensate for the death that was sure to follow. Tired of arguments leading whithersoever the contemporary winds listed, Halevi determined to "see" for himself, convinced as he was that in Palestine the gift of prophecy was ready and waiting for those eager to receive it. The return of prophecy to Israel would signalize the beginning of the redemption. "For the divine power comes to one in accordance with his preparation, whether much or little, and if we had readied ourselves for the God of our fathers with a perfect heart and an aspiring soul, we should have encountered the same wonders as our ancestors in Egypt." Of this preparation, no element was as important as that of a personal pilgrimage to Zion.

So, the Khazars having been converted, the Jewish missionary, feeling that his mission was completed, determined to go to Palestine, for the "*Shechinah* that is visible to the eyes is lacking" elsewhere, even if the "hidden, spiritual *Shechinah*" attends those of true faith in all lands. What is death in the face of so glorious an experience crowning a lifelong search for the nearness of God! Furthermore, through his journey to Zion he would attain not only personal salvation, but also pave the way of redemption for all Israel. "For Jerusalem will indeed be built when the children of Israel will long for it with all their might and favor its sands and stones."[26]

Halevi's pilgrimage to Palestine, doomed as it was from the start to end in martyrdom, was in a sense the seal and stamp of his defense of Judaism. Through this final proof of sincerity the *Kitab al Khazari* ceased to be just another book and became an undying clarion call, reverberating through the ages, calling for a return unto the God of Abraham who is nigh and close unto them that call upon Him in truth, and unto Zion, the dwelling place of His glory.

Several students of Jewish thought have labored hard to produce a full-scale metaphysical system out of the scattered hints in Halevi's writings. Actually, Halevi did not envisage philosophy in general as an inimical discipline, contesting the essential doctrines of a religious view of life. Distinguishing between philosophy as the application of reason to the basic questions in life and Aristotelian philosophy, which comes armed with the pride of its syllogisms and hypotheses, he favored the former study and subjected the latter system to a careful scrutiny. Philosophy was simply "human wisdom," which is good enough so far as it goes, but it does not and cannot encompass the ultimate mystery of the divine will. Its "first principles" are necessarily unprovable assumptions and therefore arbitrary. On the other hand, he refers to Socrates in the most respectful terms and he accepts the philosophical critique of crass anthropomorphism. Romantic and traditionalist as he was, he did not, like the Christian theologian Tertullian, maintain that religious faith must be set over against reason in accordance with the maxim, "Credo quia absurdum est." On the contrary, he wrote, "Nothing that is false may be attributed to the Deity." Hence, the Torah cannot possibly teach doctrines which reason rejects and declares to be false.

Halevi did not belong in the company of the naïve dogmatists who envisaged God in material terms. The first of the Ten Commandments is the precept to believe in God, and the second is the warning not to serve other gods; not to make idols, pictures or images; that is, not to attribute to Him any material quality. How can we fail to exalt Him above anything that is of matter, seeing that some of His creations are immaterial, such as the soul of the person who speaks to us, which is really his true personality?

> For the Moses who addresses us, teaches and guides us, is not the combination of thought, heart and brain, these again being only the instruments of Moses. . . . At the same time, it is right for us not to reject what we have received concerning the revelation at Sinai. We say that we do not know how the immaterial Word of God became an audible sound, which our human ears could perceive, nor how the universe was created out of the naught, nor how He removed for His special Providence some of the things of creation. For this we do know, that He does not lack any power. . . .[27]

The truths of revelation supplement, but do not supplant, those of philosophy:

> Let it not be incongruous, in your sight, that we compare the Creator to a man, for, in the category of reason, it appears that we should think of Him after the analogy of light, since it is the sense which is most all-embracing in its scope, most inclusive, important and subtle. But, as we think of the qualities appertaining to Him, either truly or by analogy, such as those of life, power, knowledge, will and design, giving all beings their due and judging righteously, we cannot find a closer likeness than that of the rational soul . . . and the philosophers have already compared the universe to a man magnified, and man to a microcosmos. . . .[28]

It was necessary for God to reveal His will in detail to mankind, for philosophy in itself is insufficient. "For the arguments mislead, and out of the juggling of arguments, people might arrive at Epicurean notions and corrupt ideas . . . there being many different paths of reasoning, some accurate, some perverted, of which the most exact is the discipline of philosophy. . . ."[29]

But even the best philosophic systems are founded upon a series of assumptions, which are regarded as axioms. "For the first principles of the philosophers are not themselves deduced from reason and capable of being proved. Furthermore, you will not find two of them agreeing on the same basic principles. . . ."[30]

Judaism is founded not upon reason, but upon the direct testimony of experience—the collective experience of the Jewish people and the individual experience of prophets, which may be designated as an intuition for things divine:

> As the Creator, in His Wisdom, established a correspondence between the stimulation received by our senses and the material object from which it is derived, so He set up a similar correspondence between the mystical sense and the realm of the immaterial. Then He gave to those He chose a mystical eye, capable of seeing things just as they are. . . . The great proof for the truth of their reports is the circumstance of all the people belonging in this category, namely, the prophets agreeing in their testimony. . . .[31]

To be sure, the descriptions of the divine carriage in the book of Ezekiel and the divine throne in the Book of Isaiah are not to be taken literally, since no bodily qualities may be attributed to the Deity. Those expressions are " true " in the human sense, conveying to us a notion of the ineffable mystery, for we cannot think without images. " Don't believe the sophisticate who maintains that he can order his thoughts, level after level, to the point of reaching the concept of the Deity, without including in that concept aught of the senses. . . . You cannot even count up to a hundred, for example, in thought alone, without speech. . . ."

The existence of spirit may be postulated by reason, but the nature of spirituality can only be directly apprehended by the suprarational intuition of the prophet. " Thus, the majesty of the Lord, His power, wisdom, mercy, permanence, substantiality, unity and holiness are conveyed to the prophet in one second by the vision of a created form. . . ."[32]

The intuition of the prophets is capable of seeing God as He is envisioned in Jewish tradition (YHVH), while to human reason only the God of nature (*Elohim*) is conceivable.

> No sensible person denies God as *Elohim* [the principle of order in nature], but some deny His quality as the living God of Israel [YHVH], for prophecy is a rare phenomenon . . . For this quality cannot be attained by reasoning, only by prophetic insight, by means of which a person is virtually separated from his species and lifted to the category of the

angels. . . . Then the prophet comes to love His Master, being ready to offer his life for the sake of his love, since in his union with God he finds unique sweetness and great sorrow in separating from Him, in contrast to the philosophers, who find worship to be only an ethically desirable exercise. . . ."[33]

As stated before, this gift of intuition, in a mild and nascent sense, is shared by all Jews, though it cannot flourish in the lands of exile. Non-Jews, Halevi maintained, cannot experience the immediate presence of the Deity. "In truth, He is called 'the God of Israel' because this insight is not to be found outside their ranks, and He is called, 'the God of the land' because it possesses a special potency, in its air, soil and heavens, especially in connection with the precepts that are observed only in it. . . ."[34]

In this view, the *mizvoth* of Judaism are seen to be devices for the bringing down of the divine presence, in some slight degree. The purpose of human life is to attain contact with the divine and the *mizvoth* were especially so designed as to lead to the consummation of this goal. Hence, the many "dos" and "don'ts" of the Torah are not to be regarded as so many arbitrary ordinances of the King of Kings, but as concrete marks of His love, capable of serving as rungs on the infinite ladder leading from earth to heaven. As the human soul requires the physical configurations of the body for its functioning, so the immanence of the divine presence requires that the physical and psychical circumstances of land and people be properly adjusted, in accordance with the specifications of the Torah. "Indeed, the divine quality is ready to bring its good to all who desire it. When things are properly ordered and prepared for the divine Providence, it does not refrain from bestowing upon them light, wisdom and knowledge . . . entering into them, in the sense of Providence, not place. . . ."[35]

This is the deeper significance of the sacrifices and all the holy vessels in the Temple, each of which was designed for a special phase of the divine light.[36]

In general, Halevi operates within the categories of nature and biology in interpreting the objective efficacy of each religious ritual. Just as the chain of cause and effect in nature is not inherently rational, but simply a divinely established sequence, so the rituals, too, exert their effect upon the cosmos directly and automatically according to a preordained harmony of Torah and nature.

> The divine quality was associated with all these activities, for the rites of the Torah are accurately designed by the Creator, even as are all physical objects. It is not possible for a human being to figure out the right proportions of each act, as in all activities of nature a special combination of circumstances is required for each event. . . .
>
> For it is impossible to come close to God, save by His directions, and it is impossible to know His commandments save through the tradition that merits credence. . . .[37]

But, though it is on the basis of the credibility of his tradition that the Jew accepts the practices of his faith, his loyal observance leads to their authentication by the experience of near-prophetic visions. " But our destiny it is to cleave to the divine quality in prophecy and in states of mind that are close to it. . . ."[38]

This union with the divine quality is occasionally described by Halevi as a felt mystical yearning for the divine presence. At times, too, he thinks of the divine presence as an implicit power manifested in the conjunction of a series of historical events. The Torah does not promise the rewards of immortality and heaven for the observance of the *mizvoth*; instead, it details a number of earthly compensations, rain in its season, extraordinary prosperity and amazing success in war—events which demonstrate that " our affairs are not conducted according to the customs of nature, but in line with His will." In this manner, the feeling of the nearness of God is cultivated to the point that " whosoever reaches this level is not afraid of death."[39]

As to the rewards of heaven, we can rely upon the justice of God to dispense them equitably; certainly, those who feel the nearness of God on earth need have no fears of being separated from Him in the hereafter. " We deny to no man the reward for his good deeds, no matter which creed he belongs to, but we see the perfect good which comes to the people that are close to Him in their lifetime [the comforting feeling of God's nearness], and we are thus able to appreciate their worth in the sight of God, after their death. . . ."[40]

> The pious man is a governor, who is obeyed by his senses and by his faculties. . . . He subdues his passions and restrains them from excesses, but he allows them their proper portion and due satisfaction as regards food, drink, bathing, etc. He subdues further the urge toward superiority, but

allows it as much freedom as it requires for the discussion of scientific or practical views, as well as for the rebuke of the wicked. . . . He arranges his troop in the same manner as Moses arranged his people round Mount Sinai. . . . His will directs first the organs of thought and frees them from the worldly ideas which filled them before; then it charges the imagination to produce, with the assistance of memory, the most splendid pictures possible, in order to come near the divine presence—for instance, the scene of Sinai, Abraham and Isaac on Mount Moriah, the Tabernacle of Moses, etc. . . . It directs all his faculties to work with alertness, pleasure and joy.

This hour of divine service constitutes the maturity and essence of time, while the other hours represent the road which leads to his goal . . . he prays for the sake of his soul as he takes nourishment for the sake of the body. . . . But, the further the soul of the pious man is removed from the time of prayer, the more it is clouded by the pressure of worldly matters. . . .

On the Sabbath, therefore, the body makes good what it lacked during the six days, and prepares itself for the work to come. . . . He further observes the Three Festivals and the very holy Fast Day, when he repudiates his former sins and atones for all that he might have failed in. . . . The fast of this day is such as to bring him near the angels, because it is spent in humility and contrition, standing, bowing, praising and singing. . . .

So the good man does not act, speak, or think without knowing that he is observed by eyes which see and take note, keeping an exact account of all his words and deeds. Walking and sitting, he is therefore at once fearful and happy, ashamed and proud of his actions. . . . He wears the phylacteries on that part of the head which is the seat of mind and memory . . . he wears the *tzitzith*, warning him against the allurement of the senses. . . . By such means, the love and fear of God enter the soul, being balanced by the specifications of the law, lest joy on Sabbath and holy days degenerate into extravagance, debauchery, idleness and neglect of the appointed hours of prayer, and lest fear deepen into the despair of attaining forgiveness.

He will be so powerfully persuaded of the justice of divine Providence, that he will not be disheartened by the misfortunes of life. Like Nahum of Gimzo he will learn to accept the miseries of his lot and to say, " this too is for the best." He will even welcome tribulations, if he is conscious of a sin, which they help to cleanse.

Remembering all these thoughts, with every movement that he makes, it is as if the *Shechinah* is with him continually and the angels keep him company; if his piety attains high levels, and he abides in places worthy of the *Shechinah*, they will be with him in visible form so that he can behold them with his own eyes, rising to a degree just below that of prophecy. . . .[41]

It is with the Greek ideal of harmony that Halevi begins his description of the pious man, and with the Jewish ideal of prophecy that he concludes it. Yet this consummation could only be attained in the land of Israel which was to him and to his contemporaries not just a place on the map, but an unreal, unearthly embodiment of heaven, a domain of soothing myth and pious fancy, a legend and a dream.

CHAPTER NINE

THE QABBALAH

IT was in the eighties of the thirteenth century that the classic text of Qabbalistic literature, the *Zohar*, appeared. The scholar, Rabbi Moses de Leon, is now presumed to have written the major portion of the *Zohar*, which is not really one systematic work, but a collection of many books and brochures, varying in clarity and emphasis and held together by an inner unity of theme and ideology. This vast compendium of esoteric lore is a pseudo-epigraphic composition, attributed by its editor to Rabbi Simon Bar Yohai and a coterie of his "illuminated" disciples. This second-century Palestinian rabbi was believed to have spent thirteen years in a cave, studying the hidden mysteries of Torah, with the direct aid of the "spirit of holiness." What more natural than to ascribe to him the authorship of a book which is replete with visions and revelations!

Soon after its appearance, the authenticity of the *Zohar* was questioned, by mystics no less than by their opponents. Rabbi Isaac of Akko reported the testimony of de Leon's widow to the effect that her husband was the ghost writer of the *Zohar*, in all its complex subdivisions. But this testimony was ignored and later controverted with the utmost vehemence. So congruous was the comforting message of the *Zohar* with the overriding needs of the contemporary Jewish consciousness that all critical objections were set aside. Fundamentally, the Zoharic mentality was "true" to the increasing impetus of the dogmatic and romantic phases of contemporary Judaism; ergo, it had to be an authentic revelation. For two centuries, the rise of the *Zohar* in popular acceptance was slow and steady. Then, when the travail of Spanish Jewry reached its climax in the fateful expulsion of 1492, the *Zohar* was catapulted to canonical holiness, attaining a degree of authority that was third only to the Bible and the Talmud.[1]

While the *Zohar* is the central text of Qabbalah, there was a great body of esoteric lore antedating it, which was incorporated in the Talmud, the *Midrashim*, and in a number of Qabbalistic works of which the *Sefer Yezira* (*The Book of Creation*), attributed to the patriarch Abraham, was the best known and most revered. Altogether, the term "Qabbalah" comprises today a vast literature, containing more than three thousand volumes. While some of the classic works contain elaborate metaphysical systems, most of these volumes spin the ancient threads in endless variations, with the view of uncovering the "inner secrets" of the Torah or proposing a quasi-magical formula of "holy names" for the propitiation of angels and the banishment of demons. Yet, in all its vast variety, Qabbalah contains certain basic intellectual principles and concepts, which its devotees employ with virtual unanimity.

While some rationalistic students of Jewish thought regard the Qabbalah as a temporary aberration, born of ignorance and despair, which could rightfully be excluded from the history of Judaism, we cannot overlook the fact that, for many centuries, the Qabbalah constituted the regnant philosophy of the Jewish faith. From Crescas to Mendelssohn, no Jew dared venture into the field of metaphysical speculation without treading the approved pathways of Qabbalah. Nor can it be said that Orthodox Judaism in our day has repudiated the organic complex of Qabbalistic ideas, for so authoritative a religious personality as the late chief rabbi of Palestine, Abraham Isaac Kuk, framed his ideas in the molds of Qabbalah. And the Hasidic movement of the eighteenth century was essentially a reassertion of Qabbalistic thought. As will appear in the sequel, Hasidism converted the esoteric lore of Qabbalah into a mass movement, preaching its doctrines in public and applying them in practice.

The degree of authority and prestige enjoyed by the Qabbalah may be gauged by the circumstance that Rabbi Joseph Karo, author of the *Shulhan Arukh*, was not only a devotee but also a living "channel" of Qabbalistic revelation. *Maggidim*, or holy souls from heaven, would visit him when he was in a trance and bring him tidings from "the world of truth." Rav Hai Gaon believed in the authenticity of the mystical visions of his contemporaries, the *yordai hamerkabah*, who were precursors of the Qabbalah. Nahmanides, whose commentary on the Torah was widely read and whose influence on Spanish Jewry was unsurpassed, was one of the master builders of Qabbalah. Rabbi Joel Sirkis, author of the classic halachic work, *Baith Hodosh*, asserted flatly that "he who denies the truth of the wisdom of Qabbalah is called a heretic."[2] Rabbi Moses Isserles, the greatest halachic authority of Polish Jewry, allowed himself considerable latitude in the interpretation of Qabbalistic doctrines and deplored the tendency of improperly trained scholars to venture into the dangerous domain of the "wisdom of the hidden." Yet he too agreed that Qabbalah was authentic tradition, received by Moses at Sinai and "transmitted from mouth to mouth."[3] The Gaon of Vilna and his disciples were staunch believers in the revelations of Qabbalah, insisting only on the relative independence of the realm of *Halachah*.[4]

On the other hand, a few bold voices even in medieval times dared to challenge the pretensions of Qabbalah. Rabbi Isaac ben Sheshet Barfat took issue with the Qabbalistic method of directing different prayers through different channels or *sefiroth*, insisting that childlike naïveté is the best attitude for prayer.[5] The sixteenth-century Italian rabbi, Leo de Modena, condemned the whole Qabbalistic theosophy as spurious, identifying it as pagan in origin.[6]

The eighteenth-century rabbi, Jacob Emden, accepted the general texture of Qabbalistic ideas in his introduction to the prayer book; yet, worried by the possible misuse of Qabbalah by sectarians, he asserted that the text of the *Zohar* was corrupted, so that it can only be used with the greatest of caution.[7]

From all the above, it would appear that although the Qabbalah dominated Jewish thought for several centuries, there was never a time when its authority was entirely unchallenged.

The term "Qabbalah" means "tradition." Unlike the discipline of philosophy, the Qabbalah is founded upon the testimony of revelation, not the axioms of reason or the wisdom of experience. The Qabbalists maintained that their "hidden wisdom" was charged with cosmic potency and given over to the safekeeping of chosen individuals. The basic books of Qabbalah were alleged to be written by ancient revered sages, or by heavenly beings such as "Raziel, the angel."

Enthusiastic adherents of the "wisdom of truth" maintained

that Elijah the prophet revealed the principles of Qabbalah to Rabbi David of Provence, who was the father of Rabbi Abraham (RabD), famed as the bitter critic of Maimonides. The son was also privileged to behold Elijah in his visions. His disciple Rabbi Yizhak was similarly blessed, transmitting his lore to Ezra and Azriel, " who were the fourth generation, receiving direct information from Elijah."[8] Another Qabbalist maintained that a certain Rabbi Keshisha Gaon brought this secret lore from the ancient academies of Babylonia to *Rabbi Yehudah he-hassid* of Germany.[9]

Rabbi Jonathan Eibshitz, one of the leading rabbinical figures of the eighteenth century, declared categorically that " the Qabbalists received their doctrines directly from the prophets."[10]

Modern scholars encounter no difficulty in finding parallels between the central concepts of Qabbalah and the Gnostic systems of the ancient world, which in turn were compounded in diverse combinations out of the floating debris of pagan mythology and Judeo-Christian elements. But the building blocks of philosophic systems are not as significant as the cement of thought and inspiration that holds them together. At its noblest reaches, Qabbalistic thought is rich in profound insights and noble sentiments, though it is never entirely free from the clinging " shells " of superstition. So thoughtful an author as Rabbi Joseph Irgash did not disdain pragmatic " proofs " for the truths of Qabbalah. Proceeding on the principle that truth is that which works, he challenged the philosophers with this clinching argument: " Which philosopher ever created a calf, as the Talmudic sage, Rovo, is reputed to have done? "[11] The classic Qabbalists believed in the possibility of the miracle, but scorned the employment of lofty principles for such lowly tasks, contending that only a " calf " would bother to make a calf. This was the aspect of Qabbalah which Maimonides particularly resented as rank stupidity and madness.[12] The Qabbalists retorted in time by inventing a letter in which the aged philosopher is said to have repented of his errors.

In its essential motivation, Qabbalah sought to re-establish the validity of the Jewish ritual against the challenge of rationalistic philosophy. It represents, therefore, a reflective formulation of the principles of naïve faith, a blend of the philosophic passion for analysis and systematic consistency with the religious yearning for the assurance of divine favor, humanly won and securely held.

This mighty effort to provide solid intellectual scaffolding for the tender tremors of naïve piety underlies all of Qabbalah. And this effort was directed through several channels, for, as we have seen, the rational philosophy of the Middle Ages emasculated the sinews of piety and assigned to religious ritual a subordinate role in the attainment of intellectual perfection, exalting the virtue of philosophic reflection above that of strict ritual observance. Compelled to live in perpetual readiness for martyrdom, Jewish people could ill afford the corrosive effects of rational criticism.

A mild but ever-present undercurrent in Qabbalistic writings reflects the hurt pride of the Jew. How could Maimonides possibly be right in his description of the " alien " wisdom of the Greeks as the essence of Jewish teaching? If profound essences are hidden in the Torah, they would be revealed to great Jews, not Gentiles. Are loyal, observant Jews to be compared to those who wander about the palace, while the Greek philosophers were safely inside?

> Rationalistic wisdom is not at all peculiar to Israel, but is the portion of all nations, reflecting as it does human efforts. Thus, the other nations had among them greater philosophers than we, even when our people were seduced by this wisdom. But the wisdom of Israel is inward, divine, received from the Almighty and not shared by the other nations.
> Jewish reason is different from the reason of the other nations, even as the Jew is different in the possession of a different soul, as is known to the wise, and Jewish reason is perfected through the study of Torah, its mysteries and secrets and through the dialectics of the true wisdom, which is far above the wisdom that is derived from experience. This level the philosophers did not attain and did not merit.[13]

To be sure, we are bidden to make use of our speculative and reasoning faculties, but the Qabbalists agreed with Halevi that every rational system starts out with a number of unproved axioms or assumptions. We may make use of our powers of reasoning only when the " tools " of basic intuitions are made available to us by revelation. All philosophers base their speculative systems upon one or more " first principles," and these " first principles " are extra-rational, deriving either from the illusions of human imagination or the truths of God. " For Torah and wisdom were both derived from the divine reason, and are substantially one, complementing each other, and the believer requires both for his perfection. But the first principles upon which the philosophers build their systems are not derived from the divine reason. Hence, all their conclusions are false, incapable of providing salvation."[14]

On a deeper level, the Qabbalists were concerned with the task of reconciling the personal philosophy of Jewish monotheism with the implicit mechanistic naturalism of Greek philosophy.

In Judaism, the fundamental analogy for the bonds between God and man in all their variation and complexity is the relationship between two personalities. There is God, the Master, the Father, or the King who commands, instructs, pleads, demands, promises or punishes. None of the seductive impulses of the flesh affect Him, for He is spirit, and none of the forces of nature prevail against Him, for He is the creator of the totality of existence out of the naught. Still, in all His omnipotence and omniscience, God is a person. The Talmudic sages shied away from attributing material qualities to Him, but they did not envisage Him without the temperamental and psychical qualities of a human being. It is significant that Rabbi Abraham of Posquieres, who opposed the Maimonidean conception of an abstract Deity, arguing that material qualities are applicable to the nature of God, was deemed to be one of the inspired fathers of the Qabbalah.[15]

But even those who shunned the coarse attributes of the flesh conceived of God as the ideal saint, who learns, prays, judges and administers His domain, so that His every action might serve as a model for human action.

Upon this basic insight, the entire world view of Judaism was founded. The tortuous and uncertain course of the human adventure in history is explained as the result of the perpetual tension between God and men. There is no fundamental force that is arrayed against the Deity, even Satan serving His purpose in some way, but from time to time the free human will sets itself in direct opposition to the divine will. The consequences of this human rebellion are not automatic or necessitous, for the Lord may, according to His Wisdom, elect to act in accord with the "policy of mercy" or the "policy of law." Typical of the personal concept in Judaism is the rejection of the pagan-magical view of guilt as an intangible slimy substance clinging to a person as well as the philosophical view of punishment as being causally related to its corresponding crime. The concept of *teshuvah*, repentance and reconciliation, reflects the genuine nonmechanistic impetus of Jewish genius—the causal chain is set aside by God, who forgives the sinner out of His goodness and His love for His creatures.

In Jewish monotheism, nature was not conceived as operating in accord with laws that were forever fixed in its very being. All the forces of nature are His "servants," with the sun "rejoicing" to do His bidding and the stars being "counted" upon their disappearance from the sky. The heavens are His "chair" and the earth His "footstool"; still, He speaks to man "out of the hair on His head," and "looks upon the poor and those that are contrite in spirit."

It is through speech that He reveals Himself to man, for speech is the fundamental form of communication between two rational beings. While God cannot be seen, He can be heard, with all the Israelites hearing His words at Sinai; later, His words were restricted to the prophets and still later the sages heard the "echo" of His voice (*Bath Kol*). In all these relationships, there was no basic difficulty for the religious imagination, since God was conceived as the epitome of a free spirit, able to move about wherever He pleased.

It was Aristotle's concept of a natural law operating in the whole of nature that provided the basic antithesis to the personal concept of Judaism. Man's relation to the universe about him could now be conceived in terms of the necessitous laws of cause and effect, which, once postulated, could not be terminated at any arbitrary point. The inner bond between the logical process and the concept of causality opened up a way of reasoning which sought to find necessitous connections between all events. Even the world exists by necessity, and if man is to rise above the destiny of the animal kingdom, he must achieve his goal by using the laws of necessity to his advantage, avoiding the downward pull of the material and the fever of desire in favor of the truly human exercise of philosophical contemplation. The principles of necessity and of will are polar opposites; each is capable of being stretched so far as to account for the whole of existence, and the two philosophies so generated are perpetually in conflict. The Jewish concept exalts freedom and God as the source of all life, seeing nature as a pale reflection of His dynamic will; the Aristotelian allows necessity and nature to absorb God, as it were, leaving the whole of existence in the iron grip of an inexorable machine.

While Maimonides sensed the ominous implications of this fundamental conflict, nevertheless he yielded to the Aristotelian conception of mechanism and necessity. He concurred in the description of the Deity as "alive, powerful, wise and purposive," but he emptied these adjectives of any real content by declaring that they were only to be taken as negations of negations; i.e., God is not not-alive, not not-wise, etc. To Maimonides, the way to reach God is to declare concerning all things: "They do not apply to the Deity." Accordingly, the relation between man and God, so simple and natural in prephilosophical monotheism, becomes an insuperable problem. "How then can one conceive the relation between Him and that which is outside of Him, thus postulating a dimension of existence including them both?"[16]

Man's rise in the scale of being occurs in accord with the necessitous laws of nature. As his mind grows into unison with the Active Reason of the universe, man achieves a kind of "nearness" to the divine being and a measure of liberation from the swirling currents of passion and the universal sway of death. But it is man himself who thus achieves the ascent, so that at the level of prophecy, a direct intervention of the Deity is required in order to prevent prophecy. Philosophical contemplation is, in this view, the crown of the good life, with the laws of morality and the regulations of piety serving only as the necessary preparation and context for the art of contemplation.

The *mizvoth* of the Torah are interpreted as fulfilling their function in a necessitous manner, by affecting the mind of the worshiper or the social pattern of society. The inner mechanical logic of Aristotle reigns supreme within the Maimonidean conception of Judaism. The dynamic concept of personality, in which fundamental reality is in continuous tension between the human qualities of love and domination, justice and mercy, wrath and forgiveness, is replaced by the static concept of a self-perpetuating machine in which no change ever occurs. The prophetic declaration, "I, the Lord, did not change," was intended only to describe the reliability of His character, asserting that God does not forget His promises. But when the rational spirit came to prevail within the "tent of Shem," this verse was interpreted as referring to the rigid inflexibility and unchangeability of the divine nature;

hence, it meant also that God was not moved by prayers, petitions or penitence.[17]

To many saintly souls, the austere and heroic synthesis of philosophical Judaism could only appear disastrous. As a Qabbalist of the eighteenth century put it, "This concept is in truth desolation and death; whoever accepts it should be separated from the community that is in exile, and he should not bother with *mizvoth*."[18]

This tension between freedom and necessity, personality and mechanism, is overcome in Qabbalah by the assumption of an infinite chain of being, in which personality constitutes the one direction and necessity the other. It is the progressive diminution of the "grace," emanating from the source of divine personality, that permits reality to freeze into a rigid system of inexorable "laws." There are no dichotomies or absolute divisions in existence, with the total character of the universe shading off progressively from the source of all meaning that is God to the Satanic naught.

If reality is infinite, then all that is finite partakes of unreality and every line of demarcation is only relatively true. Hence, we are led to the conclusion that all separable categories are not really separate, but united by some mediating categories. "Between every two categories there is always a middle category," and "It is of the nature of existence to have a mediating entity between two opposites."[19] The principle of continuity furnishes us with the master key for the understanding of the universe, which bears in all its ultimate constituents the double seal of both freedom and necessity, spirit and matter, personality and mechanism. This duality, the *Zohar* points out, is reflected in the divine name, *Elohim*, which frequently stands for the Deity as reflected in nature, the numerical equivalents of its letters being equal to those of the Hebrew word for nature (*teva*). This name consists of two words, *aile* and *mi*, standing respectively for the "many" of existence and the "who" of personality. The inference that is drawn from this quaint juggling is that nature consists of a continuous flux of phenomena, moving between these poles of being.[20]

In all likelihood, this organic concept was derived from the contemplation of the human personality, which is spiritual in essence and physical in appearance; free in its own consciousness, yet subject to the operation of a multitude of mechanical laws. " For man is a microcosm, therefore it is right and proper to take him as an analogy and archetype of all the worlds."[21]

While the Qabbalists derived their teaching from many sources which were not always mutually consistent, they rarely dispensed with the principles of continuity and polarity. In respect of the doctrine of God, they envisaged the Deity in the most " negative " terms, referring to Him as *Ain Sof* ("Endless"), and denying to Him any physical attributes whatsoever. " For the single Master, called *Ain Sof*, cannot be said to possess will or desire, intention or thought, speech or action."[22]

At the same time, they envisaged the *Ain Sof* as identified in some way with primal man (*Adam Kadmon*), which is the spiritual archetype of personality, and it was considered rank heresy to separate these elements in thought. As will appear in the sequel, they also conceived the primal man, in his lower representations, as functioning in automatic response to the performance of *mizvoth* on earth. Mechanism leads into personality and beyond—on to the inscrutable and the incomprehensible. The primal man consists in his turn of ten *sefiroth*, which were conceived as being both God and not-God. " For that which is infinite and boundless could not make that which is finite and definite; therefore, it was necessary to postulate ten *sefiroth* in the middle, which are both finite and infinite."[23]

Similarly, the human soul was regarded at its lowest as quasi-material, ascending thence by degrees to higher levels which receive " light " from its " roots " in primal man. Whatever man does on earth strikes echoes in the upper reaches of his soul, reverberating in the " upper worlds," bringing about either the " hardening " or the " sweetening " of the " laws."

Fundamentally, the religious content of the principle of continuity is best seen in the practical inference of the supreme importance of every human action. Qabbalistic symbols, which are generally coarse and frequently intricate in detail, were not intended to be merely symbols, but to be taken as the lowest links in the chain of being, which when moved " below " effect changes " above." Nothing that man does is unimportant, for he was designed to be the custodian of the vast palace; that is, the universe, "constricting" or "expanding" the channels of grace by his obedience to the law or his rebellion against it. "The Lord is thy shadow" was interpreted to mean that the Deity reacts in automatic fashion to the actions of men. (While we employ the term "man" in this connection, we must remember that for most Qabbalists only an Israelite deserved this designation. The souls of other nations were not connected by "channels of light" to the upper worlds and were therefore incapable of affecting the operation of the sefirotic world by their deeds or misdeeds.)[24]

Thus, the absolute dichotomy between matter and spirit, between this earthly world and the divine being, was overcome in Qabbalah by the assumption of a host of mediating and connecting entities. The metaphysical difficulties posed by philosophical analysis were solved by the bland denial of the logic of contradiction and the law of the excluded middle. The world is one; hence, all opposites are dynamically related by entities that were at once of one category and of its opposite. For our abstractions are not metaphysically ultimate. "They reach and do not reach" (mo-to v'lo moti).

The problem of a change having occurred in the eternally changeless nature of the Infinite, when the universe was created by His will, is resolved by the assumption that creation took place at levels that were far removed from the inner being of God, with the extent of volition required diminishing as the current of Divine influence is traced back to its ultimate source, so that virtually no effort was needed at the end of the infinite chain of causation. ". . . so that when we come to the ultimate Emanator, we find that no change occurred in Him, because of the chain of will leading to will. . . . At the source, we find that which is midway between potential and actual functioning."[25]

In the same manner, the Qabbalists solved the paradox of God's spirituality and mercy leading to the materiality, harshness, and satanic uncleanliness of this world. In the endless chain of being, things get "coarser" and more evil in proportion to their "remoteness" from the source and in direct relation to the number of "garments" in which the holy spark is hidden. "Just as all the laws are love in their source, so the unclean are clean, and everything is rooted in the will of wills."[26]

The Qabbalistic logic of continuity obliterated all distinctions between intellectual concepts and the physical world, by the assumption of intermediate essences, with the result that seemingly naïve primitive ways of thinking were reinstated by the supreme subtleties of their dialectics. The term "spirit" for instance, which originally meant breath, came to be reidentified with the breath of the spoken word, especially the spoken Hebrew words of prayer.

> For, behold, the letter is a palace and fortress for the spirituality to which it points, and when a man mentions or moves one of the letters, that spirituality is necessarily aroused. Also, holy forms come to be made out of the breath of the mouth which are uplifted and bound together in their roots within the domain of Emanation. Not only this, but in their physical existence; that is, in their writing, spirituality rests upon the letters. This, indeed, is the reason for the holiness of the Scroll of the Law.[27]

By the same token, the ethereal realms of spirituality were conceived to be fashioned in forms corresponding to the Hebrew letters, the alphabet being elevated to the rank of a cosmic, eternal pattern.

> They said that the higher intelligences are precious lights, of the utmost purity, fashioned in the form of letters. This association applies to all forms of light, for even physical light consists of letters, as the masters of the wisdom of magic testify, for when they make fire they see letters, by means of which they comprehend diverse branches of knowledge and are enabled to foretell the future. And if this be true in the case of physical fire, how much more is this applicable to the case of the higher lights, which contain the forms of letters and *sefiroth*, with little letters subsisting within big letters. . . .[28]

This concept enabled the Qabbalists to interpret the actual Torah as an earthly embodiment of a corresponding "spiritual" Torah, consisting of divine "lights," functioning as the key to the upper realms of grace.

"The verse, 'Torah is light,' is to be interpreted as meaning real light, not illumination in the sense of analogy, and not wisdom only but actual light, for this is the form of its existence above."[29]

It follows that the earthly domain of time and matter was bound by a chain of mediating essences unto the spiritual realm of eternity and spirit. The *sefiroth* were at once God and not-God, spatial and nonspatial, temporal and eternal.

We say that it is true that the realm of Emanation is not body and not matter, but that from it body and material issue. Thus, the masters of Qabbalah believed that the four elements are " pointed to " in the *sefiroth*. . . . Not that the actual elements are to be found in them, heaven forbid, but the roots of the elements out of which they issue; even so, with the dimensions and concepts of body. That is why we are justified in saying, length, width and depth, for we mean the power whence length issues, the power of width and the power of depth.[30]

From all the foregoing, the net religious substance of the Qabbalistic world view becomes clear. The observant Jew was assured that his every action was charged with endless " cosmic " ramifications. Upon him and his fellow Jews, the cosmic order in all its vastness and complexity hung breathless. Every *mizvah* he performed helped to effect an " improvement " in the upper spheres, while, at the same time, it provided an additional " thread of light," out of which he would eventually accumulate those " garments of light," in which his soul might be clothed when it dwells in the " lower paradise." By the same token, every *avera* (sin) constituted a " blemish " in the higher "realms of purity," which redounded ultimately to the injury of the entire world, besides daubing his soul with a diabolical stain, which would have to be removed by pain and repentance, before the soul could ascend back to its source. This ascent was conceived as an infinite adventure, continuing in the various domains of paradise in the hereafter, until the soul attains a higher degree of beatitude than it had before creation. And all these effects are virtually automatic, with the " above " domain of the spiritual responding mechanically to the actions of the Jewish people here " below." To the believers, the psychological motivations for the utmost exertions of piety were manifestly all-embracing. They labored at the salvation of their own souls, yes, but at the same time they fulfilled the most crucial function in the total economy of the universe. Their prayers were for the sake of " the world above " and for the well-being of mankind generally. Their piety partook of universal, even cosmic, idealism and of the urge to sacrifice one's own comforts in behalf of the salvation of all men.

The Qabbalistic mentality was saved from the danger of sinking to the level of theosophic juggling by constant emphasis on the psychological attitude of the worshiper. The old virtue of humility was conceived to be the master key to every forward step in the domain of Qabbalah. In all their fantastic flights to the upper realms, the Qabbalists did not forget to extol the simple and fundamental virtues of Jewish piety, guarding against the insidious sins of pride and complacency. As they strove for the powers "above" they did not neglect the moral struggle of men here "below."

Furthermore, their concept of the cosmic "mission" of the Jewish people was so exalted that they were kept from indulging in the cultivation of their own individual piety. While individual "saints" are capable of moving the worlds, the Jewish people as a whole constituted the major link between the upper and lower worlds. Though every nation possesses a governing "genius," the Jewish people represent an earthly embodiment of the *Shechinah*, which is the tenth *sefirah*, and is called *malkhuth*, or dominion. Not humanity, but Jewry in its totality, is the center of the cosmic drama, and it is for Israel to bring about by its actions the "union of the worlds," the return of the fallen *sefirah* back to its source. The individual Jew was thus bidden to unite himself in thought and sentiment with the totality of the Jewish people, performing every *mizvah* for the sake of "the unification of the Holy One, blessed be He, and His *Shechinah*, in the name of all Israel, through Him who is hidden and inconceivable."

The particularistic loyalties of the Jew were exalted in the most superlative terms. While philosophic Judaism labored to widen the common intellectual and moral ground of all faiths and peoples, the Qabbalah sought to isolate Israel from the culture of "the other nations," which is derived "from the worlds of uncleanliness." By its general doctrine of things in this world "pointing to" essences in the higher worlds, the Qabbalah was able to assign supreme importance to every Jewish custom and practice, and to give added impetus to the growth of fanaticism and ethnic self-exaltation. Rabbi Shalom Sharabi, author of a "holy" Qabbalistic prayer book, which is still used by pietists in Jerusalem, boasted in his introduction that he had never looked at any book which was not written by the great Qabbalists, Isaac Luria and Hayim Vital and their authentic disciples; i.e., the "purity" of his vision was not dimmed, God forbid, by the "shells" of "impurity" dwelling on unholy letters.[31] Thus did those who aimed so high, seeking to encompass the daring of philosophy along with the depth of piety, occasionally sink so low in fanaticism and self-aggrandizing dogmatism. The Qabba-lists tapped new wells of enthusiasm and devotion in behalf of the Jewish faith, raising the pitch of piety to feverish heights and strengthening the resistance of the Jew during the dismal, torment-filled centuries of the later medieval and the early modern period. But this good was purchased at a price, a price which all but extinguished the sweet rationality and even-tempered humanity of Judaism at its best.

CHAPTER TEN

THE RESURGENCE OF HUMANISM

WHILE the somber shadows of Qabbalah overspread almost the entire horizon of Jewish thought, brave souls came forward here and there, penetrating the haze of dogmatism, and daring to think in the universal terms of reason and humanity. The humanist movement, emerging in Italy, radiated its message of artistic beauty and intellectual vigor to the lands of Western and Northern Europe. Faint were the rays of rationalism in the writings of the humanists, confounded as they were by the ubiquitous pressure of superstition, hemmed in by the rigidity of feudal society, and frustrated into cynicism by the seeming futility of their efforts. Nevertheless, there was wafted into the cultural atmosphere of Europe a renewed appreciation of the purity and dignity of the human personality, untrammeled by the prison chains of dogma. The classical works of Greece and Rome were made available to the Western world, introducing the accents of the universal language of truth and beauty, and softening the fanatical harshness of dogma-ridden Judaism and Christendom.

Modern historians no longer regard the cultural renaissance in fifteenth- and sixteenth-century Italy as an unprecedented phenomenon in European life. It is possible to recognize feeble anticipations of cultural revival in almost every medieval century, beginning with the eleventh. Nevertheless, the Italian Renaissance, dated roughly from 1453, the year of Constantinople's capture by the Turks, to 1530, marking the commencement of the " pacification " of Italy under Spanish rule, was pre-eminent in the quality and extent of its cultural productivity. A new spirit appeared in the air, affecting both Jews and Christians. Let us briefly note its chief characteristics:

(1) *The rebirth of faith in human power.* It was an age of marvelous adventures leading to the discovery of new lands and

new inventions such as gunpowder, paper, printing and the mariner's compass. The horizon of man was expanded suddenly in all directions. Inevitably, people began to repose more faith in man's works on earth than in God's wonders in heaven. More and more people were willing to undertake a fresh appraisal of the sum of human knowledge. Scholars became more critical of the past, more disposed to undertake fresh voyages of discovery in the domain of learning and wisdom. There were grave errors in the works of the past; there were great opportunities in a fresh vision of the present.

(2) *The rebirth of faith in man's worth.* Not only man's reason and man's soul, but the total personality of man was a thing of dignity. In Scholastic circles, man's reason was like a deeply rutted, dry and dusty one-way road, leading to the merry-go-round of historically patented dogmas. Nor was man's soul a living, anxious, pulsating and aspiring reality, but only the bearer of a single-minded quest for other-worldly salvation. During the period of the Renaissance, the fullness of human nature was recognized. Hence, the renewed passion for beauty and art. Man was no longer simply an object of dogmatics; he had become a subject of new values, independent of any religious tradition.

(3) *The rebirth of faith in the objective judgment of collective humanity.* Culture and humanity were regarded as synonymous. For a brief moment, before the fanaticism of the Reformation and the Counter-Reformation cast Europe back into darkness, there was kindled the flame of faith in reason and conscience, common to all men, as against the artificial barriers of dogmatics.

Consequently, Erasmus (1466-1536) could project the critical, historical method in the study of the Scriptures. In the spirit of gentle wisdom he protested against the exaggerations of the doctrines of " indulgence " and " original sin," gently chiding the self-righteous zealotry of both Catholics and Lutherans. Scholars turned to the pre-Christian world of Greece and Rome in order to find a fulcrum for their view of man as man. In a later generation Montaigne was to express the spirit of the Renaissance in words that cut the ground from under the medieval mentality: " It is an absolute perfection and, as it were, divine for a man to know how to enjoy his own being, loyally."[1]

In philosophy, the change of mood was reflected in the shift from Aristotle to Plato, from the sterile logic of the Scholastics to a new vision of the mystery and dignity of the human soul. While this sense of mystery favored the re-emergence of faith in magic and the " science of the occult," the rediscovery of Plato helped to break the chains of dogma and to open new horizons for speculation. Nicholas of Cusa could point to the paradoxes in the heart of reality, " the coincidence of opposites," and ridicule the " Ignorant Learnedness " of the Scholastics. Men were urged to wipe clean the slate of learning and make a fresh start in all domains of wisdom.

The spirit of the Italian Renaissance stirred new and restless forces in the nearly isolated streets of the Ghetto. Jews began voluntarily to visit Christian churches in order to listen to famous preachers. At the same time, many Christians thronged to hear the sermons of the renowned liberal rabbi, Leo de Modena. Isolationism in religion was no longer considered to be the highest virtue. Italian Jews ceased to observe the stringent laws prohibiting the drinking of wine prepared or served by Gentiles. Rabbis and priests began to debate their respective faiths amicably. Many Christian scholars undertook to learn Hebrew and Qabbalah from Jewish teachers. Rabbi Leo de Modena translated and reworked for his co-religionists a popular Christian classic. Elijah Levita produced the first romances in the Yiddish language.[2]

The critical spirit was born. Solomon de Virgo wrote the little book, *Shaivet Yehudah*, in which the problem of anti-Semitism was discussed objectively. The author dared ask his contemporaries to consider whether Jews were not themselves in part responsible for the vile ideology of anti-Jewish hatred, by their heedless practice of ruthless usury, by their failure to delete objectionable passages from the Talmud, by their occasional ostentatious luxury and by their self-isolation from their host-nations.[3] This newly-born spirit of criticism found its ablest representative in Azariah de Rossi (1513-1598), who wrote a massive work re-examining the chronology of the Talmud, critically comparing historical data from Jewish, classical and Christian sources, and uncovering some of the nearly forgotten treasures of Hellenistic Jewish literature. While the zealous defenders of Orthodoxy banned the famous book of this great scholar, *Meor Ainayim*, as their spiritual confrères had previously banned the philosophic work of Maimonides and the exegetical commentary of Gersonides, the revolutionary spirit of bold research could not be quenched altogether. In the dark and narrow alleys of the Ghetto, Jewish humanism took firm root and flourished.

Perhaps the most interesting book of this period is *The Philosophy of Love* by Leone Ebreo, known to Jews as Judah Abrabanel (1470-1535). Son of the famous Jewish financier, statesman, scholar and philosopher, Don Isaac Abrabanel, Judah was born in Portugal and inducted into the best traditions of Spanish Jewry. He stood beside his noble father in all the varied struggles which preceded the final expulsion of the Jews from Spain. Admired by Spanish and Portuguese princes and adored by the Jewish people, the noted family was offered inducements by the courts of Spain and Portugal to remain in their respective countries. Judah followed the example of his father in refusing to abjure his faith for the sake of any earthly gains. Father and son placed themselves at the head of the ragged and incredibly brave host of exiles, traveling to Naples in southern Italy where Don Isaac achieved prominence as the physician to the Spanish Viceroy. It was in Venice, Italy, that Isaac and Judah found leisure and peace of mind for creative activity. Judah's life was shadowed, however, by a dark cloud, for his beloved six-year-old son was kidnapped by Christian fanatics in Portugal, brought up as a Catholic, and never permitted to see his illustrious, unhappy father.

Judah attained fame as a physician and a philosopher, his *The Philosophy of Love* becoming a popular and influential work in European literature. At its publication it was described by the publisher as the work of an author converted to Catholicism at the end of his life. It is possible, indeed probable, that this statement was made by the publisher in order to win acceptance for the book, which could not have been published otherwise, written as it was in the Italian language. However, there is no certainty on this score. This much is unquestioned: Judah writes as a Jew, referring frequently and with loving devotion to the Jewish faith as his own. That his book could have been taken as the work of a Christian is evidence of the broadly human spirit that pervades its argument, abounding in illustrations selected from the treasury of world literature. In all the varied writings of the

Renaissance, it is difficult to find a more fitting expression of the gentle philosophy of humanism.

The theme of the book can be stated very simply: *Human love at its noblest is the fundamental clue to the mystery of existence.* The cosmic current of love issuing constantly and with renewed vigor from the Creator flows down the graduated shafts of creation, to their lowest depths; then, reversing direction, the current of love flows up again from the fullness of the physical universe to the realms of the spirit and thence to the transcendent being of God. Abrabanel operates within the Platonic concept of the universe, recognizing in Ideals and Ideas the substance of all things and in The Good the source of all ideals. In his work, Platonism was purged of the various unhealthy accretions of superstition that it had acquired during the Middle Ages. His work was like a breath of fresh air that invigorated the mental climate of Europe.

Written in the form of a dialogue between Philo and Sophia, representing the philosopher and wisdom respectively, the author presents the love of man for woman as the fundamental analogue of divine love. In the austere tradition of Judaism, this attitude toward the feminine sex was revolutionary. To Maimonides and the rationalist school, every expression of erotic love was either sinful or disgraceful. While the Qabbalists esteemed the physical consummation of heterosexual love as a mystical act, fraught with cosmic consequences, they ignored the higher elements of human, romantic love and described woman as the source and symbol of the principle of evil in the universe. Abrabanel takes romantic love, as distinguished from sheer eroticism, to be the noblest clue to the mystery of existence. Love is the current of reality behind the façade of phenomena, the impulse toward perfection at work in the soul of things. In erotic love, there is a phase of this cosmic reality hovering above the sexual appetite. Thus, the attraction of sex is terminated by the climax of possession, whereas true love between men and women, partaking of the eternal current of reality, is an infinite advance toward perfect happiness, mellowing and deepening through the joy of union.

The union of the mind with the ideas of God corresponds to the ecstatic climax of erotic love. In surrendering his self to God, a man finds the consummation of his true self. But God is embraced only through Sophia, wisdom, the ideas through which His being comes to us. Thus, the pursuit of divine knowledge corresponds to an act of love. As the true love of men and women grows through the years, being periodically consummated in the ecstasy of union, so the love of man for God increases through the steady acquisition of insight and learning. As human love is both physical and spiritual, so the quest for the divine is both a hunger of the mind and a thirst of the soul. We reach out toward the source of our being by the twin pathways of thought and feeling. To love Him is to know Him; to know Him is to love Him. " For the intellect is nothing but a tiny beam of the infinite splendor of God. . . ."[4] " It follows that we love Infinite God in the measure of our knowledge of Him. . . ."[5]

As to whether the avenue of emotion or understanding should be given priority in the quest for union with the Deity, Abrabanel retains a noncommittal attitude: " About these two activities wise men have differed: namely, as to whether happiness really lies in knowing God, or in loving Him. But you must be content to know that both activities are necessary to happiness."[6]

Actually, the two activities follow one another like night and day, knowledge leading to love and love leading to the kind of knowledge of God that is otherwise unattainable, " the love that is unific, the enjoyment of perfect union."[7] In truth, love is a form of knowledge, a kind of perception, " for the true knowledge of bread lies in tasting it. . . ."

Thus, the love of God is the ultimate goal of all human aspirations toward knowledge, leading the earnest seeker of wisdom to the loftiest heights of ecstasy.

> This great love and desire of ours ravishes us into such contemplation as exalts our intellect, till, illuminated by the special favor of God, it transcends the limits of human capacity and speculation and attains to such union and copulation with God, most High, as proves our intellect to be, rather a part of the essence of God than an instrument of merely human form. . . . Yet may love and desire well persist . . . for continuance of the enjoyment of such union with God; and this is truest love. . . .[8]

Abrabanel follows Plato in assuming an intimate correspondence between the physical and spiritual realms of being. Love has this double aspect of mind and body; even so, man's ascent toward the Deity consists in the acquisition of knowledge of physical reality and in the cultivation of a sympathetic understanding of the entire range of creation. Every increment of knowledge is a step on the infinite road of love.

"Furthermore, when two spirits are united in spiritual love, their bodies desire to enjoy such union as is possible, so that no distinction may persist, but that the union be in all ways perfect; the more so as a corresponding physical union increases and perfects the union of the spirit. . . ."[9]

This intermingling of physical experience with divine reality leads Abrabanel to an enthusiastic appreciation of the mood of paganism, as it was reflected in Greek mythology. It is indeed amazing to note the gusto with which he allegorizes the ancient myths, seeking to discover the profound truths embedded in them. Unlike the great Jewish thinkers who preceded him, he was not horrified by the mere suggestion of pagan sentiments. The mythology of the classical world echoed for him the thought that all physical reality "participates in" and reflects the divine nature, and that love is the fundamental current of existence. His universalist approach was so advanced that he was able to identify the inner meaning of the myths concerning Jupiter's loves with the true intent of the Scriptural account of creation.[10] To his harmonizing mind, which seemed to be totally devoid of the capacity to perceive dissonance and discord, Moses and the Qabbalists were at one with Homer and Plato, differing only in methods of expression.[11]

Abrabanel described both Philo and Sophia as being of "the faithful," who are obligated to accept the truth of the Jewish tradition that the world was created *ex nihilo*. Nevertheless, he favored in theory the Platonic conception of a pre-existent chaos, which persistently resists and thwarts the transforming and creative operation of divine love. Manifestly, his interpretation of the Jewish faith was of unusual subtlety and universality. It was rare indeed for a Jew of his day to have conjoined St. John the Evangelist with Enoch, Elijah and Moses as the four who have achieved immortality in body and soul.[12] In his enthusiasm for the spirit of universal harmony, the barriers between Judaism, Christianity, and paganism appeared to be of minor importance. With equal and marvelous felicity he selected the building-blocks for his system from the Qabbalists, the philosophers, and the myth-makers.

This passion for harmony was reflected in Abrabanel's whole-hearted endorsement of the Platonic conception of beauty as the reflection of divine reality.

Do not marvel, Sophia, that beauty should be that which makes every beloved thing to be loved and every lover to love, and that it should be the beginning, middle and end of all love. . . . For, since the supremely beautiful is the most high Maker of the universe, the beauty of every created thing is the perfection of the work of the master craftsman. . . .[13]

For just as spectacles are good, beautiful, and prized insofar as their strength is proportioned to the eye and assists in the imagery of the visual forms, and if they are too strong and out of focus they are not only useless, but harmful and an impediment to sight; so knowledge of sensible beauty is good and is the source of love and pleasures insofar as its end is in knowledge of intellectual beauty and induces love and enjoyment of the latter.[14]

In Judah Abrabanel, sixteenth-century humanism acquired one of its staunchest exponents. Man's noblest impulse was also the most potent cosmic reality. Hatred and ignorance of all kinds were alike the protean shadows of "nonbeing," comprising the residual margin of darkness, which steadily gives way before the advancing light of God. Only love is real and divine, rising in the scale of holiness, as it unfolds progressively into the passion for understanding, the hunger for beauty, the thirst for the fullness of human dignity. Even the dumb animals instinctively perceive and obey the "circle of love," of which they are part.[15] But in man love unfolds its intellectual, esthetic and imaginative faculties, becoming an infinite current and rising in rare instances to the noblest heights of prophecy.

There appeared to be no special reason in this universal symphony of love for the tenacious, stubborn loyalty of the Jew to his unique tradition. All rites were only tokens of adoration, all forms of worship only instruments of divine love, and all theological histories only beautiful mythology. So it is not inconceivable that Judah Abrabanel did indeed provide a bitter ironic ending to the martyrdom of his family by embracing the dominant faith. In this failure to resolve the tension between a universalist outlook and a particularistic faith, he foreshadowed the paradox that troubled Jewish thinkers of the age of the Emancipation. Yet in his great work he was hardly aware of the magnitude and pathos of this tension, differing in this respect from the great intellectual luminary of a Northern clime and a later century, Baruch Spinoza, who consciously chose a lonely destiny in the thin and uncertain no man's land between Jewry and Christendom.

Baruch or Benedict Spinoza (1632–1677) combined in his amazing genius the prophetic fervor of an Isaiah along with the icy logic and lofty objectivity of an Aristotle. The dominant purpose of his life was not simply " to walk with certainty," but to discover and to teach the saving truths, by which men might live and attain blessedness and immortality. His bold excursions into the lofty realms of metaphysics were not for a moment separated from his lifelong goals: to improve human understanding, to uplift the dignity of the human personality, to bring the bliss of philosophical peace and the joy of the love of God to the strife-ridden, superstition-laden children of men, and finally to found the ideal society, in which free minds can attain the fullness of their stature. To the intellectual concerns of the philosophers, Spinoza added the burning passion for the achievement of the good life, subordinating in fact his seemingly objective speculations to the " moral certainties " of his soul.

But this rare prophet-philosopher lacked the human warmth to sense with sympathy the limited loyalties that motivate and inspire living people. Unlike the great Jewish rationalists who preceded him, he was totally insensitive to the aspirations, sentiments and compelling necessities of Jewish life. He devoted the passion of his great soul and dedicated his luminous genius to the uplifting of man in general, but he viewed with an icy, uncomprehending stare the actual life of his own people. Thus, he towered as a lonely mountain in the panorama of Judaism, representing the loftiest peak of the rationalistic tradition; yet standing apart, in the farthest corner of the receding horizon, gloomy and awe-inspiring.

At the young age of twenty-four, Spinoza was excommunicated by the rabbis of Amsterdam, who must have remembered the success of their predecessors in silencing the deistic heresies of Uriel Acosta. The Amsterdam community consisted of refugees and descendants of refugees from the terror of the Inquisition, who carried over insensibly into Judaism the ruthless rigors of penance and the fanatical dogmatism of their enemies in their native lands. The audacity of the young philosopher in subjecting the Holy Bible to a thorough criticism aroused the ire of the leaders of the little, precarious community, which had emerged only recently out of the depths of tragedy and depended for its existence on the slender thread of faith. Perhaps, too, they feared to harbour in their midst an atheist, who might bring down upon them the wrath of their Calvinist neighbors. Spinoza did not bemoan his enforced isolation from the Jewish community, building up contacts in the course of time with some of the leading figures in Dutch political life.

But while he severed his bonds with the faith of his Jewish contemporaries in Holland, he did not seek the protective covering of Christianity, refusing an appointment as professor of philosophy in Heidelberg, in order to remain untainted by the dogmas of any Church and uncommitted to the forms of any religious body. In his personal life he practised the ethics of Judaism in their noble purity, revealing to his friends a sensitive, generous, and sympathetic nature that shrank from giving the least offense. Yet he would not compromise with truth, for only by truth can mankind be saved. In keeping with Jewish tradition, he insisted on supporting himself by the labor of his hands, achieving a good reputation for his skill in the polishing of lenses. To assert his right to inherit from his father, he entered a lawsuit against his sister, who sought to take advantage of his isolation. When he won his suit, he voluntarily surrendered his patrimony to his sister. A gentle and noble sage, seeking inner purity and peace amidst outer passion and strife, he endeavored to live and to think as an unparticularized human being, a herald of a new age still unborn, that would eliminate the barriers of creed and race which divide mankind.

In spite of the ban of the Amsterdam rabbinate and his own self-alienation, Spinoza belongs in the total panorama of Judaism, for his sentiments as well as his thoughts derived from the philosophical tradition in Judaism and reflected the exigencies and experiences of Jewish life. While he was thoroughly versed in the philosophy of Descartes, who opened the modern era in philosophy by his bold, thoroughgoing method of questioning the foundations of knowledge, Spinoza did not follow the Cartesian method, but brought to full development the inner logic that was inherent in the great tradition of Jewish medieval thought. Though his works exercise a perennial fascination, he actually represented the culmination of an era of research. One of the master builders of the modern mentality and the modern secular society, he was more the sage, summarizing and criticizing and rebuilding the wisdom of the past, rather than the prophet, boldly announcing a new vision. In the sense in which every work of philosophy is a commentary upon the works of previous philosophers, the *Tractate* and the *Ethics* are extended commentaries upon the writings of the great Jewish masters, insisting upon a revolutionary revision here and there of the tradition in which his mind was nurtured.

Because his criticism was frequently too radical for the tolerance of the contemporary Christians, Spinoza was compelled almost uniformly to employ the pious language of his age in order to cloak his heretical thoughts in acceptable garments. Hence the occasional contemptuous references to Judaism and hence too his seeming acceptance of certain Christian judgments concerning Jews, the Hebrew Bible and the New Testament. The austere lover of truth was forced at times to say " yes " to the convictions of his interlocutors, adding bravely a devastating " but," that was meant for the intellectuals and that was not always understood even by them.[16]

Of the great ideas of Spinoza, the one which he pressed most ardently in his lifetime is the assertion that the essence of divine revelation is to be found in the unerring dictates of mind and conscience, not in the rites and dogmas of any organized religious body. In his preface to the *Tractatus*, he sums up his argument as the attempt to prove that freedom of religion is indispensable to the genuine piety of the individual, let alone the general welfare and the efficiency of the government. ". . . not only can such freedom be granted to the public peace, but also without such freedom, piety cannot flourish nor the public peace be secure."[17]

Spinoza sought to prove his argument for a secular state by demonstrating the historic limitations and inevitable failings of the human agents of revelation. The expressions and applications of timeless truths are time-conditioned and of strictly temporary validity. True revelation consists of the inner core and general intent of the prophetic teachings—namely, of their passion for justice, their reverence for humility, their unvarying advocacy of the ways of gentleness, kindness, and peace. The actual words in which the prophets addressed their messages partook necessarily of their own shortcomings and of those of their contemporaries. Hence, true piety consists in the cherishing of the prophetic spirit, rather than the prophetic words, and in the application of the spirit of truth and humility to the varied tasks of life. For the encouragement of truth, freedom is absolutely necessary, and for the cultivation of the attitudes of humility and obedience, the state need only be concerned with the maintenance of even-handed justice for all individuals, punishing those that disturb the well being of others.

In order to propound these fundamental ideals of liberalism in an age when theological dogmas were considered to be the foundation stones of society, Spinoza found it necessary to hammer home with chapter and verse the thesis that what is true in Scripture is neither the literal meaning nor a hidden secret doctrine guarded by a chain of authorities, but the living voice of conscience that is also inscribed on the "tablets of the heart" of all mankind. In launching a devastating attack against literalism, Spinoza followed in the wake of the entire procession of Jewish philosophical exegetes, from Philo down. However, he went far beyond his predecessors in his refusal to wrap the mantle of philosophy round the rites and dogmas of any church. Specifically, he repudiated bitterly Maimonides' method of deliberately interpreting Scripture in such a manner as to make it serve a double purpose —echo the contemporary accents of the voice of reason and sanction an existing body of doctrines and practices. With the burning wrath of a prophetic reformer, he branded as dishonest the Maimonidean dictum: "the gates of interpretation are not closed to us," pointing out the arbitrariness, artificiality and even downright cynicism of this method of interpreting. In all honesty and reverence, he insisted, Scripture should be studied and evaluated only in its own terms.[18]

It is important to recognize that Spinoza shunned the well-grooved pathways of the philosophical exegetes, not so much in the name of abstract truth as for the sake of the new ideal of a free society. The time-honored Maimonidean method was useful for the preservation of an existing society, not for the creation of a new democratic state. Naturally Spinoza was well aware of the pernicious use to which clerical dogmatists put the clever sophistries of philosophers. Scholasticism merely sharpened the sword of medieval fanatics. When a philosophical thought is put in Scriptural garb, official dogmatism is hardened and provided with a respectable façade. The cause of human freedom is not helped when philosophical doctrines are enthroned any more than when the dogmas of naïve faith are extolled, so long as the inflexible structure of an authoritarian faith is allowed to govern the policies of a state. Thus, in the intervening centuries between Maimonides and Spinoza, scholastic philosophy frequently whetted the sword as well as the appetite of ruthless inquisitors.

Philosophy must be separated from theology, Spinoza asserted; the human mind must be allowed to search for truth, unhampered by dogma, for the free activity of the mind is the highest form of piety. ". . . the nature of the human mind is a primary cause of divine revelation."[19]

The cogency and the passion with which Spinoza expressed this thesis are best conveyed in his own incisive words:

> I show that the Word of God has not been revealed as a certain number of books, but was displayed to the prophets as a simple idea of the divine mind, namely, obedience to God in singleness of heart, and in the practice of justice and charity; and I further point out that this doctrine is set forth in Scripture in accordance with the opinions and understanding of those among whom the apostles and prophets preached, to the end that men might receive it willingly, and with their whole heart.[20]

When Scripture speaks of God being nigh unto Israel and preferring it above other nations, " It speaks only according to the understanding of its hearers who . . . knew not true blessedness."[21] The entire concept of a " chosen people," whenever it arises, is a human perversion of the divine doctrine of human equality. For truly religious people derive no satisfaction from the circumstances of their being uniquely favored; in humility, they recognize their own limitations and in love they seek to share the gift of divine favor. But, human, all too human, are the words of Scripture, in spite of the divine inspiration that is contained in it. So Spinoza directed biting barbs of satire at the Calvinists of Holland, who considered themselves to be the contemporary "chosen people," the legitimate heirs of all Scriptural promises. "Lastly, prophecy varied according to the opinions held by the prophets. . . . For, as Moses believed that God dwelt in the heavens, God was revealed as coming down from heaven onto a mountain, and in order to talk with the Lord, Moses went up the mountain, which he certainly need not have done, if he could have conceived of God as omnipresent."[22]

Accepting enthusiastically the rabbinic dictum, "the Torah spoke in the language of human beings," Spinoza dealt ruthlessly with the naïve concept of literal inspiration, castigating the manifold weaknesses of Biblical figures and relegating all wonders and miracles to the realm of imagination. "It speaks inaccurately of God and of events, seeing that its object is not to convince the reason but to attract and lay hold of the imagination."[23] He even suggested that a few particularly objectionable passages may have been interpolated "by irreligious hands."

The tale of Joshua's stopping the sun in its course is a good example of the besetting sin of ethnic arrogance, unless it be interpreted as a parable, designed to teach the principle of God's superiority to the sun. "Thus, partly through religious motives, partly through preconceived opinions, they conceived of and related the occurrence as something quite different from what really happened."[24]

Spinoza's attitude toward the massive heritage of Jewish rationalism was paradoxical. On the one hand, he followed the lead of the great philosophical commentators in his interpretations of the Biblical miracles as so many parables. On the other hand, he sought to lay the theoretical foundations for a new democratic society, while they aimed at preserving the hard-pressed Jewish community. Yet it was through him that the Jewish contribution to the emergence of modern society was made effective. Towering in the splendor of loneliness, he was really the heir of a long tradition, bringing to fruition the seeds of criticism that abounded in the writings of the philosophical Jewish commentators. Thus he referred to the commentary of the twelfth-century scholar, Abraham Iben Ezra, for proof of the thesis that Moses did not write the Torah, but that an editor, most probably Ezra, collected and collated the various classical writings that now constitute the Pentateuch. There is scarcely a critical remark that Spinoza suggested which was not anticipated by the bold commentators who labored in the rationalistic tradition. Though he may be justly regarded as one of the master builders of the science of Biblical criticism, Spinoza did not depart as radically as he himself believed from the tradition of philosophical exegesis. He too saw a divine core in Scriptures, and he too regarded everything else—the tales, the wonders, the ceremonies—as so many embellishments of the basic truth. In Spinoza's view, the core of truth in Scripture was the command to love God and to obey His moral will. "The sum and chief precept, then, of the divine law is to love God as the highest good."[25] ". . . we have shown that the divine law, which renders man truly blessed, and teaches him the true life, is universal to all men . . . ingrained in the human mind."[26]

Spinoza differed from all exponents of the Jewish tradition by his negation of the worth of the external expressions of the Jewish faith. To make possible a secular state it was necessary to affirm that all rites and ceremonies are totally irrelevant to the good life; like language and social mores, religious practices are not intrinsically significant and therefore interchangeable. For if ceremonies are essential to faith, may not the dominant creed arrogate to itself the right of insisting on its own particular pattern of rituals? But by the same token, minorities should not zealously insist on their own rights and should manifest a decent respect for the practices of the dominant faith. All zeal in religion is misplaced if it ignores the substance and consecrates the shadow of faith. Spinoza therefore goes to great lengths to prove that "ceremonies are not aids to blessedness."[27]

From this vantage point, Spinoza could not but esteem the Jewish millennial insistence on the centrality of ceremonies to have been a grievous error. The laws of the Mosaic code were intended only for the government of the Jewish people, so long as they lived in their own country. Their purpose was twofold—to cultivate the habit of obedience, and to aid in "the preservation of a society." Hence, when the traditional structure of a society is broken up, the ceremonies and the laws which belonged to that tradition may be regarded as obsolete. For this reason he considered that the ritual laws of Judaism were no longer binding and that Jews were in all conscience free to adopt the rites of other faiths or to get along without any religious observances, as they pleased. In the lands of dispersion, Jewish insistence on their own ceremonies, at the price of lifelong martyrdom was, according to Spinoza, motivated by a perverted zeal and sheer stubbornness. Proponent of religious freedom as the lonely Amsterdam philosopher was, he was not entirely free from the seventeenth-century insistence on conformity, which was expressed in the succinct principle of the Treaty of Westphalia: "*cuius regio, eius religio.*" He preferred the blessedness of peace to zealotry of any kind, except the zeal for truth. He admonished Christians as well as Jews to ignore the ceremonies of their own respective faiths when they ventured into regions dominated by a different religion. "Nay, those who live in a country where the Christian religion is forbidden are bound to abstain from such rites, and can none the less live in a state of blessedness."[28]

Some Jewish critics have pointed out that Spinoza treated the New Testament with extreme gentleness, concentrating his attack on the Hebrew Bible. Did the great sage fail to be even-handed or did he fear the wrath of the church? Actually, in his eagerness to establish the principles of the separation of church and state, he had to direct his fire at the Old Testament, which outlines the life of a politico-religious community, whereas the New Testament deals with the salvation of individuals. Second, his method of Scriptural interpretation required that the books of the Bible be discussed in their own terms. For the same reason that he ranked Moses above all other prophets in keeping with the declaration of the Torah to this effect, he described Jesus in the language employed by the Gospels. In the New Testament, Jesus speaks as the voice of God incarnate, as the way and the life; therefore, he must be so interpreted. But in the final analysis, the dogmas relating to Jesus are to be judged in terms of their effectiveness as symbols. "Lastly, it follows that faith does not so demand that dogmas should be true as that they should be pious —that is, such as will stir the heart to obey."[29] "A thing is called sacred and divine when it is designed for promoting piety, and continues sacred so long as it is religiously used; if the users cease to be pious, the thing ceases to be sacred."[30]

With this pragmatic evaluation of religious symbolism, Spinoza was appalled by the senseless dogmatism of the Christian theologians of his day. "I must at this juncture declare that those doctrines which certain teachers put forward concerning Christ, I neither affirm nor deny, for I freely confess that I do not understand them."[31]

Furthermore, Spinoza was a Hebrew scholar, thoroughly familiar with the Old Testament and its commentaries, while he knew himself to be sadly deficient in the knowledge of the Greek language and Greek sources. However, he laid it down as a general rule for the study of both Testaments that the living word of God may not be equated with the actual opinions, much less the words, of the sacred authors. " Still, it will be said, though the law of God is written in the heart, the Bible is none the less the Word of God, and it is no more baneful to say of Scripture than of God's Word, that it is mutilated and corrupted. I fear that such objectors are too anxious to be pious, and that they are in danger of turning religion into superstition, and worshiping paper and ink in place of God's Word."[32]

True religion, which Jews may call Judaism and Christians Christianity, is essentially the very opposite of the rancor and intolerance of dogmatists. It is " love, joy, peace, temperance and charity."[33] In greater detail, he lists the principles of universal religion as being the following axioms: (1) the existence of God; (2) His unity; (3) His omnipresence and omniscience; (4) His unlimited dominion; (5) His worship, consisting in justice and charity; (6) Only those who serve Him are saved; (7) He forgives the sins of those who repent.

It will be easily seen that these principles describe a real and sincere faith, which is in polar opposition to either agnosticism or even deism. As to the grounds of this faith, we shall revert to them presently.

Spinoza's dominant purpose, that of advocating the creation of a free society, made it necessary for him to reduce the stature and importance of the people of the Bible as well as to negate the worth of Jewish rituals. The less that was made of the builders and citizens of the theocratic state of the Hebrew Bible, the less reason there was for the Dutch Calvinists to emulate their example. Also, the recipients of revelation had to be blamed for every imperfection in the content of the Bible. Whatever was eternally true in the Holy Bible was the voice of the living God; whatever was defective and backward was a reflection of the intransigence of the Jews. " For a true knowledge of faith it is above all things necessary to understand that the Bible was adapted to the intelligence, not only of the prophets, but also of the diverse and fickle Jewish multitude."[34]

The more "fickle" the "Jewish multitude" was conceived to be, the easier it was to discredit the ideal of theocracy and to disentangle the true seeds of faith from the encrustations of popular prejudices, fables and dogmas. Thus, strangely enough, the exegetical compulsions of liberalism frequently required that " the people of the Book " be depicted in the most lurid and contemptible terms. Spinoza, like Renan and Wellhausen in the nineteenth century, sought to bolster the liberal cause by minimizing the contribution of Jewish people and maligning their characters, outflanking the contemporary advocates of theocracy and clericalism by an indirect attack on the Jews, who constituted the remnants of the Biblical community. If the Book was to be debunked, the people who gave it had to be defamed.

In yet another respect Spinoza set the tone for the contemptuous attitude of liberal writers, like Voltaire, toward the Jewish people. Eager to break down the barriers of exclusiveness that vitiated the religions of Western Europe, he set out to dissipate the aura of being the special object of divine Providence that Scripture builds up about the Jewish people. He maintained that the Jewish people were not chosen in any concrete sense, any more than every people may be regarded as having been chosen for a unique historical destiny and assigned to one or another country. This derogation of Israel's glory was needed, in his view, in order to combat the zealotry of latter-day fanatics. All men are part of the " chosen people." Every people was to be made to feel that it was the special object of divine concern. " Now, inasmuch as their election has regard to true virtue, it is not to be thought that it was promised to the Jews alone to the exclusion of others, but we must evidently believe that the true Gentile prophets (and every nation, as we have shown, possessed such) promised the same to the faithful of their own people, who were thereby comforted."[35]

The deeper meaning of this passage is part of the insistent

theme of the philosophy of liberalism: revelation is but another name for mind and conscience at their inspired best; the Bible is like any other great book, human in its narrowness, divine in its universality; the Jews are as any other people, not "witnesses of God," in either the Christian or the Jewish sense.

As to the wondrous survival of Israel, which was construed by the Jews as evidence of God's special concern and by the Christians as proof of divine wrath, Spinoza takes pains to demonstrate that Jewish history could be explained in terms of natural causes. "For they so separated themselves from every other nation as to draw down upon themselves universal hate, not only by their outward rites, rites conflicting with those of other nations, but also by their sign of circumcision."[36]

To Spinoza, Jewish exclusiveness was not a noble virtue but a stigma of narrowness and zealotry. He was probably the first Jew of the species that is now quite common, who classify humanity according to different faiths, but who describe themselves as "non-sectarian." Anxious to establish society on secular foundations, he deprecated every social barrier that did not reflect natural, geographic conditions. Only in Palestine would Jewish people be justified in clinging to Biblical law. Nor did he rule out the possibility of an eventual restoration of the Jewish people to dominion in their native country, though he was not thrilled by such a prospect.[37] Governed as his thought was by an austere and ruthless monistic passion, Spinoza regarded the fragmentation of humanity into nations as an offence to reason and he particularly deplored the stubborn "exclusiveness" of his own people. In the Diaspora, it is only Gentile hatred and Jewish stubbornness that combine to preserve the Jewish law and the Jewish people, though Jewish existence no longer possesses any rhyme or reason.

What, then is the faith by which man might live? Spinoza offers in his writings two answers, both of which he considers true, the one designed for the common people, the other for the master thinkers. The first answer is the essential message of Scripture—"that men may be blessed through simple obedience, without understanding."[38] The second answer is the one argued in his *Ethics*, that blessedness is to be found through the sustained exercise of reason, which leads to "the intellectual Love of God."

This double answer, already foreshadowed in the classic writings of medieval rationalism, was justified by Spinoza in terms of the two sources of human knowledge—mind and conscience. It was his life's ambition to merge the voices of reason and morality into one clarion call for the good life, in which each emotion is governed by will, each fiat of will is controlled by reason, and each flash of reason sees the particular events of time and circumstance under the aspect of eternity.

Thus, the path of faith rests upon "the moral certainty" that is afforded by the voice of conscience. Scripture's great merit consists in the formulation of the doctrine "that simple obedience is the path of salvation." This teaching cannot be proven by reason, "with mathematical certainty," though it is demanded by our moral nature. In clarifying this vision of the good life, and bringing it within reach of the masses of the people, "Scripture brought a very great consolation to mankind"—a consolation which pure reason could not have produced out of its own resources.

"We should, however, make use of our reason, in order to grasp with moral certainty what is revealed—I say, with moral certainty, for we cannot hope to attain greater certainty than the prophets."[39]

In this concept of "moral certainty" as a source of knowledge, Spinoza anticipated the thesis that the great philosopher of the Enlightenment, Immanuel Kant, was to develop with surpassing brilliance more than a century later. In Spinoza's system, this concept remained in its germinal state, but the pathway leading from reason to salvation was developed with the utmost energy in his *magnum opus*, the *Ethics*.

While the majestic structure of Spinoza's philosophy belongs to the general history of thought, we shall proceed to describe briefly the elements of his system which pertain to the general tradition of philosophical Judaism. First, concerning the idea of God, Spinoza accepts Crescas' critique of Aristotelianism, describing God as infinite. Furthermore, God is substance; that is, infinite in every one of His infinite attributes. But from the infinity of God's being, Spinoza does not infer that it is impossible for the human mind to grasp the nature of the divine will. On the contrary, God is manifested through reason in the mind, as He is revealed through the laws of necessity in nature. To our human knowledge, God is expressed in the two infinite attributes of extension and thought. Whenever the human mind attains "a clear and adequate idea," it is true of reality, because mind and reality are two phases of the infinite substance of God.

But, and here Spinoza's attack is most powerfully centered, God does not order nature to suit human purposes. All things operate by necessity, there being no final cause to the chain of events that determine human life.

This denial of human purposiveness in nature is motivated by the passion for the purity and nobility of the God-idea. True love of God, Spinoza insists, does not demand God's love in return, "for, if a man should so endeavor, he would desire that God whom he loves, should not be God."[40] To love God is to surrender to His will, not to bend His will toward one's own temporal gain; it is to know and to feel in the depths of one's being " that everything in nature proceeds from a sort of necessity, and with the utmost perfection."[41]

Second, the manner of worshiping God: Man is just another creature or " mode," subject to the laws of necessity, save that he also participates in the divine nature by his reason and by his capacity for self-surrender, which is love. By permitting the power of reason to operate freely in his mind, seeing every event in the light of its total context, man may cultivate the love of God, which is true blessedness.

All the feelings of man are either active and joyous or passive and painful. For we feel pleasure when our vitality is enhanced and suffer pain when it is diminished. Now, God is all activity and pure joy. Man as creature is the victim of outer forces, but man as transformed by surrender to God shares in the divine activity and joy. Human misery arises from the turbulence and irrationality of the emotions, reflecting man's helplessness in the grip of the iron meshes of necessity; but emotion pales and fades in the light of reason, since reason is an expression of the divine nature; sharing in the activity of God, man can arrive at the steady feeling of joy that accompanies thought in its purity. For joy is the twin brother of reason, in man as in God. Through the examination of each and every emotion in the light of reason, man can achieve not only control over his impulses, but their actual transmutation into the joyous acceptance of reality, which is the love of God. " He who clearly and distinctly understands himself and his emotions loves God, and so much the more in proportion as he more understands himself and his emotions."[42] So man worships God by allowing his reason to master all emotions and all self-feeling, arriving at the joyous acceptance of the divine will and the whole-souled adoration of His majesty.

Third, the ideal of perfection: The power of understanding is not merely a process of logical reasoning from proposition to proposition, but, at its highest level, it becomes intuition, enabling man to behold things from the standpoint of God, as it were. Through the faculty of intuition, man automatically follows the dictates of reason, without any conscious effort and without any inner struggle. It is this faculty of intuitive judgment that constitutes the process of reasoning in its most divine form, " subduing the emotions and uniting the mind of man with God."[43] Thus the attainment of intuitive flashes of insight is regarded by Spinoza as the mark of human perfection, corresponding to the estimate of prophecy in philosophical Judaism. But, while prophecy involved an act of will on the part of God, Spinoza's intuition is wholly a human achievement. As in learning to read we first put letters and words together, then study the syntax and structure of a sentence and eventually learn to grasp the meaning of a whole paragraph at a glance, so the senses show us the elements of the universe, reason its logical structure and intuition its total meaning.

" We may thus readily conceive the power which clear and historical knowledge, and especially that third kind of knowledge, founded on the actual knowledge of God, possesses over the emotions: if it does not absolutely destroy them insofar as they are passions, at any rate it causes them to occupy a very small part of the mind. . . ."[44] " Consequently . . . he who knows things by this kind of knowledge passes to the summit of human perfection and is therefore affected by the highest pleasure."[45] " From this third kind of knowledge necessarily arises the intellectual love of God."[46]

". . . the intellectual love of the mind toward God is part of the infinite love wherewith God loves himself."[47]

Fourth, as to the immortality of the soul: Spinoza holds out the hope of immortality only for that part of the mind which has become habituated to thinking in the terms and laws of eternity. The rational part of the human personality, insofar as it was applied and refined to the point of intuitive insight, is deathless. In this respect, Spinoza remained true to the tradition of medieval rationalist philosophy. "Again, since from the third kind of knowledge arises the highest possible acquiescence, it follows that the human being can attain to being of such a nature that the part thereof which we have shown to perish with the body should be of little importance when compared with the part which endures."[48]

From all the above it appears clear that Spinoza not only expounded a profound metaphysical system, but that he also believed himself to have marked out a pathway to salvation. Indeed, the first title of the *Ethics* was, *On God, the Rational Soul and the Highest Happiness of Man.* In its initial stages, this path consists in the cultivation of the simple virtues of humility, kindliness and obedience. Man learns to curb the expressions of self-feeling, to consider the welfare of humanity as a whole and to submit to the will of God. In its later stages on the highway of reason, simple obedience is progressively refined into a rational understanding of the laws of the universe, which are expressions of the attributes of extension and mind, the immutable character of God. Man learns to delight in the austere purity of reason and to thrill in the joy of total surrender to the divine will. He begins to experience moments in which he enjoys the " blessedness that is not the reward of virtue, but virtue itself." On its highest levels, obedience becomes automatic, direct and intuitive; man learns to love God for His own sake, to sense the exquisite rapture of intuitive thought penetrating the mysteries of the universe, to revel in the ecstasies of the " intellectual love of God." In a word, Spinoza teaches the doctrine of salvation by self-surrender and self-transformation. Caught in the grip of necessity, man must learn to experience the divine will in the operation of reason, which is both human and divine, conquer his self-feelings by the aid of reason and learn to view all things "under the aspect of eternity." Then he will learn the supreme delight of adoring the awesome majesty of God, " living only for Him and thinking only of Him."

> For the ignorant man is not only distracted in various ways by external causes without ever gaining the true acquiescence of his spirit, but moreover lives, as it were, unwitting of himself, and of God, and of things, and, as soon as he ceases to suffer, ceases also to be.
>
> Whereas the wise man, insofar as he is regarded as such, is scarcely at all disturbed in spirit, but, being conscious of himself, and of God, and of things, by a certain eternal necessity, never ceases to be, but always possesses true acquiescence of His spirit.
>
> If the way which I have pointed out as leading to this result seems exceedingly hard, it may nevertheless be discovered. Needs must it be hard, since it is so seldom found. How would it be possible, if salvation were ready to our hand, and could without great labor, be found, that it should be by almost all men neglected? But, all things excellent are as difficult as they are rare.[49]

CHAPTER ELEVEN

HASIDISM

THE complex tapestry of Qabbalah was woven from many and varicolored threads. So vast a movement of visionary specula- tion, growing furtively through the centuries in the shadowed caverns of mystery, inevitably absorbed and assimilated different and even conflicting elements. In the course of time, the following three strands became discernible, through the varying emphases given them by different movements, though they were never completely separable.

The first strand in Qabbalah reflects the impassioned piety of the deeply religious soul, the so-called *homo religiosis*. Its component elements are: the sense of wonder at the magnificent richness of creation; the poetry of the believing soul rent asunder by the tragic dichotomy between the sorrow-laden, iniquity- bedeviled world as it is and the exalted vision of what society ought to be; and the feeling of divine awe and sublimity experi- enced in tremors of holiness and deepening into the glowing ecstasies of mysticism. For the Qabbalist of this type, the structure of myths and fables in Qabbalah was merely an articulation of the poetry of faith, relating the essentially ineffable in symbolic language and concretizing in mythical form a radiant vision of the profound realms of being that extend beyond the grasp of reason. The details of the theosophic cosmogony and theogony were of secondary importance since they were simply coarse and concrete approximations of an ineffable visionary experience, seen as "through a glass, darkly"; the basic reality was the immediate experience of the divine reality. While Qabbalah came dressed in bold myths and fantasies, its inner core was the secret life of the soul, in all its oceanic mystery.

The Qabbalists of this type tended to become master teachers of folk piety, expatiating in word and deed on the beauty of holiness and outlining the steps whereby the average person might learn to scale the heights of piety.[1]

The second strand in the richly variegated complex of Qabbalah consisted of the dryly prosaic, naïvely literal and uninspiring mentality of orthodox theosophy. Here was an extensive body of exact and authoritative knowledge, containing, as the Qabbalists thought, all the right answers to the baffling mystery of existence in this world and in the whole range of the beyond—how could one dare ignore it? Revealed by Elijah and other heavenly beings, this " knowledge " not only offered the one key to the solution of all conceivable cosmic riddles, but it also furnished specific information on the manner in which prayer could be made effective and the agonizingly slow process of redemption hastened and consummated. Verily, to the believers, the fate of the world hinged on their studies of this " hidden wisdom " and the major events of contemporary history could be understood by means of the occult map of its basic co-ordinates. So, obeying a strictly literal interpretation of the classic sources, the study of Qabbalah could continue to flourish on the narrow plateau of frozen concepts kept strictly apart from the advancing currents of thought in the modern world. Naturally, this tight little world of isolationist Orthodoxy had long ago been hardened to the point of complete irrelevance—the nemesis of all fanatical dogmatists.[2] The third strand consisted in the eschatological emphasis, which degenerated into pseudo-Messianic movements. The exile of the Jewish people was only the earthly reflection of the exile of the *Shechinah*, the imprisonment of " sparks of holiness " in the power of " shells." If only the " sparks " could be redeemed, Israel would speedily emerge triumphant. In the wretched circumstances of Jewish life, the hunger for immediate redemption through the Messiah was nearly always the predominant mass emotion. It became necessary for the great sages of nearly every generation to foster the belief that the Messiah would come in their day and age. By various devices the year of the Messiah's advent was calculated afresh in every epoch and the result, understandably enough, was always such as to reassure the people that the Messiah would come in their lifetime. Since the cultivation of the " hidden wisdom " nourished the hope of attaining varied states of prophetic inspiration, it was almost inevitable that illuminates would arise, proclaiming the imminent arrival of the

Messiah or of one of his precursors. A book published in the thirteenth century warned that Satan might mislead the Qabbalists who make practical use of holy names, giving them false information concerning the Messiah.[3] The tragic débâcle of the hopes thus raised would lead to mass despair and frustration, but not for long. For hope springs afresh in the human breast.

While these ideational strands in the uneven texture of Qabbalah were never completely separated, they were sufficiently distinct to inspire three different movements of thought.

The third, or eschatological strand, became prominent in the middle of the seventeenth century when Sabbatai Zevi proclaimed himself the hoped-for Messiah. While this deluded visionary and many of his followers embraced Islam, the Sabbataian movement did not disappear from Jewish life for at least a century, assuming varied forms and drifting steadily toward moral nihilism. In the middle of the eighteenth century, the Frankists represented the final, foul fruit of eschatological, nihilistic Qabbalah. To them, an act of sin became the means of redemption, since " the spark of holiness" contained in it must needs be "liberated." Inured to the logic of paradoxes, they reveled in contradictions, urging their followers to renounce Judaism in order to fulfill its hopes; to see the utterly incomprehensible Deity in the concrete shape of vulgar, lustful, fantastic charlatans and to make a sacrament out of heinous sins.

The Sabbataian movement was the most widespread of all pseudo-Messianic upheavals, and its effects were felt among Jewish people for more than a century. It emerged from the theosophic-mystic circles of Qabbalah, demonstrating the revolutionary impetus and the deep psychical roots of Jewish mysticism. In a study of Jewish thought, the Sabbataian heresy is an illustration of the extent to which the sober piety of Judaism could be turned upside down by ideas belonging to the tradition and forces deriving from the intrinsic pressures within the Jewish community.

Sabbatai Zevi, a Qabbalistic scholar, was convinced early in life that he had been chosen for a great purpose. Gradually he came to think of himself as the predestined Messiah, son of David, due to be revealed in the summer of 1666, or a few years later. A young visionary, the " prophet" Nathan of Gaza and other " prophets" in other cities similarly heard voices announcing that Sabbatai Zevi was the Messiah. The movement spread very rapidly throughout the Jewish Diaspora. The masses of the people believed, even when their spiritual leaders hesitated. Women and children fell into trances duplicating the ecstatic phenomena of mass enthusiasm in the early years of Christianity. In 1666 the movement was suddenly deflated, like a punctured balloon, when Sabbatai Zevi yielded to the threats of the Turkish Sultan and accepted Islam. However, a sect of believers remained, some persisting within Islam as a secret society (Donmeh), others living as Jews and guarding their secret "knowledge." The leaders of the Jewish community banned the movement as heretical after the conversion of Sabbatai Zevi.

Some three generations later the Sabbataian followers in Southern Poland were rallied together by another pretender to the Messianic throne, Jacob Frank. His followers, numbering at least fifteen thousand, accepted Catholicism in 1759 and disappeared within Polish society.

For our purpose, it is important to note the following elements in the Sabbataian-Frankist heresy.

(1) *The movement drew its roots from the lush soil of Qabbalistic theosophy.* It was through the influence of Qabbalah that attempts were made by different pietists to achieve high states of "holiness," when they were inspired by the *Ruah hakodesh* (Holy Spirit) and heard the voices of heavenly beings. Sabbatai Zevi's followers nourished their inner fires with the fuel of Qabbalistic speculations. The Frankists carried this emphasis to its logical conclusion when they declared their Holy Scripture to be the *Zohar*, the classic book of Qabbalah, and as "Zoharists" they fought against the rest of the Jews, whom they termed Talmudists.

(2) *The ecstatic phenomena of "prophetizing," "speaking in tongues" and more rational forms of "prophecy" were generated within the Sabbataian movement.* In a city like Ismir, in Turkey, there appeared several hundreds of so-called "prophetizers," who fell into trances, beheld fantastic visions and declared that Sabbatai Zevi was the Messiah. Once again, the peculiar power of mass delusion and mass intoxication was demonstrated on a global scale, both in Moslem and in Christian countries. Sabbataism emphasized the potency of faith and it appealed to a direct

"religious experience." When Sabbatai Zevi was asked for a "sign" by the Jews of Salonika, he replied that the "sign" would be the fact that the community will obey his order to observe the Fast of the Ninth of Ab as a festival, without a sign.[4]

(3) *The peculiar combinations of extreme asceticism and orgiastic revelry.* In the first years of the movement, when the momentary appearance of Sabbatai Zevi as the Messiah was expected, the people fasted and mortified their flesh with incredible zeal. Even then, the fasts were turned into feasts. New festivals and rites of celebration were established. Dances were developed as effective means of inducing collective ecstasy.

(4) *The paradox of doing the divine will by means of transgressing the divine law was promulgated as a secret doctrine within the movement.* On the one hand, the Sabbataians laid special stress on two *mizvoth*—the wearing of an untrimmed beard and a *tallith kattan* (the traditional garment with fringes). In their petition to the Archbishop of Lwów, the Frankists begged permission to wear "Jewish garments," untrimmed beards, to continue to observe the Sabbath, and to refrain from the eating of pork. On the other hand, the doctrine of redeeming "the sparks of holiness" from the grip of the "other side" led them to perform various sinful acts as ways of serving God. According to some historians, they even ordained on occasion acts of adultery as "hidden" deeds of piety.

(5) *The supernatural character of the Messiah.* Sabbatai Zevi referred to himself in grandiloquent terms, not merely as a heavenly being but also as an incarnation of an aspect of the Deity. He applied to himself several of the traditional names of God. Among the rites that he ordained was a requirement to visit the grave of his mother. Later the Frankists asserted that they believed in the trinitarian character of the Deity.

It is easily seen that the Sabbataian-Frankist movement had many points in common with the rise of early Christianity out of Pharisaic-Essenic Judaism. It also parallels the development of the Anabaptist and Quaker sects in early Protestantism.

The Sabbataian-Frankist movement demonstrates the malignant potentialities of the myth-building impetus in Qabbalah. If the chief authority of Lurianic Qabbalah could assert that it was not Queen Esther, but her "evil desire that became incarnate in the shape of a woman and lived with King Ahasuerus, giving birth to Darius," why was it not possible for some of his like-minded followers to imagine that the *sefirah* "*Tifereth*" was incarnate in a man?[5]

Indeed, a similar doctrine was preached by the early followers of Sabbatai Zevi—namely, that the spirit in his shape took up the Moslem faith, while he himself went up to heaven.[6]

In desperation, the rabbis sought to limit the study of the *Zohar* and the writings of Luria, insisting that only those who have attained the age of thirty or forty be allowed to peruse these "dangerous" volumes. However, they did not dare deny the supreme truth of Qabbalah. Caught in the entangling meshes of Qabbalistic dogma, they reaffirmed its supreme sanctity even while they built fences to protect the unwary from its double-edged sword.[7]

The theosophic strand of Orthodox Qabbalistic speculation continues to be cultivated today amidst an ever-narrowing circle of unworldly devotees in Jerusalem. In their prayers every phrase is intended to cleanse either the outer or the inner phase of a "shell," or to "improve" the inner or outer phase of a *sefiro*. With meticulous exactitude, they follow the immensely complex list of "intentions" which have been elaborated in the writings of the Lurianic school, fancying fondly that they keep the heavenly channels open for the flow of divine grace.

Even today in Orthodox circles, their influence is hardly felt. Not repudiated and yet not followed, this pathetic band of the faithful continues to spin the ancient threads, waiting for the fullness of divine redemption. Yet, for all their self-imposed isolation, their influence in the long run is not altogether negligible, since for the uncompromising Orthodox believers no ideology is permitted other than the one which is grounded in the Qabbalistic tradition.

It was out of this Qabbalistic circle and in conscious rebellion against its dry dogmatism that the late Chief Rabbi of Palestine, Abraham Isaac Kuk, evolved a world-view synthesizing the best of the "hidden wisdom" with the massive achievements of the human mind. The sheer nobility and scope of Kuk's faith demonstrates that the creative impetus in Qabbalah is not yet altogether extinct. Yet Kuk was as much a rebel against the rigid canons of the Orthodox ideology as he was a faithful representative of the rare piety that it inspires. At this point, we need only note the continuance of Orthodox Qabbalah in the total complex of modern Judaism.[8]

The psychological trend in Qabbalah, which sought to arouse and to cultivate the feelings of piety, developed into the mighty stream of Hasidism in Russia and Poland. Concentrating attention upon the inner life of the soul, it served to counteract the overly external and mechanical emphasis of Jewish law (*Halachah*). Aiming at the attainment of the loftiest peaks of devotional piety, the Qabbalists of this school were no longer concerned with the legalistic minutiae of the Talmud. To them, the rise and fall of the soul, in its longing for divine love, was the decisive focus of interest. Hence they dedicated themselves to the task of cultivating the inner life of their followers, deepening the wells of faith, and teaching their people to perceive the reality of the Supreme Being in all walks of life. The "saints" among them attained various stages of mystical illumination.

The classic work of this type, revealing the intimate bond between the mysticism of Qabbalah and folk piety, is the little volume, *The Path of the Righteous*, written by the renowned Qabbalist of the eighteenth century, Moshe Hayim Luzzatto (1707-1747), and widely used in study circles to the present day. Luzzatto began to experience mystical trances while he was still a youth, with a strange voice speaking through his mouth, dictating "revelations" in the artificial language and archaic style of the *Zohar*. While a considerable group of admirers clustered around him, the rabbis of Central Europe feared the revival of a pseudo-Messianic movement and prohibited Luzzatto from practising any mystical "unifications" (establishment of contact with a heavenly being by means of the manipulation of certain names), and from publishing his inspired writings.[9] Only if he settled in the Holy Land could he expect to resume his "unifications." Yet, as he reports in his letters, Luzzatto attained even more exalted mystical states when he simply let his mind wander into heavenly spheres, without making use of the approved letter-juggling devices of the Qabbalah. "Since then, I have received double."[10] Later some of his Qabbalistic works were published and came to be highly prized in esoteric circles. His manual met with universal acclaim and speedily achieved the rank of a popular classic.

In this brilliant work of tender piety, Luzzatto defines the purpose of man's life as being the attainment in the hereafter of the joy of " contemplating the radiance of the *Shechinah*, which is the one true joy."[11]

" For the soul (*neshamah*) does not love this world at all but, on the contrary, despises it. Therefore the Lord would surely not have sent a creature down for a purpose that is contrary to its nature and repugnant to it."[12] It follows that the purpose of human life is fulfilled not in this world, but in the hereafter.

Consequently, the purpose of all our disciplines and actions is to fit the soul for its eternal bliss in the hereafter, by purging it of all earthly desires. The soul is not exalted by mortifying the flesh, for the body is the indispensable instrument of fulfilling the *mizvoth* on earth, but the wants of the body must be severely restricted, " so as not to take of the things of this world that which is not compelled by necessity."[13]

True piety is of the spirit, bearing no relation whatever to mortifications of the flesh—such as " baptism in ice and snow." Its general principle consists in the readiness of the soul to do God's will and in the perpetual search for opportunities to be of service, carrying every *mizvah* beyond the limits described in the Torah,[14] inventing new instruments of service to Him.[15] To love God is not merely to obey the law, not even merely to find new ways of pleasing Him; above all, love is a joyous anticipation of union, a yearning for His " nearness," in transports of exaltation.

But the path of holiness can be pursued at will by unaided man only in its initial stages. For the successive milestones of progress in holiness the specific and direct help of God is needed— and when it comes, the Hasid is lifted into a higher realm of being, his holiness becoming effortless and automatic so that " even when he deals with the physical needs of his body, his soul is not severed from its adherence to the upper spheres." This stage of holiness, sublimating the instincts of the body for the uses of the soul, is a direct gift from God, since the human soul can only struggle against the body, never winning a decisive victory. Effortless, serene and confident piety, with the body serving the soul, as a violin serves the musician, is the quality of the saints chosen by God for His service.

This mystical state of "unitive" piety is described by Luzzatto as follows:

> He who has been made holy by being touched with the holiness of his Creator, even his physical deeds are transmuted into acts of sheer holiness. . . . To the one who has only attained the level of purity, physical acts are indeed only necessities. . . . But to the saint, whose soul clings steadily to God, trembling in fear and love of His dominion of truth, it is accounted to him in this life, as if he walked before the Lord in the realm of eternal life. Such a person is to be esteemed as the sanctuary, the temple and the altar. . . . Thus our sages remarked that the saints constitute the "divine carriage," for the divine presence rests upon them even as it dwelt in the Holy Temple. It follows that the food which they eat is as a sacrifice consumed in the flames of the altar. . . . Whatever use they make of the things of this world, once they have become united with His holiness, is an elevation and promotion for that thing which merited the privilege of being of use to the saints. . . .
>
> With the help of God thus given to him, his soul grows in strength, overcoming the impulse of the body and clinging to His holiness; attaining ever higher levels—such as the Spirit of Holiness [*Ruah hakodesh*], whereby his understanding is lifted above the natural powers of man. . . . So much so that even the key to the resuscitation of the dead may be given over to him. . . .[16]

In this popular classic of Qabbalistic piety, we find the basic ideas of the great mass movement of Hasidism which emerged in the southern provinces of eighteenth-century Poland—life is for the sake of the love of God, and love is best cultivated in joy, and in the discovery of new, individualistic ways of serving Him. Love is an anticipation in feeling of union with the beloved. It can become so intense and deep as to make every action a sacrament of the faith, with the living saint becoming a "dwelling place for the *Shechinah*."

The Hasidic movement reflected a widespread and powerful upsurge of mystical piety, which infused a new and revolutionary impetus into the practice of Judaism. The ideas of Hasidism were essentially those of the Qabbalah generally; however, in Hasidism, the esoteric ideology, heretofore locked in a maze of labyrinthine symbols, was transmuted by the magic of mystical experience into a popular movement of genuine, creative piety. The dry bones of theosophic abstractions were now merely the theoretic substratum and ideological undergirding of a newly released stream of religious consciousness, fed by the fresh springs of mystical experience and fervor.

A religious genius of the first order set into motion the massive popular movement of Hasidism; yet of his inner life we know but little. Beginning his career as a writer of amulets and as a master of Holy Names, Israel Baal Shem Tov (Master of the Good Name) 1698-1760, soon emerged as a master teacher of Jewish piety. A rare and genuine mystic, he gathered a host of faithful disciples about him, all of whom cultivated the arts of saintliness and developed a characteristic pattern of mystical piety. The Baal Shem was thus the first of a long line of *zaddikim*, saints, who strained for the lofty heights of mystical rapture and who were venerated as living "channels" of divine grace. The masses of pious people, known as Hasidim, gathered in loose societies round their beloved *zaddikim*; so there was evolved a unique social unit, with a living exemplar of holiness as the center, and a specific concept of the pathway to the perfection of holiness as the common centripetal force. All Hasidic societies insisted upon the self-renewal of the worshiper, either through his experience of mystical fervor in isolation, or through his surrender to the infectious mass-enthusiasm of the group. The great *zaddikim* developed their own unique patterns of worship and discipline, for to each of them faith was a fresh and living experience. Through their common efforts, the peculiar mood of mystical piety assumed diverse shapes and entered into the mainstream of Judaism.

Down to the rise of the Hasidic movement, we rarely encounter in Jewish literature the frankly announced quest of the mystic to break through the veil of phenomena and to achieve direct union with the living current of divine holiness. The prophets of the Old Testament were indeed "filled" with the "spirit of the Lord," but in the rabbinic period, who dared aspire to a like achievement? The rabbis of the Mishnah and Talmud strongly discouraged any attempt on the part of their contemporaries to attain the storied heights of prophecy. While they hoped for the renewal of prophecy and the outpouring of the Holy Spirit, they associated this consummation with the arrival of the Messiah and the supersession of the normal world of everyday existence. They allowed that a reflection of the divine presence was to be found wherever scholars prayed or studied, but it was a mere reflection. In a real sense, the divine presence abided only in the Holy Temple. On the whole, they taught the doctrine of a transcendent Deity, whose power and vision permeated the universe, but who is Himself different from and removed from every human faculty. Consequently, they wondered at the command of the Deuteronomist " to love the Lord and to cleave unto Him." How can a creature of flesh and blood cleave unto Him who is " as a consuming flame "? In their interpretation, to " cleave unto the Lord " could only mean associating oneself with the followers of the Lord, by assisting and supporting the scholars of Torah, or by taking the Lord to be the ideal model for human conduct.[17]

Since the pattern of ideas in the Jewish faith did not countenance the interpretation of the mystical experience as the attainment of actual union with the transcendent Deity, the experience itself was viewed with suspicion. Nevertheless, we read of occasional ventures in this direction. A Talmudic sage, Rabbi Nathan, enjoyed the privilege of discoursing regularly with Elijah. In the Gaonic period there were " descenders into the carriage " (yordai Merkabah) " who, after fasting many days, would put their heads between their knees, murmur into the earth many hymns and psalms, and get to the point of peering into the inner halls. They would feel as if they saw with their own eyes the seven palaces, beholding themselves go from palace to palace, seeing what there was to see."[18]

Records of such visions are encountered occasionally in the long sweep of Jewish literature, but it is difficult to draw the line between the profuse creations of sheer fantasy and the genuine reports of a chaste mystical experience. Qabbalah provided the ideological framework for the quest of the mystic and the wide range of his experiences. According to its teaching, the human soul is not completely enclosed within the body. Rooted in the divine being, it is like an infinite shaft of light, extending from God to man. Hence the higher reaches of a person's own soul, or neshamah, may be revealed to him. Thus, Karo's Maggid, which we described before, is, in a sense, his own soul, speaking with his own voice, yet revealing heavenly things that are unknown to his conscious self. The Maggid announced himself to be the Mishnah that he studied. It has been noted that the

Hebrew letters of Mishnah and *neshamah* were identical. Thus, the "voice" was actually introducing itself as the higher ego of Karo.

The Lurianic doctrine of the transmigration of souls, especially the principle stating that one's soul may be "impregnated" with the soul of a deceased saint, opened up new vistas of mystic-prophetic experiences.[19] "There are souls which come to the aid of man, in the mystery of impregnation. . . . Thus, you will see that it is possible for everyone to achieve ever higher states of inspiration up to the very highest level, and every man can rise to become the equal of Moses our teacher, if he should but will to do so."[20]

The Baal Shem refused to describe in writing the psychical pathway that he himself followed, or to allow his disciples to do so, in the belief that the experience of mystical "adherence" (*devekuth*) was essentially incommunicable. The way could be indicated only by direct, oral exposition over a period of many years. We are told that a disciple once attempted to take notes of the Baal Shem's lectures, and he was sharply rebuked when the master glanced at the notes and said, "There is here not one word that I spoke." It was only many years after the master's death that the first collections of the Baal Shem's maxims appeared in print. Yet even these sketchy remnants allow us to glimpse the exalted nature of his mystical piety.

He would fall into a trance, becoming seemingly unconscious; yet, he remained fully aware of the overwhelming presence of the divine being.

" At times, one may sit or lie, appearing to sleep, when he is really alone with his Master. This is indeed a high level."[21] "When the holy spark of one's own higher soul kindles one's spirit, then the words that he speaks come forth of their own account. It is as if the *Shechinah* were speaking out of his throat and not he himself, saying the words."[22] Or, as his famed successor, Dor Ber, expounded the same thought, "I shall teach you how best to preach the Torah. When you are completely unconscious of your own self, turning yourself altogether into a listening ear, you begin to hear how the "realm of speech" speaks through you, as if you were not the one that is speaking at all. But the moment you begin to hear your own words you should stop."[23]

We note here the characteristic quality of utter passivity and the complete absence of any consciousness of self.

"The true adherence is attained beyond the reach of sensitivity, when one no longer perceives any one thing save the reality of faith itself. We might describe it as the state of negating all existence. No one can understand its meaning of his own accord, or explain it to others. It comes to each person in accordance with his level of piety."[24]

"Whoever has not himself experienced the love of God and the fear of Him and the taste of clinging to Him and being bound up with Him, in all gradations that transpire within the heart, will never understand these things no matter how much they are expounded to him verbally and in writing."[25]

Hasidic faith is primarily an attitude of receptiveness to the divine flow of love and teaching. When man cancels out his self, God appears. The Hasid endeavors to subdue all thoughts of self, to overcome all feelings of self. As soon as he succeeds and in the measure of his success, the light of God appears within him. "True fear, an overwhelming feeling of awe, falls upon a person suddenly, so that he does not know where he is, and the tears of his eyes flow of their own accord."[26]

This state of "adherence," however it is experienced, is far more than just an emotional upheaval; it is accompanied by an assurance of being face to face with naked reality. The Hasid feels that in those blessed moments he has been favored and approved. Furthermore, the false veil of appearance has been pierced, he feels, and he has come to see the throb of love in the personal source of all existence. What he perceives in the flow of mystical exaltation provides the one certain foundation of knowledge which it is possible for man to have.

"The inwardness of the Torah and *mizvoth* is clear and self-authenticated, for certainty belongs to His name, while doubts flow from the shells and from the outwardness of things."[27]

It follows that the insights which come to the Hasid in moments of illumination may be regarded as data of prophetic revelation. "When one speaks while in a state of adherence, and a thought enters his mind, it is a kind of small prophecy."[28]

Indeed, the Baal Shem would occasionally lapse into trancelike states of mystical devotion, when he would preach in total unawareness of the people around him. "When my thought adheres to the Creator, blessed be He, I permit my mouth to say whatsoever it wills, for I relate the words to their upper source in the Creator. All things here below have their roots above."[29]

Nevertheless, in the very highest states of exaltation, there are no words, but an ineffable silence surcharged with the flow of thought in its fullness and purity before it is "contracted" into speech. "The guard of wisdom is silence, for in silence one may unite himself with the supervening domain of pure thought."[30]

The Baal Shem and his followers quoted frequently from the classic work of Elijah De Vidash, *Reshith Hokhma*, especially the passages in which the dialectic of love between man and God is expounded in great detail. Man's love may be reciprocated with divine love to the point where it is difficult for the worshiper to return to mundane reality. "And he will not be quickly separated from the holiness of His love, for the king holds him with the bonds of love. So he grows in holiness more and more. It is as if one throws a rope to a friend to pull him closer to oneself, and this friend reciprocates by similarly throwing back a rope so that they are quickly bound together in one knot, strong and tight, without any separation between them at all. He who merits this love is without a doubt bound up with and adhering to the life above. . . ."[31]

In the ecstasy of mysticism there is "the flow of holiness," ineffable joy and an intense aura of unearthly light. "He may then see with the eye of reason all the upper lights, and he senses continually intense joy, second after second, without interruption, for the root of his soul adheres above. . . ."[32]

Like all mystics, the Baal Shem was not always in a state of exaltation. His psychic life alternated between moments of greatness, when he felt himself transported into the higher realms of being, and moments of relative depression when the glow of illumination would depart from him. Operating on the principle that "wherever a person's thought reaches, there he is," he regarded himself as alternately rising and falling in the scale of being, acquiring immense power by ascending in spirit to the "source of his soul" and sinking back in utter exhaustion to the level of a "shell"-imprisoned human.

"At times the saint is in a state of greatness, praying and learning in fear and love, feeling that he faces the great King and adheres to him," but there are times when even the saint is in a "fallen" state as it were, "unable to pray with intense fervor." In the long run it will appear that every "fall was for the sake of an ascent." Nevertheless, the "dark night" that follows the "state of illumination" is all too painful and real.

In characteristic fashion, the Baal Shem explained this rhythm of mystical feeling with the aid of the following parable: "A father, teaching his son to walk, faces him with outstretched arms to keep the baby from falling. Then the father steps back a step or two, in order that his son should take a few steps and learn to walk."[33]

At times, too, the descent of the saint is needed in order that he may retain his bonds of intimacy with the common run of humanity. "Whoever desires to pull his friend out of the mire must be willing to step into it himself."[34]

How grievously this principle can be abused! Yet its formulation was but another indication of the fact that faith, in all its emotional turbulence, was to the Baal Shem not a reasoned dialectical system, which could always be contemplated "under the aspect of eternity," but a living experience, subject to the varying rhythms of all vital faculties.

It has been well said that nothing is so powerful as an idea whose time has arrived. The devotional ecstasies of the Baal Shem proved to be of revolutionary import to the evolution of Jewish thought, for their psychical impetus happened to coincide with the dynamic forces of his contemporary situation. Complex and rare as was his personality, the fundamental melody of his heart reflected the dormant longings of the oppressed Jewish masses in Eastern Europe. Paradoxical as it might seem, mysticism in all its exotic beauty and esoteric mystery speaks the language of the masses. For the deep answers unto the deep. In addition to the fascination of mysticism as such, the Baal Shem acquired a mythological aura of a wonder-working saint. His novel ways were amply "proven" to the people by the miracles which he was said to have performed. He incarnated the hero image of popular piety.

In the poverty-stricken and fear-ridden villages of the fertile

Ukraine and in the wild foothills of the Carpathian mountains there had long been brewing an inarticulate revolt against the *remoteness* of salvation. Of the pleasures of this world the Jewish masses tasted but little, crushed as they were between the restive serfs and the grasping lords. They desperately needed the sweet solace of redemption to justify the grinding misery of their everyday existence. But redemption in both its eschatological and other-worldly phases seemed so remote as to be virtually inaccessible. The advent of the Messiah in all his glory was passionately longed for, but, having been delayed so long, this vision no longer seemed real or close at hand. By the same token, the promised joy of the hereafter was predicated on the basis of such harsh and rigid demands that the average person had little hope of sharing in its delight. The rabbis, whose privilege it was to consecrate all their energies to the accumulation of Torah-merit, were still so agonizingly uncertain of their rewards in the hereafter that they spent years doing penance for imagined sins and mortified their flesh for every hour that they failed to devote to the study of the Torah. Thus Nathan of Gaza, who later became the " prophet " of the pseudo-Messiah Sabbatai Zevi, underwent a series of fasts to purge his soul of its sins in previous incarnations. In his letters to the far-flung communities, announcing the imminence of redemption, Nathan imposed on mass penitents the penance of fasting from Sabbath to Sabbath. Pious rabbis would undertake " the penance of exile," traveling as wandering mendicants in order to atone for involuntary infractions of the law. Life was harsh and the rigid exactions of piety harsher still, so that even the pietists were perpetually in fear of the coming judgment. How much less could an ordinary Jew expect to enjoy his share of bliss in the hereafter, driven as he was from pillar to post in the daily struggle against the ever-stalking specter of starvation, unable to study the Torah or to abide by its multiple requirements?

Characteristic of the psychology of rabbinic piety in this age is a popular anecdote, which recurs in many variations: A traveling peddler was caught in a blizzard while pursuing his trade. Stumbling through mountainous drifts all day, he finally succeeded by midnight in finding his way to a village, where one house only was still lit. It turned out to be the house of the rabbi, who, as was his habit, studied far into the night. The rabbi received the peddler hospitably, with offers of hot tea and a comfortable lodging. But, now that his physical needs were no longer pressing, the peddler sensed his spiritual perplexity and inquired of his kind host whether, lacking the pleasures of this world, he, wretch that he was, would at least enjoy the delights of the hereafter. The rabbi, conscious of the mountainous burden of demands that were built up by a host of casuists, replied not unsympathetically as follows: "You labor so hard for the things of this world which nevertheless elude you—how then can you expect to share in the bliss of the hereafter for which you labor not at all?"

Thus, the harassed masses of Jewry saw themselves deprived of all consolations, with the redemption of the Messiah looming in the far distance and the bliss of the hereafter dependent on gifts of talent and the luxury of leisure that were not available to them. The very maturity of the Jewish faith, which led it to esteem so highly the exercise of intellectual disciplines, made its compensations seem remote and unreal to those who hungered most passionately for the bread-and-butter consolations of popular faith.

These repressed resentments and frustrated hopes of the impoverished Jewish masses generated the revolutionary ardor which found expression in the pseudo-Messianic movements of Sabbatai Zevi and Jacob Frank. The belief that the Messiah had already come, waiting only for the right moment to reveal himself, served to assuage the bitterness of the people and to kindle within their breasts the bright assurance of the immediacy of salvation. Consequently, the masses of Polish Jewry were carried along for one brief moment on the crest of enthusiasm of the Sabbataian movement of the seventeenth century, and at the very time when Hasidism enjoyed its most creative phase, the believers in the Messiahship of Jacob Frank succeeded in ensnaring multitudes into their fantastic sect, which set the Zohar over against the Talmud and the so-called "God of Israel" over against the infinite source of all being. The Frankists arose in the very same province of southern Poland as the Hasidim, channeling the same social frustrations, but in different directions. Whereas the Frankists allayed the silent protest against the "remoteness" of salvation by pointing to the presence of the incarnate Messiah, in whose presence it behoved all worshipers to rejoice and to delight in the foretaste of the Messianic era, the Hasidim taught the masses to perceive the reality of the divine presence everywhere, especially in the personality of the *zaddik* or saint, where the spirit of God had already achieved its final triumph over the impulses of flesh and blood. The *zaddik* who is "bound" to his followers by bonds of affection is a living precursor of the perfect world to come. A pseudo-Messiah raises high hopes only to shatter them into fragments. A *zaddik* raises the hopes of the people without plunging them into despair, and there may be not one but several *zaddikim* in every generation. In both movements, redemption was not merely a promise and a hope, but a near and present reality. Hasidism was thus able to provide a genuinely religious substitute for the eschatological mythology of the Frankists, which thrived so long on the festering frustrations of the illiterate Jewish masses.

To be sure, Hasidim did not weaken, much less repudiate, the intense hope for the arrival of the Messiah, but it set the popular experience of the nearness of the divine being and their participation in the heaven-storming labors of the *zaddik* as the condition for his advent. Accordingly, they transferred emphasis from sheer idle speculation to a program of arduous labors, leading to the psychological goal of "adherence to the Holy One." In one of his visions the Baal Shem declared that he ascended to one of the highest "palaces" in heaven, where he saw the Messiah teaching the "secrets of the Torah" to the "seven shepherds." Interrupting the discussion, the earthly visitor inquired, "When will you arrive?" and the Messiah replied, "This is how you will know. When your teaching will become widely known and accepted, and the learning which I helped you to attain will be shared by many, so that they too will be able to achieve 'unifications' and 'ascents of the soul,' even as you, then the dominion of the 'shells' will end and there will be a time of favor and salvation."[35]

In other words, the key to salvation is the attainment, by increasing numbers, of the exalted ecstasies and blessed intuitions of the mystic. The congregation of Israel was to be transformed into a community of saints, enjoying "ascents of the soul" to the palaces of heaven. At least, all the people were to be "attached" in body and soul to those *zaddikim* that had mastered the art of achieving "unifications." The Messiah will not come suddenly nor without effort. His advent needs to be hastened by the labors of mystical piety.

Round the Baal Shem was formed a growing band of devoted disciples who practised the arts of mysticism, learning to attain those states of spiritual exaltation when the reality of God appears to be as near and immediate as "that of a person staring at us." Does not Qabbalah teach that the physical universe, in all its obdurate stubbornness, is nothing but a "garment" for the indwelling light of the divine? Why, then, should we not learn to see the "spark of holiness" in all things, which is also their vital power, since all power is from God? The ideological basis of Hasidism, then, consisted primarily in the axiom that the presence of God, not merely His power and providence but His very presence, was to be found in the inner substance and vitality of all things. The Baal Shem accepted this corollary of Qabbalistic metaphysics as a direct and immediate intuition, tested, made real and proven true in the glowing fires of his mystical ecstasy. It was a familiar saying among Hasidim that while the Qabbalistic visionary, Isaac Luria, revealed God in the heavens, the Baal Shem revealed Him here on earth.

As was his wont, the Baal Shem expressed the kernel of his metaphysics in a beautiful parable:

> A great king, who was very wise, caused it to be brought about through the magical power of suggestion that a palace was established with many walls, towers and gates. He then commanded that he should be approached through the gates and towers, scattering of his treasures at the entrances of each tower. Most people would go through one or another gate, taking whatever money they found there, and return to their homes. . . . But when the beloved son of the king approached the palace, he was not satisfied with the gates, which seemed to lead in labyrinthine ways so far but no farther. He refused to rest content with anything short of standing directly before the king. So he closed his eyes and made a supreme effort to reach the king; then he opened his eyes and behold—there was no partition between him and his father, there were no walls and no gates, for it had all been brought about through the power of suggestion.[36]

To attain the rank of a "beloved son" one must learn to see the universe from the point of view of God, to whom all of creation is merely an elaborate testing ground for the souls of man. The world which our senses reveal to us is nothing but appearance, while the reality behind it is the divine presence, and by a supreme effort we might be enabled to perceive the *Shechinah* directly, without any intervening " curtains."

Does it mean then that we must disregard the sensible universe as mere appearance, disparage the *mizvoth* as offering only limited rewards, and concentrate altogether upon the cultivation of the direct approach of mystical intuition? The Baal Shem and his followers stoutly resisted any such temptation. While the mystic in rare moments rises above that "power of suggestion" which conjures up this realm of appearance, he remains human for the rest of his life. Hence the Baal Shem urged that God be sought *through* the world, not in spite of it. Since there are no things and events that do not draw their vitality from the divine presence, there is literally nothing that may not be employed as a vehicle leading toward Him.

> The Holy One desires us to serve Him in all ways. Sometimes we find ourselves in the company of people when, unable to learn Torah, we may still adhere in thought to God and effect " unifications." Especially in travel one may serve God in ways other than praying and learning. Let no one grieve over these and similar interruptions, for the Lord desires to be served in all ways, sometimes in one way, sometimes in another. His situation was purposely so arranged, that he might serve God precisely by the opportunities that come to him in his travels or in the company of people.[37]

The Qabbalistic doctrine of " the redemption of the sparks " that are to be found in all things served for the Baal Shem as the ideological foundation for a multidirectional piety, which employs every occasion and every event as an opportunity for a new form of worship. Hasidic legendry embellished this thought in a number of incidents, telling of saints who effected " unifications " and redeemed lost souls, when they were prevented by unforeseen contingencies from performing their usual devotions. There is nothing that is purely accidental; all things call to us in behalf of the Creator, and we must respond in a worshipful attitude, in whatever situation we may be placed. To confine worship to stated times, fixed forms, and uniform patterns is to desecrate the sacred unity of God's creation.

We are called upon " to unite our thought, speech and deed with all the events that come our way in simple-minded devotion to God, for nothing is outside His realm and His unity. Thus, whosoever does anything at all, with no relation to the service of the Lord, separates that event from unity with Him, God forbid."[38]

It follows that every physical deed must be performed "with the thought of uniting the Holy One, blessed be He, with His Shechinah."[39]

Not only is man able to endow with sacramental significance every action of his daily life, but he is in duty bound to regard himself as standing in a perpetual dialogue-relationship to divine providence, with the external impressions impinging upon him from without as well as his own inner impulses calling him in their several ways to the service of the Lord. "If a pious man feels a particular urge for some article of good food, it may well be that the holy spark which is related to his soul is concealed and 'dressed up' in that object."[40]

To the holy men, all actions are highways opening unto the Infinite. The consumption of food is not merely a permissible enjoyment, nor yet a necessary indulgence to our physical constitution, but it is designed to be an act of divine service, for it is through eating, while in a state of "adherence to the divine being" that the holy sparks are "liberated." While the pietists who preceded him argued only that it is a *mizvah* to maintain one's health for the sake of retaining the ability to serve God, the Baal Shem taught that the taste of the food reflects the "holy spark" in it, and that pious people, "attaching" themselves to God, "liberate" these imprisoned sparks of holiness. The act of eating itself is thus conceived as a holy performance, akin to the eating of the sacrifices in the Holy Temple. "And he should bear in mind that when he eats or drinks anything at all, the taste which he feels in his mouth while chewing or swallowing is the inwardness of holiness."[41]

If the attractiveness and beauty of things is a spark of the divine, it follows that God may and should be worshiped through all forms of esthetic enjoyment. Yet the Baal Shem did not teach that the perception of beauty is itself "the seal of God," as is the perception of truth and the practice of righteousness, but only that it might be included in acts of worship, by being referred to the source of all beauty.

> If one should suddenly behold a beautiful woman, or other things of striking beauty, he should immediately reflect as follows: "Whence does this splendor derive? Is it not due to a divine power immanent in the

world? But if so, should I not be attracted to the whole and the root of which this splendor is a part and a branch? . . ." Also, when one tastes something good and sweet, he must bear in mind that the sweetness derives from a higher power. . . . The basic rule is that the vital essence of things is that which a person enjoys.[42]

With this thought in mind, the Baal Shem interpreted the Psalmist's verse, " I put the Lord always before me " as follows: Since the Lord is always before me I regard all things as equal in value.

The possibility and indeed the duty of worshiping God through every facet of experience was predicated on the belief that all creation throbs with an upward surge of spiritual impulses, seeking to find their way to the divine source. The " sparks " may be " fallen " and " imprisoned," but they contain the vital essence of all things—and their one yearning is to be " redeemed " through contact with the heaven-storming soul of the saint. So vivid was this concept of the universal craving for the " nearness of God " to the Baal Shem that he believed he heard from time to time snatches from the symphony of creation. Song is the articulation of the soul's longing for the "return" to its own source; as it soars into the " highest realms " the song of the soul takes on the overtones of a cosmic symphony, and the saint, in his exalted moments, perceives this wordless melody of creation, which echoes the inward piety of the universe. This frequently repeated thought is best expressed in the words of the great-grandson of the Baal Shem, Rabbi Nahman of Bratzlav:

> Know that every wisdom in the world has its own peculiar melody, which is distinctive to it, expressing the relation of that wisdom to its source. . . . But the melody which is peculiar to faith in the Infinite who is transcendent to the universe, supervenes above all forms of wisdom and faith in lesser ideals, and is the source of all the melodies which correspond to the other branches of wisdom. . . . Only the saint of the generation is able to perceive this supreme melody of faith, which is indeed the melody of silence, rising as it does beyond the grasp of thought and speech. . . .[43]

Every blade of grass has its own distinctive melody. . . . Know that when one prays in the field, the flowers and plants associate themselves with the voice of prayer, adding of their yearning to the worshiper's hymns.[44]

Another great mystic, who described in detail the various stages in the "ascent of the soul" to its source, declared, "Every soul, rising to the source of its being, advances only through a kind of song . . . in which the consciousness of self is utterly lost."

And in the highest level of the mystic's existence, when he no longer alternates between states of illumination and depression, there is the perception of "an abstract song," a song which is undetermined by any categories whatsoever and is the source of every kind of delight.[45]

This intimate association between music and the mystical experience of Hasidism led to the development of original songs and dances which reflected the yearning of the pietists for "adherence" to the divine being. Braving the ridicule and contempt of their soberly rationalistic opponents, the Hasidim regarded the group singing of wordless melodies as an exalted form of worship, and they esteemed the dance as a pure expression of religious enthusiasm.

The Baal Shem was fond of the following parable, which expounds the need of "listening" to the melody of faith and expressing it through dance and other physical gestures:

> Once, a master violinist and singer played a melody and sang a song to its accompaniment with surpassing sweetness. All who heard him were so overcome with the beauty of the music that they began to dance with utter abandon, jumping in their enthusiasm almost up to the ceiling, and striving to come ever closer to the masterful player. Those who succeeded in reaching closer to the heavenly musician were more overpowered by the sweetness of his song, until they seemed to lose themselves altogether in the rhapsody of the dance. In the meantime, a deaf man came along who was not able to hear the melody and sense its sweetness. Seeing people caught up in the intoxicating frenzy of the dance, he was forced to conclude that they were mad. Why all this joy? But if he were wise and knew that they danced because of the compelling sweetness of the melody, he would have associated himself with the dancers and would have joined their company.[46]

The implication of the final sentence is that those who are presently "deaf" to the cosmic melody of faith should nevertheless join in the ecstatic dancing of the mystics, in the hope that their infectious enthusiasm and spiritual sensitivity would in time be transmitted to them.

Having cultivated the capacity to sense the benign presence of God in all types of experience, the Hasidim concluded that sorrow was the root of all evil. It is the duty of the pious to be ever joyous, in the realization that God is near to them. While it is impossible for a human being to remain forever in the ecstatic state of exaltation and illumination, it is his duty to rouse himself from the depths of depression and force himself, if need be, to be joyous.

That joy is the attendant quality of faith is already asserted by the Psalmist: "Light dawns for the saint, and joy belongs to those who are straight at heart."[47] More pointedly, the Talmud declared, "The *Shechinah* rests upon a person, not when he is sad, depressed, hilarious, lighthearted or trivial, but only when he is joyous in the awareness of doing the will of God."[48] The pantheistic piety of the Qabbalists brought fresh emphasis to this ancient principle of Judaism, encouraging the pietists to keep themselves perpetually in readiness for the descent of the *Shechinah*, by cultivating the mood of joy. Isaac Luria, the famed Qabbalist of sixteenth-century Safed, managed to retain the quality of joy, in spite of his unflagging ascetic disciplines. "The disciples of this exalted man of God relate that he used to attribute his achievement of obtaining the Spirit of Holiness [*ruah hakodesh*] to the circumstance of his being extremely joyous whenever he would perform a *mizvah*.[49]

The Hasidim converted this emphasis on joy into a veritable cult. In a pious puritanical age, when the rabbis and the common folk sought to outdo each other in heaping up mountains of prohibitions, "enlarging their phylacteries" in a thousand different ways, the Baal Shem insisted on the inseparability of joy from piety.

> Let no man indulge in the multiplication of additional prohibitions and refinements of the *mizvoth*, for this is the intention of the evil desire, to insinuate the fear that one has not fully carried out the divine commands. This fear leads in turn to sadness, which is the most powerful obstacle to the service of the Creator. Even if one has stumbled into sin, he should not give way to sadness, which negates the value of anything he might do, but let him confine his regrets to the sinful act and return in joy to the service of the Creator, may He be blessed.[50]

While the Baal Shem and his followers did not disavow altogether such ascetic practices as fasting, self-flagellation and the various modes of the mortifications of the flesh which were then popular, they pointed out the two dangers inherent in this procedure—the probability of lapsing into gloom and depression, and the possibility of acquiring the bitter, invidious pride of the ascetic. Thus, the Baal Shem wrote to his favorite disciple: "When I learned of your intention to undergo a series of fasts, I became deeply disturbed. I beg you in the name of all that is holy not to subject yourself to the danger of sinking into the gloom of melancholia, for the *Shechinah* avoids a person when he is depressed, and inspires him only when he is joyous in the consciousness of doing the will of God."[51] In this letter to Rabbi Jacob Joseph the Baal Shem does indeed speak out against ascetic practices, but this condemnation of the excesses of asceticism must be placed within the total context of the prevailing piety, where asceticism was regarded as the one sure way to holiness. While reducing its importance in their design for living, the Hasidim did not give up asceticism altogether, and many of their saints were noted precisely for their numerous fasts, such as Rabbi Abraham the Angel, son of the Baal Shem's successor, and Rabbi Nahman of Bratzlav, great-grandson of the Baal Shem.

Gloom and depression are the marks of the state of "littleness" of the soul, when it sinks back into itself, but when the soul rises to its "root," attaining the state of "greatness," joy is as inevitable as light in the daytime. "The spiritual vitality of man is subject to the principle of alternation, for man was fashioned in the polar category of 'littleness' and 'greatness.' Through joy, sometimes even through a joke, man arises from 'littleness' to 'greatness,' learning to cleave unto God through study and contemplations."[52] The alternation from states of darkness and depression to states of joyous illumination was a feature of the Baal Shem's own life. It is reflected in a persistent dream he had of being alternately seated on the highest throne in heaven and cast down into the gloomiest cavern of hell.[53]

Some of the Hasidic saints encouraged their followers to indulge in playing practical jokes and in telling tales of coarse humor, prior to public worship, in order to induce the mood of joy.[54] It takes but little imagination to realize how easily this advice could be corrupted and vulgarized. In the second generation, the movement was severely criticized by the Mithnagdim (opponents of Hasidism) on account of the vulgar excesses to which the hilarity of the Hasidim was occasionally carried.[55]

At the time of the Baal Shem, there existed as yet no organized opposition to the new teaching, though the newness of Hasidic piety was clearly sensed. The entire import of Hasidism is reflected in the following question and answer: " 'What is the essence of divine worship? Our opinion and that of our fathers has long been that, in ancient times, men of piety would fast from Sabbath to Sabbath. You abolished this practice, maintaining that one is to be held accountable for depriving his body of its due and that he who torments his flesh is a sinner. Tell us, therefore, what is the essence of divine service? ' The Baal Shem replied to them: ' I came to this world to point out another way—namely, that one must seek to draw into himself the following qualities, the love of God, the love of the Torah and the love of Israel. It is thus not necessary to resort to self-mortification.' "[56]

The Hasidic type of piety esteemed the pathway of love above that of fear, the sublime feeling of holy joy above the anxious shudder of the trembling worshiper. And the pathway of love was double-pronged—directed earthward toward the living community as well as heavenward toward the Infinite. The piety of the dogmatist is generally a yearning to escape from an inner contradiction, a struggle to resist and to overcome the temptations of the flesh. This dichotomy is reflected in his asserting as true, doctrines which with half his mind he knows to be untrue. In contrast, the Baal Shem was a wholesome, harmonious personality, whose piety was the longing of the whole soul of man for greater stages of wholeness—i.e. incorporation into the congregation of Israel and into the soul of the universe which longs to be reabsorbed into its source.

The mystical ecstasy of " adherence " to the divine will, and the " putting off of materiality," is achieved through love and joy, but these feelings are in turn based upon total self-abnegation, humility, and the cultivation of the capacity to look to the " inwardness " of things. As to humility, the numerous saints who headed the movement in the last two hundred years elaborated every facet of this supreme virtue and devised a variety of disciplines for the guidance of their followers. Their impassioned insistence upon the primacy of humility was grounded in their metaphysics. If the entire range of creation is nothing but the " garment " of the Deity, then the creature separates itself from the sea of eternity, when it rises above the all-inclusive current of life and dares to be conscious of itself as a separate person.

Man's assertion of his individuality, even in mere speech, is the primary sin. How dare we say "I," when only the Almighty is entitled to the use of this personal pronoun? Yet almost everything we say assumes a world in which our self is the vital center.

"This is the basic rule: The essential distinction between the domain of holiness and 'the other side' is the category of self-dissolution in holiness, which is expressed in the statement, 'there is no I at all.' So we understand the difference between a man of piety like Maimonides and a philosopher like Aristotle. Though each presumably formed the same idea of God, Maimonides negated his self, as his knowledge grew, while the philosopher grew in pride and self assurance."[57]

To learn to unsay "I," man must learn to realize that all his perceptions and conceptions are not ultimate realities, but only the sheen of the outer façade of existence. We approach reality to the extent to which we recognize the "nonbeing" of the sensed universe. What is "naught" to our sense-bound understanding is in truth reality. To sense this truth, we must acquire the capacity to transmute our consciousness of self into an awareness of "nonexistence." For it is only when we sink back into the universal silence of the "naught" that we enter the "inwardness" of things that constitutes their divine, vital spark.

The Hasidim created a vast folk literature, extolling the virtues of humility and the consciousness of being "naught"; yet they eschewed resolutely the Buddhist goal of reducing the consciousness of self to the vanishing point. Along with the practice of self-abnegation, they taught the obverse principle which is the centrality of the human soul in the cosmic drama. The Baal Shem went so far as to cite frequently a virtually blasphemous interpretation of the phrase, "The Lord is thy shadow"—to wit, "The Lord reflects mechanically whatever you do, even as your shadow reflects the doings of your person." This combination of utter humility and fantastic pride is not rare in the history of human thought. We cannot strive to reach any goal without taking pride in its attainment, and the attainment of the goal of humility is no exception. The Hasidim taught that supreme, reason-transcending wisdom is drawn from the attainment of the utter passivity of the mystical trance, so that the saint is at once the power-charged "foundation of the world" and the humblest of all men. As to the common people, the basic advice of Hasidism is best reflected in the following aphorism: "A person should always carry with him two verses in his two pockets. In the one, he should carry the verse, 'I am but dust and ashes,' and in the other, the maxim, 'It is for me that the world was created.'" Man is nothing in himself, but to the extent to which he realizes this truth he becomes the bearer of the divine purpose, the focal center of the divine drama.

If "adherence to the divine being" is the essence and final goal of worship, why concern oneself with the observance of *mizvoth*? We encounter here essentially the same predicament as in rationalistic Judaism, where ethical perfection and intellectual contemplation constitute the vital essence of religion. To the philosophers, the *mizvoth* were disciplines, symbols and social instruments for the achievement of a form of spiritual excellence, which was obviously attainable also by secular and direct means. Even so, we may inquire whether with the mystical goal of "unification" posited as the supreme end of piety, it is not possible for people to attain this lofty height without the aid of *mizvoth*.

Within the Hasidic pattern of piety, it is indeed possible to detect many nuances of impatience with the rigid canons which regulate the life of the Orthodox Jew. The art of popular story-telling was revived, with one of its major themes being the supremacy of the ignorant and the superficially irreligious over those whose piety was impressive in external appearances, but lacking in true inwardness. The ancient legend of Hanoch (Enoch) was revived with embellishments, telling how he attained the rank of angelhood as a shoemaker, without the aid of *mizvoth*, simply by praising the Lord with every blow of the hammer.[58] The shepherd, lost among the heathen, was featured once again; he who "stormed the heavens" by his impassioned whistling, or singing, or dancing, or by simply reciting the alphabet and begging the Lord to compose fitting prayers out of it, or by expressing so naïve a sentiment as, "Oh, Lord, if you had sheep and goats, I should gladly tend them for nothing." References were frequently made to the supreme piety of the patriarchs who understood the "roots" of each *mizvah* and did not therefore find it necessary to perform the actual deed. In the folk literature which was inspired by Hasidism, publicans outweighed scholars in the scales of piety much as in the stories of the New Testament. The saint who failed to attend the synagogue was engaged in chopping wood for a helpless, sick widow, thereby ascending to heaven, " if not higher." The man who in his ignorance violated every law of the Sabbath, remembering only to rejoice on that day, was destined for the highest throne in heaven, while the rigid and unimaginative ascetic who refrained from any activity on the Sabbath lest he desecrate the holiness of the day was consigned to the lowest depths of hell, because his Sabbaths were gloomy and fear-ridden.[59] The "common man" in Judaism was brought into his own, since the gentle pathway of feeling and devotion was now seen to be preferable to the austere pathway of formal schooling. Thus, Jewish piety, made rigid by centuries of continuous emphasis on the minutiae of the *mizvoth* was unlimbered, so as to reflect once again the basic psychical reality of faith.

On the intellectual plane, Hasidism introduced the concept of the heavenly pattern of the Torah, which, unlike the earthly or "revealed Torah," did not consist of stories, laws and precepts, but of some inscrutable, suprarational essences, which a person could only grasp when he was caught up in the ecstatic state of "adherence." In its literal form, the Oral and Written Laws are the earthly "garments" of the true Torah, which appears in ever more rarefied representations in the various levels of the ascending scale of being, so that in the hereafter the saints advance perpetually in the comprehension of the "secrets of the Torah." On earth it is through "inwardness" that Torah is understood, its inner light illumining somehow the native yearnings of the heart, with faith and trust, purity and love, while its outer shell was crystallized gradually through the centuries and formulated finally in the detailed specifications of the *Shulhan Arukh*.

"The Talmudic statement, 'The *mizvoth* will not apply in the time to come,' means that then they will no longer appear in their material garment, but in their spiritual essence, being no longer valid in their physical form." "Also, today, if there should be found a man able to comprehend the *mizvoth* in their essence, he would be free from their actual observance."[60]

The belief that the Torah is but a "garment" of that spiritual reality which is the ideal pattern of the universe is of course adumbrated in Midrashic literature. The Zohar popularized this concept, asserting that "he who declares this garment to be the real Torah, and not something else, will forfeit his soul and have no share in the world to come."[61] The Hasidim endowed this abstract conception with vibrant, contemporary relevance by their conviction that the saints could ascend in their ecstasy to the "roots" of the Torah. Thus, the Bratzlaver Hasidim believed that the inspired tales of Rabbi Nahman were "taken from a very high place, indeed from the same place as the Torah of Moses."[62]

As was his wont, the Baal Shem expounded this thought of a heavenly Torah, subsisting in the shape of ineffable ideals, in the heavenly realms, with the aid of a parable:

> A king sent away his son to distant places for his own good, in order that he might be prepared to enjoy greater delights in the future. But as many years elapsed, the son forgot all the pleasures of the palace and did not wish to return. Though the king persisted in sending messenger after messenger to his son, the latter remained indifferent until the king chose a messenger who was clever enough to assume the guise, manners and speech of the son, talking to him on his own level, with the result that the son agreed to return to his father. This tale explains the appearance of the Torah in the form of material stories.[63]

The point of this parable is that the king's son begins with the disguise assumed by the king's messenger, but he soon advances beyond the disguise to its real purpose, heeding the call to return to the palace. Just so must man learn to regard the observance of the Torah, not as an end in itself, but as the instrument of mystical piety, leading to the ecstasies of "adherence," when the saint perceives the "roots" of the Torah.

Speaking of Abraham's vision of the heavenly Torah, prior to its crystallization in the Five Books of Moses, one of the first Hasidic masters declared, "But we perceive the root of the *mizvah* and its source in the holy Torah, when we study it with the right intentions. For the Lord had so designed both the Torah and our capacity for 'adherence' through it that we might be enabled to rise, from the bottom upward, until we attain the root and source of every *mizvah* . . . for all the perceptions of Abraham are possible for us also."[64]

This concept of an inner or heavenly Torah, underlying the practical precepts and historical tales of Scriptures, prepared the ground for the emergence in the latter part of the nineteenth century of the Ahad Ha'amist doctrine of *Torah Shebelev* ("Torah of the heart").

Strange as it may seem, the Hasidim, extreme pietists though they were, insisted on the discrimination between the shadow and the substance of religion, the vital seed and the dead shell —ideas which were utilized by Ahad Ha'am in his philosophy of the Jewish national genius, even as they were employed by the reformers of Western Europe in the formulation of the ideology of the Reform and Conservative movements.

Yet the Hasidic movement itself did not develop the antinomian impetus that its teachings concealed. Though God could be worshiped in all ways, the movement settled down soon enough to the established regimen of "Torah and *mizvoth*," adding to them the obligation to attach oneself to a Zaddik, travel regularly to his court, and follow the pattern of piety developed by him. The *mizvoth* remained the core and substance of piety, in spite of the sanctification of ecstatic dancing, pilgrimages to the "saint," and even, in some groups, confessions to the saint.

How, then, were the channels of piety confined to the trodden pathways of Judaism? Manifestly, the ideology of Qabbalah, interpreting every *mizvah* as a channel of divine grace, militated against any attempt to bypass the *mizvoth* and stifled every bold attempt to develop original ways of worship. Also, the unstable character of mystical piety needed to be balanced by fixed and unvarying forms of worship, like the *mizvoth*, which are suitable for people in states of "littleness." Descending from the ecstatic state of "adherence," the saint articulates his devotion through the standard *mizvoth* of the Jewish faith, thereby bringing renewed power to these "channels" of divine grace.

> As soon as the love of God or the fear of God comes to a man, he should immediately perform a *mizvah*, so that he might bring the love or the fear of God into the "contracted" realm [i.e. into the world, which came into being when the Creator "contracted" His Being, leaving "empty" space]. For as long as he does not perform a *mizvah*, he is caught in a restless struggle. But when the *mizvah* is done by means of this love or fear the inner struggle ceases. Thus the *mizvah* is as a vessel, which keeps safely locked the heavenly stimulus which has come to him. . . .[65]
>
> This stimulus from above is of the moment only, reaching us and yet not reaching us, but man should strive to hold on and cling to it with all his might—that is, to perform immediately some *mizvah*.[66]

But why insist on restricting the expression of the love of God to the performance of ritual acts? Why not concretize it through any and all actions which seem best at the moment? Both the Qabbalistic source of Hasidism and its own originality are revealed in the answer to this question:

> It is well known that love derives from the irradiation of the divine being [the letters of the Hebrew word for " love " form the vessel for the indwelling splendor of the Creator]. Thus, when one loves anything material, that object is like a vessel for the love of the Creator, but if one embraces it in physical lust, then he holds the splendor of the Creator in a vessel concealed within a vessel. However, should he love the Creator through a perfect vessel [i.e. a *mizvah*] then the splendor is embraced by him, through the mediation of only one instrument.[67]

This distinction in the degree of immediacy between the love of God in Himself and the love of Him through the things of this world is in itself unconvincing, especially since the *mizvoth* too were regarded as the earthly "garments" of divine essences. A more pertinent observation is made by the same author and others; namely, that pure love must be altogether free from selfish taint, and no love expressed and fulfilled here on earth can be that pure and absolute. Hence the need for worshiping God through the forms set by Him.

" But true love is one in which a man separates himself from all his qualities, serving the Holy One, with all his limbs and movements, leaving nothing for himself."[68]

Or, as another *zaddik* put it, "The light of the *Shechinah* is compared to the light of a candle which does not cling to the wick, save with the aid of oil. So, too, the *Shechinah* does not rest upon a person unless it be through his performance of good deeds. . . . For the soul of man, even of the perfect saint who serves the Lord in both fear and surpassing delight, is not lost in existence altogether, so that it might be completely absorbed in the light of God, becoming one with it in the utmost degree of unity. A residual consciousness of self remains in the mind of him who loves God and fears Him. Not so the *mizvoth* and good deeds, which constitute His will and the source of all life . . . through them, the light of God rests without any hiding of the Face. . . ."[69]

The *mizvoth* afford the worshiper the opportunity to lose his self altogether in utter surrender to the will of God. Nor is this consummation conceived solely as a psychical phenomenon, but in the terms of the Qabbalistic metaphysics, which describe the *mizvoth* as so many occult chains, assuming the shape of physical acts here on earth and existing in the form of "lights" in the true world. The ritual act performed by the Jew makes possible the accession of fresh power to the *Shechinah*.

Hasidism introduced the goal of mystical ecstasy into Jewish worship, trained its devotees to seek the "inwardness" of piety, aroused the feelings of joy and enthusiasm in prayer and, in general, translated the legalistic chores of Judaism into living expressions of a felt religious reality. Yet its influence was not confined to the spirit of revivalism that it had engendered. In line with the practical genius of Judaism, the Hasidic movement directed its impetus into the community, bringing into being the Hasidic society, which consists of a loosely organized band of families, scattered in various cities, who "travel to" and follow the guidance of a spiritual master, called a *rebbe* or a *zaddik*. The members of this society bring voluntary offerings to the *zaddik*, who maintains a huge establishment where his followers can visit as his guests, sharing certain meals with him. In this society, people contribute in accord with their means, and receive financial help from the *zaddik* whenever needed, as well as spiritual guidance. Organized primarily in common reverence for a *zaddik*, the society frequently took on the character of a mutual benevolent society, or, seen from another point of view, that of a feudal lord with his knights. In the "courtyards" of the *zaddikim* there were to be found *yoshvim*, men who had given up the responsibilities and pleasures of "the world," dedicating themselves to prayer, meditation and study under the aegis of their revered masters. Also, newly married men would spend months or years in the courtyards of these *zaddikim*, in order to fortify their spirits against the corruption of the secular world, which they were preparing to enter. For the most part, however, the Hasidim would gather into the towns of their *zaddikim* for weeks at a time, generally for the celebration of a festival and in particular for the observance of the High Holidays. To "attach" oneself in unquestioning adoration to a *zaddik* became a primary *mizvah* to the Hasidim.

As a great master of mystical piety, who left an indelible

impression upon his followers, put it, "To eat or not to eat, to sleep or not to sleep, to pray or not to pray, but for Rosh Hashanah you must stay with me."[70]

The Hasidic societies served to build up the self-respect of the scattered masses and to endow each follower with the reflected glory as well as the presumed merit of the central saintly figure. Since it is the purpose of life to worship God with every ounce of one's energy, only the saints can fulfill this purpose. The common people, however, share the merit of the saint by their "attachment" to him. This sociological character of the pietistic societies gave the movement tremendous political power, which in the first generations was employed against the dominance of the rabbis and their allies, the communal leaders. The revolutionary impetus of the Jewish masses was gathered round the *zaddikim*, as in similar movements in the early years of the Protestant Reformation. Hasidism occasionally took on the aspect of a mass revolt against established authority within the Jewish community.[71] However, the primary function of each Hasidic society was to cultivate by mutual encouragement the original ideas and unique pattern of mystical piety which its founder developed. In an atmosphere of true brotherhood, the members of every society would cherish the special features of the teachings of their masters, and assist each other in mundane matters as well as in their common spiritual concerns.

> In previous generations, before the light of the Baal Shem was disseminated, people would seek to worship God in loneliness, secluding themselves from human society in the month of Elul, in fearful anticipation of the High Holidays. . . . But the essence of true piety and the right pathway of penitence is to be found, on the contrary, in the association of friends, in their cultivation of mutual affection and their adherence to the saints of the generation. The faith of each one is likely to be fortified by the fiery enthusiasm and devotion of the other Hasidim, whose inspiring example will lead him to return in perfect penitence.[72]

In the center of the Hasidic society, there was the *zaddik* or saint, who acted as the spiritual mentor of the group. Yet the *zaddik* was not merely a teacher, but a "fountain of holiness and blessing." Traditionally, the rabbi was not the successor to the Biblical priest or prophet but to the Talmudic sage; he was the teacher, judge and spiritual guide in the community. Hasidism represented the *zaddik* as a living exemplar of the perfected

Messianic world, in which all that is evil and material has been overcome by triumphant holiness and the Spirit of God has come to rest upon all men. The driven and distraught masses composing the landless and rootless Jewish proletariat saw in the mere appearance of the wonder-working *zaddik* an assurance of the eventual advent of the Messiah. God may be far, but the *zaddik* who is able to avert "the harsh decrees of the Holy One, blessed be He," is here in all his manifest "power." The Messianic hope does not seem infinitely distant and unreal when a "miniature Messiah," to coin a new phrase, is close at hand.

"Whoever did not see this," writes a faithful disciple concerning the joyous piety of his master, "did not ever behold genuine goodness. Whoever was present [with the *zaddik* on the Sabbath] used to say that there will not be such a consolation until the coming of the Messiah of righteousness."[73] As we remarked previously, Hasidism rejected the Sabbataian-Frankist heresy concerning the existence of a living incarnation of the Messiah, but it fostered the belief in the presence of Messianic men, in whose nature the predicted conquest of "the power of holiness" over the "forces of the other side" had already taken place.[74] But if a living token of ultimate victory is with us, should we not sense the tremor of the Messiah's wings in the air and perceive the "illumination of the Messiah" lighting up the horizon?

So the need of channeling the longing for redemption away from the delusions of the Sabbataian-Frankist heresy led the founder of Hasidism to represent the *zaddik* as a precursor of the Messianic world, in whose person the Spirit of God had already triumphed over the impulses of nature, and whose will is capable of overcoming the laws of nature. The pressures of Jewish life brought about these exaggerated and superstition-laden concepts of the *zaddik* in Hasidism.

The Baal Shem was represented in folk literature as capable of performing all the stock miracles of the popular imagination —crossing the river by the power of faith, reviving the dead, seeing distant events, participating in the discussions of the heavenly academies and even giving birth to his son, by the sacred name.[75] These and similar fantasies conveyed the assurance of ultimate redemption by way of popular symbolism. The Messiah is not yet here, but the wonder-working *zaddik* gives a foretaste of the coming glory.

"The essence of the *zaddik*'s perfection consists in the circumstance that his 'adherence' [to the Almighty] is not cut off, even for a second. Thus, when he speaks to people regarding mundane matters he must not terminate his adherence." His worldly nature is completely transmuted by the divine soul; even as in the Messianic era, this world will be similarly transformed.[76] The Baal Shem and his disciples found it necessary to account for the states of "depression," when the glories of mystical illumination seemed to desert the *zaddik*, so that he reverted to the normal weaknesses of flesh and blood. The usual explanation was that these "descents" were needed for the establishment of spiritual contact with the masses, so as to uplift them along with him, on his periodic "ascents." The "strange thoughts" which the *zaddik* gets—i.e., the normal sentiments and longings of human beings —are indeed inconsistent with the dogmatic assertion of his being in a state of perfect holiness, but, the Hasidim insisted, these incursions of natural desire reflect the impulses of the *zaddik*'s disciples and followers, not of his own impulses. For, the *zaddik* is all spirit, but he is the mind and soul of the organic entity that is the Hasidic society. In this manner, the theoretical perfection of the *zaddik* is saved, in defiance of all appearances. Nor may any person dare to view the actions of a saint in the light of the unredeemed nature of common humanity. "Only he who is on the same level is able to understand the degree of a *zaddik*."[77]

"But it is necessary to understand why it is that *zaddikim* do get carnal desires and materialistic ambitions. Since his one desire is to serve the Creator, whence do these lusts derive? In view of the *zaddik*'s function to uplift the wicked, their evil, materialistic thoughts come to him that he might pick out the holy sparks in them. . . ."[78] This attribution of the *zaddik*'s "strange thoughts" to the influence of the carnal men that he endeavors to save may appear ludicrous today, but this doctrine fitted in perfectly with the dogma of the *zaddik*'s victorious holiness, and it answered the social need of the people to feel the imminence and nearness of redemption. Some men must succeed, if others are to try, and the reward of success can only be tremendous mystical power.

The *zaddikim* who adhere to the Torah and its wisdom have it in their power to modify both the spiritual and physical laws of nature. . . . By means of the light hidden in the Torah they can see from one end of the world to the other. . . .

When in love he rises to adhere to the living God, all Israelites are drawn after Him, for they were created for His sake. . . .

Since people cannot raise themselves to His service, the Holy One, blessed be He, in His mercy, causes the saint to commit a sin, so that he might fall into a state of " littleness "; then, as the saint gathers his energies and lifts himself to a state of holiness, he will uplift the world along with himself. This is why our sages said, " Happy is the generation whose leader sins," for it is through his return unto holiness that the whole world is exalted.[79]

Or as the Baal Shem is quoted by his great-grandson, " It is through their 'littleness' that the saints uplift the sparks which are caught in the depths."[80]

It follows that, in the pathos and travail of the saint, the inner drama of the world is enacted. It is through the saint that the blessings of this world are channelized, " for if the Lord Himself had distributed His blessings, the world would not have had the capacity to sustain so boundless an outpouring of grace."[81]

But while mundane blessings flow to the world through the mediation of the *zaddikim*, their major function is to bring their associates to their own level of piety so that the Holy Spirit (*Ruah hakodesh*) might rest upon them also.

" By following the paths of the *zaddikim* a person may draw upon himself holiness in abundance, to the point where the *Ruah hakodesh* might rest upon him, even here in exile."[82]

For many centuries, the opinion prevailed that the creative potency of the Holy Spirit belonged to the distant and great past of the Jewish people, when the *Shechinah* rested in the Holy Temple. Even so rare and genuine a pietist as Halevi did not extend the sway of the Holy Spirit to his own time and place, though such an interpretation would have greatly uplifted the spirit of his contemporaries. But the Hasidim had no hesitation in interpreting their own mystical experiences in terms of the descent of the Holy Spirit. The famed " preacher," Dov Ber, the successor of the Baal Shem, undertook to explain the amazing phenomenon of the rebirth of quasi prophecy.

How is it that now while we endure the bitterness of exile, people attain *Ruah hakodesh* more easily than at the time of the prophets, when mighty efforts were required for the attainment of prophecy and *Ruah hakodesh*? The answer may be gathered from the following parable: So long as the king dwells in his own palace, all amenities are strictly observed. The king would surely not accept an invitation to dine in someone else's home and would even resent the mere mention of such an invitation. It is therefore necessary for several advocates and go-betweens to prepare the road for such a request. But when the king is traveling and looking for an inn to rest at, then it is only necessary for the inn to be clean and the innkeeper to be ready. . . .

The analogy is clear: When the Temple was still standing the *Shechinah* was in the Holy of the Holies, many labors were needed. . . . But now, in the bitterness of exile, the holy *Shechinah* wanders disconsolately looking for a dwelling place. If then it finds a person pure and holy, it builds a dwelling place within him.[83]

In this bold fashion, the tables were turned upon the time-hallowed dogma of the remoteness of the Deity in exile. On the contrary, it is here and now, amidst persecution and national humiliation, that the presence of God is immediate, as immediate as the tragedy of that humiliation, affording mankind living proof of the reality of redemption. The Baal Shem was consoled by this assurance when his efforts to journey to Palestine ended in failure. The details of this journey are not known. It is certain that he set out on a journey to reach the Holy Land and that he gave up the attempt. He interpreted this failure as a divine mandate to stay in the Diaspora, coupled with a promise that the highest states of inspiration will be accessible to him and to other *zaddi-kim* in the lands of exile. For the *zaddik* is a representative of both the congregation of Israel and the Messiah. Hence he must stay with the people.[84] " In every genuine *zaddik* there is the self-revelation of the Messiah."[85]

" Our sages said that the Messiah must endure manifold agonies in order to atone for Israel, as it is said, ' and he is wounded for our transgressions.' Therefore the *zaddik* of the generation must suffer pains for the sake of Israel in order to lighten their burden, for he is in the category of the Messiah."[86] It is interesting that the fifty-third chapter of Isaiah, which was applied by Christians to Jesus and by Jewish commentators to the Jewish people as a whole, was applied by the Hasidim to the personality of the *zaddik*.

With so transworldly a concept of the personality of the *zaddik*, the Hasidic movement came perilously close to popular superstition and risked the danger of degenerating into a kind of saint-worship. The Hasidim of Bratzlav, for instance, introduced the practice of confessing regularly to their beloved saint, as if he could "forgive sins."[87]

"The basic principle is to bind oneself to the *zaddik* of the generation and to obey his words, in all matters great and small; not to deviate from his counsel to the right or to the left, to forsake all arguments and to act as if one had no opinion or knowledge at all, save that which he obtains from the *zaddik* and master of the generation. So long as a residue of independent reasoning is left with him, he is not perfect and not yet fully bound to the *zaddik*."[88]

Even after death, the *zaddik* was not forgotten. The Hasidim of Bratzlav continue even today to venerate their *zaddik*, as if he were alive and working for them. Indeed, it was believed that on every *yahrzeit*, the anniversary of the *zaddik*'s death, his soul rises to a higher level in the upper realms, where it continues to exert its potent power in behalf of its followers on earth. So the *yahrzeits* of the *zaddikim* became festive occasions of celebration for their followers.

"And the soul of the *zaddik* passes by the gateway of hell in order to uplift the souls of those who are attached to it, even as it did in his lifetime."[89]

Yet, on the whole, these outbursts of fantasy constituted only the frills and adornments of the central concept of Hasidism, in which the *zaddik* is not primarily the miracle-worker but the living proof of the possible triumph of holiness, the master of mystical piety and the unfailing "channel" of divine grace.

If now we wonder how humble men could bring themselves to think so much of their role as *zaddikim*, we should look for the answer primarily to the complex psychology of mystical piety. We have noted already the quasi-Messianic character of the *zaddik* and the need for combating the pseudo Messianism of the Frankists. We need to remind the reader, too, that each Hasidic teacher disclaimed the rank of a *zaddik*, ascribing it to other teachers and to his ancestors, though in actual practice they functioned as *zaddikim*. We note, too, a conscious effort to build up faith in holy men as a means of fortifying faith in God. But the chief explanation of the self-exaltation of the *zaddik* is the peculiar paradox of the surpassing pride of the self-abasing pietists. One's self may sink into the Naught, but then it becomes a revelation of the Deity. Thus we find that the German mystics of the school of Meister Eckhardt glorified their own "littleness" to the point of virtual self-deification. Ruysbroek writes, "All men who are exalted above their creatureliness into a contemplative life are one with this Divine glory—yea, *are* that glory." And Tauler adds, "Could such a man behold himself, he would see himself so noble that he would fancy himself God . . . and have all the knowledge of all men that ever were."[90]

Since Hasidism implied a profound transformation of Jewish piety, it could not have been launched without violent opposition. The Mithnagdim or opponents of Hasidism, repudiated the central purpose of mystical piety—i.e., the achievement of the ecstatic state of "adherence"; nor did they approve of the intermediate steps in the Hasidic pathway, the pilgrimages to the *zaddikim*, the indecorous outbursts of fervor, the constant expectancy of miracles and wonders.

In detail, the most significant contentions of the opponents (Mithnagdim) may be summarized as follows:

(1) The Zaddik-worship of Hasidism is inconsistent with the basic doctrine of Judaism that every man may approach God directly, without the need of any intermediary. The Mithnagdim were willing to allow that certain geniuses may attain supremely high states of exaltation, by their single-minded devotion to prayer and study. But, they pointed out, it is not necessary for the individual worshiper to "attach" himself to any particular saint in any way.

Traditionally, in Judaism, the rabbi was the teacher of the law, guiding and instructing his people in ways of piety. But no rabbi is entitled to claim the power to dispense God's blessings. The *zaddik* of the Hasidic societies was actually a throwback to an older form of Jewish leader, the prophet and the "prophetizer." Furthermore, the Mithnagdim feared that the grossly exaggerated reverence of the Hasidim for their *zaddikim* might eventuate in a new pseudo-Messianic movement. New departures in religion are generally effected by the rise of a living source of authority, claiming the power of a prophet or of a "man of God." The *zaddikim* were believed to be recipients of the Holy Spirit (*Ruah hakodesh*) and transmitters of divine blessings; what if they should enjoin their followers to adopt laws and customs at variance with the accepted tradition? Because of this widely prevalent fear, the Mithnagdim on their part opposed with excessive passion every deviation from the existing norms which the various Hasidic societies instituted.

(2) The Mithnagdim rejected the pantheistic interpretation of Judaism which the Baal Shem taught. To be sure, Hasidism did not create the complex fantasies of Lurianic Qabbalah, which reflected the conviction that the world and its fullness are in truth nothing but the "garments" of the Deity. The Hasidim built their ideology upon the foundations of Qabbalah, which they interpreted in accord with the insight of the mystic that reality consists in the "inner light" of things. The esoteric and fantastic doctrines of Qabbalah were taught by them as a living experience, accessible to all. The apparent obduracy and independence of the visible universe was explained by them as being due to the pervasive delusion of appearance and even sinful acts were merely "garments" of the "garments" of the Deity. But, if so, the Mithnagdim wondered, where is the line to be drawn between the holy and the secular, the pure and the impure, the moral will and the impulse of lust? Aren't they all "garments" of the Deity, impelled by "sparks of holiness"? The Mithnagdim, too, felt constrained to accept the teachings of Qabbalah as authoritative, but they were more critical in their approach, maintaining that some of the classic sources of Qabbalah were corrupted by scribes and copyists.[91] In line with the genuine tradition of Jewish monotheism, they insisted on the transcendence of the Deity.

While His "power" and Providence permeated the universe, His being was removed from the lowly world in which we live "so that He adheres to and borders on the realm of Emanation alone."[92]

(3) The Mithnagdim considered the Hasidim guilty of neglect of Torah-study. The rationalistic tradition in Jewish thought placed extreme emphasis upon the ideal of Torah-study. It was through the steady refinements of Torah-thought that the mind of the Omniscient was to be approached. Hence no sin was as momentous as that of *bittul Torah*, the neglect of Torah-study, and no virtue could compare with Talmud Torah, the study of Torah. When the Hasidim elevated the goals of mystical piety and devotional enthusiasm above the sheer glory of Torah

learning, they brought about a transvaluation of all traditional values in Jewish life, a transvaluation that was particularly offensive to Torah scholars as a social class. If piety is primarily an inner attitude of the soul, a matter of " feeling," will not the rigid landmarks of Torah piety, in all the exquisite detail of their legalistic perfection, be doomed to lose importance and appeal? For many centuries Judaism eschewed the excesses of pious enthusiasm, concentrating instead on the methods of legalism; should Judaism now reverse its emphasis? Would it not then be running a poor second in its race against other faiths that have always laid stress on enthusiasm and on the virtues of blind belief?

(4) Finally, the Mithnagdim expressed the innate resistance of the traditionalists to every innovation in matters of faith. To concretize their teachings, the *zaddikim* instituted a number of changes in the liturgy and in the ritual observances of Judaism, which were indeed minor in themselves, but which reflected their conviction that the *Ruah hakodesh* was guiding and inspiring their *zaddikim*. Here, then, was a new source of authority, capable of setting aside the established codes.

Though the legal issues involved were minor even from the point of view of an Orthodox believer, the fires of hate that blazed around them were fierce and widespread, with the Mithnagdim and Hasidim putting each other under the ban. The real question at issue was not this or that detail of the law, but the right of the *zaddikim* to claim the authority of the Holy Spirit. Though the Hasidim encouraged the growth of new superstitions, they were pioneers of a new dynamism in Jewish life, for they contested the principle that all was finished and perfect in Judaism. They carried the impetus of a new groping for a fresh vision of God and faith. They were willing to break the " cake of custom." Said a first-generation protagonist of Hasidism: " When people say, ' Why was not this or that practice of Hasidism observed in the life of my father or grandfather? ' we reply by asking, ' Did they bring the Messiah? ' " The legitimacy of the new was staunchly denied by the " opponents," and defended with equal vehemence by the Hasidic *zaddikim*, who felt themselves to be charged with the task of mapping new pathways for their ancient faith.

Indeed, there was an antinomian trend in the early literature of Hasidism, an insistence on the search for new ways of religious expression and a condemnation of the rabbinic practice of multiplying legalistic prohibitions. Said Rabbi Zussia, in the "world of truth, I will not be asked, 'Why weren't you like Abraham, like Moses, like David?' but I will be asked, 'Why weren't you truly yourself?'"

Mysticism is both revolutionary and conservative in its impact. When the glory of a new religious experience is felt, a new source of authority and a fresh way of evaluating all things comes into being. But when the climax of the mystic's way is no longer experienced as a reality and is remembered only as a tradition, then the emotional enthusiasm and the single-minded ardor of the mystic's way become anti-intellectual and reactionary. Dogmas take possession of the mind when the living faith dies. In Hasidism, the conservative tendency was strengthened first by the long struggle against the Sabbataian-Frankist heresy, second by the extreme isolation of the Jewish community from any contact with the Gentile world. The third generation of Hasidic leaders took steps to fortify the barriers of Jewish isolation. In a letter outlining the duties of a spiritual leader, Rabbi Menahem Mendel of Vitebsk cautions, "to remove the people from the customs of the nations and their laws very far, that they may not be defiled by these practices, for any such influence is the beginning of all uncleanliness and a surrender to the dominion of the 'shells.'"[93]

The Polish Hasidim in particular became the champions of a rigid traditionalism in the nineteenth century, insisting on the rejection of all secular learning and on the retention of specifically "Jewish garments."

In the course of time the wide chasm between the Mithnagdim and the Hasidim was bridged. In part the breach was healed by a series of events which led to the disintegration of the remnants of Jewish communal authority. The *Vaad Arba Arozoth*, the Committee of Four Lands, a central body which at one time controlled the communal as well as the religious life of the Jews of Poland and Lithuania, was abolished in 1764, six years before the first great ban against the Hasidim. The successive divisions of Poland further cut into the self-governing power of the Jewish communities. The numerous bans against Hasidism proved powerless, since Jewish communal authority was nonexistent.

In part, the two movements were reconciled because they drew inspiration from the same tradition. Qabbalah, the source of Hasidic authority, was foreshadowed by many passages in the Talmud. In the complex texture of the tradition, legalistic monotheism could not be separated with precision from pantheistic mysticism.[94] So, slowly and by degrees the chasm was narrowed down by mutual concession until it became of mere historic interest. Hasidism became progressively more intellectualized, ossified, less creative, less mystical, while rationalistic Orthodoxy, however reluctantly, took over some of the insights of Hasidism. This movement from the extremes toward the center may best be illustrated by the analysis of the ideas contained in the two classic works of Jewish piety, produced respectively by the two most prominent leaders of the two camps in the first decade of the nineteenth century.

Rabbi Hayim Volozhin (1749-1821) beloved disciple of Elijah Gaon (1720-1797) formulated his philosophy in a posthumous volume, which was reprinted many times, under the name of *Nefesh HaHayim*. Regarding the pantheistic assertions of Hasidism, the author declares that a distinction must be drawn between the appearance of the universe from the human point of view and its existence in the mind of God. True, to God the world is both existent in the very manner in which it appears to us, and at the same time it is absolute nothingness, which does not affect His being in the slightest. It is as a word, spoken for the sake of communication, but of no significance in itself in comparison with the thoughts of the Speaker. But to us human beings, it is possible to climb up to God only through the ways He alone has indicated. In other words, the pathway of the " beloved son," in the parable of the Baal Shem, is but a snare and a delusion. We are encompassed by the manifold barriers of experience, and we dare not disregard the sober message of Torah, in the idle belief that " all the fences and the gateways were nothing but appearance."

" Even though from His side, who understands His own being, the Whole is filled in absolute evenness, without any divisions, graduations or differentiations, enduring in perfect unity as before creation, we are neither able nor allowed to contemplate this incomprehensible paradox, much less to act upon it."[95]

Accordingly, it is incumbent upon us, as human beings, to

follow the pedestrian pathway of divine worship as outlined in the Torah, and not to storm the heavens by the grandiose attempt to see God in all things and to worship Him in all ways.

Rabbi Hayim grants the importance of cultivating a sense of reverence within the process of Torah-learning and of evoking the sentiments of fear and love in prayer. But he insists that the intention of the worshiper should be fixed upon the actual words that he utters.

> The essence of divine service consists in the practice of articulating every word, with the intention of employing it as the means of adding holiness in the upper realms. For this reason, he should strive to become completely forgetful of his body, abstracting his soul from his body, as it were, and rejecting all thoughts of bodily pleasures, until he will get to the point of despising the body, as if he were not composed of flesh and blood at all, and it is his soul alone that is uttering its prayers. And when he speaks any word in prayer, he should pour his will into it to the point of willingness to give his soul away with it . . . he should really feel the desire of his soul to leave the body and to cling unto Him. . . .[96]

The piety of Rabbi Hayim was that of a split soul, the spirit yearning to free itself from its imprisonment in the body of flesh and blood. In contrast, as we noted previously, the Baal Shem saw no opposition between body and soul.

To feel the desire for " adherence " rise to the breaking point is the acme of prayer, but in actuality " adherence is never reached within the body. Those whose souls rise to their upper roots depart from this world as did Elijah the prophet."[97]

Similarly in the study of Torah, the central motive must be the comprehension of the divine will, not "adherence" to Him. For understanding is an end in itself, not a means to the end of piety.[98] Indeed, Torah-study is the highest sacramental exercise available to man, for by its merit, " all sins are forgiven."[99]

Insisting upon the traditionally pragmatic character of Judaism, Rabbi Hayim deplored the excessive emphasis upon the ideal of " adherence." " Do not be misled by the strategy of the evil desire, which insinuates the thought that Torah-study or a *mizvah* is of no consequence if it is performed without adherence. . . . Such thoughts may well lead to the battering down of all fences, for you will no longer be concerned with the details of the laws. . . . Remember that the essence of all *mizvoth* is the actual performance. . . ."[100]

As to the aim of Hasidism to achieve the state of continuous "adherence," the author warns, "Do not delude yourself by the ambition so to purify your thought as to be in a state of unceasing adherence to thy Creator."[101]

Disbelieving in the achievement of the unitive state of mystical ecstasy by the *zaddikim*, he declared, "To subject oneself or to attach oneself in divine service to the Holy Spirit that is presumed to rest on any man who pretends to be a prophet or a Master of the Holy Name is sheer idolatry."

In this warning we hear the mild echoes of the mighty warnings of Rabbi Hayim's revered teacher, Elijah Gaon, who referred to Hasidism as a "new covenant" and a form of idolatry. But this mood is not typical of the rest of the volume, which is written largely in a conciliatory tone. Still, the author cannot concede the principle of a continuous revelation of the divine will, through the agency of the *Ruah hakodesh*, without opening the floodgates to a vast spate of reforms. In his eagerness to resist change, Rabbi Hayim took up an incredibly reactionary attitude, extolling every word in the established prayer book, as if it were capable of functioning automatically through a kind of pre-established harmony. "Every word of the prayer book or of the blessings ascends into the upper realms . . . where it functions through its upper roots . . . building new worlds. . . . The 120 elders, among them many prophets, saw through the Holy Spirit exactly where the luminous pathway of each word is attached. . . . Indeed, the words of the prayers are fixed in the upper realms."[102]

The members of the Great Assembly (convoked by Ezra *circa* 449 B.C.E.) were alone in possession of all the secrets regarding the ethereal structure of the heavenly realms and the function of each word. Hence, one must not change the prayers in the slightest or add new prayers to them. For even the vast esoteric knowledge of Luria is as a drop in the ocean compared to the wisdom of the authors of the prayer book, who so designed the prayers as to effect ever fresh "improvements" in the upper worlds.[103]

Apart from these objections to the ideal of "adherence" and the dynamic principle of *Ruah hakodesh*, Rabbi Hayim accepts wholeheartedly the entire world view of Qabbalah. He conceived of the purpose of the *mizvoth* as being their effect upon the inner substance of the cosmos, the "union of all the powers and the worlds," and he imagined that "all the worlds" were dependent upon the "food" of the Torah and the *mizvoth*, for the whole range of existence reflects the actions of men. "Without Torah and *mizvoth*, He would withdraw His being from the worlds so that they would return to the abyss of the naught."[104]

So the question at issue was solely the possibility and importance of the ecstatic "adherence" of the *zaddikim*. A new concept of "adherence," calculated to meet the criticism of the Mithnagdim was stated by Rabbi Sheneur Zalman of Liadi, founder of the HaBad school of Hasidism.

That the attainment of mystical states of ecstasy is not only possible but absolutely essential in the divine design is the main burden of Sheneur Zalman's philosophy. In a bold attempt to found a psychology of piety upon the traditional theosophy of Qabbalah, he analyses the various degrees of piety that are attainable by most people, leaving the central role of cosmic intermediary for the *zaddik*.

We recall that, in the myths and symbolism of Qabbalah, the central focus of the cosmic tragedy is not primarily a human act of "original sin," but the failure of the world to contain the fullness of the divine light. When the Lord poured His light into the forms of creation, so the myth runs, the forms or "vessels" broke. The fragments of the old "vessels" constitute the "shells" or forces of evil in our present world. Hence, evil is the result of the fragmentation of The Good, which took place before Creation. No act of conscious sin is here involved, even on the part of the world, but simply a cosmic catastrophe, which it is the business of man and God to overcome. "The soul itself does not require to be redeemed," deriving as it does from the divine being. But it is sent here on earth in order to conquer the "shells," by resisting the impulses deriving from them and then transmuting the power of the "shells" into the love of God.

The cosmic tragedy and its redemption are re-enacted within the soul of man. The "shell" attains consciousness in the human personality where its one fundamental desire is pleasure and its basic attitude is that of overweening pride. Against these impulses of the flesh, the "divine soul" comes armed with the power of divine love, which impels it to seek its source. Also, the light of God continues to shine upon it, so that it is able at any and every moment, by prayer and humble submission, to obtain the power to resist the evil desire and to suppress it below the level of consciousness.

The tenacious optimism of the Jew is manifested even in its mystical versions, which at times come closest to the defeatist mood of early Christianity. For Sheneur Zalman insists that the balance of forces within the human heart is so constituted that goodness is always likely to be triumphant in the domain of conscious thought and action, with the aid of divine favor, while evil is condemned to the dumb violence of the unconscious. This conclusion is necessitated by the concept of divine grace as a continuous ray of light, uniting the human soul with its source in the divine being. Within the human heart, goodness must triumph over evil, since the realm of holiness is the one positive force in existence, while the "shells of uncleanliness" form only the shadowy chaos of privation and nonbeing. "For within the soul the light of God dwells, which is not subject to the variations and determinations of time; inhering in the realm that is beyond time, it is capable of dominating the impulses originating in time."[105]

But while the impulses of the flesh cannot gain the ascendency in the conscious self of the "average" person, the spiritual forces are unable to vanquish the flesh completely and to convert it into an instrument of divine service. The virtual stalemate within the personality of the "average" person is actually a defeat for the cosmic design, even though the "average" person has never committed an overt sin. For the "shells" remain unbroken and uncowed, the imprisoned "sparks" unredeemed and the divine design unfulfilled.

Sheneur Zalman's description of the "average" person reflects the lofty standards and the intense puritanical bias of Hasidism.

> The average person is the one in whom the evil impulse has not ever prevailed to the extent of being expressed in conscious thought, speech or action . . . and he never committed a sin, not even the sin of neglecting Torah-study, nor is he ever likely to commit one, so that the designation "wicked one" does not apply to him even for a second. . . . In moments of prayer the evil desire is subordinated entirely, but when the devotional exercises are over it rises to the surface in the form of yearning for the pleasures of this world. Yet the evil desire is checked at every turn. . . . The average person is not a saint, for in appearance his evil impulses remain unchanged, and he continues to be capable of lusting after material pleasures. . . . To be sure, sinful thoughts are rejected by him the moment

they enter consciousness, for he is called wicked if he entertains them will-ingly even for a second. . . . Or if jealousy or anger invades his conscious-ness, he repudiates them immediately, disdaining even to repay evil for evil, but, on the contrary, he makes an extra effort to show kindness to those who hurt him. . . .

Now, this description of the average person applies really to all people, in the sense that it is possible for all Israelites to reach this level of piety at any moment. For even when lustful passions appear to be dominant, it is possible for the person to say, " I do not want to be wicked even for one hour and thereby to erect a barrier between God and myself. . . . Even the lowest of the low in Israel is capable of sacrificing himself for the sake of God; why then should I despair? "[106]

The faith of the " average " person derives from the divine sphere of *Hochmah*, which supervenes above reason. . . . This is why the average person, even if he be ignorant or willful, is ready to endure excruciating agonies so as not to deny the one God. . . . "Without knowledge or contemplation, they are pre-pared to sanctify the name, as if it were absolutely impossible to deny the one God, no argument or reason being needed. This axiomatic acceptance is due to the light of God which shines upon and illuminates the soul, molded as it is in the category of Hochmah, which is above reason and knowledge."[107]

Living in an exceedingly pious age, Sheneur Zalman found it possible to believe that the " average " person was virtually a sinless individual—especially the average Israelite. The soul of every Israelite was a " spark " from the divine being; hence, pure piety was a native, incorruptible quality of the Jewish soul, acquired through the merit of Abraham. When it was not mani-fested in overt actions and sentiments, this ethnic heritage continued to function in an " unconscious fear and love of God " which kept every Israelite true and loyal in spite of his own will, in spite even of his overt deeds and his momentary concerns.

It is even possible for the " average " person to achieve a measure of mystical " adherence," and thus to touch temporarily the level of the *zaddik*. " For it is only one's will which stands between his soul and its adherence unto the divine light. . . . But as soon as a person wills to cling unto the Lord, his soul is immediately taken up into unity with Him."

Since man is thus able to emerge out of the confines of his own self, he need not be disturbed by the harsh sting of evil.

Seen from the standpoint of God, there is no evil, since all things are good in their "roots." Why, then, should those who "adhere" to God fail to see things in His light?

> How can he assume that he is really afflicted by evil, in such matters as grief from children, lack of sustenance or sickness or any other kind of pain? Doesn't he know that the naught which is His wisdom is the source of life, goodness and pleasure, being the fountain of delight which supervenes above the world to come? He imagines that he suffers because he does not think of the Ultimate Source of his vicissitudes. This is why evil and pain appear in his imagination. But in truth no evil descends from above; everything is good, though it is not understood because of the magnitude of the goodness contained in it. This is the essence of the faith for the sake of which man was created—to believe that no place is empty of Him.[108]

Still, the "average" person does not transmute the "shells" into holiness; what, then, is his function in the cosmic plan? Sheneur Zalman questions very seriously the reason for the existence of the "average" worshiper. "We must try to understand even to some extent the purpose of the creation of the average worshipers, since they can never succeed in vanquishing utterly the shells. . . . Why then did their souls descend into this world where they labor in vain, battling against the evil desire which they cannot subdue altogether?"[109]

The answer to this strange question brings us back to the fear of the Mithnagdim concerning the possible loss of importance of the *mizvoth* in the Hasidic scale of values. The "average person" can certainly observe the *mizvoth*, yet this task appears to be relatively unimportant for the goal of cosmic redemption in Hasidic ideology. Counteracting this charge, Sheneur Zalman points out that for the "average" Israelite, the performance of the *mizvoth* is indeed the only way of entering into the divine cycle of cosmic redemption. Through the *mizvoth*, the divine presence is made to enter *into* this world, giving added power to *zaddikim*, whose task it is to uplift the "holy sparks." In the cyclical ebb and flow of divine grace, the "average" Israelites armed with *mizvoth* play their part in the descending curve of holy power, but only *zaddikim* are able to complete the cycle by "breaking the shell" and returning the "sparks" to their source. Thus a compromise was effected between the normative piety of Judaism and the mystical world view of the Baal Shem. The latter's maxims were to be understood as referring to *zaddikim* only. They were to worship God "in all ways," to redeem "strange thoughts" and to uplift the "sparks" in all things. Ordinary Israelites should study Torah and observe *mizvoth*.

The *zaddik* in HaBad Hasidism plays the same decisive role in the cosmic drama as in the other trends of the movement. It is through him that the flow of divine blessings is channeled. The souls of the *zaddikim* constitute the "heads" of the generation, "the sustenance and vitality of the people deriving from them." Hence those who attach themselves in devotion and veneration to them "cling to the *Shechinah*," as it were. But the "average" Israelite also fulfills a worthy function, through his loyal observance of the *mizvoth*. The distinguishing characteristic of the *zaddik* is the ability to "adhere" to the divine being uninterruptedly, since in his nature the evil desire had been completely converted into holiness, the impulses of flesh and blood had become absorbed into the one all-encompassing purpose of loving God. "Among the saints, the evil which dwells in the animal soul, which in turn is incarnated in flesh and blood, is converted into goodness and made part of the holy, divine soul."[110]

It follows that the saint does not have to strive actively to worship God, for the faculties of his soul know no other delight than that of clinging to the Almighty. His capacity for enjoying pleasure, originally deriving from the animal soul, is now confined to the uses of holiness. In utter passivity he functions as a "channel" for divine grace, as it rises up from the world and as it courses down from heaven.

Since the saint can take delight only in holiness, he instinctively despises all the pleasures of the flesh. "The incompleteness of a saint is in direct proportion to the lack of hatred in him for 'the other side,' and lack of repugnance for its pleasures. . . . To despise utterly the pleasures of this world. . . ."[111]

A later protagonist of the same school defined the highest rungs of love for God in these words: ". . . to forsake all desires that derive not from the soul but from the flesh and to acquire only one will—the will to be one with God. He should learn to say, 'I want nothing else but Thee alone.' . . . Let him be sick with love and despise his own life, yes, even the worldly goals of children, life and sustenance. . . . For this did the soul descend into the body, that it might resist and overcome it."[112]

At this point, Sheneur Zalman deserts the whole-souled piety of the Baal Shem and returns to the dualism of traditional piety, in which the human soul was constantly at war with the desires of flesh and blood.

To placate the "opponents" still further, Sheneur Zalman indicated in effect that the Baal Shem and his teachings were unique and unparalleled. Ordinary *zaddikim* do not claim to be constantly in a state of "adherence." The ultimate goal of "self-negation" is reached only by the very great *zaddikim*, "those who constitute themselves into a divine carriage, in complete oblivion of their existence."[113] And even they have moments when they worship God like other Israelites.

"The adherence and worship of the saints of every generation follows the principle of alternation—that is, their soul rises to the loftiest peak of adherence and then descends therefrom to serve God through the study of Torah and the performance of *mizvoth*."[114]

Or, as his grandson, the leading spokesman of Hasidism in his day, put it, "In the upward movement there operates the fiery enthusiasm of the desire to escape from the darkness of the body and to be dissolved and lost in the source of life; in its return, the soul concretizes its obedience in the performance of the *mizvoth* and in the study of the Torah."[115]

Through Torah-study, God is embraced, as it were, for the Torah is the earthly "garment" of the will of God. When the mind of man thinks the same thoughts as God, there is a unity of "adherence" that can hardly be surpassed.

"It is as if the King were embraced. Pursuing this analogy, does it make any difference whether in this act of love the King is dressed in one garment or in many? . . . Actually, this intellectual union is a wondrous unification, the like of which is scarcely to be found in the material world."[116]

Adherence through Torah-study is indeed the unique goal of HaBad Hasidism. To seek the goal of mystical unity through the turbulent pathways of feeling without making use of the ready-made, evened and paved pathway of the Torah is absurd to Sheneur Zalman, though this was precisely the teaching of the Baal Shem. "The love of God results in a surpassing delight of the soul, which yields us a foretaste of heaven. . . . But he who feels the thirst burning within him and has not yet sensed the delight of satisfaction should plunge into Torah-study. Else he is like one who is overwhelmed by pangs of thirst, and standing in the midst of a fresh-flowing stream, he cries, ' Water, water.' "[117]

Thus the intellectual activity of Torah-study was reinstated as an integral element within the approved pattern of the mystical piety of the *zaddikim*.

HaBad Hasidism developed a unique type of mystical ecstasy. The letters *HaBad*, standing for the three words, " wisdom, understanding and the contemplation of love," reflect the threefold source of the state of ecstatic piety. Wisdom is the intuitive knowledge of faith, coming to us from without and revealing to us the majestic reality of the divine being in utter immediacy. We are suddenly confronted with this sublime reality, as the central fact of existence, quite apart from any reasons, arguments or proofs that we may entertain. Understanding is the contribution which our mind makes to the realization of the meaning of the idea, allowing the light of our intelligence to play upon it from the manifold angles of our creaturely nature. The contemplation of love is the response of our whole being to the divine presence. As one climbs upon the rungs of piety, this response becomes more and more automatic, for it is really implied in the category of wisdom. God has taken the initiative, and our love for Him is merely a reflection of His love for us.

" This love which wells up in our being is like a mighty flame which seeks to rise above the wood and the wick. . . . The fire turns into a thirst, which deepens progressively into a melody of love, rising and falling between agony and ecstasy . . . in a manner that only music can capture. . . . For the soul seeks to escape from its bodily prison and to return to the lap of its Father."[118]

In greater detail, Dov Ber, the son of Sheneur Zalman, described the various levels of ecstatic piety. He stresses again and again the *passive* quality of the mystical phenomenon. It is not even an experience, strictly speaking, for the worshiper does nothing but wait and listen, in complete self-abnegation. " He is caught up in an enthusiasm that is paradoxical in character, for it is both sensed and yet not sensed, since it affects him, though he takes no part in it, . . . without intention or action, it invades the soul, while he is hardly conscious of this invasion."

This incipient enthusiasm gradually pervades the entire consciousness, affecting all the senses "with intense light and heightened vitality."

The loftiest peak of mystical ecstasy is reached when the "adherence of thought" rises to the point where ideas dissolve in the blaze of unity, leaving only the yearning of delight, which is an undifferentiated melody, "a simple song."

"The simple song is the hylic matter of delight, the substance of all forms of pleasure . . . supervening in every way above taste and knowledge, for there is neither taste nor will to this undifferentiated and unqualified, hylic delight."[119]

So, in this form of Hasidism, contemplation and love form jointly the path of the soul's ascent. Then grace, streaming down from above, inundates the consciousness of the mystic, lifting him to the uttermost peaks of delight, where love and thought merge into the mysterious oneness of the song of faith.

The Hasidic movement was burdened from the beginning by the cultural isolation of the Jews and the intensity of prevailing fanaticism. In a short time it had become the champion of both. Nevertheless, we cannot fail to recognize that this mystical movement virtually rejuvenated the psychological springs of Jewish piety. As a mystical movement, Hasidism compares favorably with the popular mystical movements in both Christianity and Mohammedanism, especially in its inveterate practicality and this-worldliness, its healthy joyousness and its ethical emphasis. The variety of emphases within the movement is particularly remarkable, and arose since every *zaddik* knew himself to be called upon to evolve his own unique blend of contemplative and emotional elements in piety. While the regimen of Jewish piety was determined by the law, the Hasidim sought and found ample room for variations in emphasis, restoring the vital force of creativity to the religious life of the Jew.

In this reintroduction of the dynamic impetus of originality into Jewish life, Hasidism evolved the notion of the continuity of inspiration which had been allowed to lapse. No longer was religious authority to be confined solely to the written letter, but faith as an experienced reality in the hearts of the *zaddikim* was to be regarded as a living fountain of guidance. The *Ruah hakodesh* which had inspired the authorities of the past is a distinct possibility even now, Hasidism declared, so that Jewish piety need not be frozen forever in the dead molds of the past.

In addition to the gifts of creativity and originality, Hasidism added the dimension of inwardness to the practice of Jewish life. It summoned its adherents to return to the basic values of religion and to esteem all acts of devotion in terms of their psychic motivations and intentions. The legalistic bias of Judaism directs attention to the fundamental virtues of ethics, since it inculcates the spirit of obedience to a law that is absolute and rational even as it is voluntarily undertaken. But this bias is liable to distortion. Jewish piety is constantly in danger of becoming petrified with sheer legalism. The loving obedience of walking humbly with God might be turned into a cold calculation of heavenly merits and demerits, and the living orientation of the soul to God might be frozen into a set of external practices. In spite of its subsequent development into a dark force of reaction, Hasidism constituted a movement of self-renewal, insisting on the revitalization of the tradition by going back to the original confrontation of the human soul with the divine imperative. The conception of an ethereal heavenly Torah, of which the visible one is only a "garment," prepared the ground for the distinction in modern Judaism between the eternal principles of faith and their legalistic representation at any one time. Hasidism was the mightiest of all periodic rebellions against the process of legalistic petrification in Judaism.

On the whole, Hasidism turned its back on philosophy and science, yet it provided the one solid base upon which religion could make its stand in defense against the onslaughts of the modern spirit. By identifying religion as primarily a psychological experience, it confronted the challenge of modern secularism from an unassailable position. The data of experience form the building-blocks of our modern world. Science may arrange and rearrange these blocks in ever-varying shapes and structures to suit the changing fashions of the prevailing philosophies. It cannot deny the reality of these data. Indeed, the weapons of rationalistic philosophy were blunted by modern criticism and the authenticity of tradition was put under a cloud by the new methods of research—but who can resist the testimony of experience? Thus Hasidism paralleled the emergence in Christian thought of the philosophies which were grounded in the actual experience of the worshiper. "Adherence" as a felt reality parallels Scheiermacher's *Gefühl*, Kierkegaard's "creaturely" feeling, Otto's apprehension of "the holy," anticipating also the "existentialist" approach of modern theology.

CHAPTER TWELVE

THE AGE OF REASON

IN the generation preceding the French Revolution, Moses Mendelssohn (1729-1786) was one of the foremost spokesmen of the German Aufklärung-movement, struggling for the emergence of a free, secular and democratic society. Continuing the line of reasoning developed by Spinoza, this eighteenth-century exponent of rationalistic Judaism maintained that the unnatural union of church and state was a stumbling block in the path of human progress. Only in a secular society, permitting all citizens to pursue the insights of their mind and heart, can true religion grow freely and naturally, as " truth springs out of the soil."[1] Both thinkers maintained that the truths necessary for salvation were implanted by God in the soil of nature and in the mind of man. The good God built into every man all that he needs for the attainment of happiness on earth and bliss in the hereafter. Salvation is but another word for self-fulfillment. Most men attain salvation by the practice of the simple virtues of humble piety, while the philosophers achieve it by means of their quest for truth. The reasonable virtues of common sense and the unfettered adventure of reflection constitute together man's vocation and service of God. The first duty of society is to permit men to grow into the fullness of their stature in accord with the inner light that God had implanted within them. Hence it is for the sake of religion, in the deepest sense of the term, that the state must withhold the aid of its " secular arm " from any religious group.

But though Mendelssohn followed Spinoza's lead in developing the ideological foundation for a free and secular society, he stood at the opposite pole from the great and lonely seventeenth-century sage in regard to nearly all other issues bearing on Judaism and religion. For Mendelssohn considered Spinoza's identification of God and nature as a grave error and a fundamental distortion of

Jewish monotheism. In the exuberance of Spinoza's pantheism, Mendelssohn felt that all moral distinctions were erased and the essential difference between man and the beasts of the field was obliterated. If everything was of God, then no action is more divine than another; there can be no good and evil, only wisdom and folly.

Mendelssohn was willing to pursue the path of reason, as far as it goes, but he remained withal a passionately loyal Jew, believing that the law was binding upon everyone who was born into the Jewish faith. Far from deeming it necessary to discredit the basic documents of Judaism in order to undermine the foundation of Christian dogmatism, Mendelssohn maintained that insistence on the rights and dignity of the Jew was a potent and indispensable means of demonstrating to the Christian majority the undogmatic character of true religion and the inherent freedom of the human mind. Every Jew in the Christian world was a living protest against the reign of dogma and a challenge to the enslavement of the human mind by the fetters of myth and bigotry. For Judaism was, to Mendelssohn, nothing more than unadulterated philosophical religion. In his loving zeal, Mendelssohn ignored the romantic, mystical currents of Jewish thought, as Spinoza in his day did scant justice to the rationalistic current in Judaism. Both philosophers addressed themselves to the Jewish and Christian communities, but in different ways. While Spinoza demanded from the Jew total surrender to the natural processes of assimilation, and from the Christian a rationalistic reinterpretation of the dogmas of the church, Mendelssohn conducted his valiant battles in the name of Judaism, which he believed to be pure philosophical religion, and he challenged the Christian world to bring their tradition into conformity with the demands of reason.

Born in Dessau, in the year 1729, Mendelssohn settled in Berlin early in life, where he acquired a thorough grounding in the Talmud and in the secular learning of the time. In his twenties he became the friend and intellectual associate of Gotthold Lessing, who was one of the leading protagonists of the German Enlightenment. The publications of the young Jewish thinker in the fields of philosophy and literary criticism earned him the title of " the Jewish Socrates." For a generation he towered as a leading figure on the intellectual scene of Germany, laboring tirelessly for the betterment of the lot of his brethren and the improvement of their cultural tastes. Standing on the threshold of the Emancipation and remaining subject to the manifold indignities and disabilities which weighed heavily upon Jewish people in pre-emancipation Prussia, he represented a perfectly harmonious blending of intense Jewish loyalties with the emergent liberal culture of the West. It was not until the last years of Herrmann Cohen that the same synthesis was achieved again in all its perfection. A gentle, intellectual aristocrat who exerted wide influence by the sheer force of personality, Mendelssohn did not suffer from the tragic conflict of loyalties which marred the lives of many modern Jews. The demoniac spirit of German nationalism was still in its incipient stages and Jewish nationalism was still unborn, while in philosophy the rationalistic-theistic approach was virtually unchallenged. It was therefore altogether natural for Mendelssohn to labor as a Jew in the building of German culture and to work as an exponent of Western culture for the enlightenment of his own people.

That religion need not be a divisive force among men, Mendelssohn demonstrated by his writings, as well as by his life. In his little book, *Jerusalem*, he maintained that a religious society must depend solely upon the voluntary consent of the individual, renouncing the intervention of the state. The "secular arm" freezes the living body of faith into the cold corpse of forced conformity. Since religion is an affair of the mind and heart, "it must have no relation to properties and possessions." "Under no circumstances may it resort to the methods of compulsion. Nor may its members exert compulsion within the church. All its judgments and concerns can only consist of inspiring, teaching, fortifying and consoling. . . . Either the activities of the church issue out of the free will of the soul or they amount to nothing at all. . . ."[2]

For this reason the teachers of faith must not be paid professionals. The Talmud says of God, "As I teach for naught, so should you." Every attempt to intervene in the spiritual life of others, no matter how well meant, must be recognized as an unmitigated evil, "for it is impossible for me to possess the right to govern the thoughts of others, as if they belonged within my private domain. . . ." Every individual works out his own salvation by allowing his thought freely to orient itself among the poles of truth and falsehood, without being swayed by considerations of expediency. Hence the marks of a true faith are as follows:

(1) It ordains rituals as action-symbols, expressive of true ideas, not as sacraments important on their own account.

(2) It renounces the power of compulsion to maintain norms of discipline among its own members.

(3) It appeals solely to man's innate feelings of piety, his love of God.

(4) It does not make use of false and degrading devices, such as promising earthly rewards for obedience and threatening the fires of hell for disobedience.

In maintaining the impropriety of a religious society employing any form of intimidation, Mendelssohn was not unaware of the frequent use of the ban (*herem*) within the Jewish community. Admitting that at various times in the past Jews were compelled to make use of the ban as their only means of enforcing a measure of discipline within the walls of the ghetto, he maintained that this method belonged to the socio-political character of the Jewish community, not to its character as a religious group. In the evolving free society of Europe, where Jews and Christians share in civil and political life, there is no room for compulsion by social ostracism or seduction by privilege.

But if true religion repudiates the use of force, why does the law of Moses specify diverse punishments for the violation of numerous ordinances? How can a believer in the Hebrew Bible advocate the separation of church and state when the Jewish state as described in the Holy Scriptures undertook to regulate all domains of life, enforcing the Mosaic code as if it were a political constitution? To these and similar questions, Mendelssohn replied that the Biblical state was a unique phenomenon, designed for only one period in the life of one people when it lived in one land. " This state existed only once in the world. Call it the Mosaic society, by its proper name. It has already disappeared from the earth. Only God knows in which people and at which time we shall again see a similar situation."[3]

It was not difficult for Mendelssohn to maintain the unparalleled nature of the Mosaic state, since the Christians concurred in this belief. For Christians as for Jews, the laws of the Bible represented the commands of God for a specific situation, and were not to be regarded as models for legislation by men.

The Mosaic Code was a body of laws and precepts imposed upon the Jews as the covenanted people. Hence, the Five Books of Moses define what is right and what is wrong in action, not what is true or false in belief. The laws of the Torah were, according to Mendelssohn, comparable to the social and civil regulations which prevail in our society, not to the affirmation of a religious principle. Does it not rather confine itself to the teaching of maxims of behavior and the legislation of righteous ordinances? Manifestly, the Torah eschews the realm of dogma, leaving the field of ideas and faith to the intelligence of the individual, as indeed it must, for the essence of belief is the free acceptance of the searching human mind.

"Jews have revealed Torah, laws, commandments, ordinances, precepts, teachings revealing the will of God, not a revealed faith. . . . I do not admit any universal, eternal truths other than those which are not only comprehended by human reason, but which can also be proven and verified by reason."[4]

The first of the Ten Commandments, for example, does not read, "I am the Lord, maker of heaven and earth." Instead, the Lord is described as the One "who hath taken thee out of the land of Egypt." Thus, the Torah steered clear of the issues of metaphysics, basing its appeal to the Jewish people upon their actual historical experiences. All right-minded men and women are given the same opportunity to acquire those truths out of their own experience and reflection. They are also endowed with the strength of character that is needed to live by them.

Since the Torah contains precepts that are meant for Jewish people only, its appeal is directed to specific Jewish experience. On the other hand, the Torah does not specify the principles of faith and action that are binding on all men and that are validated by the universal experience of mankind. Only the latter category of principles is indispensable for salvation. Accordingly, the Torah assumes the principles of humanism and of the universal truths of faith. Hence, Mendelssohn concludes, the Jews were not granted a monopoly on faith, but were given a set of supplementary precepts, governing the actions of the Jewish individual and determining the character of the Jewish community. Whatever the purpose of God may have been in singling out the Jews as the objects of special legislation, He cannot have intended to make the observance of the Torah a prerequisite for salvation. For any doctrine confining salvation to a select group is unjust, Mendelssohn argues, and injustice may not be imputed to God. If the Holy Bible be regarded as the sole repository of divinely revealed truth, we are entitled to inquire, " Why did He withhold His revelation from the Hindus? "

Did Mendelssohn then assume that the Mosaic Code had no validity in modern times? If Torah is the pattern of laws designed for the Jewish state, and the Biblical state is no longer in existence, why should the Jews of eighteenth-century Europe feel obligated to continue their subservience to the laws of Judaism? At this point, Mendelssohn dissented vehemently from Spinoza, whose lead he followed in restricting the domain of Torah to rules of action. A fundamental distinction must be drawn, Mendelssohn contended, between the Torah as the constitution of a state and the Torah as a set of rules governing the life of the individual. It is true that the Mosaic laws, insofar as they forged a religio-social community, no longer applied in the contemporary world, since the Jews did not constitute any longer a self-governing nation. But the precepts which referred to the life of the individual were never specifically abrogated. Since they were revealed at Mount Sinai, in thunder and lightning, and in the presence of a vast assembly, how can we dare ignore them, unless and until they shall have been rescinded officially, as it were, by means of public and similarly impressive ceremonies? While Spinoza maintained that every Jew was free to resign from the community and thus to remove himself from the dominion of the laws of Torah, Mendelssohn insisted on the continued validity of those precepts which regulate the conduct of individuals.

" Even if one of us accepts Christianity, how can he liberate himself from the Torah and the *mizvoth*? Jesus the Nazarene never said it. . . . He observed the rabbinic ordinances as well as the precepts of the Torah. . . ."

" He who is born in the faith is compelled to live and die in

it "[5] It follows that the breakup of the Jewish state in the year
69 C.E. invalidated the national legislation of the Torah, leaving
intact the manifold individual obligations described in the Bible
and Talmud. Jews must now learn " to render unto Caesar what
is Caesar's and unto God what is God's," accepting the dominion
of the state for their socio-political life and the rule of the Torah
for their personal conduct.

The re-establishment of the Jewish state in our own day poses
the question whether Mendelssohn would have advocated that
the modern state was compelled to live in accord with the ancient
laws of the Torah, which ordained severe penalties for infractions
of the ritual observances of Judaism. Even the major Orthodox
organizations today moderate their vision of a theocracy with a
good dose of liberalism. In any case, Mendelssohn did not envisage
the possibility of the establishment of a Jewish secular state. He
affirmed his faith in a Messiah, who would restore Israel to its
homeland, but who would at the same time transform the entire
structure of the mundane world. The Messianic era was " transhistorical," a vision and a dream that transcended the boundaries
of common sense.

If the laws of the Torah are not indispensable for salvation,
why should Jews feel constrained to abide by them? To be sure,
according to Mendelssohn, these laws are divine in origin, but
if they had already served their historical purpose, why does
the good Lord still expect Jews and only Jews to continue under
the burden of the law? In answer, Mendelssohn asserted that
the mystery of the divine will in imposing a unique destiny upon
the Jew is no greater today than it was in the past. He refused to
concede that modern man was more amenable to the guidance
of reason than were the contemporaries of Moses. Living before
the rise of the great historical schools in Germany, he did not
believe that mankind had made any real progress in the domain
of ethics and faith. Whatever it is that prompted the good Lord
to single out Jews for a special pattern of life in ancient times
was as valid today as ever before. While the external circumstances of human life may and do change with the lapse of time,
the general pattern of human life remains virtually the same. To
Mendelssohn, the line of human progress was circular and oscil-
lating, not straight and ascending.

Furthermore, Mendelssohn believed that the Divine Torah was designed to aid the Israelites in the attainment of the good life here on earth. To be sure, Torah was law, not faith, but law is an expression of a philosophy of life. Indeed, law is to the great virtues of life as the body is to the soul. The great ideals and virtues of humanism are accessible to all men, but is it not true that most people glimpse their truth only occasionally and sporadically? History proves, Mendelssohn contended, that the great philosophers of ancient times failed to convey their truths to future generations without distortion. The Torah sought to remedy this human weakness by ordaining laws that would create a society in which the great truths of mankind would always be understood and cherished. The precepts of the Torah were designed by God to express His truths through the pattern of observances of a living people. These truths are indeed available to all men, but while mankind is liable to forget and distort these truths from time to time, the people of Israel will never forget and never pervert these teachings of reason. At all times, Mendelssohn concluded, the great truths of religion will be treasured and illustrated by the " very existence " of the " Jewish people."

" The ceremonies constitute a living kind of script, which quickens heart and spirit, which is deeply meaningful and inspiring, standing in the closest possible relation to the speculative truths of religion and the teachings of ethics."[6] Sometimes the value of one or another religious ceremony is manifestly clear to us; but even when we do not see any value in a particular ritual observance, Mendelssohn insists that we must not presume to judge the words of God. " Weak and near-sighted is the eye of man! Who can say, I have entered into His holiness and have pierced through the whole design, so that I can now tell the measure, purpose and limit of all things? "[7]

Again, Mendelssohn averred, the law cannot be abolished save by a direct and public act of God. Only the author of the law is entitled to revoke it. Hence, the law is for Jews fate, as well as faith, a divine imperative as well as a freely chosen regimen of living. " All other nations can change their laws in accord with time, circumstances, needs and convenience; but for me, the Creator Himself prescribed certain laws. Should I, weak creature that I am, dare to modify divine laws, to suit the darkness of my understanding? "[8]

Mendelssohn had many occasions to defend the validity of the laws of the Talmud for the people of his day, for he lived at the time when the full impetus of modern liberalism was beginning to be felt. The liberal rationalists maintained that all religions were equally meritorious. The German Protestants scorned any emphasis on external actions, stressing the inner life of the soul. At the same time, evidence was beginning to accumulate tending to support an evolutionary concept of religion and a critical approach to the study of the Bible.

Conceding the liberal claim that God made it possible for all men to achieve salvation, Mendelssohn denounced the doctrine of exclusive salvation. Judaism, he declared, asserts no claim to a monopoly on true faith. The central ideas of religion were alone necessary and sufficient for the bliss of the soul here and in the hereafter, and these central ideas constituted the " seven principles of Noah " which all men discover by searching their hearts. Mendelssohn knew that Maimonides, in his Code, gave a dogmatic interpretation of the doctrine of the Noachide faith, alleging that a person could achieve salvation by loyalty to the universal principles of ethics and religion only if he accepted the dogma of revelation at Sinai.[9] With some bitterness, he repudiated Maimonides' interpretation, extending the doctrine of the Noachide faith to its logical conclusion. He even declared that the laws and practices of other faiths might be considered God-given, for the Lord gave guidance and inspiration to all nations as He gave the Torah to the Jews. " The Jewish faith is best for us, but it is not the best absolutely . . . which is the best form of worship for other nations? . . . who knows, perhaps the Lord gave them guidance through their understanding or by means of prophets."[10]

For Jews, the law is binding forever and irrevocable, save by another Sinaitic covenant. Mendelssohn rejected decisively the attempts at Biblical criticism that were being made in his day and he had no sympathy for the evolutionary concept of religion.

The ceremonial law was obligatory for all born Jews, and being divine in origin, it could not be devoid of supreme significance. In the first place, Torah made certain that the universal truths of religion will always be a living reality, guarded by a dedicated people. He quoted approvingly from the commentator, Seforno, "while the pious of all nations are doubtless precious to Me [i.e., God] you will be my special treasure, for you will function as a 'kingdom of priests' to teach all mankind to serve God."[11]

As against the challenge of the Protestant emphasis on inwardness, Mendelssohn made good use of Rousseau's educational philosophy. It is through the totality of his experiences that a person is educated, not through the accumulation of book learning. For this reason the Torah embodied the ideals of piety into a solid structure of concrete rites and ceremonies, embracing all of life. By obeying his daily regimen of prescribed precepts, the Jew inscribes the wisdom of piety and ethics upon the tablets of his heart. The Torah, being the work of God, consists of depths upon depths of divine wisdom that are revealed to us with the progress of our understanding. Also, the ceremonial laws serve to bind together the masses of the people and their philosophers. In a religious community, all loyalties hang together, and the neglect of the ceremonial laws lead inevitably to the weakening of the moral tone of the community as a whole.[12]

With all his genuine love of and loyalty to the law, Mendelssohn did not cite the penalties cited in Torah and Talmud for violations of its precepts. Impelled by the logic of his rationalistic faith, he could not accept either the recital of earthly punishments or the horrors of hell as being anything more than fables for the masses. While he spoke of the Torah as laws, he really thought of it as a body of ideals and standards reflecting profound truths and high values. But in this mundane world, truths and values enjoy no immunity from the rigors of logic and the pressures of life. In the narrow portals of our existence, all truths and values cannot pass at one and the same time. Choices must be made between different facets of truth and different combinations of value. Thus Mendelssohn's defense of the law was to be severely tried and tested by his disciples and successors.

In Mendelssohn's own time, his views were challenged from the standpoint of believing Christians. If Mendelssohn considered a religion as true, providing its inner content agreed with the universal principles of faith, why does he not accept Christianity in this light? Furthermore, if he accepted the truth of revelation at Mount Sinai on the ground of the wonders and miracles with which it was associated, why did he refuse to accept the miracles of the New Testament, telling of the appearance of the Christ? These questions were posed to Mendelssohn by a popular preacher named Lavater, but in essence these two questions, of which one was directed at the open gate of reason, the other at the firm pillars of dogma, constituted the double challenge of philosophy and Christianity to Judaism. From the point of view of the philosopher, there is no essential difference between the two monotheistic faiths. Therefore, the pressure of life may be allowed to tip the scales against Judaism. At the same time, the Christian dogmatist, taking the miracles of his own faith to be self-evident truths, resented the fact that the believing Jew did likewise, particularly when the Old Testament, as he thought, was chockfull of " evidences " for the Athanasian creed. So, in an enlightened Christian atmosphere, which Mendelssohn was the first to face, the Jew was challenged both by the liberals and the believers, though in different ways.

Both arguments were countered by Mendelssohn as follows: on the philosophical plane, he maintained that the ideal of " one shepherd and one flock " could be realized only through a slow process of evolution, not by any drastic step of compulsion or conversion. Short of the " end of days," religion in general can have no reality, only specific religious communities. And the philosopher is in honor bound to reverence the rites and symbols that hold together the religious community of which he is a part. Like Maimonides before him, he admitted that Judaism as a concrete historical community contained ideas which were in themselves untrue but which served to fortify the faith of the masses of the people. A philosopher should respect and publicly acknowledge these concessions to the masses, for he too, is part of the community.[13]

In a letter to H. Obereit, written during his controversy with Lavater, Mendelssohn listed the following criteria for the determination of the best faith: (a) tolerance of other faiths; (b) universality in the love of humanity; (c) absence of any restriction on the availability of salvation; (d) offers no contradiction to free human thought. He implied that, tested by these and similar standards, Judaism was far superior to Christianity. As he later wrote to Elkan Herz, "Blessed be the Lord who gave us a true Torah. We have no dogmas which are opposed to reason or above it."

True to the impetus of philosophy, Mendelssohn retreated somewhat in his letters from the dogma of the inflexibility and unchangeability of the law that he expounded in *Jerusalem*. He wrote that "the inner service of God" in Judaism is universal and eternally valid, while "the outer service" is dependent on time and place; it is only the spirit of the law that is eternally valid, while its specific content may well be subject to change. Anticipating the position of the later reformers in this liberal attitude toward the law, he went even further in a letter to the French scholar, Bonnet, where he stated that "the difference between Judaism and Christianity is as that between Cartesianism and Leibnitzism," i.e., between rationalism and a mystical type of philosophical idealism. In the letter he wrote to the Duke of Braunschweig in January, 1770, he declared that when the New Testament will have been properly explained, a common faith for the Jew and Christian will become possible.[14] The genuine core of the Christian faith, Mendelssohn believed, was very close to the spirit of Judaism. As its complex mythology evaporates into the golden aura of symbolism, Christianity comes to resemble its parent-faith. In the course of time, he suggested, Judaism will find room for the ethical and pietistic teachings of Jesus, and the rigid dogmas clustering about the concept of the "son of God" will be dispelled.

As against the challenge of Christian dogmatism, Mendelssohn restated the traditional Jewish arguments, which coincided, in many instances, with the rationalistic trend of the times. To blame contemporary Jews for the crucifixion of Jesus, he argued, was a fantastic theological dogma. "I do not wish to assume responsibility for the action of Jerusalem judges centuries ago." He ridiculed the doctrine of "original sin" and the belief in eternal punishment of the unredeemed; he exposed the injustice of the dogma of vicarious atonement and criticized in detail the so-called "testimonies" to the Christian faith. Carrying home the battle against Christian dogmatism, he pointed out that liberal Jews may well accept the general truth of the New Testament account of Jesus' ministry, without yielding any ground to the Christian faith. In other words, liberal Jews are likely to read the

Gospels in a humanistic way, separating the kernel of divine truth from the encrustations of myth and popular superstition. Anticipating later developments in Christian thought, Mendelssohn drew a clear distinction between "the religion of Jesus" and official Christianity. He thought he could prove that Jesus never sought to be recognized as God; that he did not think of himself as a son of God; that he did not order people to pray to him and that he did not intend to destroy the Jewish faith.

Mendelssohn and his associates became the champions of a humanistic interpretation of the personality of Jesus. Many years later, David Friedlander, a disciple of Mendelssohn's, was to write an open letter to an evangelical minister, offering to accept Christianity providing the dogmatic interpretation of Jesus as a son of God was eliminated from its official credo. The seeds of this paradoxical proposal may be found in the writings of Mendelssohn, who was, however, also cognizant of the intimate bonds that are forged in childhood between the essence of faith and its concrete historical forms. Did he not endorse Maimonides' concept of the place of "necessary ideas" in the structure of a religious community? Dogmas which may be "offensive" to the mind of an outsider become the fundamental axioms of thought to those who were brought up in the faith. That is why religious dogmas cannot be discussed in a purely objective manner. Is not a certain bias inseparable from any living faith, Mendelssohn inquired, even as a measure of egotism is indispensable to one's happiness? Referring to his own acceptance of the miracle of revelation at Sinai and his rejection of the miracles of Jesus, Mendelssohn stated that he was not aware of his own prejudices in behalf of Judaism "any more than a person is conscious of his own halitosis." Effective religion is part of one's own very being; therefore, sincere conversion from one faith to another is psychologically an impossible feat.[15]

Though Mendelssohn reserved the domain of metaphysical ideas and beliefs for the dominion of human reason, restricting the proper sphere of revelation to laws governing action, he did not subscribe to the naïve notion that he, or his contemporaries, did indeed possess a "clear and adequate idea" of the nature of the universe or the character of God. It is the function and duty of man to reflect on the mystery of existence, and reflection is possible only in freedom. But man was not designed to solve with absolute certainty the riddles that engage his attention. Speculative reflection is the noblest of human activities, even if its results are not susceptible of mathematical proof. So Mendelssohn eschewed dogmatism of any sort, in theology as in philosophy, esteeming the brave search of truth to be the cardinal and all-embracing virtue.

For this reason, the ancient and unconditional Greek philosopher Socrates was chosen by Mendelssohn to be the spokesman for his own views, in the beautiful little book *Phaedon*, which deals with the immortality of the soul. Socrates was the great seeker after knowledge who knew that he did not know, and who dedicated his life to the clarification of the fundamental ideas of his countrymen. To the eighteenth-century Jewish thinker, the bold Greek thinker seemed to be the precursor of a natural or universal religion, in spite of its residual paganism. Socrates' " demon " to which Plato refers in the famous *Apology* was merely a symbol, the personification of his keen sense of duty toward the Creator. Though he was a pure monotheist, Socrates mentioned the promptings of his demon several times in the course of his great oration to the people of Athens. In Mendelssohn's view, Socrates as the ideal philosopher was in duty bound to respect the beliefs of his countrymen. Similarly, the Eleusinian mysteries, which the Athenian philosopher commended, were simply the teachings of natural religion, garbed in priestly symbolism and ceremonialism. His seemingly unnatural " love " for Alcibiades was merely the currently fashionable way of referring to normal friendship. In sum, Socrates emerges in Mendelssohn's work as the exponent of the secular " common ground " of enlightenment and culture, on which both Jews and Christians can stand equally, while according in public due regard to the myths and symbols of their respective communities.

Mendelssohn's proofs for the immortality of the soul were couched in the terminology of the then prevailing idealistic school of Leibnitz. An infinite number of souls or monads, as Leibnitz called them, were conceived to be the inner substance of the universe. All that happens anywhere in the world happens everywhere, for every single monad reflects the entire cosmos. Hence the succession of ordered events that we behold in life takes place in all monads at the same time, in accord with a law of "pre-established harmony" that the Creator had fixed from the beginning of time. Monads reflect all possible changes, but they never perish. In this view, the soul of man is simply the most developed and most nearly perfect of all created substances. It cannot die, because the transition from existence to nonexistence is inconceivable as a continuous process. Since the human mind is Godlike, reflecting in its reasoning the grooves of the Creator's "pre-established harmony," a change which is not humanly think-able is not possible in existence.[16] The force of this argument can only be felt in the context of a philosophy which describes the final atoms of existence not as material entities, responsive to force, but as souls, reflecting the laws of the divine mind.

Mendelssohn fortifies this argument by calling attention to the simplicity, unity and all-pervasiveness of the soul. If there is any bedrock for the stream of experience what else can it be but a soul? Does not the soul permeate all the facets of the human personality, imposing upon them the unifying pattern of a living whole, co-ordinating their separate functions for the good of the organism? Yet, with all the transformations which it makes possible, the soul itself remains one and pure. Since it is the soul which imposes a unifying pattern upon the many elements of an organism, the soul itself cannot be a composite. But if the soul is an ultimate simple unity, it cannot be divided or broken up. Hence it is not weakened by age or negated by death.

Finally, the soul of man is endowed with a consuming hunger for perfection. For Mendelssohn, as for Plato, it appeared certain that the soul could not obtain its complete fulfillment in the dark dungeons of this world, where only the palest reflections of the perfect ideal of goodness and beauty are to be found. The vision of perfection that is implanted in the soul of man could not have arisen out of the chaos and confusion that is the normal lot of humanity. It may therefore be inferred that God endowed man with a vision that could be realized in another domain of exis-tence. Surely the good God would not provide the pangs of hunger without creating the corresponding bread for its satis-faction.[17]

In the final analysis, the belief in human immortality depends upon faith in the goodness of God, but how is the existence of

God to be proven? Mendelssohn's favorite proof was a modification of the ontological procedure. We find the concept of God in the core of our consciousness. This idea of a Supreme Being, perfect in every way, could not have arisen out of the sadly limited experiences of mankind, since we have no direct knowledge of anything remotely resembling the ideal of divine perfection. It is therefore an *a priori* concept, preceding all experience; one of the basic concepts of the mind that enable us to comprehend the outside universe; a category of thought similar to that of space, time and causality. These concepts are in our minds, but they are not subjective or limited to the individual's interior awareness, since they determine the character of universal experience. But this ideal of divine perfection includes necessarily the quality of existence in its own right; otherwise it would be dependent on some other force and therefore imperfect. So the divinely perfect being exists.[18]

Taken by itself and considered apart from the context of ideals with which Mendelssohn operated, this proof appears to be inconsequential enough. But in its time it seemed to carry conviction, since the scientific study of the history of religious ideals was not yet begun. Also, in this proof Mendelssohn anticipated the approach of his great contemporary, Immanuel Kant, who interpreted the task of philosophy to be the study of the structure of ideas in the human mind.

Between Mendelssohn and Kant there was interposed the keen analysis of the Scots philosopher, David Hume, who, after analyzing the flow of consciousness, arrived at the conclusion that all human reasoning was only subjective and that all ideals were mere illusions. To counter the reasoning of Hume, Kant embraced Mendelssohn's argument that the human mind was itself an objective fact. Though the Jewish thinker prepared the ground for the great work of Kant, Mendelssohn did not take kindly to the latter's *Critique of Pure Reason,* principally because it limited the area for the dominion of reason.[19] His own living philosophy was based upon the simple axiom that the good God has given us sufficient gifts of mind and heart to understand this universe and our place in it.

" No individual capable of happiness is predamned; no citizen in the state of God is condemned to eternal sorrow. Everyone pursues his way, going through a series of determinations and reaching, from level to level, toward that degree of happiness that is suitable for him."[20]

"You know how very inclined I am to regard all the disputes of philosophical schools as merely verbal quibbles, or at least as deriving from verbal misunderstandings."[21]

"What people require as people, God has given to all; what they require as certain people, he has given to certain people [i.e. for example, to Jews, the Torah]."[22]

Apart from the specific ideas that were embodied in his philosophy, Mendelssohn served as the vital center of the *Haskalah*, or Enlightenment movement in Germany. While this movement assumed different guises in the successive generations of the nineteenth century, it was in its beginnings the Jewish form of the general European movement toward the transformation of society along rational lines. In the Age of Reason, the forward-looking thinkers of Europe believed that all the ills of humanity could be solved if the structures of the church and of the state were rebuilt along rational lines; that is, in keeping with the principles of natural morality and universal religion. The society of the ancient regime was divided into rigid classes, with time-honored barriers between them. The "enlightened" of all faiths and nationalities demanded a thorough re-examination of all institutions in the light of reason and before the bar of conscience. In France this emphasis on the dominion of reason and the values of universal humanity led to the political doctrines of "the rights of man," the social principles of "equality, liberty and fraternity," and, in its extreme form the worship under the Convention of "the religion of reason." In Germany the same movement assumed milder forms among the philosophers of *Aufklärung*, such as the plea for tolerance in Lessing's *Nathan der Weise*, the importance of the ideals of beauty and harmony in Goethe and Schiller, the supremacy of moral values and the ideal of an all-embracing world government in the philosophy of Kant.

In view of the special circumstances of Jewish life, the *Haskalah* movement developed certain distinctive features. Animated by faith in the power of reason and the native goodness of all men, *Haskalah* aimed to batter down the inner and outer walls of the ghetto. For the "iron curtain" which Christian fanaticism had erected against the "killers of Christ" was supplemented by Jews in the course of time with a thick and impenetrable "legal fence," which served to keep out all foreign influence from the Jewish community. Through the double action of Gentile exclusion and Jewish isolationism, the medieval Jewish community constituted an obdurate, alien body, thrust into the midst of a living organism. The very continuance of the Jewish community, as a social caste, was a powerful symbol of the myths of the *ancien régime*. Hence a rational solution of the Jewish question appeared to Christian liberals to be the acid test of enlightenment. For the Jews, the promise of liberation constituted a challenge to the sense of distinctiveness and alienism which had been carefully nurtured during the long night of "exile." To be "chosen" by God and rejected by "the nations" was to the medievalist the peculiar Jewish lot. How were Jews suddenly to think of themselves as simply human beings, no longer rejected but also no longer "chosen"?

On the surface, the *Maskilim* did not attack the Orthodox mentality by a frontal assault, contenting themselves with the exposition of the new values. To this end they undertook to revive the Hebrew language and to use it as a vehicle of secular learning and expression. They emphasized especially the esthetic and intellectual virtues of European humanism, which they called "the Torah of man." To cultivate a sense of beauty among their brethren, they hoped to eliminate the use of the Yiddish vernacular, which they despised as a "jargon." They thought of culture in terms of surface phenomena, such as the use of classical, grammatical language. Hence German and Hebrew were good, while the use of Yiddish was a mark of barbarism. In literature they aimed to cultivate a taste for stylistic expression, for a rational ordering of ideas and the attainment of a harmonious pattern of religious and secular values. In religion they were zealous rationalists, seeking to banish all superstition and mysticism so as to permit the healthy values of philosophical Judaism to come to the surface. A relatively minor issue, whether or not interment of the dead could be delayed for a few days, loomed large in the disputes between the Orthodox and the Enlightened.

The major effort of the *Maskilim* was directed toward the awakening of a sense of human dignity, which would lead to an appreciation of secular values and a secular society. They sought to persuade Jewish communities to permit their children to study secular subjects, on the ground that the cultivation of the rational faculty is indispensable for the emergence of a higher, reflective type of Jewish piety. To this speculative argument they added the practical consideration that the self-transformation of isolationist Jews into Jewish humanists would lead to complete political and social emancipation. To serve all these purposes, Mendelssohn and the circle of scholars that gathered around him proceeded to translate the Old Testament into German, providing an exhaustive commentary for each of the Five Books of Moses. The German translation was printed in Hebrew characters so that the Jewish readers might learn the German language even as they studied the Torah, while the commentaries were intended to counteract the Qabbalistic vagaries which had accumulated through the centuries. Mendelssohn's works were promptly banned and burned by the Orthodox leaders, who sensed that their own narrow and rigid piety could not flourish in a society that was open to outside influences. In spite of his desire to shun controversy, Mendelssohn and his disciples became the focus of the struggles within the Jewish community in regard to the challenge of the new, secular society.

In its deeper currents *Haskalah* was a Messianic movement of redemption, aiming to redeem the Jew from the status of perpetual homelessness and alienation and teach him to strike roots in the lands of Europe. All through the long dark night of exile, the aspirations of Jewish people for redemption were oriented toward the other-worldly dreams of the Messiah. In time to come, the Messiah would arrive to right all wrongs, gathering the Jews into Palestine, waking the dead from the grave, punishing the wicked nations and establishing a reign of justice and peace. The Messianic hope was not merely a speculative affair or a theological dogma; it was the conscious foundation for Jewish life and the justification for day-by-day existence. The finest efforts of the best people were directed toward the hastening of the Messiah's advent. The mundane world was only a temporary stage and the "world to come" was just around the corner. The Torah was studied as a lifelong occupation, not only as a guide to the meticulous observance of the Commandments, nor yet simply as a pious practice that served to accumulate merits for the individual in the sight of God, but also as the noblest form of life for the Jew, providing an earthly abode for the *Shechinah* and "making ready" the path of redemption for the "totality of Israel."

As the spirit of *Haskalah* unfolded among the Jewish people, the yearning for redemption was directed insensibly into the outward channels leading toward the great society of the western world. The Messiah in all his mystic splendor receded into the background as a "theological" concept that was no longer relevant to the problems of daily living, while the hopes for deliverance were fastened upon the forging of links between Jews and their neighbors. The battle of emergent liberalism against the domination of the church gave promise of the birth of a secular society, in which both Jews and Christians would live in amity. But the new society would come stillborn if it were only a makeshift arrangement, good for business and prosperity, but devoid of deep roots in the realm of eternal values. The new democratic way of life must be embraced as an all-encompassing faith, built round the spirit of reverence for the human values of beauty, order, harmony, rationality and tolerance.

Thus the Jew accepted the world view of liberalism not merely as a beneficent social philosophy, but as a faith, a way of life and a substitute for the Messiah.

The liberal philosophy was for the Jew a continuation and an extension of the rationalistic trend in his sacred tradition; the concepts and values of philosophical Judaism now became charged with the electric energy of a liberating movement. The horizons of human reason had expanded immeasurably from the days of Maimonides to those of Mendelssohn. Esthetics generally and European culture in particular, were now embraced within the perspective of human reason, and the outlines of a new society based upon the common ground of reason were becoming visible. But if the domain of reason grew apace, the sphere of Torah had to shrink accordingly. Torah was now but another handmaiden to the redeeming mistress that was reason. Already the great rationalist of the thirteenth century had shocked the Orthodox of his day by stating that he had written his great code in order to enable the pious to learn all the needed laws of the Torah in a relatively short time, leaving leisure and energy for the cultivation of science and philosophy. For Maimonides, secular wisdom was a worthy goal of life, by no means inferior to Torah. The subsequent intensification of folk piety and the rise of Qabbalah to power as a mass movement in the succeeding centuries elevated the practice of Torah-study to the position of a supreme and exclusive ideal, and made a singular virtue of the enforced isolation of the Jew from the emergent culture of the Christian world. With the emergence of *Haskalah*, the implicit humanistic ideals in Maimonidean thought were revived and the liberal philosophy was embraced with the fervor of a newly-born faith.

The coincidence of ideological liberalism with the impetus of social evolution was demonstrated in the deliberations of the so-called Sanhedrin, which was convoked by Napoleon in Paris, in February of 1807. While the emancipation of the Jews in France was accomplished previously by the National Assembly in 1792, the great humanitarian advance was achieved simply on the strength of the general principle of " the rights of man." The Jews were granted the rights and duties of citizenship, as individual human beings, who differed only in religion from their fellow citizens, having no national aspirations of their own. The defenders of the Jewish people, from Abbé Grégoire, the progressive Catholic, to Mirabeau, the great liberal, saw Jews as forming not a national or political community, but as disenfranchised human beings, who desired only to merge their destiny with that of the French nation. As these liberal statesmen saw it, the hope for victory and triumph under the leadership of the Messiah was in Judaism only a "theological" dogma, of no real significance in the day-by-day concerns of Jewish people. The liberal orator, Clermont-Tonner, spoke for all the advocates of Jewish emancipation when he formulated the intentions of the Assembly in the words: "To the Jews as a nation, nothing; to the Jews as individuals, everything."

Napoleon, actuated by complaints of Alsatian merchants and farmers against the usurious practices of some Jewish loan sharks, set out to re-examine the question of Jewish status. Are Jews really distinguished from their countrymen only in matters of religious faith, or are they truly an alien body among the nations of Europe? Is it only the "hope of Zion" that reflects the separatist sentiments of the Jews? Did not the Jews build up a mighty "inner wall" behind the outer walls of the ghetto—a wall of self-isolation, indifference and even hostility to their host nations? Are the Jews willing to batter down this wall of self-segregationist sentiments in the event of emancipation? Napoleon and his advisers were not clear as to which practices represented the bitter animus of ethnic isolationism and which were simply ritual expressions of the Jewish faith. Was Jewish usury an expression of the state hostility that exists among different nationalities? Were the dietary laws instruments of holiness or devices of separatism? These and similar questions were naturally complicated by the anti-Semitic bias of the majority population, which took its own customs for granted and regarded all deviations from the culture of the majority with suspicion.

To allay all these doubts, Napoleon convened an assembly of rabbis and notable laymen and put to them twelve questions, which may be summarized as follows:

(1) Are the Jews willing to accept the jurisdiction of the civil government in matters of marriage and divorce—specifically, to renounce polygamy (which had been renounced by European Jews in the tenth century); to grant no divorce, save in the event that a civil divorce had been obtained; to recognize the marriage of Jews and Christians as valid?

(2) Are the Jews willing to regard Frenchmen as their brothers and to accord them the status of monotheists in Jewish law; to regard France as their homeland and to fight for it; to accept the civil code of France as binding?

(3) What is the character of the inner source of authority within the Jewish community; specifically, does it seek to control the social and economic activities of its members; does it prohibit Jews from entering any trade or profession?

(4) In regard to usury, are Jews permitted to take usury from other Jews; are they permitted to lend money on interest to non-Jews?

It is easily seen that the purport of all these questions is one—namely, are Jews willing, on their part, to consider themselves as sons of the emergent French nation?

On the formal plane, it was easy enough for the members of the Sanhedrin to answer the above question in an affirmative fashion, consistent with the spirit of liberalism and the demands of the rising nation-states. They declared that the ban of Rabenu

Gershon on polygamy is binding for all time; that the rabbis would not grant any divorce unless the couple had been previously divorced in the civil courts; that the ban against intermarriage in the Torah and the Talmud did not refer to the peoples of Europe, and that a Jew who married a Christian civilly did not therefore subject himself to the punishment of the ban; that the Jews of France considered France as their homeland and the Frenchmen as their brothers; that the congregation of Israel was no longer a nation, harboring the ambition of territorial concentration and self-government, so that the Jews of France could be regarded unequivocally as part of the French people; that the laws of the Talmud against the heathen did not refer to Christians, since they are monotheists; that Jews would willingly fight for the defense of France as their homeland. In regard to the structure of authority prevailing within the Jewish community, the Sanhedrin declared that, following the Revolution and the consequent Emancipation, the rabbis no longer possessed any powers of compulsion and that they exercised strictly "religious" functions. They further issued an appeal for the Jews of France and Italy "to engage in agricultural work, buy farms and fields, learn trades and study the professions," so as not to be confined to junk-peddling, pawnbroking and the other ghetto occupations of pre-Emancipation days. The Biblical prohibition of usury among Jews was not an expression of a double standard of morality, the one toward Jews, the other toward Gentiles; it was one of a group of laws aiming to establish among Jews a greater measure of mutual helpfulness than citizens normally uphold within the confines of a nation. Also, in Biblical days loans were not productive of profit as they are in a capitalistic society. In the case of commercial loans it is permitted for Jews to charge interest to one another. As to usurious rates of interest, Jewish courts and assemblies during the Middle Ages prohibited such abuses, even when the borrower was a Gentile. It was the harsh pressure of necessity which compelled the Jews of the Middle Ages to resort to the business of moneylending, since other sources of income were denied to them.[23]

Formally, these responses of the Sanhedrin were fully in accord with Jewish law. Nevertheless, the decisions of the Sanhedrin implied a fundamental reorientation of Jewish community feeling from the center to the periphery. The dynamism of the Jewish faith was to be directed toward the building of the great democratic society, not toward the nurturing of the specific hopes of the Jewish community. Throughout our discussion in the previous chapters, we noted how all-pervasive the feeling of kinship and the sense of being part of a self-enclosed community are in the Jewish religion. To both Mendelssohn and Spinoza the rituals of Judaism were not religious sacraments or even concrete expressions of personal religion, but solely instruments of a communal or national covenant with God. Mendelssohn took for granted the separateness of the Jewish community, affirming that it was a unique synthesis of social and religious elements, but now the Napoleonic Sanhedrin sought to separate the community from the faith of the individual. And the Sanhedrin reflected without doubt the longing of the modern Jew to end his " abnormal " status and to take his place as a member of the emergent western democratic community. If, then, the separate corporate existence of the Jewish community is no longer esteemed as a supreme value, what point is there in the continued struggle to maintain the Jewish faith? Since the ideas of Judaism are those of the universal mind of man while the practices reflecting the identity of the community and the spirit of separatism are now disavowed, how can the struggle for Jewish survival be justified?

As a matter of record, great numbers of Jewish people accepted Christianity in Germany and France in the first decades of the nineteenth century. One third of the Berlin Jewish community forsook Judaism in the single decade of 1802-1812.[24] While an honest intellectual like David Friedlander wished to make certain that he was not asked to swallow any Christian dogmas in the process of conversion, most people were not so squeamish. A wave of conversion engulfed the Jewish masses of Germany, aided by the continuing disabilities of Jews in most German states and European countries.

A new concept of Judaism was needed if it was to survive as a vital faith in the western world—a concept that would uncover its essential truth and validity in the modern world, its distinctive idealogy *vis-à-vis* the Christian world, and its relevance to the life of the Jewish individual.

For a while it seemed as if Judaism in western Europe would

not be able to withstand the double-headed challenge of the new era—the challenge of the spirit of rationalism to the faith of the individual and the challenge of the new secular society to the communal structure of Jewry. However, as happened so frequently in the past, Judaism never rose to such noble heights as when its very existence was questioned. Its amazing vitality was demonstrated in the nineteenth century by the rise of two massive movements in Judaism, each reasserting the worth of tradition in its own way: the Reform-Conservative movement, defending the faith of the individual, and the new Zionist movement, reaffirming the intrinsic value of the Jewish community.

EPILOGUE

HAVING surveyed the main currents of thirty centuries of Jewish thought, we bring this volume to a close at the threshold of the modern era. The emancipation of the Jews of western Europe, proceeding apace from the first decade of the nineteenth century, brought the individual Jew to the fore, liberating him from the pressure of enforced communal loyalties. In the course of time the bonds of communal loyalty were weakened; the congregation, a voluntary association of free individuals, came to take the place of the overall community which one entered by birth and left by death or an act of conversion. As a result all the cleavages in Jewish life were widened and deepened.

In the nineteenth century the meaning of the term "Jewish thought" became both wider and narrower than in all previous centuries. It was now wider since the resonant voices outside the pale of the community would not be ignored. Is it justifiable to leave out of our discussion, for example, such men as Heine, Börne and Bergson, whose inspiration derived at least in part from Jewish sources as well as from Jewish experience?

On the other hand, "Jewish thought" came to embrace a necessarily narrower compass than in the past, for the Jew as man is now part of the European community, and the Jew *qua* Jew is such only by virtue of his theology and his "misfortune," the burden of anti-Semitism.

In our next volume, dealing with the last century and a half of Jewish thought, we will need to employ a wider canvas and a fuller array of brushes and colors than heretofore. Each of the currents comprising the variegated stream of Jewish thought is intensified and deepened by the massive challenge of modernists. Rationalistic Judaism has eventuated in the modern movements of Reform and Conservatism, with the latter group adding a strong dose of nationalist romanticism and a dash of mysticism to its rationalistic approach. Orthodox Judaism in the eastern countries has become more isolationist than in previous centuries, barricading itself against the incursion of secular learning and the solvent effects of the rationalistic spirit. In eastern Europe the dark cobwebs of Qabbalistic mysticism remained undisturbed well into the twentieth century, while in western Europe Orthodoxy embraced an uneasy alliance with modern culture, seeking support from the anti-intellectualist trends of modern thought and continuing the traditional current of romanticism, in both its ethnic and affective forms.

But the divergent trends do not separate into independent denominations or even independent schools of thought; they continue to affect, influence and mold one another. We encounter in Judaism the phenomenon which sociologists call the "cultural lag"—namely, the fact that only the upper layer of any society changes culturally with the times, while the medium layer changes more slowly and a large portion of society continues its slumber virtually undisturbed. Accordingly, no matter how far the advanced elements of Jewry developed in their quest for a new synthesis of Judaism and the modern spirit, a remnant of the old mentality persisted in every generation. Consequently, in Orthodox ranks today all shades of the premodern spectrum of beliefs can still be found, and individual thinkers, beginning their intellectual adventure in the Orthodox community, are compelled to find their own way to a tenable philosophy of life out of the darkly shadowed, tortuous paths of medievalism.

Secularism is distinctly a new phenomenon in "Jewish thought." Created in the first place by the impact of rationalism, it assumed a Jewish garb under the influence of ethnic romanticism. While the secularists in the first half of the nineteenth century generally accepted the "entrance ticket to European culture," converting to Christianity, those of the latter half of the past century remained as a rule officially within the Jewish community. In the last decades of the century they provided the leadership and impetus of the Zionist movement.

Nothing demonstrates the complex interaction of opposing intellectual forces in Jewish life so much as the emergence of Zionism. In the first place, it was made possible by the influence of rationalism, which undermined the old faith in the eventual coming of the Messiah. On the other hand, its reassertion of

Jewish ethnicism drew inspiration and vitality from the romantic current in Judaism, which described the people of Israel as a uniquely endowed nation, set apart by divine decree or by the fatalities of history from all the families of the earth. At the same time, the mystical trend in Orthodox Judaism rediscovered in Zionism a quasi-magical device for hastening the steps of the Messiah. While rationalistic Zionists sought to build a homeland for the Jew as a means of overcoming the Jewish "abnormality" of status in the lands of the Diaspora, and of encouraging the "normal" processes of assimilation in the Diaspora, romantic Zionists sought to employ a Jewish homeland as a means of preserving the "abnormal" status of a "unique" people, countering the trends of assimilation. As this is written, this issue is still unresolved.

Now that the State of Israel is a reality, the exponents of rationalistic Judaism look upon it as a creative center of Jewish faith and culture, not as a means of liquidating the Jewish communities in the Diaspora. Accordingly, they encourage the moral stature of the state rather than its military might, just as they favor the promotion of the spiritual values of Judaism in every country where Jews are found. And they see no good purpose served in the world-wide effort to encourage emigration to Israel, undercutting the psychological rootedness of the Jewish Diaspora so as to bring about its degeneration and disappearance. On the other hand, those who draw their inspiration from the romantic current of Judaism see the Jew as "unique" and "different," forever arrayed against the "nations," with no hope of peace for him, except in his own land, where the strength of his arms will protect him from his enemies. Thus do the issues of today reflect the impetus of the divergent currents of yesterday.

As we turn back for a synoptic view of the different currents within the stream of Judaism we note first the fallacy of all monolithic renderings of this tradition. Friends and foes loved to write of Judaism as if it had a single view of life, providing one answer to all-important questions. Not only psychopathic anti-Semites, painting Judaism in the darkest hues, but even philosophical interpreters of culture, too, construed the Jew as one psychological type and Judaism as a monochromatic picture on the unfolding scroll of human history. Hence, the potent fantasies concerning the characteristics of the " Semitic mind."

Renan saw the Jewish spirit as one of surpassing but monotonous brightness, like the glare of sunlight in the desert, oblivious of the variety of shade and color in nature, seeing the upper surface of things with harsh clarity, but ignoring the reality of depths and shadows. A whole school of historians goes back to Fichte and Schleiermacher for inspiration. In their view, the Jewish faith is the reflection of the peculiarity of Jewish genius, which consists of a calculating cleverness and business shrewdness; incapable of profundity, inventiveness or the appreciation of the romantic nature of man. Wellhausen conceived the difference between prophecy and mysticism in terms of this concept. Mysticism is an expression of the piety of the Aryan soul, in which man surrenders all of himself in the fullness of love. The Semite, according to this school, is capable only of receiving and taking, not of loving and giving. Accordingly, the Bible envisions the prophet as filling himself up with the divine spirit.

Even in socialist circles this mischievous conception of a peculiar Jewish mind was given fresh currency and the semblance of authority by Karl Marx, who maintained that the god of the Jew was the dollar bill and his worship a form of bargaining and haggling.

To counter this nonsense, many Jewish writers set up opposing fantasies of their own, extolling the Jewish " genius " and soothing the wounded vanity of their people. For example, Abraham Geiger, with all his liberalism and sober rationality, wrote of the existence of a Jewish " genius " for religion, shared by no other people; Samuel David Luzzatto asserted that pity was the unique quality of the Jewish soul; and Ahad Haam maintained that the rational quest for the dominion of absolute justice was the underlying impetus of the Jewish mind.

Need poison be countered by antipoison drugs, or can mankind be educated to dispense with the drug of collective egotism and learn to take life as it is, without the sinister solace of artificial concoctions? After all, counterpoisons are also drugs. We believe that the best defense against the barbs of bigotry is the serenity of objective thought, not the fevered passion of superheated ethnic zealotry.

We have seen a wide variety of theological positions in the long and winding pathways of Jewish thought. How broad is the panorama thus unfolded! How rich is the spectrum of colors ranging from the twilight moods of mysticism to the stark clarity of rationalism, from the lofty heights of universalist idealism to the dark depths of collective "sacred egoism"!

We find exponents of both alternatives in the discussion of such central issues as the following:

(1) The transcendence of God versus His immanence

Rationalists like Maimonides asserted that God was remote from earthly concerns and far beyond the grasp of human faculties. His Providence does not extend to the masses of people, "the poor and the broken in spirit," but only to the well-proportioned and well-disposed, those reflective and saintly souls whose lines have fallen in pleasant places, and who undertake the arduous philosophical disciplines leading to the comprehension of His difference from the material world. All Biblical miracles were predetermined in advance of creation, built into the inflexible system of iron necessity that governs the universe. The only pathway to God is that of reason, and this pathway is impersonal, consisting in the elimination from our mind of human interests and the actual stuff of experience.

On the other hand, the doctrine of divine immanence is well represented in the stream of Jewish thought. In the ethnic romanticism of Halevi, God is portrayed as being in direct communication with the people of Israel, when they are gathered in the land of Israel. A divine effulgence was visible, at least to the sages and to the prophets, and a divine voice could be heard at critical moments. In Qabbalah, man's power to affect the divine pattern of *sefiroth* was deemed to be so direct and immediate as to be virtually automatic, the Deity acting toward man, "like a shadow." The material world was only the lowest garment of the substance of reality. And man's soul is not entirely enclosed in his body, being rooted in the realm of *sefiroth*.

In naïve or unreflective Judaism, both concepts of the Deity could be found side by side. Consequently, the Talmud and a huge mass of popular pietistic literature employ rationalistic and mystical concepts, almost interchangeably, for their "religious value," if we may coin a new phrase, without any awareness of their mutual incompatibility.

(2) *Human dignity versus human sinfulness*

Does a person best reflect the "image of God" within him when he is made aware of his dignity or of his sinfulness? This question points to a psychological cleavage that cuts deep. On the one hand, there is the "active" piety of those who consider man to be "a partner of the Lord" in the establishment of His kingdom on earth. God is best served by the fullest assertion of man's faculties and gifts. Man is bidden to use his faculty of rational judgment, in the determination of right and wrong, and in the amelioration of existing evils. When men assert their perceptive powers in the domains of thought and action, they give concrete expression to the divine element in their nature. For man and God are united in rationality, love of goodness and gentleness, and in reverence for law. In general man is the agent of the divine *nisus* for perfection.

This way of thinking is reflected not only in the rationalistic school but also in the sober mood of the Talmudic sages. The concept of a covenant between man and God in which both parties to the agreement undertake to abide by certain actions is a perfect expression of "active" piety. God does not compel man to accept any law, but man does what is right out of loyalty to his own higher nature, which is Godlike. And this concept underlies the reasoning of *Halachah*, Jewish law. If the children of Israel had not voluntarily undertaken to observe the law, they would not have been obliged to abide by it, for in the domain of reason and ethics all rational and moral beings are equal.

But while the mood of "active piety" is well represented in Judaism, the opposite mood of total surrender to the divine will is also rather frequently encountered. This attitude is permeated with a deep awareness of human failure. Man's greatest achievements are but vanity and naught. It is in sin that we are born. "And if thou dost act righteously, what does thou give unto Him?"

"What are we, what is our life, what our kindness, our righteousness, our salvation, our power, our heroism? And the superiority of man over the beast is naught, for all is vanity."[1]

In this mood we feel that God's only demand is man's self-abasement. Not by being "like unto God," but by total surrender, by "a broken heart," by the practice of humility so thoroughgoing as to approach self-negation, does God take delight in us. By active striving we achieve nothing, for God neither desires our good right arm nor can we exert any of our faculties to good effect without falling victim to the perverting and ensnaring forces of pride and sin.

Several historians of religion take the contrast between the active and the passive moods of piety to be the fundamental distinction between Judaism and Christianity. But actually many variations of passive piety are found not only in the romantic and mystical currents of Jewish thought, but also in the pietistic literature (*Mussar*) of popular Judaism.

The opposition of several leading Orthodox rabbis to the introduction of an organ in the synagogue was motivated by the belief that beauty and dignity minister to man's sense of self-importance, discouraging the penitential mood of sinfulness. "A sinner must not bedeck himself with beauty, a sinner must not take on the garments of pride."[2]

As a rule, the doctrine of "original sin" is not central in Judaism, but at various times it has been strongly affirmed. In the Talmud we find the dogmatic assertion that all who did not stand at Sinai suffer from the "corruption of the serpent."[3] In Qabbalah the souls of all non-Jews are presumed to be "rooted" in the domain of the "shells."

In Halevi's philosophy, even converts cannot expect to achieve equality with born Jews following the advent of the Messiah nor to become recipients of the "gift of prophecy." The capacity for the "divine quality" is denied by Halevi to non-Jewish mankind as a whole, which is doomed to grope in the darkness. Also, the proposition that it is possible for man, unaided by revelation, to live a life of goodness and attain a share in the world to come is both affirmed and denied in Jewish tradition.[4]

(3) *Is the content of religion some things to be done or something to become?*

This question probes deep into the nature of piety. When religion consists of a number of rites to perform and commandments to execute, we have a pattern of piety that is external to man's true being. It may be dogmatically asserted that the rites in question exert a quasi-magical effect on the soul and in the cosmos, "purifying" man's inner nature and providing "food for the upper worlds." But in the actual performance of the rites there is no inherent sequence of effects upon the psyche of the worshiper. In this pattern of piety the supreme value of the ritual is asserted, and the value of any universal ethical and esthetic virtues is questioned.

Such a completely externalized religion may be softened by the additional requirement of "duties of the heart," supplementing those of physical performance. But, characteristically, these obligations of the mind and heart are not conceived of as mandatory and essential to the rite itself.

This nonspiritual concept of piety is certainly encountered within the sacred literature of the Jewish faith. It is virtually assumed in the stream of *Halachic* (legalistic) nonphilosophic Judaism. It is justified somewhat hesitantly in the romantic current of Jewish thought. In Qabbalah we find elaborate rationalizations for the belief in the cosmic effects of the performance of the *mizvoth*.

But the opposing concept of the nature of piety is also well represented in Judaism. In the rationalistic school, the *mizvoth* are conceived of as instruments of piety embodying universal, ethical and esthetic values. The *mizvoth* were intended to train men and women in the acquisition of good habits, noble ideas and lofty sentiments. The context of religion is not the execution of certain commands, but the fulfillment of the divine potential in human nature. God is not a king, intent upon the enforcement of His orders, but our Father, concerned with helping us to attain the fullness of our stature. Religion is not a burden on our backs, but an aspiration in our souls to grow into our ideal likeness. Understood in this way, the virtue and truth of other religions may be honestly acknowledged without giving up the belief in one's own religion. Faith becomes not the guardianship of "eternal verities," but the quest for the truths of eternity, a search for wider horizons for the life of the soul, a courageous ascent and an endless task.

Both types of piety have been illustrated in the preceding pages.

(4) *Is man completely free to work out his own salvation, or is his future predetermined?*

The predominant emphasis in Judaism is unquestionably on the side of man's freedom. The Torah affirms that man is free to choose between good and evil, the blessing and the curse, life and death. In the Talmud, we are told that everything in a person's life is fixed in advance save his righteousness. "All is in the power of heaven, save the fear of heaven."[5] Rabbi Akiba set the stage for a philosophical riddle that occupied all the masters of Jewish philosophy when he asserted, "All is foreseen, but the choice is given."[6] The power of repentance is infinite in scope; even the greatest sinners can, if they will, transform their lives and attain the greatest heights of piety.[7]

On the other hand, Crescas, who has been called "the most Jewish of all the philosophers," declares that even a person's piety is predetermined and human freedom is only an illusion. In Qabbalah, non-Jewish humanity, drawing its sustenance from the "shells," can hardly be expected to do anything that is genuinely good. Those who become converts to Judaism, so the legend goes, possess souls which were present at Sinai when the covenant was concluded. A verse from Proverbs (14:34) is an oft-quoted maxim: "Even the kindness of the nations is sinful."

The advent of the Messiah, who will usher in the Kingdom of God, is both fixed in the mind of God and also dependent on Jewish repentance. If Jewish merit and penitence do not succeed in hastening the arrival of the Messiah, then he will come in the previously appointed time.[8]

In the rationalistic current of Jewish thought, it is assumed that man's reason is free and untrammeled and that man can attain the good life by the exercise of his native endowments of intelligence and conscience. Both assumptions are contested in the romantic and mystical schools of Jewish thought. Reason is declared to be the shameless servant of the will, and the will in turn is "rooted" by birth and early upbringing either in the spheres of holiness among loyal Jews or in the unclean dominion of the "other side," among the rest of mankind. Halevi introduces the argument in his famous book by telling of an angel that appeared to King Bulan and warned him, "Thy thoughts are acceptable but thy deeds are not." Acceptable deeds, for Halevi, are spelled out in the codes of the Jewish faith. Non-Jewish humanity is for the ethnic romantics, by and large, precluded from salvation.

For the rationalists, divine grace is not needed as the condition for man's goodness, since this favor is granted to man at birth and by education in the shape of the twin lights in his soul, conscience and intelligence. For the romantics and mystics, divine grace and the " merit of the fathers " is of the essence. For man's soul is virtually besieged by the malicious forces of Satan. And those which are not "rooted " in the divine pleroma are almost inevitably steeped in sin.

(5) *Is the Divine Will inherent in the normal and natural processes of history, or is it " transhistorical," breaking into the flux of historical events with predetermined results?*

This question seems labored and casuistic; yet, it points to the real issue between those who believe that human progress is a gradual result of the strains and stresses of social forces and those who envision the high points of peace and prosperity as being attained by unpredictable incursions of God's grace. When the question is asked, " Does Judaism believe in human progress? " the answer cannot be given in the simple syllables of "yes " or " no."

The vision of the Messianic era was born in Judaism, a many-splendored vision of hope and beauty incarnate. But this vision represented not the upward path but the ultimate goal, the situation at " the end of days." Nor did that vision stand alone, unassociated with other eschatological hopes and fantasies. After a period lasting from forty years to four hundred years, according to different traditions, it was believed that the human personality would become metamorphosed and life in all its aspects would be completely transformed, ushering in the wondrous era of " the world to come."[9] Perfection in body and soul would then be the unfailing rule—but the human body would then be transformed into a new, heavenly substance, no longer a thing of flesh and blood.

Is the goal reached through the processes of history? A rationalist like Maimonides believed that the Messianic era would be attained by the normal processes of history, for God had pre-arranged all human events and, through the prophets, had made known His will. Even Maimonides did not see any progress toward this goal in the events of his day, looking for confirmation of his faith to the verses of Scripture and the traditions of his family. In his letter to the Yemenites he tentatively expressed the hope that the Messiah would appear in his own generation.

Nevertheless, we can find in Maimonides the seeds of a philosophy of historical progress. For he affirmed the Resurrection and the fantasies of the " world to come " not as true ideas, but only as beliefs necessary for the maintenance of the community. And in both Christianity and Islam he saw the divine impulse at work, preparing the ground for the ultimate triumph of the " true faith."

Nahmanides and his school did not envision the fulfillment of the Messianic dream in any progressive manner. The belief in the Messiah was a dogmatic assertion, of the same type as the Resurrection, and as little given to progressive realization. The authors of the apocalyptic *Midrashim*, one and all, envisioned a series of catastrophes, taxing human endurance and culminating in disasters from which only a few survivors will escape. The help of the Lord will come suddenly.[10] Human repentance can hasten the coming of the Messiah, but repentance was conceived by the romantics and the mystics in purely dogmatic terms.

In general, the pietists of Judaism did not see any progressive improvement in the behavior of their contemporaries—either Jews or Gentiles. It is of the essence of Orthodoxy to idealize the past, not the future. " If the people of early times were like angels, we are like men, and if they were men we are donkeys."[11] Even the wicked men of the past like Balaam and Nebuchadnezzar were conceived to be great in their own way, so that miracles could be performed for their reproof or enlightenment.

A doctrine of the cumulative merit of redemption was contained in Qabbalah, especially as taught in the Lurianic school. But the accumulation of merit was believed to be taking place in the occult essence of the universe, not in the unfolding of the visible events of history.

(6) *Is faith an extension and anticipation of the lights of conscience and intelligence, or is it the acceptance of traditional dogmas outside the dictates of reason and ethics?*

This question might be phrased in many different ways. Indeed, it underlies almost every issue in theology. The Scholastics distinguished between faith as " trust in God " and faith as " assent " to a proposition. For the believers of the first category, faith is a blend of love, trust and intuition; hence, they will interpret the documents of revelation in accord with the precepts of reason. They will eschew literalism in practice and dogmatism in theory, interpreting the legendry of their faith as parables and the rites of their religion as action-symbols of faith. If, however, faith is conceived not as an insight of the soul but as its submission to an external fiat, reason will not be allowed a decisive role as the source of truth, and moral principles too will be subverted to serve the worldly interests of the "chosen people," who are pledged to maintain the one and only true faith. The mentality of fundamentalism, deriving from an insistence on the literal truth of the documents of revelation, is inescapably zealous and exclusive. Fundamentalists may accommodate themselves to the pressures and needs of modern society, but they cannot in truth acknowledge the rightness of the values upon which it is founded.

Was Judaism, then, prorational or antirational? Was it a religion of dogmas, affirmed on the testimony of tradition, or was it a religion of faith in the inspired guidance of prophets and saints, sages and philosophers?

Here again the answer depends on the particular school of thought within Judaism. The rationalists maintained that revelation and reason concurred fully in their essential import; that revelation provided instruction in those areas where the testimony of reason was indecisive and uncertain; that the documents of revelation needed to be interpreted in the light of reason; that the purpose of revelation was to fortify man's intellectual moral adventure, assuring him of the ultimate success of his efforts, for man's highest values are rooted in eternity.

The romantics and mystics, on the other hand, labored hard and continuously to assert the contrary claim. God takes delight in confounding man's pride of reason. This is why Abraham was tested by the command to sacrifice Isaac. Would Abraham follow the rationalists and refuse the demand of God on the ground of its unreasonableness, or would he slaughter his son in obedience to God and in defiance of reason?

The battle between the rationalists and their opponents can be traced in Judaism to the Biblical period, the contest between the true prophets and the numerous contemporary "prophetizers." The prophets identified the insights of a keen conscience with the will of God, whereas the "prophetizers" sought to find God in an emotional frenzy that extinguished the light of consciousness. And this battle is by no means over. For the human situation renews for us perennially the choice between placing our faith in the testimony of a revered tradition or in that of our heart and mind.

There is an active, open-eyed, open-minded and open-hearted type of piety, arising out of the projection of man's highest values against the cosmic curtain of eternity. Opposed to this piety of the harmonious personality there is the religion of those who are predominately moved by fear—fear of the dark depths of their own souls. Psychologically speaking, they need a faith of closed horizons, shutting the doors tight against the longing of the soul; hemming it in by the barriers of dogma and by a rigid regimen of conduct that is presumed to be unalterable. The affirmation of a dogma is for them an action-symbol, setting limits to the restless dynamism of heart and mind which they deeply distrust.

Proponents of both alternatives and of some mediating positions as well will find in the treasures of Judaism ample support for their views.

(7) *Is Judaism a universal religion, employing a nation as its historical vehicle, or is it the "way of life" of the Jewish people, the expression of the culture and sancta of the Jewish people?*

This question is couched in modern terms, reflecting distinctions which are meaningful only in a society where religion and politics are separated. Nevertheless, in our survey of the development of Jewish thought we have dealt continuously with the wider implications of this distinction. On several different occasions we distinguished between Judaism as a structure of universal ideals and sentiments, rites and symbols, and Judaism as sublimated ethnicism, refined by a high ethical tradition and associated with a great religious tradition.

In the current of rationalistic Judaism, the motives of ethnicism dwindle into relative insignificance. Maimonides' interpretation of the Jewish faith does not assume a wide gulf between Jews and the rest of mankind. The *mizvoth* of the Torah are only educational devices. Judaism is an excellent school. But some men will go through the best schools, learning very little, and others, studying in mediocre institutions or even self-taught, will find their way to the presence of the Almighty. Even the Messianic era was conceived by Maimonides not primarily as an epoch of national triumph but as an era of universal good will, when all men will accept the "true faith," surrender the follies of national ambition and devote themselves to philosophical meditations.

"The sages and the prophets longed for the days of the Messiah, not in order that they might govern the whole world, lording it over the pagans and being exalted by all nations; nor that they might eat, drink and rejoice, but in order that they might enjoy the leisure to engage in the study of Torah and wisdom, free from interference and oppression, attaining thus to life eternal."[12]

Albo spoke of the general category of a "Divine Torah," allowing the possibility of several divine faiths, each suited to the varied circumstances of people living in different portions of the globe. To be sure, in his Epistle to the Yemenites, Maimonides hews close to the line of ethnic zealotry, forced as he was to appeal to the sentiments and mentality of simple-minded people, "of women and children." Similarly, we encounter concessions to popular prejudice in all the writings of rationalistic Judaism. But essentially and in principle, philosophical Judaism was universalistic and free from the zealotries of ethnicism. In this respect the current of philosophical Judaism continued, widened and deepened the sparkling mountain streams of prophecy. For the great prophets, too, defined religion by means of universal and ethical standards; combatted the ethnic pride and prejudice of their contemporaries; conceived of the "congregation of Israel" in the ideal terms of the loyal remnant and looked forward to the conversion of all mankind.

To be sure, in the books of prophecy we occasionally encounter verses reflecting ethnic pride and prejudice. The prophets were children of their time as well as geniuses of faith. Ethnic zealotry was after all part of their environment. Their genius was manifested, however, not when they yielded to the sentiments of the people, but when they confronted their contemporaries with new ideas and sought to redirect national zeal into spiritual channels.

On the other hand, there is no lack of support for the ethnic conception in the central ideas of nonphilosophical Judaism, in the romantic and in the mystical currents of thought. The Talmud operates consistently on the supposition of a wide and deep chasm, yawning between Jewry and "the nations."

The sages of the Talmud differed on such issues as whether Jews are called "children of God" regardless of the quality of their piety and the ethics of their conduct; whether the "pious of the nations" do or do not have a share in the "world to come"; whether the term "man" in the Torah refers to Israelites only or to all men; whether the severe laws in the Pentateuch regarding the neighboring nations of Palestine were to be applied in the centuries following the destruction of the Temple; whether or not proselytes should be sought out and welcomed; whether or not the dietary laws should be made progressively more stringent, so as to interpose a more forbidding barrier between Jews and Gentiles. The liberal position was never lacking in Judaism, but at times it was overwhelmed and overruled.

In romantic and mystical Judaism, the Jewish people is elevated to the rank of a "superhumanity" which alone is capable of communing with God. The term "the God of Israel" is interpreted literally to suggest an intimate, organic and exclusive relationship, as if God could be revealed to mankind only by the agency of the people of Israel. As we noted before, the Qabbalists taught that only the souls of Jews were derived from the Supreme Being. Gentiles were even forbidden to study the Torah, according to the authorities belonging to this school, for the Torah was the private possession of the one people that God loves and protects by His Providence. Even the lofty concept of the Messianic era was frequently perverted in popular literature and distorted by the proponents of this view so as to express the bitter frustration of a persecuted people rather than the noble vision of inspired prophets. The Messiah was to avenge the wrongs perpetrated against Jewish people and compensate them for their years of suffering, restoring to Jews their rightful position as "sons of Kings." This caricature of the Messianic vision, however, was rarely allowed to stand unchallenged, uncorrected and untransformed by the refining genius of philosophical piety.

(8) *In view of the manifold tensions and polarities in Jewish thought can we speak of the "mainstream" of Judaism?*

Subjectively, it is certainly quite natural and almost inevitable for contemporary writers to identify their own interpretation of Judaism as the "mainstream." Throughout our discussion, we have not failed to make clear our own alignment with the rationalistic school, which is sometimes also designated as the current of philosophical Judaism. We believe that God reveals

Himself primarily through the twin lights of conscience and intelligence and that the written documents of revelation need to be interpreted in the light of the living Word of revelation. We believe that this recognition of the primacy of the living Word is the central insight of Judaism, a faith that was hammered out of teachings of prophets and sages. While the "prophetizers" of the Bible and of Canaanite culture were presumably passive vessels in the grip of their "frenzy," the Hebrew prophets identified the "still, small voice" of a sacred, sensitive conscience with the voice of the Lord.

At the same time, we must not forget that Judaism is far larger than any school of thought. Objectively, we cannot ignore nor make light of the other currents of Judaism. Nonphilosophical Judaism, with its rigid, legalistic mentality, was at all times a potent reality. The vast, darkly shadowed halls of Qabbalah constitute part of the Jewish tradition, and the self-exalting works of the Romantic school, rhapsodizing on the "unique" glories of the Jewish soul, are among the treasured possessions of the faith. We may, if we choose, consider the philosophical interpretation as the "mainstream," or the "essence," or as being "normative"; but then we need to acknowledge frankly that we follow our own personal preference.

In the modern period there have appeared a plethora of popular books, all purporting to describe the "essence" of Judaism. As a rule the author's private interpretation of what is "true" or "authentic" is given as the "essence," and all that does not fit into his category is dismissed as relatively unimportant, unauthentic or marginal. Sometimes, too, the old casuistic skills of our Talmud-trained ancestors are made use of to prove that contradictions do not annoy the "unique" genius of the Jewish mentality, which thinks in terms of "both-and" not "either-or" categories. As we have noted, opposing points of view were due to the clash of diverse currents of thought within the tradition, not to a unique faculty or a peculiar logic. Such efforts at romantic self-aggrandizement would be laughable if they were not tragic reminders of the essential similarity of human nature the world over. It is precisely the defenders of the "uniqueness" of German genius, Polish genius, Russian genius, etc., who glory in a similar discovery of the "transrational" domain, where the categories of the intellect are inapplicable, and dreams of ethnic superiority can be indulged to the heart's content.

Actually, Judaism as a great religious tradition reflects diverse approaches and insights which are organized in different patterns to suit the varying mentalities which compose a world-wide community. In his massive work, *A Study of History,* Prof. Arnold J. Toynbee attempts to prove that the great religions reflect the different psychical structures of mankind, with each religious tradition corresponding to one psychological type. As a matter of fact, all variations of character are found in every people, and a great tradition growing over a long period of time will naturally reflect the insights and needs of every important category of human personality.

However, this reasonable approach to the mysteries of faith was countered by equally powerful trends toward dogmatism. Thus, the self-righteous dogmatist, who bans and burns the books of his opponents, is not an unfamiliar figure in the history of Jewish thought.

For a variety of historical reasons, conflicting positions were tolerated within the confines of Judaism. The awesome greatness of God was felt so powerfully that the sages were disposed to recognize the legitimacy of different approaches. The heart of so great a mystery cannot be reached by any single pathway. For the proponents of a non-dogmatic faith, it appears reasonable enough to project shafts of light into the cosmic mystery from many different angles, without being able to see how they fall into a consistent and logical pattern. The prophetic-rationalistic school of Jewish thought naturally favored this attempt to see God and His works from a great diversity of standpoints. Fortunately, the cause of tolerance was aided by the circumstances that the law can more easily take account of actions than of thoughts, and Jewish piety was molded in the patterns of legalism. So the actions of the Jew were regulated with the utmost zeal and precision, while his thoughts were allowed a relative measure of freedom.

Finally, the most decisive factor in the creation of a wide domain of tolerance within the tradition of Jewish theology was the absence of an all-powerful central authority. It is in the conflict of cultures and in the mutual confrontation of diverse points of view that philosophy comes to life and flourishes. In the

Biblical period, prophets vied against priests and against kings. By the Second Commonwealth, there was only a narrow area where Sadducees and Pharisees could agree. Besides the official academies, there was always the free proliferation of private schools, and their traditions achieved recognition in the course of time. The Babylonian Gaonate dominated the Jewish scene only for a few centuries, and their authority was challenged by the Qaraites. When the power of the Geonim was broken, Jewish intellectuals needed to take into account only the guidance of their own conscience, the opinion of their colleagues and the broad areas of agreement among the people generally.

Consequently, a rich and many-sided tradition came into being which reflected the full spectrum of colors resulting from the focusing of Divine light upon the various psychic planes of the prism of human genius.

In view of the diversity of trends within the stream of Jewish thought, wherein does the unity of the Jewish tradition consist? We find the unifying principle in the text, the context and the emphasis of all schools in Judaism. The unity of a river consists of the bedrock and banks of the channels through which it flows, the intermingling of the tributaries in the course of its flow and the impetus of direction shared by its waters. In Judaism, the unity of source is the chain of sacred literature, the unity of bedrock is the social structure of Jewish life and the unity of impetus is the quest for the realization of the Godlike qualities of the human personality. The text is the series of sacred documents, the Pentateuch, Bible and Talmud, and all the varied books of the classical tradition. All interpreters of Judaism, as far as their ideas may range, return for inspiration and guidance to the same sacred books. There exists also the unifying code of conduct regulating worship, home ritual and everyday life.

As the stream flows, some of its waters are evaporated by wind and sun; and fresh rivulets bring new waters from the country-side; stagnant pools form here and there in the low marshlands as well as rushing eddies in narrow defiles; yet the stream is one, the unpractised eye noticing scarcely any distinction among its waters, while the experienced sailor can sail up the stream, from the channels in the delta to its sources in the mountains of antiquity.

The context is the total life of the Jewish community. It is impossible to separate the evolution of ideas in Judaism from the social and economic forces in Jewish history. The unity of Jewish communal life, fashioned by many historic forces, provided a forum for the airing of opposing views and the conciliation of conflicting opinions.

The nature of the communal bedrock for the flow of Jewish thought changed in the course of time from the confederacy of twelve tribes to a unified nation and from the political unity of a nation to the social unity of a religious community. The effective meaning of the category of a religious community did not remain static. At all times, Jewishness involved awareness of a very real communal setup. The bedrock and channels were there, painfully real, even if observers differed concerning its nature and proper designation.

In addition, certain emphases belong to the tradition as a whole, characterizing its every facet in greater or lesser degree. The emphases on God's unity, on the rationality and goodness of His Will, on the freedom of the human personality, on the ethical vocation of man and his 'destiny as a " partner of the Lord "—all these emphases, different though their significance may be in the different currents of Jewish thought, belong to the spiritual impetus of Judaism as a whole.

These emphases are of special significance in the consideration of the place of Judaism within the larger context of the Judeo-Christian tradition. As against the Christian challenge concerning the divine nature of Jesus, all branches of Judaism upheld the rationalistic-ethical position. We have had occasion to mention Nahmanides' contention that the "mind of a Jew " will never consent to the proposition that God became man, being born out of the womb of a woman, or that God needed to sacrifice " His son," in order to atone for the sins of mankind and compensate for the corruption of " original sin." Nahmanides belonged to the mystical current of Judaism; nevertheless, as against Christian dogma, he too employed the weapons of reason and the objective validity of ethical principles.

This contrast runs through every domain of religious expression. The rational and moral nature of God precludes His devising a method of salvation which is based on the acceptance of dogma and the surrender of the faculty of moral judgment.

Men must be judged by their "works," not by their faith. The good God could not have predetermined any individual or group of individuals for perdition. God requires from us, not the feelings of trust and total surrender, but our co-operation in the building of His Kingdom. God is love, but love is not the sheer feeling of benevolence; it is sustained devotion to the construction of the ideal society in this world. If religion be conceived as a field of tension between the pole of active, rational and moral piety, devoted to the "daytime" spirit of optimistic and constructive idealism, and the pole of passive, emotional piety, esthetic and reflective, devoted to the "nighttime" spirit of love, peace and goodwill, then Judaism, in all its diversity, will be found closer to the first pole. While the love of God in Islam is chiefly surrender to His Will, and love in Christianity is primarily an act of self-giving, love in Judaism is devotion to "the fashioning of the world into a Kingdom of God."

So the hero-image of Judaism is primarily the prophet, fighting for truth and justice, and secondarily the sage, studying and outlining the ideal patterns of the good life; the hero-image of Christianity is the mystic, whose soul has sounded the depths of the mystery of existence, and secondarily the saint who suffers in love for the sake of humanity.

The challenge of Judaism tends to make the Christian world more prophetic, more communal minded, more rational and ethical, more concerned with the "works" of love. The Christian challenge to Judaism tends to break down the self-exalting impetus of ethnicism and to caution against the externalization of religion and its hardening into a series of lifeless rituals. The rationalistic school in Judaism has always been responsive to the variety of intellectual and esthetic challenges posed to it by its daughter religion.

We cannot conclude our review of the currents of thought in historic Judaism without taking account of the question that has come to loom so large throughout the modern period: What is the significance of the Jewish tradition for western civilization and humanity as a whole?

It was the current of philosophical Judaism that placed the greatest emphasis on the concept of the Jew as the custodian of eternal truths for the sake of all mankind. But in this volume we found ourselves dealing with radically different versions of these truths. What happens to the concept of treasuring eternal truths if the exponents of Judaism differ so radically on the understanding of these truths?

Our answer to this question has been suggested throughout the discussion of this volume. We do not and cannot claim to know all about God nor all about man's need for salvation. As Jews, we do not strike the pose of all-knowing prophets, but rather "sons of prophets," determined seekers of truth. The Jews are heirs of a hundred generations of deeply earnest men and women who sought God by the feeble lights in their possession. They denied themselves many things for the sake of their faith, forswearing the luxuries of life and even life itself when the test came, but they never denied the God of their heart. The history of the Jewish faith is the magnificent tale of an endless quest by a world-wide community, a community of people remaining true to its search in spite of many temptations and refusing to compromise with its conscience.

The Jews became an eternal people because they set for themselves an endless task, a task that may never be consummated but that will be brought ever closer to realization. This task is all-embracing, presenting a challenge in every aspect of life. Because Judaism asserts the doctrine of God's unity, the task of comprehending His work in nature and in history is a never-ending challenge to human thought. God's unity cannot be comprehended within finite time, for the task of synthesizing all categories of wisdom expands as our knowledge grows. By insisting that human nature contains the "image of God," Judaism released a powerful, revolutionary force making for freedom and justice. This too is an impetus driving toward wide and then wider horizons, for the meaning of freedom and justice is unfolded only through the diverse processes of history. Because the Jewish religion is based on the doctrine of a covenant with God, the intellectual-ethical domain becomes the common ground of man and God. But the implications of this covenant at a particular time or in the vision of the future are worked out anew by every generation.

Abstract truths susceptible of verbal formulation belong to the universal society of scholars and thinkers. They can in no way be staked out as a private domain by any people or any community. A religious tradition represents the application of truth to the total life of a community, and this application of accumulated insights to the problems of life requires the agency of institutions, the charm of rites and the momentum of the love and loyalty of generations. But the task of applying eternal truths to temporary situations is never finally accomplished. Here is where the experience and wisdom of one tradition poses a challenge to and serves as a corrective for another tradition.

It is important to bear in mind the distinction between eternal truths and their embodiment in institutions. Abstract truths are best conveyed through books and through instruction within the academic world. The applied truths of religion, affecting as they do the whole of life, are transmitted through the institutions and practices of a living, historical community. Eternal truths are invigorated with the sinews of life by the impetus and scope of a vital tradition, but religious traditions may hinder as well as help the continuing application of truth to the ever-changing stream of life. A tradition may hallow a temporary application and erect it as a barrier against the free interaction of thought and life. The very greatness of a tradition, recording the successful confrontation of great problems with eternal truths in ages past may cause its adherents to become unduly worshipful of instruments and institutions, unduly arrogant toward other faiths and psychologically unable to meet fresh situations with creative vigor. The wholeheartedness and finality of a religious tradition preserves the spirited momentum of the past, but it tends to hallow the static solution rather than the ever-dynamic method. Hence, the mutual confrontation of two or more traditions is always helpful for the maintenance of their power of self-criticism and self-renewal.

The significance of the Jewish tradition within the larger context of western civilization consists precisely of the challenge it presents to other religious traditions. The historic stream of Judaism flows beside other streams, reflecting the same great tensions and problems within a different context and containing different solutions. It is because of the sameness of eternal truth and the difference of historic experience that Judaism confronts the other great religions with a creative and continuing challenge.

Jewish apologists felt themselves constrained in the past to insist on the "uniqueness" of Judaism. They thought that Judaism could be esteemed as being of surpassing worth only if

417

it were known as different from all other faiths in a deep and essential sense. Judaism, they felt, could be protected from the criticism that is freely directed at other traditions only if it were shown to be "unique." But the claim of uniqueness is itself far from being unique. Romantic writers of every nation and religious tradition love this word, for it seems to mark out a charmed circle, free from the revolving sword of reason. Actually, Judaism is unique in the same sense that other faiths are unique —as a compound, not as a chemical element. In the preceding chapters we have shown the variety of responses within it to the challenges of the hour. Each school of thought responded in the idiom used by the corresponding schools in other traditions. The history of Jewish thought, in all its multifarious expression, is of universal significance because it is the account of responses to perennial universal problems. Dealing with the great polar tensions of one religion, it reflects the dynamic forces in all religious cultures.

These polar tensions are threefold in character, corresponding to the three dimensions of every faith: its ideological structure and its search for truth; its institutional character, consisting of its rites and forms of worship; its sociological structure, outlining the duties of the individual to the other members of the "in" group, and the relation of the "in" group to the rest of mankind. These three dimensions correspond to a classification of Judaism attributed to Simon the Just—*Torah* (learning), *Avodah* (worship) and *Gemiluth Hassadim* (social obligations and acts of loving kindness).

The first polar tension is between the belief in one true faith and the assertion that all faiths are equally good and true for their worshipers. This tension may also be described in terms of the contrast between the subjective approach, which sanctions all that is one's own, and the objective point of view which rises above all possessive prejudices.

Both the dogmatists and the relativists, the intellectual isolationists and the champions of impartiality, find it easy to define their positions and to stake out their claims. But neither the cause of truth nor the spiritual welfare of humanity is served by them, for the spirit of man is expressed in both subjective feeling and objective thought. The authentic response of the human soul to this polarity is to find a dynamic balance of the two moods, resulting in a mediating position between the two extremes.

Within the Jewish tradition, we find several ways in which this tension was resolved. While the solutions of the past may not be entirely adequate for the problems of the present, they should not be ignored in searching for new solutions.

The second polar tension of religious tradition is that between the inner and outer expressions of the faith, between the emphasis on "the service of the heart" and the sacramental concept of ritual acts. Religions are inevitably articulated in institutions, myths and rites; else they are still-born abstractions. But the moment they are expressed in external actions, the danger arises of the external performance becoming a hallowed end in itself instead of being only an aid to piety. Hence, the dilemma: no religion without rituals; yet how often do the ritual acts stifle the inner life of the faith!

In some Christian circles, this polar tension is described as the contrast between Pharisaic Judaism and early Christianity. This hoary accusation is a delusion based upon the caricature of the ancient Pharisees and of Judaism. Actually, in Jewish tradition, as reviewed in this volume, we encountered several different ways of meeting this perennial problem of organized religion.

The third polar tension is perhaps the most important in our modern world. We find it the more difficult to visualize because we are ourselves caught up in its coils. It is the tension centering round the concept of a "chosen people." Is it the intention of this concept that the people ought to be dedicated to the ideals of God, or does it mean that the life of the people is supremely important because the ideals of God are attached to it? The two alternatives do not appear to be mutually exclusive. Yet there is a real choice between the two attitudes in every concrete situation. In the one case the community acts as a "prophet-people," gauging its policies by means of universal, ethical principles and sacrificing its own temporal welfare for the sake of its ideals. In the other case the welfare of the nation itself is ranked as the supreme value and embraced with the wholeheartedness and totality of devotion that is characteristic of genuine piety. In effect the second alternative turns nationalism itself into a zealous religion and all universal ideals are accorded only secondary significance. The posture of a "prophet-people" is still assumed, but the ideals of prophecy are no longer the goal of the nation's existence and the measuring rod of its actions, only so much guise and disguise.

The problem of a "chosen people" is not peculiar to Judaism, since every religious tradition of necessity accords supreme significance to the collective existence of its devotees. This tension is inseparable too from the impetus of nationalism, which in modern times has achieved, more than once, the devotions due religion. However, in Jewish tradition, the polar tension in the concept of the "chosen people" has had an unusually long and many-sided development. No one can expect to contribute to the resolution of this perennial problem without taking account of the variety of ways in which this problem was viewed in the long record of Jewish experience.

In sum, the significance of the Jewish tradition transcends the limits of the Jewish community.

The Jew does not claim to be the sole custodian of eternal truths, but he does set for himself the endless task of applying eternal truths to the changing problems of life. The Jewish people are heirs of a long tradition of truthful search. Within this tradition, we find different approaches to the solution of those perennial problems of a living faith, which every generation encounters afresh.

Thus we bring to a close this study of the faith that is life for the Jews and "a light unto all the nations."

NOTES

CHAPTER ONE

1. Y. Kaufman, *Toldoth Haemunah Hayisrealith*, III, 737.
2. Exodus 19:6. For a more detailed study see Kassuto, *Me-Noah ad Avraham* (Jerusalem, 1953), pp. 1-101.
3. Genesis 18:19.
4. Genesis 18:14.
5. Genesis 1:4.
6. Psalms 19:1.
7. Psalms 8:4, 5.
8. Proverbs 8:22, 23, 30, 31.
9. Proverbs 3:5, 6, 19.
10. Isaiah 44:6.
11. Genesis 18:25.
12. Isaiah 66:2.
13. I Samuel 16:7.
14. Jeremiah 12:1.
15. Psalms 92:7.
16. Job 42:10.
17. Isaiah 53:4, 5.
18. Deuteronomy 4:20.
19. Exodus 23:9. Deuteronomy 11:28.
20. Isaiah 48:10.
21. Proverbs 16:18.
22. Isaiah 10:5.
23. Isaiah 45:1.
24. Zephaniah 3:9.
25. I Samuel 26:19.
26. I Kings 8:41.
27. Deuteronomy 4:19.
28. Isaiah 14:6.
29. Jeremiah 25:15, 16.
30. Isaiah 19:22-24.
31. Isaiah 11:3.
32. Isaiah 11:9.
33. Micah 4:5. Malachi 1:11.
34. Jeremiah 16:19.
35. Micah 6:8. Jeremiah 31:31.
36. Jeremiah 12:15, 16.
37. I Kings 8:24, 25.
38. Leviticus 26:44. Deuteronomy 30:3-5.
39. Amos 9:11-14.
40. Jeremiah 31:30-33.
41. Isaiah 49:6.
42. Isaiah 56:6, 7.
43. Exodus 24:10.
44. Genesis 8:21.
45. II Samuel 22:11.
46. Genesis 6:6. Deuteronomy 1:34. Exodus 32:14. Isaiah 57:16.
47. Deuteronomy 29:19.
48. Ezekiel 1:28. Exodus 24:10.
49. Tur Sinni, *Leshon Vesefer*, Vol. III.
50. Exodus 33:20.
51. Exodus 34:6. See Maimonides' interpretation in *Guide to the Perplexed*, 1, 21.
52. I Kings 19:12.
53. Isaiah 6:1.
54. Isaiah 2:11.
55. Jeremiah 9:23.
56. Isaiah 2:12-19.
57. Amos 1, 3. Jonah 1:2.
58. Genesis 8:21. Jeremiah 17:9.
59. Isaiah 1:4.
60. Isaiah 6:3.
61. Leviticus 11:44.
62. See Gedalia Alon, *Mehkarim Betoldoth Yisroel* (Tel Aviv, 1957), p. 176.
63. Exodus 20:3.
64. Exodus 23:13.
65. Exodus 34:7.
66. II Kings 10:18-31, 18:4-6, 23:4-21. Hosea 2:4-17. Jeremiah 10:11, 25:31. Habakkuk 2:18.
67. Exodus 32:1-35.
68. I Samuel 15:22.
69. I Kings 18:1-40.
70. Deuteronomy 7:6.
71. Deuteronomy 7:8.
72. Exodus 19:6.
73. Amos 3:2.
74. Deuteronomy 4:19.

75. Numbers 23:19.
76. Isaiah 49:15.
77. Exodus 32:9-14.
78. Exodus 34:9.
79. Isaiah 10:22. Ezekiel 11:19. Jeremiah 23:3.
80. Deuteronomy 28:10.
81. Isaiah 42:6.
82. Zechariah 14:9.
83. Isaiah 2:3.
84. Zechariah 14:16.
85. Isaiah 19:23.
86. Isaiah 53.
87. Isaiah 30:15.
88. Amos 7:14.
89. Deuteronomy 18:18.
90. Deuteronomy 11:11.
91. I Samuel 26:19.
92. II Kings 5:18.
93. Ruth 1:16.
94. Exodus 25:22.
95. II Chronicles 6:36.

96. Numbers 15:38. Deuteronomy 15:1.
97. Genesis 17:11.
98. Deuteronomy 14:1.
99. Leviticus 25:5, 19:3, 25:37, 19:34, 19:32. Deuteronomy 24:17.
100. Deuteronomy 6:24, 25.
101. Isaiah 58:6.
102. Ezekiel 20:21. Isaiah 58:13. Jeremiah 17:22.
103. Ezekiel 40-48.
104. J. B. Pritchard, *Ancient Near Eastern Texts* (Princeton, N.J., 1950), p. 175.
105. *Ibid.*, p. 176.
106. Deuteronomy 24:16.
107. *Ancient Near Eastern Texts*, nos. 209-213, p. 175.
108. *Ibid.*, p. 183.
109. Deuteronomy 24:1-4.
110. Ezra 10:11.

CHAPTER TWO

1. Yoma 69 b.
2. Sukkoth 20 a.
3. Baba Kama 82 a, b.
4. Nehemiah 10:1, 30, 39.
5. Deuteronomy 18:15. Nehemiah 8:9, 15.
6. Sabbath 104 a.
7. I Maccabees 14:41.
8. Deuteronomy 33:4.
9. Travers Herford, *Pharisees* (London, 1924), p. 135.
10. Baba Bathra 12 a.
11. Bercohoth 33 a. Pirke Aboth 1: 2. *Dubnow, Divrai Yemai Am Olam*, II, 18.
12. I. Baer, *Yisroel Boamim*, p. 24. Y. Sabbath 1:3, the Mishnah of R. Pinhos ben Yair.
13. Ezekiel 44:13.
14. Jeremiah 17: 18.
15. Ezekiel 44.
16. Hagigah 3 a.

17. See Lauterbach, "Midrash and Mishnah" in *Rabbinic Essays* (Cincinnati, 1951), p. 163.
18. Sabbath 15 a.
19. Rosh Hashanah 31 a.
20. Exodus Rabba 41:6. See Hayim Chernowitz' *Toldoth Hahalachah* (New York, 1944), I, 60-80.
21. I. H. Weiss, *Dor Dor Vedorshov*, Book VI, Chap. VI.
22. Gedaliah Alon, *Mehkarim Betoldoth Yisroel* (Tel Aviv, 1957), pp. 115-117.
23. Sifri, Shoftim 175. Menahoth 99 b.
24. Sukkah 28 a.
25. Seder Eliyahu Zutta 2.
26. Deuteronomy 11:22.
27. Niddah 30 b.
28. Job 1:5.
29. Proverbs 9:10.
30. Jerusalem, Hagigah 1:7.

31. Pirke Aboth 3:17. W. Bacher, *Aggadoth Hatannaim* (Jerusalem, 1922), VII, 180.
32. Sota 14 b.
33. Canticles Rabba 1:6. Solomon Schechter, *Some Aspects of Rabbinic Theology*, p. 204. Plato, *Theatatus*, 176 b, *Republic*, 613 c, *Phaedrus*, 253 a, *Timaeus*, 90 c.
34. Isaiah 56:2.
35. Mechilta, Beshalah 4:5.
36. Mechilta, Yithro 8.
37. Sanhedrin 39 a.
38. Tanhuma, Vayigash, *Aggadoth Hatannaim*, I, 59.
39. *Aggadoth Hatannaim*, VI, 114.
40. Baba Kama 79 b.
41. Kiddushin 22 b. *Aggadoth Hatannaim*, I, 20.
42. Niddah 31 b.
43. Yalkut Shimeoni, Deuteronomy 12:31.
44. Vayikra Rabba 17:7. *Aggadoth Hatannaim*, VIII, 23.
45. *Aggadoth Hatannaim*, VIII, 23. Pesikta 192 b.
46. Amos 3:2.
47. Tosefta. Sanhedrin 13.
48. Makkoth, end.
49. Mechilta, Bo 5.
50. Genesis 15:8.
51. Bereshith Rabba 15.
52. Pirke Aboth 2:1.
53. *Aggadoth Hatannaim*, VII, 178. Pesikta 23.
54. Pirke Aboth 4:11. *Aggadoth Hatannaim*, IV, 9.
55. Vayikra Sifra 20:25.
56. *Aggadoth Hatannaim*, VI, 157.
57. Pirke Aboth 3:4.
58. Aboda Zara 5 a. Louis Ginsberg, *Legends of the Jews*, VI, 51.
59. Tosefta cited by Rav Hai Gaon in his introduction to the tractate *Tohoroth*. This comment is found in many variations, some of which indicate a rational, ethical kind of "purging." See Vayikra Rabba 13, Bereshith Rabba 44, *Aggadoth Hatannaim*, II, 45.

60. Pesikta 40, *Aggadoth Hatannaim*, I, 29.
61. Deuteronomy 17:16, 17.
62. I Kings 11:1-8.
63. *Aggadoth Hatannaim*, III, 80. Vayikra Rabba 19. Jerusalem Sanhedrin 2.
64. Ecclesiastes 7:16.
65. I Samuel 15, Yoma 22 b.
66. Leviticus 18:3.
67. Some scholars maintain that the "uncleanliness of Gentiles" antedated the beginning of the first century. See Gedaliah Alon, *Mehkarim Betoldoth Yisroel* (Tel Aviv, 1957), p. 146. Sabbath 17 b.
68. Aboda Zara 35 b.
69. Aboth 6, end.
70. Berachoth 33 b.
71. Jeremiah 33:25.
72. *Aggadoth Hatannaim*, VI, 170.
73. *Ibid.*, IV, 29, n. 65.
74. I. Baer, *Yisoel Boamin* (Jerusalem, 1955), p. 16.
75. Yoma 38 b.
76. *Aggadoth Hatannaim*, III, 50, n. 26, Sabbath 33 b, Sanhedrin 103 b.
77. Bereshith Rabba 1.
78. Yebamoth 63 a.
79. Bereshith Rabba I.
80. *Aggadoth Hatannaim*, VI, 29.
81. Aboth 5:1.
82. Berachoth 7 a.
83. Koheleth Rabba 6:12, Pesikta 192 b.
84. Bamidbar Rabba 12.
85. Sanhedrin 39 a.
86. Jerusalem Sanhedrin, end.
87. Berachoth 17 a.
88. Sukkah 49 b.
89. Pesikta 103.
90. *Aggadoth Hatannaim*, VI, 20
91. Berachoth 55 a.
92. *Aggadoth Hatannaim*, VI, 34.
93. Sabbath 88 a.
94. Aboda Zara 2 b.
95. Sanhedrin 56 a. Tosefta, Aboda Zara 9. Hulin 92 a.
96. Sanhedrin 63 b. Tossafoth "Ossur," Shulhan Oruch, Orah Hayim, 156.

97. Goodenough, "By Light, Light," Introduction *Encyclopedia of Religion and Ethics*, IX, 317; H. A. Wolfson, *Philo*, I, 7.
98. *Zion*, 1953, pp. 15-30.
99. Hulin 13 b.
100. Josephus, *Antiquities of the Jews*, 17:6, 2. Klausner, *Historia shel Habayith Hasheni*, IV, 164.
101. Maimonides' *Commentary on Mishnah*, Aboda Zara. Tossafoth, "Ossur." Yad hahazaka, Hilchoth Akum 9:4. Sanhedrin 63 b.
102. Micah 4:5.
103. Tosefta, Sanhedrin, 13. Klausner, *Historia shel Habayith Hasheni*, V, 45.
104. Klausner, *Miyeshu ad Paulus* (Tel Aviv, 1940), I, 37-45.
105. Abboth di Rabbi Nathan 52:18.
106. Sanhedrin 90 a.
107. Genesis 18:21.
108. Exodus 33:22.
109. Genesis 3:8.
110. Exodus 25:22.
111. Exodus 16:10
112. Isaiah 6:2.
113. I Kings 19:12.
114. Taanith 31 a.
115. Pesikta 20, Tanhuma, Naso.
116. For opposite views see Rosh Hashono 31 a, Tanhuma, Shemoth 10.
117. Sotah 3 b.
118. Berachoth 5 b.
119. Sabbath 12 b.
120. Hagigah 14 a.
121. Sabbath 31 a.
122. Tanna dibai Eliyahu 9.
123. Baba Bathra 15 b.
124. Berachoth 30 a.
125. Yoma 9 b.
126. Baba Bathra 12 a.
127. Yoma 9 b.
128. Airuvin 13 b.
129. Baba Metzia 59 b.
130. Taanith, 3rd Chapter.
131. Hagigah 13 a. Sukkah 28 a. David Neumark, *Toldoth Haikkarim Beyisroel*.
132. Bereshith Rabba 4.
133. Sanhedrin 39 a.
134. Midrash Shohar Tov 90.
135. Jerusalem Taanith 2. Sanhedrin 103 a.
136. Berachoth 50 a.
137. Berachoth 60 a.
138. Sabbath 152 a.
139. Nazir 23 b.
140. Berachoth 8 a.
141. Sabbath 33 a.
142. Sanhedrin 91 a.
143. Berachoth 17 a.
144. Berachoth 39 a.
145. Sanhedrin 99 a.
146. Berachoth 25 a.
147. Kiddushin 40 b Aboda Zara 4 a.
148. Berachoth 7 a. Sabbath 33 b.
149. Sabbath 55 a, b.
150. Sabbath 146 a.
151. Sabbath 33 a.
152. Baba Mezia 85 a. Sukkah 28 a.
153. Taanith 8 a.
154. Zebahim 62 a.
155. Pesikta 35.
156. *Aggadoth Hatannaim*, I, 163, II, 63.

CHAPTER THREE

1. Isaiah 44:19.
2. Ezekiel 20:32.
3. Isaiah 45:7. Isaiah 66:1.
4. See, for example, Plutarch's interpretation of the Egyptian religion in *De Iside et Osiride*;
H. A. Wolfson, *Philo*, I. 6, 7.
5. Philo, *Mission to Caius*, p. 45.
6. S. Baron, *A Social and Religious History of the Jews* (rev. ed.; Philadelphia, 1952), pp. 171-179.
7. Isaiah 2:3.

8. Josephus, *Against Apion*, II. 39.
9. Charles' edition of *Sibylline Oracles*, Chaps. 1-7.
10. *Ibid.*, 218-277.
11. *Ibid.*, 767-784.
12. Renan, *The History of Israel*, Vol. II.
13. Josephus, *Against Apion*, II, 39.
14. *Wisdom of Solomon*, 14.
15. *Ibid.*, 1:4.
16. *Ibid.*, 14:12.
17. See Romans 1:27, *Sibylline Oracles*, III, 185-186.
18. *Wisdom of Solomon*, 11:17, 7:22-8:1.
19. H. A. Wolfson, *Philo*, Vol. I, Introduction.
20. *Life of Abraham*, II, 21.
21. S. Baron, *A Social and Religious History of the Jews* (rev. ed.), I, 240.
22. Tacitus, *Annals*, V, 4.
23. Sotah 5 a.
24. *De Migratione Abrahami*, 8. *De Specialibus Legibus* 1:8.
25. Wolfson, *Philo*, II, 27.
26. *Ibid.*, I, 328.
27. Sanhedrin 11 a. Baba Mezia 59 b.
28. *De Decalogue*, 11. Norman Bentwich, *Philo* (Philadelphia, 1910), 146.
29. *De Somniis*, II, 37.
30. *Life of Moses*, II, 47, 261.
31. *De Orificio Mundi*, 2, 8.
32. *Life of Abraham*, 24, 122.
33. Phaedrus, 245, 249.
34. *De Congresu Eruditionis Gratia*, 26. 92.
35. *De Vita Moses*, II, 35, 188.
36. *Ibid.*, II, 39, 213.
37. Exodus 20:18.
38. I. Heinemann, *Darchai Haaggadah* (Jerusalem, 1950), 80.
39. *De Orificio Mundi*, 1, 3.
40. Philo, *De Fuga et Inventione*, 12, 36. Plato, *The Laws*, IV, 716. Sota 14 a.
41. *De Specialibus Legibus*, IV, 25, 134.
42. *De Migrationi Abrahami*, 16, 93.
43. *De Posteritate Caini*, 3, 11.
44. *De Cherubim*, 29, 99-100.
45. *De Providentia*, 2, 64.
46. *De Specialibus*, IV, 34, 179.
47. *De Vita Moses*, II, 7, 49.
48. Wolfson, *Philo*, II, 415-417.
49. *De Praemiis et Poeniis*, 29, 165.
50. Wolfson, *Philo*, II, 415.
51. I Maccabees 1:11.
52. *De Josepho*, II, 360.
53. Bentwich, *Philo*, p. 127.
54. *De Praemiis et Poeniis*, 44.
55. *Ibid.*, 29, 169.
56. *De Decalogo*, 20.
57. Isaac Heinemann, *Darchai Haaggadah* (Tel Aviv, 1950), p. 157.
58. *Letter of Aristeas*, 142. Another wri.er affirmed that nonkosher food was not good for the soul. " He [God] has commanded that we eat the things that will be fitting for our souls, and He has forbidden us to eat meats that will be contrary to our souls." (IV Maccabees 5:26).
59. *De Specialibus Legibus*, 11, 414.
60. *Quis Rerum Divinarum Heres*, 53.
61. Wolfson, *Philo*, I, 412.
62. *De Gigantibus*, 3, 12.
63. Plato, *Timaeus*, 42 b. *Phaedrus*, 249 b.
64. Louis Finkelstein, *Mave Limasecheth Aboth di Rabbi Nathan*, pp. 212-222. Suggests that Hillelites and Shammaites differed regarding the nature of immortality.
65. Goodenough, " By Light, Light," pp. 115, 180.
66. *Ibid.*, Chapts. 4, 5.
67. *De Fuga et Inventione*, 108.
68. Goodenough, "By Light, Light," p. 136.
69. *De Somniis*, II, 187-189.
70. *Ibid.*, 139.
71. *Questiones et Solutiones in Genesion*, 8.
72. I. Heinemann, *Darchai Haaggadah*, p. 186.
73. Wolfson, *The Philosophy of the Church Fathers* (Cambridge, Mass., 1956), Chap. II.
74. Hagigah 11 b.

CHAPTER FOUR

1. Matthew 23:3.
2. Pesahim 49 a. Definitions of *am haarez* in Berachoth 47 b. Bechoroth 30 b, on manner of receiving a *haver*, a member of the Pharisaic society, Demai, Chapter II.
3. Hullin 106 a.
4. Gedaliah Alon, Mehkarim Betoldoh Yisroel, p. 168.
5. Aidoyoth, Chap. 5. Mark 7:1-9. Matthew 15:1-3.
6. Mark 7:10-14. Matthew 15:3-12.
7. Hagigah 10 a. Y. Kaufman, *Goleh Venaichar*, I, 351.
8. Matthew 19:3-10. Mark 10:1-12. Solomon Schechter, *Fragments of a Zadokite Work*. Kiddushin 21 b.
9. Jerusalem, Nedarim, 9, 4.
10. Matthew 22:32. Sanhedrin 90 b.
11. Matthew 12:1-21. Mark 2:23-28. Luke 6:1-5.
12. Mechilta, *Tisa*.
13. Matthew 9:3-8. Mark 2:5-12.
14. Matthew 6:1-34.
15. Matthew 23:15.
16. Matthew 15:26.
17. Matthew 10:5.
18. Sanhedrin 96 b.
19. Abodah Zara 10 b.
20. Matthew 11:3.
21. Matthew 11:3-15.
22. Ethiopian book of Enoch, Chap. 45.
23. Matthew 16:13-20. Mark 8:27-29. Luke 9:18-20.
24. Matthew 12:28.
25. Matthew 10:1. Mark 3:13-16.
26. Luke 19:38.
27. Luke 19:11.
28. Luke 20:1-18.
29. Erubin 43 b.
30. Sanhedrin 89 a.
31. H. A. Wolfson, *The Philosophy of the Church Fathers* (Cambridge, 1956), p. 157.
32. *Dialogue with Trypho the Jew*, Chap. 49.
33. Sanhedrin 93 a, b.
34. It is interesting to note that this point was asserted by Rabbi Abraham ben David (Rab D) in his criticism of Maimonides' definition of the function of a Messiah. Yad Hahazakah, *Hilchoth Melochim*, end.
35. Berachoth 28 b, Aboth di Rabbi Nathan 51, 25, ed. Schechter.
36. Derech Erez Zutta 81.
37. Vayikra Rabba 34. Yalkut, *Vayaishev*.
38. Edoyoth 8:5.
39. Ginsberg, *Legends of the Jews*, VI, 322-323.
40. Baruch 83-90.
41. Enoch 45:3, 6.
42. *Ibid.*, 48:7-10.
43. *Wisdom of Solomon*, 17-21, 44.
44. I Chronicles 22:10.
45. Fourth Esdras 12:32. Words in brackets are taken from the Syriac version.
46. *Ibid.*, 13:9, 10, 38.
47. Matthew 21:12-15. Luke 19:45. Mark 11:17.
48. Luke 10:30-37. J. Mann discusses the meaning of this parable in the *Jewish Quarterly Review*, Vol. VI.
49. Luke 22:48-50. Luke 20:25.
50. John 11:47-54.
51. Joel 3:1.
52. Acts 10:45-48.
53. *Antiquities* 20:2, 4.
54. Yebamoth 46 a.
55. Acts 15:1.
56. Galatians 5:2.
57. Acts 15:20.
58. Acts 15:10.
59. Acts 6:1.
60. Acts 6:9, 7:1, 59.
61. Kethuboth 110 b.
62. J. Klausner, *Historia shel Habayith Hasheni*, IV, 260. Claude G. Montefiore's *The Synoptic Gospels*, 2 volumes, is a study of Christian-Jewish parallels.

63. Acts 5:34-39.
64. II Corinthians 12:2.
65. Romans 14:17.
66. Berachoth 17 a.
67. Berachoth 34 b. Sanhedrin 99 a.
68. Ephesians 6:5.
69. Romans 13:1, 2.
70. Quoted by Herbert J. Muller, *The Uses of the Past*, p. 269.
71. Colossians 1:14, 15.
72. Sanhedrin 38 b.
73. Hullin 91 b. Legend on Jacob discussed in L. Ginsberg's *Legends of the Jews*, VI, 271.
74. Bereshith Rabba, 77.
75. Galatians 4:6, 7.
76. "Mystery of Christ" in Ephesians 3:4. "The wisdom that hath been hidden" in I Corinthians 2:7.
77. Tosefta, Sanhedrin 13.
78. Hullin 13 b.
79. Galatians 1:8, 9.
80. II Thessalonians 2:13.
81. II Thessalonians 1:8.
82. Romans 9:3.
83. Romans 11:11.
84. Romans 11:25, 26.
85. I Corinthians 15:51.
86. Romans 13:14.
87. I Corinthians 12:3.
88. I Corinthians 3:18.
89. Ephesians 1:4.
90. Niddah 16 b.
91. Aboth 3:15.
92. Romans 7:19.
93. Kiddushin 30 b.
94. Sanhedrin 99 a.
95. Sanhedrin 99 b.
96. Galatians 2:21.
97. Romans 6:5.
98. Galatians 5:2.
99. Bacher, *Aggadoth Hatannaim*, II, 34.
100. Berachoth 7 a.
101. Vayira Rabba 17:7.
102. Menahoth 111 a.
103. Jerusalem Sanhedrin 12.
104. Aboth di Rabbi Nathan 4.
105. Zebahim 88 b.
106. Moed Kattan 28 a. Yoma 5 a. Zebahim 6 a. Sifra, Leviticus I, 4, ed. Weiss.
107. Zebahim 62 a. Hagigah 12 b. L. Ginsberg, *Legends of the Jews*, VI, 381.
108. Frazer, *The Golden Bough*, Part IV, Book I.
109. Ephesians 2:14.
110. Romans 11:11.
111. Matthew 27:25.
112. *Sefer Havikuah Lehoramban*, 12.
113. Salo Baron, *A Social and Religious History of the Jews* (1st ed.), I, 370.
114. Matthew 23:15.
115. Baba Mezia 59 b. Yebamoth 109 b.
116. Pesahim 87 b. Nedarim 32 a.
117. James Parkes, *The Conflict Between Church and Synagogue*.
118. Psalms 115:1, 2.
119. James Parkes, *The Conflict Between Church and Synagogue*, p. 63.
120. *Ibid.*
121. *Ibid.*, p. 70.
122. *Ibid.*, p. 101.

CHAPTER FIVE

1. Ch. Chernowitz, *Toldoth Haposkim* (New York, 1946), I, 25, 29. Z. H. Chayoth, *Mavo Hamishna*.
2. *Teshuvoth Hagaonim*, 56. Note also the expression, *Kach herunu min hashomaim* ("so were we shown from Heaven") in the same Responsum. B. Z. Diaburg, *Yisroel Bagolah* (Tel Aviv, 1926), pp. 133, 134.
3. The rejection of the Palestinian

Talmud by the Babylonian authorities was an immense forward step in the progressive adaptation of Judaism to the conditions of life in the Diaspora. The laws of "purity" as regards prayer and study, the system of priestly "gifts" and the laws restricting contact with Gentiles were greatly eased. The authority of the secular government in money matters was explicitly acknowledged. L. Ginsberg, *Of Jewish Law and Lore* (Philadelphia, 1955), pp. 12-19.

4. *Shaarai Teshuvah*, no. 187. Attributed to Rav Natronai Gaon.
5. *Toldoth Haposkim*, I, 19.
6. I. H. Weiss, *Dor Dor Vedorshov*, IV, Chap. 8.
7. A. E. Harkavy, *Zichron Lorishonim*, p. 139.
8. *Ibid.*, p. 176.
9. A. E. Harkavy, *Anan*, pp. 12, 13.
10. S. Pinsker, *Likutai Kadmoniyoth*, p. 31-33.
11. *Ibid.*
12. Tuvya ben Moshe, *Ozar Nehmad*. Quoted by R. Mahler, *Qaraimer* (New York, 1947), p. 309.
13. *Dor dor Vedorshov*, IV, 94. *Halizah* is the ceremony described in Deuteronomy 25:9 for the release of the childless widow of one's brother.
14. *Dor dor Vedorshov*, IV, 75.

15. *Eshkol Hakofer*, Book 4, par. 74.
16. *Dor dor Vedorshov*, IV, 86.
17. *Ibid.*, IV, 102-103.
18. *Likutai Kadmoniyoth*, pp. 31, 32.
19. *Shaarai Teshuvah*, no. 23. *Yisroel Bagolah*, II, 177.
20. A. E. Harkavy, *Anan*, p. 189. R. Mahler, *Qaraimer*, p. 214. The opposition of the early Qaraites to the study of the sciences and philosophy may also be attributed to their zealous Biblicism, i.e., their insistence that the study of the Holy Scriptures is altogether sufficient for the attainment of all that man legitimately desires.
21. *Qaraimer*, p. 178.
22. *Taanith* 30 b.
23. J. Mann, the *Jewish Quarterly Review*, XII, 285.
24. *Sanhedrin* 97 b.
25. *Likutai Kadmoniyoth*, p. 36.
26. M. Maimonides, *Yad Hahazakah*, *Hilchoth Maacholoth Asuroth*, Chaps. 12-32.
27. J. Mann, *Karaitica*, pp. 800-803. *Qaraimer*, Chap. 10.
28. *Eshkol Hakofer*, *Aleph*.
29. *Seder Tefiloth Hakaraim* (Vienna, 1859).
30. *Karaitica*, p. 169.
31. *Zichron Lorishonim*, pp. 12, 374 *Toldoth Haposkim*, I, 28.
32. I. Husik, *A History of Medieval Jewish Philosophy* (New York, 1930), p. XXV.

CHAPTER SIX

1. Saadia, *Emunoth Vedeoth*, Chap. 1, par. 3.
2. *Ibid.*, Introduction.
3. *Ibid*, Introduction.
4. *Ibid.*, 2:5.
5. *Ibid.*, 2:1.
6. *Ibid.*, 2:10.
7. *Ibid.*, 2:10.
8. *Ibid.*, 2:10.
9. *Ibid.*, 2:10.
10. Exodus 19:21.
11. *Emunoth Vedeoth*, 2:11.
12. *Ibid.*, 3:1.
13. *Ibid.*, Introduction, 6.
14. *Ibid.*, 3:1.
15. *Ibid.*, 3:2.

16. *Ib:d.*, 3:10.
17. *Ibid.*, 3:10. Leviticus 16:22.
18. *Emunoth Vedeoth*, 3:5.
19. *Ibid.*, 3:4.
20. *Ibid.*, 3:6.
21. *Ibid*, 3:5.
22. *Ibid.*, 3.6.
23. *Ibid.*, Introduction, 6.
24. *Ibid.*, 3:8.
25. *Ibid.*, 4:4.
26. *Ibid.*, 4:2.
27. *Ibid.*, 5:1.
28. *Ibid.*, 5:1.
29. *Ibid.*, 5:5.
30. *Ibid.*, 5:5.
31. *Ibid.*, 5:5.
32. *Yoma* 86 b.
33. Maimonides, *Yad Hahazakah, Hilchoth Teshuvah*, 2:2.
34. Bahya Ibn Pakuda, *Hovoth Halevovoth*, Introduction.
35. *Ibid.*, Gate 1.
36. *Ibid.*, Gate 1.
37. *Ibid.*, Gate 1.
38. *Ibid.*, Gate 1.
39. *Ibid.*, Gate 1:6.
40. *Ibid.*, Gate 1:10.
41. *Ibid.*, Gate 1:10.
42. *Ibid.*, Gate 1:10.
43. *Ibid.*, Gate 2:1.
44. *Ibid.*, Gate 2:5.
45. *Ibid.*, Gate 3:3.
46. *Ibid.*, Gate 3:5.
47. *Ibid.*, Gate 4:3.
48. *Ibid.*, Gate 4:1.
49. *Ibid.*, Gate 4:1.
50. *Ibid.*, Gate 9:2.
51. *Ibid.*, Gate 5:5.
52. *Ibid.*, Gate 9:2.
53. *Ibid.*, Gate 6:7.
54. *Ibid.*, Gate 7:8.
55. *Ibid.*, Gate 7:10.
56. *Ibid.*, Gate 8:3.
57. *Ibid.*, Gate 8:3.
58. *Ibid.*, Gate 8:4.
59. *Ibid.*, Gate 10:7.
60. *Ibid.*, Gate 10:1.
61. *Ibid.*, Gate 10:1.
62. *Ibid.*, Gate 10:3.
63. *Ibid.*, Gate 9:3, 4.
64. *Ibid.*, Gate 9:5.
65. *Ibid.*, Gate 8:3.
66. *Ibid.*, Gate 4:4.

67. *Moreh Nebukhim*, Introduction.
68. *Ibid.*, 1:31.
69. *Ibid.*, 3:51, Commentary *ad locum* of Shem Tov.
70. *Ibid.*, 3:51.
71. *Ibid.*, 1:31.
72. *Ibid.*, 1:71.
73. *Ibid.*, 2:4.
74. *Ibid.*, 2:5.
75. *Ibid.*, 2:7.
76. *Ibid.*, 2:22.
77. *Ibid.*, 2:29.
78. *Ibid.*, 1:53.
79. *Ibid.*, 1:56.
80. *Ibid.*, 1:57.
81. *Ibid.*, 1:59.
82. *Ibid.*, 1:54.
83. *Ibid.*, 1:65.
84. *Ibid.*, 1:65.
85. *Ibid.*, 1:66.
86. *Ibid.*, 1:19.
87. *Ibid.*, 1:36. See also Shem Tov's commentary to Introduction.
88. *Ibid.*, 1:37, commentary of Afudi, *ad locum.*
89. *Ibid.*, 1:46, commentaries of Afudi and Shem Tov, *ad locum.*
90. *Ibid.*, 2:16.
91. *Ibid.*, 2:36.
92. *Ibid.*, 1:34.
93. *Ibid.*, 2:32.
94. *Ibid.*, 2:36.
95. Abraham J. Heschel, *Haeemin Horambam shehigia linvva?*, in *sefer Hayovel Lichvod Prof. Ginsberg.*
96. *Ibid.*, 3:33.
97. *Ibid.*, 2:31.
98. *Ibid.*, 3:28.
99. *Ibid.*, 3:28.
100. *Ibid.*, 3:36.
101. *Ibid.*, 3:34.
102. *Ibid.*, 3:28, commentary of Shem Tov *ad locum.*
103. *Ibid.*, 3:32.
104. *Ibid.*, 3:29.
105. *Ibid.*, 3:32.
106. *Ibid.*, 3:37.
107. Leviticus 2:11, 13.
108. *Moreh Nebukhim*, 3:46.
109. *Ibid.*, 3:46.
110. *Ibid.*, 3:45.
111. *Ibid.*, 3:47.

112. *Ibid.*, 3:47.
113. *Ibid.*, 3:48.
114. Numbers 5:18.
115. Deuteronomy 25:9.
116. *Moreh Nebukhim,* 3:49.
117. *Ibid.*, 3:41.
118. *Ibid.*, 2:48.
119. *Ibid.*, 3:11.
120. *Ibid.*, 2:47
121. *Ibid.*, 3:17.
122. *Ibid.*, 3:18.
123. *Ibid.*, 3:23.
124. *Ibid.*, 1:70.
125. *Ibid.*, 3:51.
126. H. Auerbach, *Albalag* (Breslau, 1906).
127. I. Albalag, *Deoth Hapilosophim,* p. 52.
128. *Ibid.*, p. 47.
129. I. Zinberg, *Geschichte fun Yidisher Literatur,* Part 4, Book I, Appendix.
130. Gersonides (Ralbag), *Milhamoth Hashem,* Introduction.
131. Gersonides, *Toaltioth,* commentary on the Bible.
132. Gersonides, *Milhamoth Hashem,* 4:5.
133. *Ibid.*, 3:4.
134. *Ibid.*, 1:11.
135. *Ibid.*, 1:13.

CHAPTER SEVEN

1. H. A. Wolfson, *Crescas' Critique of Aristotle* (Cambridge, 1929), Introduction.
2. H. Crescas, *Or Adonoi,* Book I, Section 3, paragraph 5.
3. *Ibid.*, 1:3, 5.
4. *Ibid.*, 2:1:6.
5. *Ibid.*, 2:4:3.
6. *Ibid.*, 2:4:3.
7. Nahmanides, *Perush at Hatorah, Bereshith,* 2.
8. *Or Adonoi,* 2:1:6.
9. *Aboda Zara* 22 b.
10. L. Ginsberg, *Legends of the Jews* (Philadelphia, 1942), V, 254.
11. *Or Adonoi,* 2:6:1.
12. *Ibid.*, 2:2:4.
13. *Ibid.*, 3:8:1.
14. *Ibid.*, 2:5:6.
15. *Ibid.*, 2:3:1.
16. *Ibid.*, 3:3:3.
17. *Ibid.*, 2:1:1.
18. J. Albo, *Sefer Haikkarim,* Book I, paragraph 24.
19. *Ibid.*, 1:5.
20. *Ibid.*, 1:8.
20a. *Ibid.*, 1:25.
21. Ch. Chernowitz, *Toldoth Hahalachah* (New York, 1944), Vol. 4, Appendix.
22. *Sefer Haikkarim,* 1:2, 3:29.
23. Maimonides, *Perush al Hamishnah, Makkoth,* end.
24. *Sefer Haikkarim,* 1:21.
25. *Ibid.*, 1:18.
26. *Ibid.*, 1:19.
27. *Ibid.*, 1:21.
28. *Ibid.*, 1:24.
29. *Ibid.*, 3:14.
30. *Ibid.*, 3:14.
31. *Ibid.*, 3:16. A play on words in Hebrew.
31a. *Ibid.*, 3:23.
32. *Ibid.*, 3:3.
33. *Ibid.*, 2:15.
34. *Ibid.*, 3:32.
35. *Ibid.*, 3:31.
36. *Ibid.*, 3:4.
37. *Ibid.*, 3:28.
38. *Ibid.*, 3:31.
39. *Ibid.*, 3:33.
40. *Ibid.*, 3:36.
41. *Ibid.*, 4:50.
42. *Ibid.*, 2:11.
43. *Ibid.*, 4:41.
44. *Ibid.*, 4:22.
45. *Ibid.*, 2:13.
46. *Ibid.*, 1:51.
47. *Ibid.*, 4:48.
48. *Ibid.*, 4:38.

49. *Ibid.*, 4:35.
50. *Ibid.*, 4:34. Kethuboth 103 a.
51. *Sefer Haikkarim*, 4:19.
52. *Ibid.*, 3:7.
53. *Ibid.*, 1:18.
54. I. Arame, *Akaidath Yizhak*, Gate 7.
55. I. Arame, *Hazuth Kashoth*, Chap. 10.
56. *Ibid.*, Chap. 8.
57. *Ibid.*, Chap. 8.
58. *Akaidath Yizhak*, Gate 12.
59. Nahmanides, *Perush al Hatorah*, Shemoth 21:19.
60. *Akaidath Yizhak*, Gate 26.
61. *Ibid.*, Gate 18.
62. *Ibid.*, Gate 56.
63. *Ibid.*, Gate 44.

64. *Ibid.*, Gate 48.
65. *Ibid.*, Gate 82.
66. *Ibid.*, Gate 88.
67. *Ibid.*, Gate 88.
68. *Ibid.*, Gate 44.
69. *Ibid.*, Gate 58.
70. *Ibid.*, Gate 58.
71. *Hazuth Kashoth*, Chap. 4. *Akaidath Yizhak*, Gate 22.
72. *Akaidath Yizhak*, Gate 60.
73. Joseph Ya-abetz, *Or Hahayim*, Chap. 1.
74. *Ibid.*, Chap. 2.
75. *Ibid.*, Chap. 2.
76. *Ibid.*, Chap. 5.
77. *Ibid.*, Chap. 4.
78. *Ibid.*, Chap. 4.

CHAPTER EIGHT

1. Husik, *A History of Medieval Jewish Philosophy* (New York, 1930), pp. 59-79.
2. *Mekor Hayim,* Hebrew translation (Tel Aviv, 1950), Gate I, Chap. 6.
3. *Ibid.*, I, 7.
4. *Ibid.*, I, 14.
5. *Ibid.*, I, 16.
6. *Ibid.*, II, 2.
7. *Ibid.*, V, 24.
8. *Ibid.*, V, 39.
9. *Ibid.*, V, 39.
10. *Ibid.*, V, 40.
11. The comparison of creation to writing is found in the selections from *Shem Tov ben Palkira*, no. 62.
12. Selection from *Shem Tov ben Palkira*, 44.
13. Historians are divided on the date of Halevi's birth, which occurred in 1075 or 1080 or 1085. The date of his death is also unknown, although it is placed after 1140.
14. *Kusari*, I, 1.

15. *Ibid.*, II, 50.
16. *Ibid.*, III, 67.
17. *Ibid.*, III, 49.
18. *Ibid.*, IV, 16.
19. *Ibid.*, I, 196.
20. *Ibid.*, I, 103.
21. *Ibid.*, II, 54.
22. *Ibid.*, II, 44.
23. *Ibid.*, II, 8.
24. *Ibid.*, II, 34.
25. *Ibid.*, II, 23.
26. *Ibid.*, V, 27.
27. *Ibid.*, I, 89.
28. *Ibid.*, V, 3.
29. *Ibid.*
30. *Ibid.*, IV, 25.
31. *Ibid.*, IV, 3.
32. *Ibid.*, IV, 5.
33. *Ibid.*, IV, 16.
34. *Ibid.*, IV, 17.
35. *Ibid.*, II, 26.
36. *Ibid.*
37. *Ibid.*, III, 53.
38. *Ibid.*, I. 109.
39. *Ibid.*
40. *Ibid.*, I, III.
41. Selected from *Ibid.*, III, 3-11.

CHAPTER NINE

1. See introduction to J. Tishbi, *Mishnath Hazoar.*
2. *Teshuvoth HaBah Hayshonoth,* 5.
3. *Torath Haolah,* III, 4.
4. *Nefesh HaHayim,* IV; see also the introduction of Rabbi Hayim Volozhin to the commentary of Rabbi Elijah of Vilna to the *Safro Dizniuta.* Printed in *Shiveath Hameoroth* (Vilna, 1913).
5. *Teshuvoth Ha-Rivosh,* 157.
6. *Ari Noem,* 15.
7. J. Yavetz, *Mitpahath Seforim.*
8. Rabbi Meir Ibn Gabbai, *Avodath HaKodesh,* III, 18.
9. R. Shem Tov ben Shem Tov, *Sefer Hoemunoth,* IV, 14.
10. J. Eibeshutz, *Shem Olam* (Vienna, 1891), p. 11.
11. *Shomair Emunim,* I—Dispute. See also beginning of *Sefer Ha-Peliah,* where a human being is created by a combination of letters and then restored by reversing the formula.
12. *Guide to the Perplexed,* I, 62.
13. *Avodath HaKodesh,* III, 17.
14. *Ibid.*
15. See reference above to chain of authority; also, *Meirath Ainim,* Beshalach; commentary of *Rikanati on Torah,* Nasso.
16. *Guide to the Perplexed,* I, 53.
17. *Ibid.,* III, 28:36:32.
18. Basila, *Emunath Hakhamim,* Chap. 13.
19. Commentary of RabD to *Sefer Yezirah,* p. 54; also R. Hayim Vital in beginning of *Aitz Hayim.*
20. See *Zohar,* Hakdomo.
21. *Shomair Emunim,* p. 27.
22. Quoted in the name of Rabbi Isaac the Blind in *Shem Olam,* p. 77; see also commentary of RabD to *Sefer Yezirah.*
23. *Shem Olam,* p. 41.
24. See *Shefa Tal,* Chap. 13; *Tanya,* Chap. 6; *Nefesh Ha-Hayim,* I, 4. On the other hand, note the opposing view of R. Elijah Ginazina: " But know that the other nations can also effect some improvements in the channels, when they observe the seven Noachide *mizvoth,* but their improvements are not as perfect as those of the 613 *mizvoth.*" (*Iggeret Hamudoth,* p. 37.)
25. *Alima Rabati,* ain Kol Tamar, I, 15.
26. *Ibid.,* II, 6-18.
27. *Pardes Rimonim,* shaar haotiot, II.
28. *Shem Olam.*
29. R. M. Ch. Lazzato, *Kelach Pithhai Hokhmo,* introduction.
30. *Pardes Rimonim,* shaar taam hoaziluth. Some Qabbalists referred to the *Sefiroth* as quasi-spatial entities. See *Kelach Pithhai Hokhmo,* 29: " But, before space came into being, it was impossible for anything to exist; only after space came to be, the *sefiroth* emerged in accordance with the nature of space." Of particular interest is the manner in which the category of space is derived by some writers from the ten *sefiroth.* As the infinitesimal point " expands " out of the naught, it asserts itself along three dimensions, each of which possesses a beginning, middle, and end, thus reflecting the number ten. This derivation has its philosophic parallel in the " critical " philosophy of Hermann Cohen, particularly his *Category of the Source.*
31. *Nahar Shalom,* in introduction.

CHAPTER TEN

1. See *Age of Adventure* (Boston, 1957), p. 167.
2. Mosheh Shulwass, *Hayai HaYehudim beItalia* (New York), 1955.
3. Solomon Ibn Virga (ed. I. Baer), *Shaivet Yehudah* (Jerusalem, 1947).
4. Leone Ebreo, *The Philosophy of Love* (London, 1937).
5. *Ibid.*, p. 34.
6. *Ibid.*, p. 47.
7. *Ibid.*, p. 48.
8. *Ibid.*, p. 50.
9. *Ibid.*, p. 55.
10. *Ibid.*, p. 144.
11. *Ibid.*, p. 296.
12. *Ibid.*, p. 330.
13. *Ibid.*, p. 375.
14. *Ibid.*, p. 397.
15. *Ibid.*, p. 106.
16. A. H. Wolfson, " Spinoza " in *Menorah Journal*, winter, 1951.
17. Preface to *Tractatus Theologica-Politicus*, trans. by R. H. M. Elwes (London, 1909).
18. *Ibid.*, Chap. 1.
19. *Ibid.*
20. *Ibid.*
21. *Ibid.*, Chap. 3.
22. *Ibid.*, Chap. 2.
23. *Ibid.*, Chap. 6.
24. *Ibid.*
25. *Ibid.*, Chap. 4.
26. *Ibid.*, Chap. 5.
27. *Ibid.*
28. *Ibid.*, Chap. 3.
29. *Ibid.*, Chap. 14.
30. *Ibid.*, Chap. 12.
31. *Ibid.*, Chap. 1.
32. *Ibid.*, Chap. 12.
33. *Ibid.*, Chap. 1.
34. *Ibid.*, Chap. 14.
35. *Ibid.*, Chap. 3.
36. *Ibid.*
37. *Ibid.*
38. *Ibid.*, Chap. 15.
39. *Ibid.*, p. 196.
40. *Ethics*, Part V, prop. XIX.
41. *Ibid.*, end of Part I.
42. *Ibid.*, Part V, prop. XV.
43. *Ibid.*, Part II, Note 2.
44. *Ibid.*, Part V, prop. XX, Note 5.
45. *Ibid.*, Part V, prop. XXVII.
46. *Ibid.*, Part V, prop. XXXII.
47. *Ibid.*, Part V, prop. XXXVI.
48. *Ibid.*, Part V, prop. XXXVIII.
49. *Ibid.*, Part V, end.

CHAPTER ELEVEN

1. Thus, for example, *Reshith Hochma*, by Elijah de Vidash, a disciple of Moses Cordovero.
2. An example of this prosaic Qabbalah is the book *Pithhai Shearim*, by Rabbi Isaac Hover (Warsaw, 1888).
3. *Sefer Hasidim* (Jerusalem, 1957), paragraph 206.
4. G. Scholem, *Sabbatai Zevi* (Tel Aviv, 1957), Vol. 2, p. 534.
5. R. Hayim Vital in *Aitz Hayim*, Chap. VI.
6. *Sabbatai Zevi*, Vol. II, p. 587.
7. The non-theological character of Halachic literature served to obscure the issues involved in the acceptance or rejection of the Qabbalistic world-view.
8. For a detailed description of the world view of A. I. Kuk, see J. B. Agus, *Banner of Jerusalem* (New York, 1946).
9. David Kahana, *Even Aifel*, p. 8.
10. *Iggeroth Ramahal*, II, 232.
11. *Ibid.*, Chap. 1.

12. *Ibid.*
13. *Ibid.*, Chap. 14.
14. *Ibid.*, Chap. 18.
15. *Ibid.*, Chap. 19.
16. *Ibid.*, Chap. 26.
17. *Kethuboth*, III b; *Sotah*, 14 a.
18. Note 44 in Rapaport's Hebrew book on Rav Hai Gaon.
19. The thesis of this paragraph is elaborated in great detail in the following articles by this author: " Hahidush b'toroso shel Habesht " in *HaDoar*, year 24, issue 30; " Ish HaMistorin " in *Talpioth*, Nissan, 5708.
20. *Sefer HaGilgulim*, 6.
21. *Tsavoath HoRivosh.*
22. *Kether Shem Tov.*
23. *Or HaMeir*, Tsav.
24. R. Menahem Mendel (of Vitebsk), *Pri Haaretz.*
25. *Kether Shem Tov.*
26. *Ibid.*
27. *Ibid.*
28. *Ibid.*
29. Lech Lecho, *Sifthai Tsaddikim.*
30. *Kether Shem Tov.*
31. *Reshith Hokhma*, shaar *Ahavah.*
32. Dov Ber Mezrich, *Or Torah.*
33. *Tsavoath HoRivosh; Toldoth Yaakov Yoseph*, Bo.
34. *Ibid.; Kedushoth Levi*, shir HoShirim, where it is maintained that souls of new converts are generated by this rise and fall.
35. Letter of Baal Shem, printed in *Toldoth Yaakov Yoseph.*
36. *Kether Shem Tov.* Quoted with many variations in the source books of the Hasidic movement.
37. *Tsavoath HoRivosh.*
38. *Beair Mayim Hayim*, Taitsai.
39. *Kethonath Passim*, shemini.
40. *Beair Mayim Hayim*, B'hukothai.
41. " Tsetel Koton " in *Noam Elimelech.* Compare with *Reshith Hokhma*, shaar Hak'dushah, 15, where the famed Qabbalist presents the same thought, but without identifying the felt taste with the mythical holy spark. This comparison is another illustration of the transformation of Qabbalistic ideology into Hasidic experience. " It is also important to bear in mind while eating that in all things there is the inwardness of holiness, which is mixed with chaff and straw because of the sin of Adam. Through the process of chewing, his soul receives the inwardness of the food which is turned into blood, while from the chaff and straw the residue is left which is given over to the ' outsiders.' "
42. *Tsavoath HoRivosh.*
43. *Likutai Maharan*, 104.
44. *Ibid.*
45. R. Dov Bar (of Liubavich), *Kuntros hahithpaaluth.*
46. *Degel Mahneh Ephraim*, Yithro.
47. Psalms 97:11.
48. " Simhah shel mizvah " in *Sabbath*, 30 b.
49. *Shenai Luhoth Habrith* (Keltz edition), p. 60.
50. *Tsavoath HoRivosh.*
51. Letter to R. Jacob Joseph in *Shivhai HoBesht.*
52. *Tsavoath HoRivosh.*
53. *Shivhai HoBesht.*
54. Autobiography of Shelmo Maiman.
55. The followers of R. Abraham of Kaliska were especially noted for their antics. " Rolling over in the streets," they aroused the wrath of Gaon Elijah of Vilna, who declared them to be idolaters. See the letter of Rav Sheneur Zalman, seeking to explain the conflict between the Hasidim and " opponents," printed in the second section of *Likutai Amorim.*
56. *Butsino Dinhora.*
57. R. Menahem Mendel (of Liubavitch), *Derech Mizvosecho*, mizvath miloh.
58. *Nefesh Hahayim.*
59. *Shivhai HoBesht.*

60. *Toldoth Yaakov Yoseph,* introduction and Bereshith.
61. *Zohar,* III, 152 a, 149 b.
62. Quoted by S. Horodetsky in *Hahasiduth Vehasidim,* III, 54.
63. *Kether Shem Tov,* 16.
64. *Noam Elimelech,* yithro.
65. *Kedushah Levi,* yithro.
66. *Ibid.,* Bereshith.
67. *Ibid.*
68. *Ibid.,* Lech Lecho.
69. Sheneur Zalman, *Likutai Amorim,* 35.
70. *Hayai Maharan,* II.
71. See Simon Dubnow, *Der Chassidimus;* also Raphael Mahler's work in Hebrew, *Divrai Yemai Yisroel,* Vol. III, Chap. 12.
72. *Maor Veshemesh,* Taitsai.
73. *Hayai Maharan.*
74. This interpretation is well presented by M. H. Amishai, *Mahashavah Veemeth* (Tel Aviv, 1939), Vol. II, p. 411.
75. Shivhai HaBesht.
76. *Kethoneth Passim,* Shemini.
77. *Tsavoath HoRivosh.*
78. *Kedushath Levi,* Noah.
79. *Noam Elimelech,* Vayhi.
80. *Degel Mahneh Ephraim,* Vayaitsai.
81. *Ibid.,* Miketz.
82. *Ibid.,* Vayigash.
83. *No-am Elimelech,* vayaishev.
84. This interpretation is elaborated in B. Dinur's *Bemifneh Hadoroth* (Jerusalem, 1955), pp. 81-227.
85. *Likutai Maharan.*
86. *Torah R. Naham* (ed. Horodetsky), p. 185.
87. *Likutai Maharan,* II, 25.
88. *Torah R. Nahman* (ed. Horodetsky), p. 188.
89. *Porath Yossef,* Lecho.
90. W. R. Inge, *Christian Mysticism* (New York, 1956), pp. 189, 190.
91. Introduction of R. Hayim Volozhin to Elijah Gaon's commentary

to the *Safro Dizniuta,* in which he maintains that Elijah Gaon did accept and revere the Qabbalah of Isaac Luria. On the other hand, R. Sheneur Zalman in his *Iggerot HaKodesh* refused to debate with Elijah Gaon on the ground that the latter did not accept Lurianic Qabbalah in its entirety.
92. R. Haymin Volozhin, *Nefesh Ha Hayim,* III, Chap. 4.
93. R. Menahem Mendel (of Vitebsk), *Peri Haaretz.*
94. This thesis is argued well in the four-volume Hebrew work of Eliezer Zweifel, *Sholom al Yesroel.*
95. *Nefesh Ha Hayim,* III, 6.
96. *Ibid.,* II, 14, 15.
97. *Ibid.,* II, 17.
98. *Ibid.,* IV, 2.
99. *Ibid.,* IV, 31.
100. *Ibid.,* IV, 4, 5.
101. *Ibid.*
102. *Ibid.,* II, 10.
103. *Ibid.,* II, 13.
104. *Ibid.,* II, 6.
105. R. Sheneur Zalman, *Likutai Amorim* (Vilna, 1923), paragraph 25. Numbers refer to paragraphs.
106. *Ibid.,* 12, 13, 14.
107. *Ibid.,* 18.
108. *Iggerot HaKodesh,* II, printed in the volume of *Likutai Amorim* cited *supra,*
109. *Ibid.,* 35.
110. *Ibid.,* 29.
111. *Ibid.,* 10.
112. R. Menahem Mendel Liubavich, *Derech Mitzvosecho* (New York, 1944).
113. *Ibid.,* p. 40.
114. *Ibid.*
115. *Derech Mitzvosecho,* hallel.
116. *Likutai Amorim,* 5.
117. *Ibid.,* 37.
118. *Ibid.,* 50.
119. *Kuntros Hahithpaaluth.*

CHAPTER TWELVE

1. Psalms 85:11.
2. *Jerusalem*, part I.
3. *Ibid.*, part II.
4. *Ibid.*
5. *Ibid.*
6. *Ibid.*
7. *Ibid.*
8. *Ibid.*
9. *Hilkhoth Melokhim*, 8:11.
10. I. Heinemann, *Taamai HaMizvoth Besifruth Yisroel* (Jerusalem, 5716), Vol. II, pp. 16, 38.
11. Commentary on Exodus 19:5.
12. I. Heinemann, *supra*, Vol. II, p. 23.
13. Ravidowitz in Ha-tekufah, Vols. 25, 26.
14. *Ibid.*
15. Ravidowitz, Ha-tekufah, Vols 25, 26.
16. *Phaedon,* I dial.
17. *Ibid.*, end.
18. *Morgenstunden; Schriften*, II, 36, 43.
19. *Schriften*, V, 704.
20. *Ibid.*, II, 432.
21. *Ibid.*, II, 341.
22. *Ibid.*, V, 497.
23. *Transactions of the Parisian Sanhedrin* (in Hebrew) (London, 1807). "Teshuvoth al sh'taim esrai ha-shailoth shel ha-Kaisor Napoleon." Rosenthal, *Talpioth*, 1950.
24. See Baron, *A Social and Religious History of the Jews*, last chapter of first edition. S. Dubnow, *Divrai Yemai Am Olam* (Tel Aviv, 1936), Vol. VIII, p. 141.

EPILOGUE

1. *Daily Prayer Book.*
2. The contrast between the active and passive moods of piety is well drawn by Josiah Royce in his *The Spirit of Modern Philosophy*. Among recent theologians, James Parkes construes the difference between Judaism and Christianity in terms of this contrast. The opinions of Orthodox authorities concerning the organ are collected in the booklet *Aile Divrai Habrith*.
3. *Sabbath*, 146 a.
4. Tosefta, *Sanhedrin*, 13. See *Masekheth Gerim*, Chap. 1, where a prospective convert to Judaism is at first discouraged, but if he persists he is told, "The world was created only for the sake of Israel, who alone are called 'sons of the All-Present' and alone are beloved of Him. All the discouraging words we spoke to you were for the purpose of increasing your reward."
5. *Berokhoth*, 33 b.
6. *Aboth* 3; 15.
7. *Aboda Zara* 10 b.
8. *Sanhedrin* 98 a.
9. *Ibid.*, 99 a.
10. Yehuda Ibn Shemuel, *Midreshai Geulah* (Jerusalem, 1954).
11. *Sabbath*, 112 b.
12. Maimonides' Code, *Hilchoth Melochim*.

INDEX

INDEX